RESCUING JUSTICE AND EQUALITY

RESCUING JUSTICE AND EQUALITY

G. A. Cohen

Harvard University Press

Cambridge, Massachusetts

London, England

2008

Library of Congress Cataloging-in-Publication Data

Cohen, G. A. (Gerald Allan), 1941–
Rescuing justice and equality / G. A. Cohen.
p.   cm.
Includes bibliographical references and index.
ISBN-13: 978-0-674-03076-3 (alk. paper)
1. Equality.   2. Social justice.   3. Communism.   I. Title.
HM821.C65 2008
305.01—dc22   2008002152

For my beloved wife,

Ganni

SHORT TABLE OF CONTENTS

LONG TABLE OF CONTENTS

I

RESCUING EQUALITY FROM . . .

II

RESCUING JUSTICE FROM . . .

PREFACE

One usually cannot identify the moment, or even the month, in which the theme of a book first appeared in its author's mind, but I think I can identify the moment in the case at hand. I am proceeding on foot, amid the glorious snow of the Princeton University campus, in the company of Tim Scanlon, to attend a seminar in February 1975. At the time, I wasn't as familiar as I ought to have been with John Rawls's *Theory of Justice*, and I said to Tim, with all due naiveté, that, while I could see that it might be sensible for all concerned to offer unequalizing incentives to the more productive when the condition of the worst off would be improved as a result, I could not see why that would make the resulting inequality *just*, as opposed to sensible. Tim was visibly reflective, but he didn't say whether or not he agreed.

The first part of this book defends my 1975 comment: it seeks to rescue equality from the Rawlsian argument against it. The second, more meta-ethical, part of the book defends a view about the concept (not the content) of justice to which I was led as a result of the nature of the defense of equality on offer in its first part. (The book is called *Rescuing Justice and Equality* rather than, according to the order of its agenda, *Rescuing Equality and Justice*, solely because the first phrase has a better rhythm.) It is a wonderful thing about philosophy, or, anyway, I find it wonderful, that you start in one place and that, "following the argument wherever it leads,"[1] you end up someplace very much else. That happened to me thirty-five years ago when I mounted a defense of Karl Marx's theory of history. In that case I started with the substance of historical materialist explanation, but I had to reach up to the pure concept

1. Plato, *The Republic*, 394d.

of explanation to support what I was doing, just as here I have found it necessary to reach up to the pure concept of justice.

I have labored long and hard on this book, and with many a temporary weakening of my resolve. In this struggle I have had the enormous benefit of the solidarity, the intellectual and emotional support, of two friends. The first of these is Mike Otsuka, against whose bracing resistance much of what follows was worked out. Thank you, Mike, for what is for sure more than a thousand phone calls (and thank you, All Souls, for paying for them). The second is Derek Parfit, whose brilliance is public property, but whose kindness is something known, in its full dimensions, only to those of us who have been lucky enough to be close to him.

I must also quadruple out for special thanks Cécile Fabre, Andrew Williams, Arthur Ripstein, and Arnold Zuboff. Cécile read the whole manuscript when it was nearly finished and raised some particularly acute questions. Andrew made excellent extensive criticisms at many times over the past fifteen years and capped his contribution with a sage report to Harvard University Press. Arthur was the other reporter, and his penetrating criticisms have affected the result. And Arnold went in for much detailed dissection of drafts at a very early stage of the book's development, before I had to compete with his wife and children for his attention.

I thank All Souls College and Oxford University for superb conditions of work, and the Leverhulme Foundation for conferring on me two years (2000–2002) of freedom from teaching and administration.

The book has been so long in the making that very many people have commented efficaciously at various times. The list of others to whom I am indebted is long: Dick Arneson, Daniel Attas, John Baker, Annette Barnes, Jerry Barnes, Brian Barry, Chris Bertram, Akeel Bilgrami, Giacomo Bonanno, Michael Bratman, David Brink, John Broome, Diemut Bubeck, Myles Burnyeat, Paula Casal, Victor Caston, Clare Chambers, John Charvet, Josh Cohen, Michèle Cohen, Miriam Cohen Christofidis, Jerry Dworkin, Ronnie Dworkin, Jon Elster, David Estlund, Colin Farrelly, Sam Freeman, John Gardner, Max de Gaynesford, Allan Gibbard, Margaret Gilbert, Keith Graham, Stephen Grover, Daniel Hausman, Ted Honderich, the late Susan Hurley, Rob Jubb, Frances Kamm, the late Jerry Katz, the late Gregory Kavka, Jeroen Knijff, Daniel Kofman, Christine Korsgaard, Saul Kripke, Will Kymlicka, Andy Levine, Kasper Lippert-Rasmussen, David Lloyd-Thomas, Hui-Chieh Loy, Steven Lukes,

Murray MacBeath, Dan McDermott, John McMurtry, Jon Mandle, David Manning, Mike Martin, Andy Mason, Saladin Meckled-Garcia, Mohamed Mehdi, David Miller, Chris Morris, Sarah Moss, Véronique Munoz-Dardé, Tom Nagel, Jan Narveson, Michael Neumann, Dilip Ninan, Richard Norman, Kieran Oberman, Bertell Ollman, Paule Ollman, Martin O'Neill, Ellen Frankel Paul, Jeffrey Paul, Chris Peacocke, Philip Pettit, Hanna Pickard, Piero Pinzauti, Thomas Pogge, Ross Poole, Janet Radcliffe-Richards, Joseph Raz, John Roemer, Miriam Ronzoni, Amelie Rorty, Miles Sabin, Ben Saunders, Geoffrey Sayre-McCord, Tim Scanlon, Sam Scheffler, Rob Shaver, Bill Shaw, Seana Shiffrin, Saul Smilansky, Horacio Spector, Gopal Sreenivasan, Hillel Steiner, Uwe Steinhoff, Joe Stiglitz, Adam Swift, Larry Temkin, Dag Einar Thorsen, Bertil Tungodden, Peter Vallentyne, Frank Vandenbroucke, Philippe Van Parijs, Nicholas Vrousalis, Steven Wall, Bob Ware, Alan Wertheimer, David Wiggins, Martin Wilkinson, the late Bernard Williams, Jo Wolff, and Erik Wright.

The kindness and wittiness of Phoebe Kosman of Harvard University Press dissolved a lot of anxieties. Kieran Oberman of the Oxford University Politics Department executed superior service as a research assistant. And I think my wife, Michele, knows how grateful I am to her.

INTRODUCTION

1. The Big Issue

As my supervisor Gilbert Ryle would have said, "You rescue something *from* something," and that from which I here attempt a rescue of justice and equality is Rawlsian liberal thought. I shall lay out the large lines of the intended rescue in section 2 of this introduction. But here is an attempt to sketch the ideological disagreement that lies behind the philosophical dispute.

The big background issue in my disagreement with Rawls and the Rawlsians is the nonliberal socialist/anarchist conviction that Karl Marx expressed so powerfully in his essay "On the Jewish Question," when he said that "human emancipation" would be "complete" "only when the actual individual man . . . has recognized and organized his own powers as *social* powers so that social force is no longer separated from him as a *political* power"; thus, only when he "has taken back into himself the abstract citizen" so that freedom and equality are expressed "in his everyday life, his individual work, and his individual relationships."[1]

The ideal liberal society is not the same as the ideal socialist society. In the ideal socialist society, equal respect and concern are not projected out of society and restricted to the ambit of an alien superstructural power, the state. If the right principles are, as Marx thought, the ones that are right for real, everyday, material life, and if they are practiced in everyday life, as the socialist ideal utopianly envisages that they will be, then the state can wither away.

---

1. "On the Jewish Question," p. 241, emphases in original. It was David Estlund's deft use of this passage as an epigraph to his "Liberalism, Equality, and Fraternity in Cohen's Critique of Rawls" that made me realize that my critique of Rawls was, in effect, an attempt to deliver some of the content of Marx's pregnant statement.

And that means more than that coercive power can wither away. In the Marxist hope, it is the *separation* of state and society, the duality itself, that goes. There is not, then, on the one hand, as there is in Rawlsian perception, an economic structure that is organized to achieve a certain form of justice, and, on the other, a set of individual economic choices that need show no respect for that justice. The Marx-inspired question is whether a society without an ethos in daily life that is informed by a broadly egalitarian principle for that reason fails to provide distributive justice. To that question, Rawls, being a liberal, says no: here is the deep dividing line between us.

Liberally minded economists take for granted that economic agents are self-seeking, or, like James Meade, they think that they should be,[2] and then they want people as political agents to act against the grain of their self-interest: pile up your earthly goods on the mundane plane of civil society but be a saint in the heaven of politics. One way out of the apparent contradiction is to generalize *Homo economicus:* hence the work of theorists like James Buchanan and David Gauthier. I am engaged in an exploration of the reverse generalization.

2. Rescuing Equality and Justice

This book attempts a rescue of the egalitarian thesis that in a society in which distributive justice prevails, people's material prospects are roughly equal: distributive justice does not tolerate the deep inequality,[3] driven by the provision of economic incentives to well-placed people, that John Rawls and his followers think a just society displays. The book also attempts a rescue of the concept of justice from the Rawlsian constructivist treatment of that concept. And that more metaethical rescue, of a concept, supports the rescue of the egalitarian thesis. If constructivism about justice is true, then, as I shall explain in a moment, the prospects for the claim that distributive justice requires equality become worse. The first rescue is pursued in Part One of the book, the second in Part Two.

If one rescues equality, and justice requires equality, then, and in that

2. See section 4 of Chapter 8 below.
3. See *A Theory of Justice*, pp. 7/7. Texts adduced at pp. 11–12 of section 3 of the General Appendix below show how deep Rawls expected that inequality to be.

sense, and to that extent, one rescues justice. But that is not the sense that "rescuing justice" bears in the title of Part Two of this book, where it rather means rescuing the *concept* (whatever may be the content) of justice from the constructivist view of how to establish its content. On the constructivist view, the content of justice is identified by the rules for social living, the rules of regulation that would be chosen in a privileged choosing situation (in the Rawlsian case, that situation is the original position). My rescue of justice denies the mooted identification on two grounds: if rules for social living are soundly based, they will reflect both values other than justice and practical constraints that restrict the extent to which justice can be applied. That being so, justice, itself, could not be what is specified by such rules.

What is the relationship between the rescue of equality in the first part of this book and the rescue of justice in its second part? To the extent that justice is distinguished from other values, the case for the thesis that justice requires equality is strengthened, because values other than justice tend against equality. And a variety of practical constraints also tell against the implementation of equality. Accordingly, the rescue of justice that distinguishes it both from other values and from implementable rules of regulation supports ($\neq$ establishes) the claim that justice requires equality.

Note that, while I criticize constructivism in particular for systematically conflating other questions with the question of justice, my discussion should be of interest to persons who are independently convinced of the falsehood of constructivism, since it is of independent interest whether or not I am right that what I consider to be the other questions truly are other than questions of justice.

3. Some Methodological Disagreements

Beyond the disagreement between me and the Rawlsians with respect to both the form and the substance of justice, there is a disagreement about how to do political philosophy, or indeed philosophy itself, a disagreement complexly explained by the fact that I am an Oxford man (of a certain vintage) and they are Harvard men and women. Oxford people of my vintage do not think that philosophy can move as far away as Harvard people think it can from pertinent prephilosophical judgment. We have different views about the analytic/synthetic distinction, and therefore about the status of philosophy itself; also about fact and value, and about the relation of theory to practice. The differences are the fruit of contrasting philosophical histories, at least decades-long, and also of differences in national character.

A *Theory of Justice* set itself against, and offered to replace, what Rawls called an "intuitionist" conception of moral and political philosophy, but, given his characterization of the conception in question, it would be better to call it "radical pluralism." In this conception, one favored by many Oxford types like me, we determine the principles that we are willing to endorse through an investigation of our individual normative judgments on particular cases, and while we allow that principles that are extensively supported by a wide range of individual judgments can override outlier judgments that contradict those principles, individual judgments retain a certain sovereignty.[4]

In my philosophically conservative view, that is the only way to go. And when we go that way, we refine, and we thereby reach, our deepest normative convictions, which, being our deepest, we find it difficult to defend (except against attack).[5] We expect to find, moreover, as we approach the completion of our task, that the normative requirements that we recognize present themselves in competitive array: they cannot all be satisfied all the time, nor do we have a method for systematically combining them. Discursively indefensible trade-offs are our fate. I do not say that such an intellectual predicament is satisfactory. But I do say that it is the predicament we are in. There are many attempts to escape it in the literature, and as many failures to do so.

As Rawls noted, the view that I prefer to call "radical pluralist" has two features, the second of which renders the pluralism more radical than the first one, by itself, does: such theories, he said, "consist of a plurality of first principles which may conflict to give contrary directives in particular types of cases; and second, they include no explicit method, no priority rules, for weighing these principles against one another: we

---

4. I thereby mean to enlist myself as a partisan of what Frances Kamm calls "standard deontology": see her "Owing, Justifying, and Rejecting," pp. 336–341.

5. As that explication of the "intuitionist" approach implies, it does not carry commitment to an epistemology that posits a faculty of moral perception. It is consistent with many views of the status of our fundamental convictions, including the view that they are noncognitive expressions of emotion or of attitude.

are simply to strike a balance by intuition, by what seems to us most nearly right."[6]

Rawls found the idea of a mass of normative requirements that we negotiate without method or compass unsatisfactory. He sought to produce something more orderly, both at the level of method and at the level of result. He offered, precisely, a *theory,* an organon for generating principles, the original position, and he identified justice with what the original-position machine produces. The theory of the original position says that whatever people would choose self-interestedly in a certain condition of knowledge and ignorance constitutes justice, because of the conditions of that choice: principles chosen in full knowledge of the character of human nature and of the laws of sociology and economics, but in ignorance of anything that distinguishes anybody (and, therefore, me) from anybody else, are said to carry normative authority.

Rawls claimed, moreover, that the principles generated by the recommended procedure would display a firm structure: they would fall into a lexical order, which would support determinate rulings in particular situations, instead of unstructured trade-offs. But just as I think (see section 2 above) that the rules-of-regulation method is inappropriate, so I think that the promise of greater system in its result isn't really fulfilled. The conflicts of conviction persist, backstage.

Rawls was not alone in finding what I believe to be our unavoidable reliance on intuitive trade-offs, in the domain of political (and other) morality, unsatisfactory. Yet everybody practices intuitive balancing without qualm when the practical question falls within the scope of their legitimate self-interested choice. Let me illustrate how people seek in moral matters a level of precision and certainty that they would not expect to find in matters that fall within personal preference.

People say that they'd like to give to charity, but that they are so bewildered as to be paralyzed by the multitude of good causes and would-be servers of good causes that they don't know to which charity to give. No similar paralysis affects them when they have a surfeit of restaurants to choose from. They simply choose one that they know or believe to be good, even if it is not the best, and they think that's good enough.

And people say that you can't *know* that a given charitable donation will do any good, thereby erecting a standard for epistemic confidence

---

6. *A Theory of Justice,* pp. 34/30.

which, if applied to their own self-interested concerns, would deprive them of a lot of enjoyment, such as that to be derived from investments that merely happen to pay off.

People also press the sorites question (where can one draw the line?) more insistently in a charities than in a self-interested context. People say "If I give them $10, why not give them $15? Where am I going to stop?" But nobody says, "If I spend $10 on a bottle of wine, then why not $15? Where am I going to stop?"

And people jib against the vagueness of injunctions of duty, such as "do your bit," which are no vaguer than calls for enjoyment whose vagueness deters no one from observing them, such as "let's go have a good time."

And then there is the issue of how to balance the various claims on one's generosity against one another. The incommensurabilities that paralyze people in that context don't bother them when it's a matter of choosing the restaurant that offers the best combination of price, taste, décor, distance, and so on.

I'm not saying that it's quite OK that things are vague, and it is undoubtedly more consequential in the moral than in the personal domain that they are. Like everybody else, I would prefer something better. But unlike some others, I don't think it's to be had. Yet, however that may be, what I find arresting is the remarkably contrasting reaction that we manifest to vagueness (and so on) when our interests are and aren't at stake. When facing our legitimately self-interested choices, we feel no need for a theory that will make everything determinate. Do we demand such theory in the moral realm in order to avoid, or reduce, our moral commitment? Recall Thomas Hobbes's remark that the "doctrine . . . That the three Angles of a Triangle should be equal to two Angles of a Square" might well have been "disputed," had a belief in its falsehood served somebody's interest.[7]

4. Justice and Fairness

While Part One of this book concerns distributive justice in particular, Part Two concerns the very concept of justice, which applies to matters outside distributive justice, such as the just and unjust treatment of individuals with respect to their liberty and their privacy. Before turning to

7. Hobbes, *Leviathan,* p. 166.

some remarks about distributive justice in particular, let me say a little, unsatisfactory though it may be, about justice quite generally.

I assume on the reader's part an intuitive understanding of the sort of principle that a principle of justice is: it is the understanding that she employs when she recognizes that the dispute between John Rawls and Robert Nozick is a dispute about justice, and when she recognizes that the principle that we should respect our natural environment is not a principle of justice, absent some pretty special background beliefs. But if, as some of my critics insist, I simply *must* say what I think justice is, in general terms, then I offer, for those who will be content with it, the ancient dictum that justice is giving each person her due.[8] For my part, however, I am not fully content with it, because, just by itself, the dictum is consistent with each of two opposed views of the relationship between justice and what is due to people. According to one of these views, a conception of justice is fashioned *out of* beliefs about what people are due; according to the other, beliefs about what people are due lie *downstream from* (independently identifiable) convictions about justice. I am not sure which view is more sound, but I do not think I need take a stand on the matter for the sake of defending any of the claims of this book.

Now as I indicated in section 3, the method that I favor investigates the shape of, and, consequently, the logical implications of, our deepest normative convictions. And my own animating conviction in political philosophy with respect to justice is a conviction about distributive justice in particular. It is that an unequal distribution whose inequality cannot be vindicated by some choice or fault or desert on the part of (some of) the relevant affected agents is unfair, and therefore, *pro tanto*, unjust, and that nothing can remove that particular injustice. It does not follow, and I do not say, that such unjust inequality cannot be part of a package of policy that is, all things considered, superior to any other (because values other than justice weigh in its favor) or even that it cannot be part of a package that is, all things considered, more just than any other (because considerations of nondistributive justice weigh in its favor). But it does follow that any package that contains that kind of unfairness cannot be through-and-through just. Thus, to take a central example, the difference principle, which in the Rawlsian conception endorses the distributions that satisfy it as just plain just, in fact, and as I argue in Chapter 4, tolerates a certain form of injustice. More generally, the Rawlsian

8. For a brief résumé of its provenance, see David Wiggins, *Ethics,* p. 284, n. 13.

approach denatures justice, since it cannot recognize that if something is unfair, then it's to that extent unjust: the identification of the best-all-things-considered rules of regulation with principles of justice excludes that recognition.

The view that accidental inequality is unjust is suggested in certain passages in Ronald Dworkin's "Equality of Resources." Dworkin did not himself go so far as to endorse the view in its full generality, but Richard Arneson and I proposed its generalization, and Elizabeth Anderson aptly dubbed the proposal "luck egalitarianism." Luck egalitarianism, the stated view, is now under intense investigation in a number of doctoral dissertations, and the ingenuity of aspirant members of the philosophical profession is exposing ambiguities and difficulties in it that were certainly never contemplated by me. I have not tried to restate the key conviction in a manner that addresses all the weaknesses that have been discerned in its opening statements. But I still believe it in a general way. So this book does not offer a full countertheory of distributive justice to the Rawlsian one, but that is not necessary for the forms of critique of Rawls that I mount, even though the conviction plays a certain role in Part One of the book, especially in Chapters 4 and 5. But the role that it plays there does not require it to be stated in any particular one of the competing possible forms of it that are now emerging. It can, moreover, be roundly rejected consistently with everything in Part Two of the book.

5. The Two Standpoints

A major theme of the present book is that, properly understood, the Rawlsian difference principle, which condemns inequalities that contradict the interests of the worst off, applies not only to the actions of the state but also to the choices of individuals that are beyond the reach of the state. Now, many Rawlsians resist that extension of the difference principle into the personal domain by pleading the propriety of a moral division of labor, under which the state sees to justice, and the individual, having herself willingly seen to justice insofar as the state requires her to do so, sees then to the imperatives and values of her own personal life. This division of labor is justified, so it is thought, by the presence in morality of two standpoints, an impersonal standpoint on the one hand, to which the state responds, and a personal standpoint on the other, to which the individual, other than in her capacity as a law-abiding citizen, may rightly be dedicated. Those who in this fashion criticize my extension of the reach of distributive justice into personal choice might be disposed to cite on behalf of their view the pregnant observation by Thomas Nagel that "institutions," such as the state, "unlike individuals, don't have their own lives to lead."[9]

I accept both the thesis of the duality of standpoints, personal and impersonal, that animates this objection, and also Nagel's point that the state contrasts with individuals in not having its own life to lead. But I reject the conclusion that impersonal justice is a matter for the state only, a conclusion that neither Nagel himself nor Rawls actually draws.

Chapters 6 and 9 of Nagel's *Equality and Partiality* articulate a more nuanced view of the matter under inspection than the one described above, but it is not relevant here to go into its details. What matters here is that the view described above is not that of Rawls: so much is evident from Rawls's assignment to individuals of a set of "natural duties," duties, that is, that lie on individuals rather than on the state, and that include the duty to respect others, to uphold and foster just institutions, to do a great good when the cost of doing so is not excessive, and so forth. These duties respond to utterances of the impersonal standpoint, but they apply at the heart of personal life: they are, expressly, principles for individuals rather than for institutions. That does not exclude a reduced statement of the moral division of labor, which restricts it to the domain of distributive justice: in this domain, Rawls indeed divides the task of the state, which is to set the just framework, from the nontask of the individual, which is to do as she pleases within that framework. The real opposition between Rawls and me, on the present issue, is therefore not whether the impersonal standpoint reaches personal decision but whether the demands of distributive justice in particular do so. And while it is quite consistent for Rawls to think both that they do not but that other deliverances of the impersonal standpoint do, the Rawlsian position about distributive justice cannot be *based* on a general bar to impersonal justice entering individual decision: it diminishes the plausibility of the division-of-labor thesis with respect to distributive justice in particular in that it cannot be said to reflect something more general.

The profound truth that there exist Nagel's two standpoints, and the

9. *Equality and Partiality*, p. 59. Typical of many, Julius ("Basic Structure," p. 327) describes the stated position as the "Rawls/Nagel ideal of a division of labor."

further truth that the state, unlike individuals, has no life of its own to lead, do not justify a moral division of labor between a justice-seeking state and justice-indifferent (save insofar as they are willingly obedient citizens) individuals. The Nagelian premises provide no warrant for the asserted division of labor, nor, therefore, for extruding the demands of impersonal justice from personal choice.

We can, in fact, distinguish three possible views, with respect to who must see to distributive justice in particular, that are consistent with the Nagelian premises of the argument, each of which contradicts the view, often misattributed to me, that the individual must be as dedicated to such justice as the state is. There is, first, the Rawlsian view that distributive justice is a task for the state alone. A second view would say that the individual must show some regard to what the state is fully dedicated to in this domain. Finally, there is my own view, which is that both the state, with no life of its own, and the individual, who is indeed thus endowed, must, in appropriately different fashions, show regard in economic matters both to impersonal justice and to the legitimate demands of the individual.

To elaborate. There are many forms of motivation along the continuum between unrestrained market-maximizing at one end and full self-sacrificing restraint in favor of the worst off on the other. The first extreme is permitted by Rawls (and I regard that as absurd), but the second extreme isn't required by me. Requiring the second extreme is, in my view, excluded by a legitimate personal prerogative. The prerogative grants each person the right to be something other than an engine for the welfare of other people: we are not nothing but slaves to social justice. But the individual who affirms the difference principle must have some regard to it in his economic choices, whatever regard, that is, which starts where his personal prerogative stops. Yet the state, too, must have regard, in its legislation, to the personal prerogative of the individual. It should not, should it happen to have the power to do so, legislate so invasively and so comprehensively that the individual lacks scope for the exercise of what belongs within his own prerogative: but, as is manifest, and as I point out in section 8 of Chapter 1 below, a state that respects that constraint is not the same thing as a society that restricts application of the difference principle to the state. The prerogative justification is a quite different justification of inequality from the difference-principle one, and the inequalities that it justifies will coincide only by accident with those that the difference principle would license under Rawls's restricted interpretation of that principle: they might be greater or smaller than the latter.

So individuals indeed have their own lives to lead,[10] and they are therefore permitted to strike a balance between the claims of the difference principle and their own legitimate concerns, but not, therefore, to ignore the difference principle[11] in their everyday lives.[12] The balance of which I speak is perforce a vague matter, and that makes it difficult to decide whether it has been achieved: the comments in section 2 above bear on that difficulty, and I canvas it at length in Chapter 8 below.

6. The Greatness of John Rawls

My friend Marshall Berman told me that the Columbia philosopher Morris Raphael Cohen would give a seminar every year on Hegel's *Phenomenology of the Spirit,* and that Cohen's contribution to the seminar proceedings was to criticize Hegel mercilessly, so that the text lay in shreds by the end of the semester. Then, when a photograph of the Columbia Department was to be taken, Cohen appeared with the *Phenomenology* under his arm, to be displayed in the picture. A surprised colleague said, "But you're always attacking it! Why did you bring *that* book?" Cohen's answer was "What other book is there?"

I feel something like that about John Rawls's *Theory of Justice.* I believe that at most two books in the history of Western political philosophy have a claim to be regarded as greater than *A Theory of Justice*: Plato's *Republic* and Hobbes's *Leviathan.* I shall not try to say what I think is great about those books. But among what contributes to the greatness of *A Theory of Justice,* and of the entire Rawlsian achievement, is that, to put the matter as Hegel would have done had he agreed with me, John Rawls grasped his age, or, more precisely, one large reality of his age, in thought. In his work the politics of liberal (in the American sense) democracy and social (in the European sense) democracy rises to consciousness of itself. (Note that to say that a philosophy represents its age is not to deny its possession of universal truth. As Hegel himself insisted, different aspects of universal truth are more apparent in different ages.)

10. As the Jewish sage Hillel said, in a widely quoted because widely admired passage, "If I am not for myself, then who will be for me?"

11. As Hillel continued, "But if I am for myself alone, then what am I?"

12. Or, as Hillel concluded, "If not now, when?"

Somebody once said to me that the reason why the thought of John Locke was full of tensions, and maybe sometimes contradictions, is that Locke saw all the problems. Well, liberal social democracy is certainly not without its problems, and they surface in the tensions that I claim to find in the Rawlsian architectonic. Some people[13] think that I exaggerate the difference between what Rawls offers and what I counteroffer. If they were disposed, as a result, to call me a left-Rawlsian, I would neither disavow nor dislike the description. There is a strong egalitarian element in Rawlsianism that I try to train against its inegalitarian conclusions.

In the penultimate paragraph of Part II of Volume I of *Capital,* which is the middle paragraph of what are, to my mind and heart, the deepest and most inspiring three paragraphs in that work, Karl Marx says of the capitalist market that "there alone rule freedom, equality, property and Bentham," "property" being understood to include (here, especially the worker's) self-ownership, and "Bentham" being understood to denote utility maximization. Whether or not Marx was right to draw a special connection between those values and the market, they are certainly the chief values of liberal capitalist civilization, and they are the values that therefore preoccupy its political philosophers. Not all political philosophers are preoccupied with all four values, but Rawls was, and the suit he tailored covered all of them. He was like the tailor in the story about the customer who comes to collect the suit for which the tailor had measured him up a week earlier. The customer tries on the jacket, and one shoulder seems higher than the other. But the tailor says that he's not wearing the jacket right and gently pushes down one of the man's shoulders. The tailor also has to turn one of his legs twenty degrees, and so forth, until the man, puzzled but compliant, leaves the tailor's shop and makes his awkward way, as best he can, onto the sidewalk. A passing woman says to her husband, "Poor man! What an affliction!" And her husband says, "Nice suit, though!"

Chief among the conflicts of value that capitalism displays is that between equality and utility. Its rhetoric endorses both, but its reality

---

13. For example, Joshua Cohen and David Estlund: see, respectively, their "Taking People as They Are?" and "Liberalism, Equality, and Fraternity."

sacrifices equality to utility: it relies on injustice to produce human happiness.[14] When Thomas Nagel declared that "what capitalism produces is wonderful," a sentence which, I must admit, jarred me, before I saw its point, he did not mean that it was morally attractive—that, as some think, it gives everyone her proper due. He meant, rather, that it delivers the goods.[15]

All responsible contemporary political philosophy must cope with both sides of the truth about capitalism, its dark truth and its brighter truth. The Rawlsian endorsement of inequality as just when and because it delivers the goods to everyone is a way of coping that, so I think, masks the conflict it seeks to resolve.

I find Henry Sidgwick's reaction to the conflict more congenial (by "this argument," Sidgwick means, roughly, the incentives argument for inequality that I criticize in Part One of this book):

> This argument is, I think, decisive from a political point of view, as a defence of a social order that allows great inequalities in the distribution of wealth for consumption. But when I hear it urged as conclusive from an ethical point of view, I am reminded of Lord Melbourne's answer to a friend whom he consulted, when premier, as to the bestowal of a vacant garter.[16] His friend said, "Why not take it yourself? No one has a better claim." "Well, but," said Lord Melbourne, "I don't see what I am to gain by bribing myself." The answer is cynical in expression, but it contains a lesson for some who profess a higher moral standard than Lord Melbourne was in the habit of professing. For when we have decided that the toleration of luxury as a social fact is indispensable to the full development of human energy, the ethical question still remains for each individual, whether it is indispensable for him; whether, in order to get himself to do his duty, he requires to bribe himself by a larger share of consumable wealth than falls to the common lot. And if one answers the question in the affirmative, one must admit one's self to belong to the class of persons characterized by George Eliot as "people whose high ideals are not required to account for their actions."[17]

14. I do not say that it succeeds. I do not reject critiques of capitalism that focus on the misery it produces. I am developing a different form of criticism.
15. *Equality and Partiality,* p. 93.
16. Which is not here a stocking holder without a thigh in it, but a knighthood without a knight in it.
17. *Practical Ethics,* pp. 108–109.

Because this book sets itself against the Rawlsian outlook on justice, I thought it important to lay out how momentous I think the Rawlsian achievement is. But it also matters to me that I should declare my admiration and affection for John Rawls the person. I was not within the circle that surrounded Rawls, but it was my good fortune that I got to know him well across many Oxford and a few Harvard occasions. I remember with particular pleasure one lunch that we took in what was, for a (too) short time, a lunchtime haunt of ours, namely, the austere and now defunct benches-only basement café of the Holland and Barrett health-food store in King Edward Street, Oxford. We were talking about Kant and free will, and I was delighted that, as it seemed to me,[18] Rawls expressed the belief that if all our choices really were causally determined, then many of our customary judgments of the moral worth of people would make no sense. Since I had been inclined to think the same for about thirty years, against the grain of the dominant compatibilist consensus, it delighted me that Jack Rawls was on our minority side. There was a satisfying sense of conspiring together against the consensus.

Jack Rawls treated everyone as an equal, and with great generosity, and as much for that reason as because his work was so profoundly far-reaching, he nourished a wonderful philosophical community. I have considered it a privilege to be accepted as an *interlocuteur valable* by that community.

7. An Outline of the Book

Four previously published pieces appear here, variously tweaked: Chapters 1 through 3[19] and Chapter 6. In the case of Chapters 1 through 3, changes in the text are merely stylistic, but some footnotes have been added and some have been altered or expanded: in each case that is indicated, except where it would be stating the obvious. In the case of Chapter 6 there has been a bit more reworking than in Chapters 1 through 3,

---

18. This may sound like a fussy caveat, but it is a necessary qualification, because Rawls often spoke from such a deep engagement in what he was commenting on that one couldn't always be sure *precisely* what he was saying, partly because one couldn't be sure that one had reached the same level of depth.

19. Chapter 3 was also in my *If You're an Egalitarian, How Come You're So Rich?*, but it needed to appear here too, to preserve the sequence of argument.

mostly in section 13, on "'ought' implies 'can,'" and in section 19, on the distinction between fundamental principles and rules of regulation.

Chapter 1 reproduces my 1991 Tanner Lectures on "Incentives, Inequality, and Community." Egalitarian liberals, and notably John Rawls, believe that an inequality is justified if, through the familiar incentive mechanism, it benefits the worst off: when paying the better off more than the worse off redounds to the benefit of the latter, doing so is justified, Rawls thinks, by his difference principle, which endorses inequality that benefits those at the short end of it. I claim that that pattern of justification of inequality is far more problematic than is generally supposed; that (at least) when the incentive consideration is isolated from all reference to desert or entitlement, it produces an argument for inequality that presupposes a model of society as a noncommunity, in which relations among human beings are construed as strategic, with people taking one another into account as so many opportunities for and, obstacles to, gain, rather than as fellow citizens by whom they can be asked to justify the way they live. Yet community, or as Rawls denominates it, fraternity, is an important value for Rawls, and one that he claims to be not only consistent with but illustrated by the incentive rationale that I criticize. I counterclaim that the manner in which Rawls applies the difference principle, in his endorsement of incentives inequality, represents abandonment of that very principle.

I question neither the difference principle itself nor the causal story about the benign consequences of unequalizing incentives in Chapter 1. I do not mean that I endorse either of those items, but, rather, that my particular line of criticism in the chapter is consistent with their truth. I argue, instead, that *even* if the causal story is true, and whether or not the difference principle is correct, the difference principle does not justify incentive-based inequality *as a feature of a just society,* on Rawls's own understanding of a just society, according to which it is a society whose citizens believe in and live by the principles that make the society just.

The anti-Rawlsian case undergoes further development in Chapter 2 (the Pareto Argument), which offers a refutation of an apparently compelling argument for inequality, one that is closely related to its aforestated (putative) justification by the difference principle. The argument begins with the claim that a proper understanding of the ideal of equal opportunity requires equality itself, as the natural *starting point* in the search for a just order: no one has a rightful claim, based on desert, or on any other antecedent condition, to have more resources than anyone else. But now suppose, what is realistic, that *everyone* would be better off under a certain scheme of *unequal* rewards. It would surely then be folly—this is the "Pareto" move—to reject that scheme. Accordingly, inequality is justified: we should not rest at the equal starting point.

I show, in main reply, that if the case for an initial *equality* is sound, then it undermines the case for replacing that equality by an inequality. For if an inequality in which all are better off is feasible, then so, too, I claim, in the relevant cases, is equality at a higher level than that at which the initial equality was pitched, one that is not Pareto-dominated by the relevant inequality. And the said Pareto-incomparable equal state should clearly be preferred to the inequality that it rivals, on the premise that justified the initial preference for equality.

The chapter proceeds to justify the inclusion of labor burden, both its quantity and its quality, in the metric of equality. It is further argued that the Pareto argument uses inconsistent metrics. A justified inequality appears to obtain, within the Pareto argument, only when, quite inconsistently, we use the primary goods metric to establish that the Pareto move produces an unequal distribution and we look to labor burden to justify that inequality.

It emerges from the criticisms of Rawls in the first two chapters of the book that distributive justice cannot be achieved solely through citizens' compliance with the laws of a state that aims at benefiting the worst off, and, therefore, regardless of how self-seeking (within the limits of compliance with the law) the behavior of those citizens is. A society that is just within the terms of the difference principle, so I conclude, requires not only just coercive *rules,* but also an *ethos* of justice that informs individual choices. Citizens do not qualify as fully committed to the difference principle unless that principle influences not only their voting behavior but also some of their behavior within the structure that their vote creates.

But that conclusion faces an objection, to wit, that the eye of justice does not focus on the decisions of economic agents in daily life, since their behavior occurs within, and does not determine, the basic structure of society, and it is only to the latter that the difference principle applies. The difference principle, it is contended, evaluates the rules within which agents operate, not the choices that they make within those rules.

I reply to the stated Basic Structure Argument in Chapter 3. I begin by reporting Rawls's principal rationale in *A Theory of Justice* for treating the basic structure as "the primary subject of justice," which is that "its effects are so profound and present from the start."[20] But, so I argue, the effect of the behavior of economic agents on people's life chances is comparably profound, and the exclusion of that behavior from the scope of the difference principle is therefore inconsistent with the grounds Rawls gives for focus on the basic structure. The harder productive people bargain, within any state-imposed structure of rules, and the less willing they are to perform with industry and zeal under high marginal taxation, the worse off the worst off will, in general, be. If economically productive people who accept the difference principle consequently accommodate themselves to very high redistributive taxation, then the worst off would be markedly better off than if the productive go abroad or knock off early in response to high taxation, or otherwise kick against it. But the difference between those two scenarios is a difference of ethos, and of ethos-governed behavior. It is not a difference between a just and an unjust basic structure as Rawls would determine the justice of the structure, which takes people's choices within it as mere neutral-as-far-as-justice-is-concerned data.

The first three chapters criticize the restricted application of the difference principle, but they do not challenge that principle itself. Yet there are elements in the argumentation of those chapters that, brought together and to the fore, sustain an argument against the difference principle itself, and not merely against the lax Rawlsian application of it.

Chapter 4 recruits those elements. It argues that the difference principle is not a principle of unqualified justice, because it endorses the injustice of inequalities whose causes are morally arbitrary. I also venture the claim that there is a radical tension between the Rawlsian *case* for the difference principle, which includes an affirmation of relational egalitarianism, that is, an egalitarianism that is fundamentally sensitive to comparisons between people, and the *content* of the difference principle, which makes that principle blind to comparisons between people, in the relevant sense. An important equivocation as between the usual informal and the canonical lexical formulations of the difference principle is explored, and a refurbished version, due to Thomas Nagel, of the Pareto argument of Chapter 2 above is dissected. Some unexpected commonalities between the Rawlsian Pareto argument and Robert Nozick's Wilt Chamberlain argument are exposed, both in respect of the structure

---

20. *A Theory of Justice*, pp. 7/7.

of those arguments and in respect of the criticisms to which that shared structure makes them liable. In a summarizing section I contrast different reasons why citizens who sincerely profess the difference principle, and applaud the state's adherence to it, might nevertheless not live by that principle. The chapter ends with a discussion of the relationship between views about human nature and Rawlsian constructivism.

Chapter 5 takes up unfinished business bequeathed by Chapter 2. In the argument that I examine and reject in Chapter 2, we begin with a favored state of equality, D1, and we are then told that it is pointless to maintain D1 when it can be replaced by D2, an unequal state in which everyone is better off. If the argument is right, the egalitarian is caught in a dilemma: he must either give up his principle or endorse a Pareto-inferior state of affairs. Pareto appears to dictate the abandonment of equality. But I say, in the Chapter 2 reply, that there is no such dilemma. For when D2 is possible, then so, standardly, is D3, a Pareto-optimal state of equality that is Pareto-superior to D1 and Pareto-incomparable with D2. We therefore do not have to choose between equality and Pareto.

But, if the egalitarian does not face a dilemma, she may nevertheless face a trilemma, and that is the topic of Chapter 5. Equality might be consistent with Pareto, but, so many would contend, inconsistency breaks out when we add freedom to the set of desiderata under one or other of two interpretations of "freedom."

The chapter addresses each of two trilemma theses. The first says that equality and Pareto are inconsistent with freedom in the sense of freedom of occupational choice: jobs will be filled Pareto-optimally, consistently with equal reward, only by forcing those who would prefer a different job for the same pay to do the job that optimality dictates. In response, I argue that appropriately motivated egalitarian citizens would choose optimal placement for reasons other than that they are forced to. If I am right, one form of the claim that equality imposes a slavery on the talented is thereby refuted.

The second trilemma thesis says that, even if everyone freely chooses her equal-to-everybody-else's-pay job in the Pareto-optimal array out of egalitarian inspiration, individuals may suffer an unfreedom in the performance of the job they choose, because it may thwart their prospects of self-realization. I show in response not that no such reduction in self-realization, relative to what would be achieved in an ordinary jobs market, can occur, but that no such reduction can justify a departure from equality of reward.

Chapter 5 concludes Part One, a brief retrospective of which now follows.

Part One is chiefly devoted to challenging both premises of the following argument:

1. Inequalities are unjust unless they are necessary to make the worst off people better off, in which case they are just.
2. Unequalizing incentive payments to productive people *are* necessary to make the worst off people better off.
3. Therefore, unequalizing incentive payments are just.

Chapters 1 through 3 develop an objection to premise 2. The objection says that the unequalizing payments aren't *strictly* necessary, since they reflect the will of incentive seekers, who would not, moreover, require the incentives in question to produce as they do if they acted in conformity with the conception of justice that is stated in premise 1.

My objection to premise 1, to which most of Chapter 4 is devoted, is that there is an incoherence in the thought behind it. You cannot make equality the natural starting point, or default point, for justice, on the *ground* that nobody deserves more than anybody else and then depart from equality because the departure benefits the worst off *and then* declare that the result is unambiguously just.

Finally, Chapter 5 asks whether there is a price in loss of freedom to be paid for the conception of distributive justice that emerges from my criticism of the advertised argument.

The entire argument of Part One is conducted at the level of the fundamental nature of justice, as opposed to the level of the rules of regulation that were distinguished from justice as such in the second paragraph of section 2 of the Introduction above. Virtually the whole of Part Two is dedicated to a defense of that distinction and, hence, to the mode in which the argument of Part One was conducted.

Chapter 6 opens that second, more meta-ethical, part of the book. It presents a general investigation of the relationship between facts and normative principles. Its principal thesis is that, whenever a fact supports, that is, gives us reason to affirm, a principle, it does so in virtue of a more ultimate principle that is not supported by any facts (which is not to say that there exists no good reason of some *other* kind, of some kind other than a set of facts, for affirming the fact-unsupported principle: that is a further question). It follows, given a further premise or two, that if facts support principles, then fact-insensitive principles are at the summit of our normative convictions.

Having set out the argument for the chapter's main claim, I defend it against a number of objections, and I show that it is quite distinct from the familiar thesis that one cannot derive an "ought" from an "is," and that, surprisingly enough, those who affirm that one *can* derive an "ought" from an "is" are constrained to accept my thesis.

My thesis bears the implication that infeasibility of application does not defeat the claim of a principle: thereby I appear to transgress against the hallowed "'ought' implies 'can'" meta-principle, so I distinguish what is true and what is false in the "'ought' implies 'can'" doctrine.

Although I believe that my thesis contradicts what most philosophers (and nonphilosophers) think, the only philosopher I know who *argues* that all principles do depend on facts is John Rawls, and he does not argue that on a constructivist basis: he believes that *all* fundamental principles, whether constructively or otherwise derived, depend on facts, so that the case for utilitarianism, for example, quite properly depends on such facts as that the institution of slavery could never be required for maximizing human happiness. I examine and refute several arguments that Rawls gives for the comprehensive fact-sensitivity of principles. In the course of my discussion of the Rawlsian view, I seek to reinforce the distinction between fact-bound principles and the fact-free principles that underpin them by identifying an important subset of the former, namely, rules of regulation, and contrasting them with the fundamental principles on which they rest.

Chapter 7 demonstrates that the identification by constructivists of principles of justice with rules to live by that would be chosen in an optimal choosing situation perverts the nature of justice, because, as I have explained in section 2 of the Introduction, optimal principles to live by are shaped both by values other than justice and by practical considerations that do not reflect fundamental principles. The operative distinction is between fundamental normative principles that express our deepest moral commitments and the rules of regulation that we adopt, either expressly or through custom and usage, and that we use, precisely, to regulate our affairs. A failure to make this distinction with clarity and force, in the right place, is central to the error in constructivism that I claim to discern, the error which means that the very concept of justice must be rescued from constructivism, whatever the content of justice may turn out to be.

According to constructivism, and across its several variants, principles of justice are those that epistemically and/or morally privileged choosers would select in answer to the question, "What are the right principles for the regulation of social life?" I make one simple point against constructivism, so conceived, and I examine its implications. That simple point is that the answer to the stated question, while depending in part on beliefs about justice, depends also on matters of fact and feasibility that do not bear on the nature of justice, and on values other than justice. The constructivist identification of principles of justice with the right answer to the stated question is therefore unsustainable both because it treats justice as sensitive to fact and because it fails to distinguish between justice and other values. The identification of principles of justice with the optimal set of principles to live by is incorrect, because the optimal principles are optimal, all things considered, and therefore not considered from the point of view of justice alone.

The stated misidentification is dictated by the question that is put to constructivism's selectors. They are not, of course, asked to say what *justice* is: it is we who ask that question, and the constructivist doctrine says that we get the answer to it when we have the answer to the different question that is put to constructivism's specially designed selectors, to wit, what are the optimum rules of social regulation? My generative criticism of constructivism is that the answer to that question could not answer the question, What is justice?

Chapter 8 considers, and rejects, the claims of *publicity* as a formal requirement of justice.

The focus on publicity arises as follows. Whether or not an individual is conforming to the egalitarian ethos that I say justice mandates is for more than one reason difficult to determine. For one thing, no one could suppose that justice demands that an individual forgo an incentive to perform a certain function where performing that function is so repugnant to him that doing so without extra compensation would degrade his life, to a point where it is worse than that led by what would otherwise be the worst off people. But it will often be impossible for others, including his intimates, to tell whether or not his performance of a certain function *is* unusually repugnant to a person: it will, indeed, often be difficult even for *him* to tell whether it is, because, in order to reckon that, he needs to compare his own level of job fulfillment with that of others at large, and that raises severe epistemic difficulties. Accordingly, the principles of an egalitarian ethos cannot be crisply stated, and whether or not someone respects them can, for that and other reasons, be difficult to determine (although, very importantly, it is less difficult for others, and for him, to determine whether or not he is making a *good faith effort* to conform to egalitarian principle).

These features of the ethos, the difficulty of stating it precisely, and the associated, though not merely consequent, difficulty of estimating how well people conform to it are the point of departure for Andrew Williams's critique of my position. For Williams insists that, in Rawlsian justice, and in truth, a principle of publicity about justice prevails, according to which it is in the nature of rules of justice that it must be possible to tell whether or not they are observed. That is because individuals are entitled to refuse the sacrifices that are, or, rather, that might otherwise be, demanded by justice if they lack assurance that others, too, are sacrificing, and they cannot readily have that assurance with respect to conformity to an egalitarian ethos, both because it cannot be made precise and because the springs of people's behavior are not fully accessible. If Williams is right, my critique of Rawls loses much of its force. There is no inconsistency in Rawls's nonapplication of the difference principle to people's job and income choices: a publicity constraint on justice forbids that application.

Now it may indeed be *desirable* that the rules governing behavior in a society possess the stated publicity property, and it is true that the rules of the ethos that I advocate lack that property in some measure. But I argue that publicity is *at most* a desideratum of the rules regulating society, and not a proper constraint on the content of *justice*. I show that in certain instances, such as the present one, representing publicity as a constraint on justice conflicts with deep intuitions about the character of justice itself, and that they must prevail when, in advance of deciding practical policy, we are seeking to formulate what justice (simply) *is*.

A General Appendix is largely given over to Replies to Critics. I have been blessed with many critics, and the supply continues apace as this book goes to press.

The Appendix appears here because intellectual ethics demands a degree of follow-through on things that one has written: one should respond to criticism and reconsideration, and, where necessary, one should amend one's position. But satisfying that demand can mean diminishing returns in quantity of illumination per unit of effort, and trade-off judgments sometimes have to be made. If I had released the text of this book only after I had satisfied myself with respect to all the important criticisms that have already been made of its reasoning, it would have remained on the computer forever. But I should like to mention that I particularly regret that I have not yet had the time to decide exactly what I think about the criticisms in Michael Titelbaum's "What Would a Rawlsian Ethos of Justice Look Like?" and A. J. Julius's "Basic Structure and the Value of Equality."

I

RESCUING EQUALITY FROM . . .

1

THE INCENTIVES ARGUMENT

> *Well-off:* "Look here, fellow citizen, I'll work hard and make
> both you and me better off, provided I get a bigger share
> than you."
> *Worse-off:* "Well, that's rather good; but I thought you were
> agreeing that justice requires equality?"
> *Well-off:* "Yes, but that's only as a benchmark, you see. To do
> still better, both of us, you understand, may require differ-
> ential incentive payments to people like me."
> *Worse-off:* "Oh. Well, what makes them necessary?"
> *Well-off:* "What makes them necessary is that I won't work
> as hard if I don't get more than you."
> *Worse-off:* "Well, why not?"
> *Well-off:* "I dunno . . . I guess that's just the way I'm built."
> *Worse-off:* "Meaning, you don't really care all that much
> about justice, eh?"
> *Well-off:* "Er, no, I guess not."
>
> —*Jan Narveson, "Rawls on Equal Distribution of Wealth"*

I: The Incentives Argument, the Interpersonal Test, and Community

1. Incentives, the Difference Principle, and Equality

In March 1988, Nigel Lawson, who was then Her Majesty's chancellor
of the exchequeur, brought the top rate of income tax in Britain down,
from 60 to 40 percent. That cut enlarged the net incomes of those whose
incomes were already large, in comparison with the British average, and,
of course, in comparison with the income of Britain's poor. Socialists

hated the tax cut, and a subsequent Labour Party policy document said that Labour would, effectively, restore the pre-1988 rate.[1]

How might the Lawson tax cut be defended? Well, economic inequality is no new thing in capitalist society, so there has been plenty of time for a lot of arguments to accumulate in favor of it. We hear from the political right that rich people are entitled to their wealth: to part of it because they produced it themselves—but for them, it would not have existed—and to the rest of it because it was transferred to them voluntarily by others who were themselves entitled to it because they produced it, or because they received it as a gift or in voluntary trade from others who were themselves entitled to it because . . . (and so on). (Some who hold that view also think that it is because it establishes moral desert that production justifies title, while others find the entitlement story compelling even when the idea of desert plays no role in it.) And then there is the utilitarian proposition, affirmed not only on the right but in the center, that inequality is justified because, through dynamizing the economy, it expands gross national product and thereby increases the sum of human happiness.

Left-wing liberals, whose chief representative in philosophy is John Rawls, reject these arguments for inequality: they do not accept the principles (entitlement, desert, and general utility) that figure in their major premises.[2] But the right and center sometimes offer an additional argument for inequality, to the major premise of which the liberals are friendly. That major premise is the principle that inequalities are justified when they render badly-off people as well off as it is possible for such people to be.[3] In one version of this argument for inequality—and this version of it is the topic of the present chapter—their high levels of in-

1. Strictly speaking, the top tax would be raised to 50 percent, but the ceiling on National Insurance contributions would be removed, and the effect of the two measures would be the same as that of raising income tax to 59 percent and leaving National Insurance alone.

2. To be more precise, they reject those principles *at the relevant fundamental level.* The qualification is necessary because left-wing liberals recognize desert and entitlement as (derivative) rules of legitimate reward in schemes of contribution and compensation that are not *grounded* in notions of desert and entitlement. (See *A Theory of Justice,* pp. 103/88–89, 310–315/273–279; Tom L. Beauchamp, "Distributive Justice and the Difference Principle," pp. 144–148; Thomas Scanlon, "The Significance of Choice," pp. 188, 203. For a later statement of nuanced views on desert and entitlement, see Rawls, *Justice as Fairness,* p. 72ff.)

3. For extensive use of this principle, see F. A. Hayek, *The Constitution of Liberty,* Chapter 3, and especially pp. 44–49.

come cause unusually productive people to produce more than they otherwise would; and, as a result of the incentives enjoyed by those at the top, the people who end up near the bottom are better off than they would be in a more equal society. This was one of the most politically effective justifications of the unequalizing policy of Thatcher Conservatism. We were ceaselessly told that movement contrary to that policy, in a socialist egalitarian direction, would be bad for badly off people by advocates of a regime that seems itself to have brought about the very effect against which its apologists insistently warned.[4]

Left-wing liberals deny the factual claim that the vast inequalities in Britain or America actually do benefit the badly off, but they tend to agree that if they did, they would be justified, and they defend inequalities that really are justified, in their view, by the incentive consideration. That is a major theme in John Rawls's work. For Rawls, some people are, mainly as a matter of genetic and other luck, capable of producing more than others are, and it is right for them to be richer than others if the less fortunate are caused to be better off as a result.[5] The policy is warranted by what Rawls calls the difference principle, which endorses all and only those social and economic inequalities that are good for the worst off or, more generously, those inequalities that either make the worst off better off or do not make them worse off: in this matter there is a certain ambiguity of formulation in Rawls, and in what follows I shall take the difference principle in its more generous form, in which it allows inequalities that do not help but also do not hurt the worst off.[6]

4. Strong support for that charge comes from Kay Andrews and John Jacobs, *Punishing the Poor.*
5. See *A Theory of Justice,* pp. 15/13, 102/87, 151/130–131, 179/156, 546/omitted in 1999; *Justice as Fairness,* pp. 76–77.
6. Statements of the difference principle display ambiguity along two dimensions. There is the ambiguity remarked in the text above, between inequalities that *do not harm* and inequalities that *help* the badly off, and there is the further ambiguity between *mandated* and *permitted* inequalities. These distinctions generate the following matrix:

	Mandated		Permitted
Helping ones are	1	→	2
	↑		↑
Nonharming ones are	3	→	4

Since what is mandated is permitted, and what helps does not harm, there exist the implications among possible interpretations of the principle indicated by the arrows

Back now to the socialist egalitarians, who did not like the Lawson tax cut.[7] Being to the left of left-wing liberals, socialist egalitarians are also unimpressed by the desert, entitlement, and utility justifications of inequality. But it is not so easy for them to set aside the Rawlsian justification of inequality. They cannot just dismiss it, without lending to their own advocacy of equality a fanatical hue that they could not themselves on reflection find attractive.

Socialist egalitarians say that they believe in equality. We might well think that they count as egalitarians because equality is their premise. But the structure of that premise is too simple to accommodate the thought that gets them going politically, which is: why should some peo-

---

above, and there are five logically possible positions about which inequalities are mandated and which allowed: all are mandated (1,2,3,4); helping ones are mandated and others forbidden (1,2); none are mandated and only helping ones are permitted (2); none are mandated and all nonharming ones are permitted (2,4); helping ones are mandated and all nonharming ones are permitted (1,2,4). Rationales can be provided for each of these five points of view, and I believe that there are traces of all of them in the letter and/or spirit of various Rawlsian texts. (Although, as I have said, I take the difference principle in a form in which it allows *all* nonharming inequalities, my critique of Rawls in this chapter is consistent with his holding any of the positions distinguished above: it depends only on his allowing helping inequalities and forbidding harming ones, and that stance is a constituent in each of the five positions).

(For passages in which variant readings of the difference principle are exposed or suggested, see the set of texts collected by Derek Parfit and presented in the Appendix of his *Equality or Priority?*.)

7. (Added, 2008) In the remaining paragraphs of this section, I am insufficiently exercised by the distinction between justice and optimal policy. Under the influence of that distinction, I would now say that distributive justice *is* (some kind of) equality, but that the Pareto principle, and also that constrained Pareto principle that is the difference principle, often trump justice. Accordingly, I would now say that although, with certain qualifications, I indeed accept the difference principle, I do not accept it *as a principle of justice*, but rather as a principle of intelligent policy. Accordingly, I now disagree with the position attributed to "socialist egalitarians" in the remainder of this section. Some who merit that title hold the position described in the section, but others, like me, think it mistaken.

See, further, sections 1–5 of Chapter 4 and section 6 of Chapter 7, below. Note that this major change of doctrine does not affect my criticism of Rawls on incentives in Chapters 1 through 3, which complain that Rawls *misapplies* the difference principle, and *not* that he prefers it, as a reading of distributive justice, to equality as such.

ple be *badly* off, when other people are so *well* off? That is not the same as the colorless question, Why should some people be better off than others? For in that question there is no reference to absolute levels of condition, hence no reference to anyone being badly off, as opposed to just *less* well off than other people are. Maybe some egalitarians would maintain their zeal in a world of millionaires and billionaires in which no one's life is hard, but the politically engaged socialist egalitarians whom I have in mind have no strong opinion about inequality at millionaire/billionaire levels. What they find wrong is that there is, so they think, unnecessary hardship at the lower end of the scale. There are people who are badly off and who, they believe, would be better off under an equalizing redistribution. The practically crucial feature of the situation is that the badly off are worse off than anyone needs to be, since an equalizing redistribution would enhance their lives.

For these egalitarians,[8] equality would be a good thing because it would make the badly off better off. They do not think it a good thing about equality that it would make the well off worse off. And when their critics charge them with being willing, for the sake of equality, to grind everyone down to the level of the worst off or even lower, they do not say, in response: well, yes, let us grind down if necessary, but let us achieve equality on a higher plane if that is possible. Instead, what they say is somewhat evasive, at the level of principle; they just deny that it is necessary, for the sake of achieving equality, to move to a condition in which some are worse off and none are better off than now. Were they more reflective, they might add that, if leveling down were necessary, then equality would lose its appeal. Either it would make the badly off worse off still, in frustration of the original egalitarian purpose, or it would make the badly off no better off, while others are made worse off to no evident purpose. Relative to their initial inspiration, which is a concern about badly off people, an inequality is mandatory if it really is needed to improve the condition of the badly off, and it is permissible if it does not improve but also does not worsen their condition.

Accordingly, these egalitarians lose sight of their goal; their position

8. (Added, 2008) They are here called "egalitarians" not because, what is manifestly false, they affirm egalitarianism (as opposed to prioritarianism) as a fundamental principle, but because they believe in promoting equality. A utilitarian, who rejects egalitarianism as a fundamental principle, who believes that the law of diminishing marginal utility justifies an equal distribution, might permissibly say: I am an egalitarian because I am a utilitarian. See, further, the last paragraph of this section.

becomes incoherent or untrue to itself, if, in a world with badly off people, they reject the difference principle and cleave to an egalitarianism of strict equality. (Given the priorities and emphases that I have attributed to them, they should, strictly speaking, affirm as fundamental neither equality nor the difference principle but this complex maxim: make the badly off well off, or if that is not possible, make them as well off as possible. But on a modestly demanding interpretation of what it means to be well off, and on a realistic view of the world's foreseeable resource prospects, the practical consequences of the complex maxim are those of the difference principle.) We might conclude that the socialist egalitarians which I have in mind should not be called "egalitarians," since (if I am right) equality is not their real premise. But that conclusion would be hasty, and I shall say more about the propriety of the name "egalitarian" in a moment.

For my part, I accept the difference principle, in its generous interpretation (see page 29 above), but I question its application in defense of special money incentives to talented people. Rawlsians think that inequalities associated with such incentives satisfy the principle. But I believe that the idea that an inequality is justified if, through the familiar incentive mechanism, it benefits the badly off is more problematic than Rawlsians suppose; that (at least) when the incentive consideration is isolated from all reference to desert or entitlement, it generates an argument for inequality that requires a model of society in breach of an elementary condition of community. The difference principle can be used to justify paying incentives that induce inequalities only when the attitude of talented people runs counter to the spirit of the difference principle itself: they would not need special incentives if they were themselves unambivalently committed to the principle. Accordingly, they must be thought of as outside the community upholding the principle when it is used to justify incentive payments to them.[9]

Speaking more generally, and somewhat beyond the limited brief of

9. Although I shall press against left-wing liberals the thought that community cannot tolerate the inequalities that they endorse, I need not deny that enormous inequalities coexisted with community in premarket societies. For if that was indeed true, then the coexistence was possible because of general acceptance, and, more particularly, because of acceptance by the less well off, of ideologies of destiny and place that left-wing liberals do not countenance. That community can go with inequality when people believe things that liberals regard as false does not show that they can go together in a society possessed of a modern consciousness.

these lectures, I want to record here my doubt that the difference principle justifies *any* significant inequality, in an unqualified way. The principle allows an inequality only if the worst off could not benefit from its removal. And I believe that it is in general more difficult than liberals suppose to show that the worst off could not benefit from removal of an inequality, and hence in general more difficult than liberals think it is to justify an inequality at the bar of the difference principle. The worst off benefit from incentive inequality in particular only because the better off would, in effect, go on strike if unequalizing incentives were withdrawn. This inequality benefits the badly off only within the constraint set by the inegalitarian attitude, and the consequent behavior, of the well off, a constraint that they could remove. And an inequality can also benefit the badly off within a constraint set, not by inegalitarian attitudes per se, but by preexisting unequal structure. Thus, in a country with state medical provision, the inequality of treatment that comes from allocating a portion of hospital resources to high-fee-paying patients who get superior care benefits the badly off when some of the revenue is used to raise standards throughout the service. The unequal medical provision helps poor people, but only against the background of a prior income inequality (which no doubt itself reflects further structural inequality and inegalitarian attitude) that has not, within this argument, itself been shown to benefit them.

The further back one goes, temporally and causally, in the construction of the feasible set, the more one encounters open possibilities that were closed by human choice, and the harder it is to identify inequalities that do not harm the badly off. Bringing together the two cases distinguished above, I conjecture that social inequalities will appear beneficial to or neutral toward the interest of those at the bottom only when we take as given unequal structures and/or inequality-endorsing attitudes that no one who affirms the difference principle should unprotestingly accept.[10]

Now if all that is right, then we might in the end, in a roundabout way, vindicate the application of the term "egalitarian" to the socialists whom I have had in mind, provided that they are willing to tolerate

---

10. We can also·say that inequalities are necessary to improve the condition of the badly off when we take for granted, not, as above, causal but moral imperatives. Thus incentives can indeed be judged necessary to raise the condition of the badly off when elements of the desert and entitlement rationales that left-wing liberals reject are affirmed.

a formulation of their position along lines just foreshadowed. For we might say that a person is an egalitarian if he applies the difference principle in circumstances in which there exist badly off (as opposed to just less well off) people *and* he believes that the principle demands, in those circumstances, equality itself, if, that is, he believes that in the long run and prescinding from rooted inegalitarian attitudes and practices, there *are* in such circumstances no social inequalities that do *not* harm the worst off. Equality appears at first to be a premise. It is then rejected, *as a premise*, when the reason for wanting equality is clarified: it is rejected in favor of the difference principle (or, strictly, the more complex maxim stated on page 32 above). But now grounded in (something like) the difference principle, it reasserts itself as a conclusion, for our world, in these times, and for the foreseeable future.

2. Nigel Lawson's Tax Cut

I return to Rawls and the difference principle in Part III of this chapter. Right now I want to focus on Nigel Lawson's tax cut, and on the incentive case against canceling it, the case, that is, for maintaining rewards to productive people at the existing high level. And I shall consider that case only with respect to those who, so it is thought, produce a lot by exercising skill and talent, rather than by investing capital. Accordingly, the argument I shall examine applies not only to capitalist economies but also to economies without private ownership of capital, such as certain forms of market socialism. Of course, there is also an incentives argument for high returns to capital investment, but I do not address that argument in this chapter.

Proponents of the incentives argument say that when productive people take home modest pay, they produce less than they otherwise might, and as a result relatively poor and badly off people are worse off than they are when the exercise of talent is well rewarded. Applied against a restoration of the top tax to 60 percent, the argument runs as follows:

Economic inequalities are justified when they make the worst off people materially better off. [Major, normative premise]

When the top tax rate is 40 percent, (a) the talented rich produce more than they do when it is 60 percent, and (b) the worst off are, as a result, materially better off. [Minor, factual premise]

Therefore, the top tax should not be raised from 40 percent to 60 percent.

It is immaterial to present concerns how the circumstance alleged to obtain in part (a) of the minor premise of the argument is supposed to occasion the result described in part (b). One possibility is that the rich work so much harder when the tax rate goes down that the tax take goes up, and more is available for redistribution. Another is that when the rich work harder, they produce, among other things, (better) employment opportunities for badly off people.

I am going to comment negatively on the incentives argument, but my criticism of it will take a particular form. For I shall focus not, directly, on the argument as such, but on the character of certain utterances of it. Accordingly, I shall not raise questions about the validity of the argument, or about the truth of its premises, save insofar as they arise (and they do) within the special focus just described. And I shall not, in particular, pursue possible doubts about the minor, factual premise of the argument. I shall question neither claim (a), that the supposedly talented rich are more productive when they are more generously rewarded, nor claim (b), that the badly off benefit from the greater productivity of the well off affirmed in (a). I do not aim to show that the minor premise of the incentives argument is false.

The critique that follows is not of everything that could be called an incentive, but only of incentives that produce inequality and that are said to be justified because they make badly off people better off. I raise no objection against incentives designed to eliminate a poverty trap or to induce people to undertake particularly unpleasant jobs. It is not constitutive of those incentives that they produce inequality. My target is incentives conferring high rewards on people of talent who would otherwise not perform as those rewards induce them to do. I believe that the familiar liberal case for incentives of that kind has not been thoroughly thought through.

3. On Uttering Arguments in Variable Interpersonal Settings

I said I would criticize the incentives argument by focusing on certain utterances of it. For I believe that, although the argument may sound reasonable when it is presented in blandly impersonal form, as it usually is, and as it was above, it does not sound so good when we fix on a presentation of it in which a talented rich person pronounces it to a badly off person. And the fact that the argument undergoes this devaluation when it occurs in that interpersonal setting should affect our assessment of the nature of the society that the incentive justification by implication recommends.

A normative argument will often wear a particular aspect because of who is offering it and/or to whom it is being addressed. When reasons are given for performing an action or endorsing a policy or adopting an attitude, the appropriate response by the person(s) asked so to act or approve or feel, and the reaction of variously placed observers of the interchange, may depend on who is speaking and who is listening. The form and the explanation of that dependence vary considerably across different kinds of cases. But the general point is that there are many ways, some more interesting than others, in which an argument's persuasive value can be speaker-audience-relative, and there are many reasons of, once again, different degrees of interest, why that should be so.

Before describing a form of dependence (of response on who is addressing whom) that operates in the case of the incentives argument, and in order to induce a mood in which we think of arguments in their contexts of delivery, I list a few examples of the general phenomenon:

(a) I can argue that the driver over there should not be blamed for just now making a right turn on a red light, since he does not know that the rules are different outside California. But he cannot, at the moment, make that very argument, entirely sound though it may be.

(b) You want the fishing rod for recreation, and I need it to get my next meal. I know that you are so unstoical that you will be more upset if you do not get to fish than I will be if I do not get to eat. So I let you have the rod, and I cite your hypersensitivity to disappointment as my reason. It would be a lot less good for you to give that as a reason why you should have the rod.

(c) I might persuade my fellow middle-class friend that, because my car is being repaired and I consequently have to spend hours on the bus these days, I have a right to be grumpy. The same conclusion, on the same basis, sounds feeble when the audience is not my friend but a carless fellow bus passenger who is forced to endure these slow journeys every day.

(d) As designers of advertisements for charitable causes know, our ordinary self-serving reasons for not giving much (we need a new roof, I'm saving for my holiday, I'm not actually very rich) sound remarkably lame when we imagine them being presented to those for whom our lack of charity means misery and death.[11]

---

11. "How do you tell a person dying of hunger that there's nothing you can do?" *Action Aid* leaflet, 1990.

(e) And such quotidian reasons also sound feeble when they are presented to people whose sacrifice for the cause is much larger than the one the speaker is excusing himself from offering.[12]

(f) Since the pot should not call the kettle black, an employee may be unimpressed when a routinely tax-evading well-heeled superior dresses him down because of his modest appropriations from petty cash.

12. An exploitation of *(inter alia)* this particular relativity occurred in an advertisement of 1943 whose purpose was to promote the purchase of war bonds. In March 1944 the advertisement won a prize for its contribution to the war effort.

The top third of the ad's space pictures an American prisoner of war in a bleak cell. Below the picture, we find the following text:

WILL YOU WRITE A LETTER to a Prisoner of war . . . tonight?

Maybe he's one of Jimmie Doolittle's boys. Perhaps he was left behind when Bataan fell. Anyway, he's an American, and he hasn't had a letter in a long, long time.

And when you sit down to write, tell *him* why you didn't buy your share of War Bonds last pay day.

"Dear Joe," you might say, "the old topcoat was getting kind of threadbare, so I . . ."

No, cross it out. Joe might not understand about the topcoat, especially if he's shivering in a damp Japanese cell.

Let's try again. "Dear Joe, I've been working pretty hard and haven't had a vacation in over a year, so . . ."

Hell, better cross that out, too. They don't even get vacations where Joe's staying.

Well, what are you waiting for? Go ahead, write the letter to Joe. *Try* to write it, anyhow.

But mister, if somehow you find you can't finish that letter, will you, at least, do this for Joe? Will you up the amount of money you're putting into War Bonds and *keep* buying your share from here on in?

(1945 *Britannica Book of the Year*, p. 22)

A word about the form of this ad, and about the sources of its motivating power (if it did the motivating it should have done to deserve the prize it won).

The ad is directed not, of course, at one person but at a large set of people, all the people in the condition of material life and personal intention of the civilian that the ad sketches. Yet the ad speaks as though to one person and it has that single person address a single member of the set of POWs. The content of the ad implies that civilians as such have some kind of obligation to POWs as such. But the ad aims to convey the obligation falling on many by selecting one individual from each of the two groups and figuring forth an encounter between them. Notice, moreover, that the ad would have sacrificed little or nothing of its purpose and power if its personal references had been pluralized, if, that is, the civilian had spoken of *our* threadbare coats, run-down sheds, and lack of vacations, to an imagined *assembly* of POWs. (Compare a first-person-plural presentation of the incentive justification, by a rich person, or by all of them in unison, to all the poor people.)

The examples show that arguments vary in their power to persuade because of variations in people's epistemic (a) or moral (e and f) or social (c) position, or because of issues of tact and embarrassment (c, d, and e), and immediacy (d), or because being generous is more attractive than being grabby (b). I shall not here attempt a systematic taxonomy of ways that arguments subside in different sorts of interpersonal delivery. Instead, I pass to a type of case that is of special interest here, since the incentives argument belongs to it.

4. The Kidnapper's Argument

In this type of case, an argument changes its aspect when its presenter is the person, or one of the people, whose choice, or choices, make one or

---

The ad makers thought they could expose the insufficiency of the reasons civilians give themselves for not buying bonds by portraying a civilian offering them to Joe. And they were right that it is easier to face yourself when you decide for the stated reasons not to buy bonds when you do not have to face Joe at the same time.

The power of the ad to move the reader is multiply determined, mingling elements that go into types (c), (d), and (e) above. The ad simulates an immediacy between the civilian and Joe, such immediacy being one rhetorical effect of casting an argument in interpersonal form. And then, immediacy having been secured, there are two or three separable things, mixed here in a powerful cocktail, on which the ad relies: that Joe and I are members of the same community, and he is suffering; that Joe and I are co-participants in an immensely important enterprise in which at least the *quality* of my life and that of the members of my family is at stake; and that Joe is a moral hero—look what he has given, for the sake of the mentioned enterprise, compared to the modest thing that I resist giving. These considerations combine to make me feel answerable to Joe. The ad says that, although it sounds quite reasonable for a person to choose a new coat before buying more bonds, the burden of wearing a threadbare coat carries no justificatory weight when it is compared to the burden Joe carries: that, so the ad implies, explains the shame a civilian would feel in telling Joe that his threadbare coat was a good reason for not buying more bonds.

Finally, a comment on the role of immediacy, which, so I noted, is one source of the advertisement's power. Immediacy can contribute to persuasion in cases where what is rendered immediate is not a person (or a group) that is addressed. We do not speak to animals, but arguments justifying their use in certain experiments might be hard to deliver in the lab while those experiments are in train. We also do not speak to trees, but it might be harder to justify the size of the Sunday edition of the *New York Times* when one is standing in a majestic forest. So having to address someone when uttering an argument is a special case of immediacy, not part of its general form, and it is perhaps not crucial to the ad's power that the POW is addressed, as opposed to just *there*, that is, here, when the argument is presented.

more of the argument's premises true. By contrast with other presenters of the same argument, a person who makes, or helps to make, one of its premises true can be asked to justify the fact[13] that it is true. And sometimes he will be unable to provide a satisfying justification.

For a dramatic example of this structure, consider the argument for paying a kidnapper where the child will be freed only if the kidnapper is paid. There are various reasons for not paying. Some concern further consequences: maybe, for example, more kidnapping would be encouraged. And paying could be thought wrong not only in some of its consequences but in its nature, since paying is acceding to a vile threat. You may nevertheless agree that, because so much is at stake, paying kidnappers is often justified. And the argument for paying a particular kidnapper, shorn of qualifications that are needed to neutralize the countervailing reasons mentioned above, might run as follows:

Children should be with their parents.

Unless they pay him, this kidnapper will not return this child to its parents.

So this child's parents should pay this kidnapper.

Now, that form of the argument is entirely third-personal: in that form of it, anyone (save, perhaps, someone mentioned in the argument) might be presenting it to anyone else. But let us now imagine the kidnapper himself presenting the argument, to, for example, the child's parents. (What will matter here is that he is doing the talking, rather than that they are doing the listening: the latter circumstance achieves prominence in section 11 below.) The argument that follows is the same as that given above, by an unimpeachable criterion of identity for arguments: its major premise states the same principle, its minor premise carries the same factual claim, and its conclusion directs performance of the same action.

Children should be with their parents.

Unless you pay me, I shall not return your child.

So you should pay me.

Notice, now, that despite what we can assume to be the truth of its premises and the validity of its inference, discredit attaches to anyone

13. As opposed to the claim that it is true, which every presenter of the argument can be asked to justify.

who utters this argument in the foregoing interpersonal setting, even though uttering the same argument in impersonal form is, in most cases,[14] an innocent procedure. And there is, of course, no mystery about why the argument's presenter attracts discredit in the exhibited interpersonal case. He does so because the fact to which he appeals, which is that you will get your child back only if you pay, is one that he deliberately causes to obtain: he makes that true, and to make that true is morally vile.

When he presents the argument, the kidnapper shows himself to be awful, but it is hardly necessary for us to reflect on his utterance of the argument to convince ourselves that he merits disapproval. Independently of any such reflection, we amply realize that the kidnapper's conduct is wrong, and we need not be especially scandalized by his frank avowal of it. Indeed, in certain instances a kidnapper's presentation of the argument will be a service to the parents, because sometimes his utterance of the argument's minor premise will, for the first time, put them in the picture about how to get their child back. One can even imagine a maybe slightly schizoid kidnapper suddenly thinking, "Omigod, I've forgotten to tell the kid's parents!" and experiencing some concern for them, and for the child, in the course of that thought.

Yet although what is (mainly) bad about the kidnapper is not his voicing the argument, but his making its minor premiss true, he should still be ashamed to voice the argument, just because he makes that premise true. The fact that in some cases he would do further ill not to voice the argument does not falsify the claim that in all cases he reveals himself to be ghastly when he does voice it.

In the kidnapper argument, there are two groups of agents, the kidnapper and the parents, both referred to in the third person in the initial presentation of the argument, and referred to in the first and second persons in its revised presentation. Consider any argument that refers to distinct groups of people, A and B. There are many different ways in which such an argument might be presented. It might be uttered by members of

14. I express myself in that cautious way because, apart from the case, if you want to allow it, in which the kidnapper himself uses the impersonal form of the argument, referring to himself as "he," there is the case of a person who puts it forth and conveys (for example, by his tone) that he is quite insensitive to the countervailing (if properly overridden) considerations, and/or that he sees nothing untoward in the kidnapper's threat, and/or that he sees human dealings on the model of interaction of impersonal forces.

A or of B or of neither group, and it might be addressed to members of either group or of neither. And all of that applies to the incentives argument, with the groups being talented rich people on the one hand and the worst off on the other. In my treatment of the incentives argument I shall mainly be interested in the case where a talented rich person puts it forward, sometimes no matter to whom and sometimes where it matters that poor people are his audience; but at one point I shall consider the opposite case, where a poor person addresses the argument to a talented rich one.

The incentives argument has something in common with the kidnapper argument, even though there are major differences between withholding a hostage and withholding labor until one gets the money one desires. But before looking more carefully at similarities and contrasts between the kidnapper and incentives arguments, I want to explain why the word "community" appears in the title of these lectures.

5. Community, and the Interpersonal Test

In its familiar use, "community" covers a multitude of conditions, and I shall introduce the particular condition that I have in mind by relating it to the concept of a *comprehensive justification*.

Most policy arguments contain premises about how people will act when the policy is, and is not, in force. Schemes for housing, health, education, and the economy typically operate by altering agents' feasible sets, and their justifications usually say what agents facing those sets can be expected to choose to do.

Consider, then, a policy P and an argument purportedly justifying it, one of whose premises says that a subset S of the population will act in a certain fashion when P is in force. We engage in what might be called *comprehensive assessment* of the proferred justification of P when we ask whether the projected behavior of the members of S is itself justified. And *comprehensive justification* of P obtains only if that behavior is indeed justified.[15]

"We should do A because they will do B" may justify our doing A, but it does not justify it comprehensively if they are not justified in doing B,

---

15. It follows, harmlessly, that penal policies adopted to reduce the incidence of crime lack comprehensive justification. The very fact that such a policy is justified shows that all is not well with society.

and we do not provide a comprehensive justification of our doing *A* if we set aside as irrelevant the question whether they are justified in doing *B*. Thus, insofar as we are expected to treat the incentives argument as though no question arises about the justification of the behavior of the talented rich that its minor premise describes, what we are offered may be a justification, but it is not a comprehensive justification of the incentives policy.

Now, a policy argument provides a comprehensive justification only if it passes what I shall call the *interpersonal test*. This tests how robust a policy argument is by subjecting it to variation with respect to who is speaking and/or who is listening when the argument is presented. The test asks whether the argument could serve as a justification of a mooted policy when uttered by any member of society to any other member. So, to carry out the test, we hypothesize an utterance of the argument by a specified individual, or, more commonly, by a member of a specified group, to another individual, or to a member of another, or, indeed, the same, group. If, *because* of who is presenting it, and/or to whom it is presented, the argument cannot serve as a justification of the policy, then whether or not it passes as such under other dialogical conditions, it fails *(tout court)* to provide a comprehensive justification of the policy.

A salient way that arguments fail when put to this test, and the only mode of test failure that will figure henceforth in this chapter, is that the speaker cannot fulfill a demand for justification that does not arise when the argument is presented by and/or to others. So to anticipate what I shall try to show, the incentives argument does not serve as a justification of inequality on the lips of the talented rich, because they cannot answer a demand for justification that naturally arises when they present the argument, namely, why would you work less hard if income tax were put back up to 60 percent? The rich will find that question difficult no matter who puts it to them, but I shall often focus on the case where their interlocutors are badly off people, because in that setting the question, and the difficulty the rich have with it, may lead to further dialogical development that carries further illumination.

When the justification of policies that mention groups of people is presented in the usual way, with exclusively third-person reference to groups and their members, the pertinence of the question why various people are disposed to act as they do is not always apparent. It becomes evident when we picture the relevant people themselves rehearsing the argument, and sometimes more so when the audience is a strategically selected one. The test of interpersonal presentation makes vivid that the justification of policy characteristically depends on circumstances that are not exogenous with respect to human agency.

And so to community. I began by observing that there is more than one kind of community, and I must now specify the kind that is relevant to present concerns. First, though, a few points about the semantics of the word "community."

Like "friendship," "community" functions both as a count noun and as a mass noun. It is a count noun when it denotes sets of people variously bound or connected (the European community, London's Italian community, our community), and it is a mass noun when we speak of how much community there is in a certain society, when we say that some action enhances or reduces, or some attitude honors or violates, community, and so on.

A community, one could say, is a set of people among whom there is community: that is how the count-notion and the mass-notion are linked. "Community" is in this respect like "friendship": a friendship is a relationship in which friendship obtains. Notice that friends can do and feel things that are inconsistent with friendship without thereby dissolving their friendship. There can be a lapse of friendship in a friendship without that friendship ceasing to be. But there cannot (enduringly) be *no* friendship in a friendship. And all that is also true of community: there can be violations and lapses of community in a community, but there cannot be no community in a community.

In addition to community in the adjectivally unqualified sense where it is analogous not only in form but also in content to friendship, there are specific types of community, some of which do, while others do not, contribute to community in the adjectivally unqualified sense. And types of community (mass-wise) distinguish types of community (count-wise). Linguistic community, or community of language, constitutes a linguistic community as such; community of nationality establishes a national community; and community of interest in stamps binds the philatelic community.

The form of community that concerns me here, which I shall call *justificatory community,* prevails in justificatory communities. And justificatory community, though something of a concocted notion, contributes to community *tout court,* that is, to community in the full (adjectivally unqualified) sense sketched a moment ago. A justificatory community is a set of people among whom there prevails a norm (which need not always be satisfied) of comprehensive justification. If what certain people are disposed to do when a policy is in force is part of the justification of that policy, it is considered appropriate to ask them to justify the relevant behavior, and it detracts from justificatory community when they cannot do so. It follows that an argument for a policy satisfies the requirement of justificatory community, with respect to the people it mentions, only if it passes the interpersonal test. And if all arguments for the policy fail that test, then the policy itself evinces lack of justificatory community, whatever else might nevertheless be said in its favor.

Now, an argument fails the interpersonal test, and is therefore inconsistent with community, if relevant agents *could* not justify the behavior the argument ascribes to them. What if the agents are actually asked to justify their stance and, for one reason or another, they refuse to do so? Then the argument in question does not necessarily fail the test, for it might be that they could justify their stance. But if their reason for refusing to justify it is that they do not think themselves accountable to their interrogators, that they do not think they *need* provide a justification, then they are forswearing community with the rest of us in respect of the policy issue in question. They are asking us to treat them like a set of Martians in the light of whose predictable behavior (be it aggressive, benign, or neither) it is wise for us to take certain steps, but whom we should not expect to engage in justificatory dialogue.

To employ the interpersonal test and to regard its failure as indicative of a lack of community is to presuppose nothing about which particular collections of people constitute communities in the relevant sense. Some may think there is no reason why there should be community between rich and poor in a society, and they may therefore regard failure of the test as uninteresting or, if interesting, then not because it shows lapse of community. Others, by contrast, might think that community ought to obtain among all human beings, so that it would stain a policy argument advanced by rich countries in North-South dialogue if it could not pass muster in explicit I-thou form.[16] The thesis associated with the interper-

---

16. (Altered, 2008) In n. 28 on p. 152 of the 1989 typescript of *Justice as Fairness: A Briefer Restatement,* Rawls expresses a view that has a bearing on how wide community can be: ". . . the allegiance to, or the motivational support needed, for the difference principle to be effective presupposes a degree of homogeneity among peoples and a sense of social cohesion and closeness that cannot be expected in a society of states." This statement implies that there is sufficient such closeness domestically. (The footnote is not reproduced in the version of *Justice as Fairness* published in 2001, perhaps because of the superior—as Rawls may have thought—development of the theme in *The Law of Peoples,* which appeared in 1999.)

sonal test is that if a policy justification fails it, then anyone proposing that justification in effect represents the people it mentions as *pro tanto* out of community with one another. Whether they should be in community with one another is a separate question. That depends on a doctrine, not to be articulated here, about what the proper boundaries of a community are. In my own (here undefended) view, it diminishes the democratic character of a society if it is not a community in the present sense, since we do not make policy *together* if we make it in the light of what some of us do that cannot be justified to others.

It is often said that it is unrealistic to expect a modern society to be a community, and it is no doubt inconceivable that there should be a standing disposition of warm mutual identification between any pair of citizens in a large and heterogeneous polity. But community here is not some soggy mega-*Gemeinschaftlichkeit*. Instead, my claim about the incentive justification is that, to appropriate a phrase of Rawls, it does not supply "a public basis in the light of which citizens can justify to one another their common institutions"[17] and that the justification is therefore incompatible with what Rawls calls "ties of civic friendship."[18]

Now some examples of the battery of concepts introduced above.

Under the premiership of Harold Wilson, some economic policies were justified by reference to the intentions of the so-called "gnomes of Zurich," the international bankers who, it was said, would react punitively to various government decisions. It was a mark of their *foreign* status that economic policy had to *placate* those bankers, and although it might have been thought that they should behave differently, it would not have been considered appropriate for the British government to call upon them to do so. But such a call would surely be appropriate in the case of people conceived as belonging to our own community. Nor should members of our own community need to be placated by our community's policies: when justified their demands should be satisfied, but that is a different matter.

An example that for some readers may be close to home: the policy argument that rates of pay to British academics should be raised, since

17. "Kantian Constructivism in Moral Theory," p. 347. Cf. Christine Korsgaard: "Part of the appeal of the difference principle is that it is the source of justifications which you can offer *to anyone* without embarrassment" ("The Reasons We Can Share," p. 50).
18. *A Theory of Justice*, p. 536.

otherwise they will succumb to the lure of high foreign salaries. We can suppose that academics are indeed disposed to leave the country because of current salary levels. The issue of whether, nevertheless, they should emigrate is pertinent to the policy argument when they are regarded as fellow members of community who owe the rest a justification for decisions that affect the welfare of the country. And many British academics with an inclination to leave who put the stated policy argument contrive to avoid that issue by casting the minor premise of the argument in the third person. They say: "Lots of academics will go abroad," not: "Lots of us will go abroad."

The connection between sharing community membership and being open to requests for justification comes out nicely in an example of current (that is, 1991) interest. The Moscow generals might address the Lithuanian independence movement leaders as follows: "Widespread bloodshed is to be avoided. If you persist in your drive for independence, we shall intervene forcefully, and there will be widespread bloodshed as a result. You should therefore abandon your drive for independence." The Lithuanian leaders might now ask the generals to justify their conditional intention to intervene forcefully. If the generals brush that question aside, they forswear justificatory community with the Lithuanians.

The Lithuanian leaders might produce a parallel argument: "Widespread bloodshed is to be avoided. If you intervene forcefully, we shall nevertheless persist in our drive for independence, and there will be widespread bloodshed as a result. You should therefore abandon your plan to intervene forcefully." And the Lithuanians too might feel no obligation to justify their intentions to the generals. If, on the other hand, both sides labor under such a sense of obligation, they will enter a justificatory exchange in which each tries to show that the other's minor premise, whether true or not, should be false.

6. Does the Incentives Argument Pass the Interpersonal Test?

The interpersonal test focuses on an utterance of an argument, but what it tests, through examination of that utterance, is the argument itself. If lack of community is displayed when the rich present the incentives argument, then the argument itself (irrespective of who affirms it) represents relations between rich and poor as at variance with community. It follows, if I am right, that the incentives argument can justify inequality only in a society where interpersonal relations lack a communal character in the specified sense.

Sometimes, as, for example, in the kidnapper case, the interpersonal test will be a roundabout way of proving an already evident point (in the kidnapper case, that there is significant lack of community between the kidnapper and the parents). But in other cases the test will illuminate, and I believe that the incentives argument is one of them. That argument is generally presented in entirely third-personal terms and, relatedly, as though no question arises about the attitudes and choices of the rich people it mentions. When, by contrast, we imagine a talented rich person himself affirming the argument, then background issues of equality and obligation come clearly into view, and, if I am right, the rich are revealed to be out of community with the poor in respect of the economic dimension of their lives. So we see more deeply into the character of the incentives argument when we cast it in the selected I-thou terms.

Now an important qualification. I say that the incentives argument shows itself to be repugnant to community when it is offered *on its own* by well off people. I insert that phrase because the present case against the argument lapses when the argument appears in combination with claims about desert, and/or with Nozick-like claims about a person's entitlements to the reward his or her labor would command on an unfettered market. I do not myself accept that sort of compound justification of incentive inequality, but I do not here contend that it fails the interpersonal test. My target here is the unadorned or naked use of the incentive justification. It is often used nakedly, and with plenty of emphasis that it is being used nakedly. That emphasis occurs when advocates say it is an advantageous feature of the incentive justification that it employs no controversial moral premises about desert or entitlement. (Notice that, since John Rawls rejects use of desert and entitlement to justify inequalities, the Rawlsian endorsement of incentives takes what I call a naked form.)

The sequence of claims that I make goes as follows: The talented rich cannot justify the fact that the minor premise of the (naked) incentives argument is true. If they cannot justify the truth of its minor premise, then they cannot use the argument as a justification of inequality. If they cannot use it as a justification of inequality, then it cannot be used as a justification within community. If it cannot be used as a justification within community, then anyone who uses it (in effect) represents society as at variance with community when he does so.

II: Testing the Incentives Argument

7. *What Makes the Minor Premise of the Incentives Argument True?*

The kidnapper argument discredits its advocate when the kidnapper puts it forward himself because, as I said (see section 4 above), he *makes* it true that the parents get their child back only if they pay, and to make that true is morally vile.

Accordingly, to discredit first-person affirmation of the incentives argument in a parallel way, I must defend two claims. First, that in a sufficiently similar sense, the rich *make* it true that they will not work as hard at 60 percent tax as they do at 40 percent: I have to show that the minor premise[19] of the incentives argument owes its truth to their decisions and intentions. (I say *sufficiently* similar because there are undoubtedly some significant differences here, which are consequent on the fact that the rich are not an individual but a group, and a group with shifting membership: in the final paragraphs of this section I address some of the complication that this fact generates.) And it also needs to be shown that, deprived as they are here of recourse to the considerations of desert and entitlement that are set aside in a "naked" (see the penultimate paragraph of section 5) use of the incentives argument, the rich cannot justify making the stated proposition true. I am not, of course, obliged to maintain even then that their making it true puts them on a moral par with kidnappers, but just that, if their posture is defensible, then its defense rests on grounds of the sort that a naked user of the incentives argument forgoes.

I turn to my first task, which is to show that the talented rich do make the factual premise of the argument true. Let us ask: if that premise is true, then why is it true? Is it true because the rich are unable to work at 60 percent as hard as they do at 40? Or is it true because they are unwilling to work that hard at 60 percent? If the truth of the premise reflects inability, then we cannot say that, in the relevant sense, the rich *make* the

---

19. Or, strictly, part (a) of that premise: part (b) is true only if others—for example, the government—act in certain required ways. But for simplicity I shall continue to speak of the rich making the factual minor premise *(tout court)* true.

premise true. An inability explanation of the truth of the premise means that the rich could not, by choosing differently, make the premise false.

There are two forms that an inability claim might take. In the first form of the claim, the rich cannot work hard unless they consume things that cost a great deal of money.

Now it might well be true that without enough money to buy superior relaxation some high-talent performances would be impossible: perhaps the massively self-driving executive does need, to be effective, more expensive leisure between one day's work and the next than he can get living in ordinary accommodation on an average wage. (When I say that he might need high-quality leisure, I refer not to his preference ordering or utility function but to what it is physically and/or psychologically possible for him to do. That kind of capacity limitation interacts causally with a person's utility function, but it is not identical with it or an aspect of it.) But the income gap which that consideration would justify is surely only a fraction of the one that obtains even at 60 percent top tax. The extra money that executives (and so forth) get at 40 percent can hardly be required to finance whatever luxuries we might imagine they strictly need to perform at a high level: they could afford those necessary luxuries with what they have left even when they pay a 60 percent tax.

In a different version of the claim that the rich could not work as hard at 60 percent tax as they do at 40 percent, what they are said to need is not the goods that only a lot of money will buy but the prospect of getting those goods or that money: the high reward is now said to be indispensable to motivation, or morale. (You eventually give the biscuit to the performing dog so that the same procedure will work again next time, and not because the dog needs the calories it gets from the biscuit to enable it to go on performing.) This motivation story does not say that, unless they are handsomely paid, the rich will choose not to work very hard: the proposition that they have a real choice in the matter is just what the inability claim is designed to contradict. What is rather meant is that the allure of big bucks sustains, and is needed to sustain, the motivational drive required for heavy effort: the rich just cannot get themselves to work as hard when they expect to be taxed at 60 percent as they can get themselves to work when they expect to be taxed at 40 percent.

Now, in my opinion, there is not much truth in this contention: it represents people of talent as more feeble than, on the whole, they are. It is not likely to be lack of power to do otherwise that causes the rich to take longer holidays, to knock off at 5:00 instead of at 6:00, or not to bother trying to get one more order, those being the things that they do when income tax rises, if the minor premise of the incentives argument is true. The tax rise means that the rich face a new and less appealing schedule of the costs and benefits of alternative courses of action, and they will, of course, find it harder to raise up enthusiasm for choices that now promise smaller rewards. It does not follow that they cannot make, and effectively pursue, those choices.

Still, I say that there is not much, not no, truth in the contention mooted here. For I recognize that a perception that reward is "too low" can cause, at least somewhat independently of the will, a morose reluctance that operates as a drag on performance. But we should ask what brings about that disabling perception. And if two of its prominent causes were its only causes, then, as I shall now try to explain, the "motivation" version of the inability contention would be disqualified.

One thing that causes a dispiriting feeling that reward is too low is disappointed expectation. Socialized as they have been in a severely unequal society, the talented rich of course anticipate a handsome return for their exertions. They will therefore be downcast when such return is not forthcoming, even when they do not judge that they deserve or are otherwise entitled to it. But it is not unlikely that they also do make judgments like that. They think that they have a right to golden rewards if they work hard, and so powerful is that belief that it can act as a further cause of low morale: it can make the thought of working hard at 60 percent tax fill them with a truly disabling dismay.

Now an inability to work hard at 60 percent tax (in people who *ex hypothesi* routinely work that hard at 40 percent) that reflects habituated expectation, or judgment of entitlement, or both, cannot count here, in rebuttal of the claim that optional decisions of the talented rich make the minor premise of the incentives argument true. Consider, first, the habituation factor. We are here engaged in a ground-level investigation of a certain justification of inequality. It is therefore inappropriate, by way of contribution to that justification, to cite mere habituation to unequal rewards. Habits can change,[20] and they are therefore beside the

20. (Expanded, 2008) If not always at the level of the individual, then certainly at the social level, through reformed structures of education.

And even if the relevant habits could not change, that would have more implications for the practice than for the theory of justice. As Rawls says, "We do not consider the strains of commitment that might result from some people having to move from a favored position in an unjust society to a less favored position (either abso-

point in a fundamental inquiry. And the causal force of belief in the rightness of high reward (which helps to sustain the habitual expectation) must also be ignored here. For we are here envisaging the talented rich uttering the incentives argument in its naked form, in which invocation of entitlement is pointedly eschewed. There would, accordingly, be a kind of pragmatic inconsistency if the rich had to cite their own belief in entitlement when rejecting the claim that the truth of the minor premise of the argument reflects what they themselves are willing and unwilling to do.[21]

If the "motivation" variant of the inability claim depended entirely on habit and normative belief, we could safely set it aside. We could say that if it is true, it is compromised in the present context by what its truth rests on, that it does not furnish an appropriate reason for saying that talented rich people could not work as hard at 60 percent tax as they do at 40. The claim might help to silence moralistic charges against the present generation of talented rich people, but it could not contribute to a robust vindication of inequality in human society.

Now I firmly believe that such truth as the inability claim possesses does depend, entirely, on factors of habit and ideology that, for the stated reasons, must here be ruled out. I think it hard to believe otherwise when one focuses on the inability claim proper, as opposed to the claim, with which it is readily confused, that the talented rich have a right not to work as hard at 60 percent tax as they do at 40 percent. Nevertheless, I have not shown that there exist no relevant deeper restrictions on motivation, and, in the seminar following the lectures on which this chapter was based, I was rightly taken to task on this score by

lutely or relatively or both) in this just society . . . The strains of commitment test applied to cases of hypothetical transition from unjust societies is irrelevant" ("Reply to Alexander and Musgrave," pp. 251–252, and see *Justice as Fairness*, p. 44, on the role of education in sustaining a just society: the relevant strains of commitment are those that survive a socialization process that instills egalitarian principles in the young).

21. That particular inconsistency would not attach to naked use of the argument by a third party who cites (without endorsing) the belief of the rich in their entitlements as what happens to explain the truth of the argument's minor premise. But reference to that belief would nevertheless be unacceptable when the argument for inequality is pitched at a fundamental level. If the rich are unable to work as hard at 60 percent tax as they do at 40 because they believe that they should be paid more if they work harder, then the stated incapacity cannot, without bizarre circularity, figure in an argument that would justify the proposition that it is *fundamentally right* that they be paid more for working harder.

Samuel Scheffler, who did not reject my conclusion but who emphasized that it had not been demonstrated, not, at any rate, in the general case, where the issue is not whether these particular people could keep their shoulders to the wheel under the contemplated tax rise, but whether *some* significant inequalities are required, in general, for optimal economic motivation.

For all that I had shown, so Scheffler said, incentives might elicit motives that could not "be summoned at will," that nothing else would induce, and that would enable agents to perform better than they otherwise could. To illustrate the form of his objection, he cited the "runner who needs competition to achieve his fastest times," and people who work best under pressure, adversity or challenge. These compelling examples warn against being simple-minded about psychological feasibility. They show that what people are able to do depends on the reasons they have for doing it: with different reasons the adrenalin flows to different extents. And Scheffler concluded that a fully adequate reply to the inability claim would have to include "at least the rudiments of a serious psychology of egalitarianism . . . a realistic account of the human motivational resources and mechanisms that egalitarian . . . institutions would expect to engage."

I accept this claim, which calls for a program of work that manifestly cannot be accomplished here. It needs to be shown that a society of people who believe in equality and act accordingly is reproducible, that it is not fated to collapse under disintegrative strains. Such societies seem to be possible on a small scale, and we need to explore what constraints of human nature and organization make them difficult—as they undoubtedly are—on a larger scale, and whether those difficulties approach impossibility. As a practical proposal, normative egalitarianism indeed requires a corresponding psychology. If the research program to which the Scheffler objection points were to deliver negative results, equality might still be a tenable value,[22] but it could not, unmodified, represent a policy goal.

22. (Added, 2008) It might indeed constitute the value of justice, one that, we should have to say, cannot be realized, because of deficiencies in the makeup of human beings. Through a misinterpretation of what, insofar as it is true, "'ought' implies 'can'" means, some philosophers have (unwittingly or otherwise) demonstrated that human beings are not by nature unjust. I don't think that can be shown *a priori*. (See Chapter 6, section 13 below on a characteristic misuse of "'ought' implies 'can,'" and the final sentence in the penultimate paragraph of section 8 of Chapter 7 for a protest against conceptualizations of justice that render original sin logically impossible.)

In pursuing such a program in the search for possible equality-supporting "human motivational resources and mechanisms," it is not inappropriate to reflect on the other (nonincentive) examples that illustrate the form of Scheffler's objection. For they all involve a drive to perform well, whether as an end in itself or as a way of impressing others and/or oneself. The motivation in question contrasts with the search for gains that, like money, are quite external to the performance itself. The examples remind us that the desire to achieve, to shine, and, yes, to outshine, can elicit enormous effort even in the absence of pecuniary motivation. Of course, many would say that such nonpecuniary mechanisms just replace money inequality by status inequality, and that is yet another large challenge to which I cannot respond fully here.[23] Notice, though, that the notion of "replacement" is somewhat unapt, since money inequality itself generates status inequality. Status is not, moreover, redistributable in the same way that material resources are, and it therefore does not raise the same issues as money inequality does for an egalitarianism whose inspiration (see pages 30–31 above) is that some people lead unnecessarily hard lives.

And there is another consideration to be borne in mind: in estimating what it would be like for a person to accept a salary that is much lower than what full exercise of market power would provide, the strain to think about is the one he would feel when, *ex hypothesi,* people like him are accepting similarly modest salaries. We are talking about an egalitarian society, not about a population of talented people each of whom is a unique moral hero.

That is the best I can do, right now, by way of facing up to the prodigious task Scheffler set me. So, realizing that some of the required case has not been proven, I nevertheless now set the motivation claim aside, and with all the relevant implied caveats I conclude that the reason why the minor premise of the incentives argument is true (if it is true) is that the executive and his like are willing to work hard only at a 40 percent top tax rate.

But before we ask whether that choice is justified, let me address the complication that, even if each talented individual chooses not to work hard at 60 percent tax, no such individual makes the minor premise of the incentives argument true, since its truth requires that many such indi-

23. For an ingenious attempt to meet it, see Joseph Carens, *Equality, Moral Incentives, and the Market.* There are substantial flaws in Carens's account, but it is in my view a profound and pioneering work. (For more on Carens, see Chapter 5 below, pp. 189–191, and Chapter 8, pp. 369–370.)

viduals make similar choices. Here, then, is a disanalogy with the case of the kidnapper, since he makes the minor premise of his argument true all by himself.

In response to this important point, I shall say only two things here. First, notice that an individual talented rich person is relevantly analogous to a member of a large band of kidnappers, who could also truthfully say: it will make no, or not much, difference if I change my choice. Yet if a member of such a band puts the kidnapper argument in the first-person plural, if he says, "Giving *us* the money is the only way you will get your child back," then the fact that he is only (a dispensable) one of the "us" who together ensure that the child is held captive does not make his posture justifiable. And it is similarly true that if what the rich together cause could not be justified if one rich person caused it, then being only one rich person and not all of them would not suffice to make one's behavior justifiable. One might not be *as* responsible as when one achieves something without assistance, but one also could not say that the result had nothing to do with one's actions.[24]

And whatever the complex truth may be about individual responsibility for a collectively produced result, I am not here primarily interested in commenting on the moral character of rich people. My primary interest is in an argument that, I claim, fails the interpersonal test. Rich people may benefit from a practice on which they have little occasion to reflect. If I here (counterfactually) imagine them trying to justify that practice by recourse to the incentives argument, it is in order to investigate not, in the first instance, how blameworthy they are, but how that argument fares in the light of a norm of justificatory community.

8. Why the Incentives Argument Fails the Interpersonal Test

In its standard presentation, the incentives argument is put forward as though it is irrelevant to its assessment whether the rich are justified in making its minor premise true, and as though it would be inappropriate

24. For a case that bears on the issue dealt with in the foregoing paragraph, see Derek Parfit's "harmless torturers" at p. 80 of his *Reasons and Persons*. If someone objects that the talented rich are unlike the just imagined kidnappers in not being an organized group, then, so I believe, reflection on Parfit's case shows that they need not be one for my purposes. And one could also put forward a persuasive case of relevantly unorganized kidnappers, where all that is essential to the analogy is restored, but I shall spare you the rococo detail.

to put that question to them. I have protested that the question can be considered inappropriate only if the rich are conceived as inaccessible third persons who do not belong to the society for which the incentive policy is proposed. It does not follow that what the rich do could not be justified, that the neglected question, having been raised, could not be answered satisfactorily. In this section I explore possible answers to it.

The relevant part of the minor premise (that is, the part that the rich need to justify, part [a]) says that if the top tax rises to 60 percent, the talented rich will work less hard than they do now, when the top tax is 40 percent. And, so we have concluded, that is because they will then choose to work less hard. As a result of that choice, the badly off will be worse off than they were before (by the truth of part [b] of the minor premise of the incentives argument), and, a fortiori, worse off than they would be if the talented rich maintained at 60 percent tax the effort they put in at 40 percent. On the factual assumptions behind the minor premise of the argument, the ordering of benefit to the badly off from the three work/tax packages just mentioned is as follows:

1 The talented rich work w at 60 percent tax
2 The talented rich work w at 40 percent tax
3 The talented rich work $w - x$ at 60 percent tax,

where w is the amount the rich choose to work at 40 percent and x the amount by which they reduce their input if the tax rises to 60 percent.

We must now ask whether the choices of rich people, which make 3 rather than 1 true if the tax rises, and thereby make the badly off worse off than when the tax is low, can be justified, consistently with their advocacy of the argument set out near the beginning of section 2 above, when notions of desert and entitlement are not allowed to figure in justifications.

In certain cases, where working just as hard at 60 percent tax as one did at 40 percent would mean an oppressive existence, the choice that the rich make is undoubtedly justified. Think of those harried and haggard yuppies or overworked surgeons who really would lead miserable lives if the massive amount of work they do were not compensated by the massive amount of income that leads them to choose to work that hard. We can set such "special burden" cases aside, not because they do not exist, but because of the nature of the justification of the talented rich person's choice in this sort of case.

Let me explain. In the present exercise the incentives argument is supposed to justify inequality. But when special burden is invoked, what we get is not a justification of an inequality, all things considered, that incentives produce, but a denial that they do produce an inequality, all things considered. That is so because, when we compare people's material situations, we must take into account not only the income they get but also what they have to do to get it. Accordingly, if the talented rich could plausibly claim special burden, the move to the 40 percent tax that induced them to work harder might also be required for the sake of equality: where work is specially arduous or stressful, higher remuneration is a counterbalancing equalizer on a sensible view of how to judge whether or not things are equal. Since I oppose only those incentives that induce unambiguous inequalities, my opposition retires in the face of the special burden case, and I acknowledge that, where special burden holds, the rich have a persuasive answer to the question why they make the minor premise of the incentives argument true.[25]

My primary target as a philosopher is a pattern of justification, one from which the incentives argument deviates when special burden holds. But as a politically engaged person, I also have another target: the real-world inequality that is actually defended on incentive grounds. And because I also have that second target, I have to claim that the special burden case is statistically uncommon. But I do not find that difficult to do, since I am confident that if talented rich people were to provide, at 60 percent tax, the greater effort we are supposing them to supply at 40 percent, then a large majority of them would still have not only higher incomes but also more fulfilling jobs than ordinary people have.[26]

25. (Added, 2008) Note that this persuasive answer doesn't justify the additional payment as an incentive. It would be similarly justified by equality under a regime of direction of labor that did not rely on incentives. For excellent remarks on the "special burden" case of which I was unaware when I was preparing the Tanner Lectures, see Alastair Macleod, "Economic Inequality: Justice and Incentives," pp. 186–188.
26. Anyone who dissents from that statistical assessment is invited to settle for the following more modest claim, which will suffice here: although it is difficult to tell how much any given individual enjoys or disenjoys his work, it is false that jobs demanding talent are, on the whole, less satisfying. Accordingly, the consideration of burden cannot justify the fact that on the whole they command much more pay.
It is an important point for Rawls that the talented are fortunate to be talented, and that is partly because the exercise of talent in work is satisfying. Accordingly,

Since I propose to cast no doubt on the truth of the minor premise of the incentives argument, I must now set aside another case, that in which well-paid talented people so enjoy their work or are so dedicated to making money that they would actually work no less hard after a tax rise. Such people are bluffing if, in the rent-seeking hope of inducing a political effect, they announce that a tax rise would lead them to work less. But in their case, and a fortiori in the case of talented people whose labor supply curve is in the relevant range not merely vertical but backward-bending, the minor premise of the incentives argument is false, since these people will *not* work less hard if the tax goes up, and this case is therefore out of bounds here.[27]

Summarizing and extending the foregoing discussion, I now ask you to look at a table that depicts three positions that the talented rich person might be thought to be in. Of the three cases that appear in the table, two are, for different reasons, irrelevant to our purposes, the special burden case because it poses no problem for the egalitarian point of view (and is in any event not widely instantiated) and the case of bluff, because in that case the minor premise of the incentives argument is false. So from now on let us focus on what is called "the standard case"[28] in the table.

In the table, w denotes the amount that the rich actually work at 40 percent, and $w - x$ denotes some significantly smaller amount:

Rawlsians are not well placed to adduce the special burden consideration in support of the justice of incentives. As Robert Nozick remarks, "Rawls is *not* imagining that inequalities are needed to fill positions that everyone can do equally well, or that the most drudgery-filled positions that require the least skill will command the highest income" (*Anarchy, State, and Utopia*, p. 188).

27. It is, however, a perfectly realistic case. Pigs don't always remove their snouts from the trough when there's less fodder there: sometimes they work harder to get at it, and that has implications for policy.

28. (Added, 2008) "Standard" was an unfortunate choice of expression, because it needlessly (for my purposes) implies that the bluff or rent case (or, as I call it near the beginning of section 4 of Chapter 2, the "*bad* case") is more rare than what I called the standard case: Joshua Cohen rightly criticizes that implication at pp. 374–375 of "Taking People as They Are." I should have said that what I called the "standard" case was more common *within* the set of nonrent cases, which is to say that it is *more* common than "special burden."

Table 1.1

Benefit to the (currently) badly off	Preference orderings of the rich across three work/tax packages
	The standard case
2	Work w at 40 percent
3	Work $w - x$ at 60 percent
1	Work w at 60 percent
	(and be much better off than others are)
	The bluff case
2	Work w at 40 percent
1	Work w at 60 percent
3	Work $w - x$ at 60 percent
	(and be much better off than others are)
	The special burden case
2	Work w at 40 percent
3	Work $w - x$ at 60 percent
1	Work w at 60 percent
	(and be worse off than others are as a result)

In all three cases the rich prefer working w at 40 percent to working $w - x$ at 60 percent. This preference may not be readily apparent, but we can demonstrate[29] that they have it. For they choose to work w, rather than $w - x$, when the tax is 40 percent, and they must prefer $w - x$ at 40 percent to $w - x$ at 60, since work is the same and income is higher in the first package. It follows that the rich prefer working w at 40 percent to working $w - x$ at 60.

The preference orderings of the rich are identical in the standard and special burden cases. The difference between those cases (which is formulated in parentheses) lies in the comparison between the lot of the rich and that of other people when the rich are at the bottom of that preference ordering. This comparison reflects both income level and quality of work experience: were they to work as hard at 60 percent as they do at 40, the rich would in the special burden case be worse off than others are, but in the standard case they would still be much better off than others are. The ordering of benefit to the badly off from the various work-tax packages (which is given by the numbers in the column on the left,

---

29. On the usual economists' assumptions, which are innocent here, that choice tracks preference, and that wide choice is preferred to narrow.

and which is the same in all three cases) is based on the assumption that part (b) of the minor premise of the incentives argument is true (so "w at 40 percent" ranks above "$w − x$ at 60 percent) and on the further assumption that, if the rich worked as hard at 60 as they do at 40, then that would bring still further benefit to the poor (so "w at 60 percent" ranks above "w at 40 percent").

The interpersonal test has talented rich people themselves uttering the incentives argument. Now for present purposes the talented rich do not fall under the bluff case, in which the minor premise is false: they really will work less if the tax goes up. And if we follow a distinction that has found favor with philosophers, the rich do not threaten anything if they utter the incentives argument, since, in the recommended distinction, you merely warn that you will do A when you are bent on doing A independently of the leverage you get from saying that you will do it. Notice that, in the recommended distinction, a kidnapper who likes children merely warns if he would actually prefer (for nonstrategic reasons) to keep the child if he is not paid: this shows that, under the recommended distinction, nonthreatening warnings can be very unpleasant.

So imagine now a set of highly paid managers and professionals addressing poorly paid workers, unemployed people, and people indigent for various personal and situational reasons, who depend on state welfare. The managers are lobbying against a rise in the tax from 40 to 60 percent, and this is what they say:

> Public policy should make the worst off people (in this case, as it happens, you) better off.

> If the top tax goes up to 60 percent, we shall work less hard, and, as a result, the position of the poor (your position) will be worse.

> So the top tax on our income should not be raised to 60 percent.

Although these argument-uttering rich may not, for one or other reason, count as threatening the poor, they remain people of superior income and form of life who could continue to work as now if the tax rose to 60 percent, and thereby bring more benefit to the poor, while still being much better off than they are, but who would refuse to do that. They say, in effect: we are unwilling to do what we could do to make you better off and yet still be much better off ourselves than you are. We realize that, at the present level of fuel allowance, many of you will be very cold this winter.[30] If the tax went up to 60 percent and we worked no less hard in response, revenue for fuel expenditure could rise, and some of you would be more comfortable. But in fact we would work less, and you would be worse off, following such a tax rise.

Having presented their argument, the rich are not well placed to answer a poor person who asks: "Given that you would still be much better off than we are if you worked as you do now at the 60 percent tax, what justifies your intention to work less if the tax rises to that level?" For these rich people do not say that they deserve a lot because of their prodigious effort, or merit more because of their higher contribution to production. There is in their approach no appeal to such controversial moral premises, and many of them would think that, being free of such premises, their argument is consequently less vulnerable. And they cannot respond by saying that the money inequality that they defend is necessary to make the poor better off, since it is they who make it necessary, and the question the poor put asks, in effect, what their justification is for making it necessary.

The incentives argument does furnish the poor with a reason to accept the inequality that it recommends. For the poor can take it as given that the rich are determined to sustain the intentions that make the argument work. But the argument cannot operate like that for the rich themselves: since they cannot treat their own choices as objective data, they cannot take it as given that the minor premise of the argument is true. Correspondingly, and unlike the poor, they need a justification not for accepting but for imposing the inequality that the argument defends.

But it might be said that the rich can indeed respond convincingly to the poor, and without advancing the controversial claims about desert and entitlement that are here ruled out. They can say: "Look, it simply would not be worth our while to work that hard if the tax rate were any higher, and if you were in our shoes you would feel the same way."[31] Would that not be a good answer to the question the poor pose?

As I shall presently allow, there is some power in this answer. But its rhetorical cast makes it seem more powerful than it is.

30. According to Robin Cook, MP, who was then Labour's spokesman on health, in the severe winter of 1991 there were four thousand more deaths of old people than are usual in such a period.

31. This piece of dialogue comes from Samuel Scheffler's seminar commentary on these lectures. Scheffler pressed the challenge to which the rest of this section is a response.

Notice, to begin with, that the first part ("Look . . . higher") of the quoted plea has no independent interest, no interest, that is, independent of the associated claim that the poor, if better placed, would feel (and act) as the rich now do. For it is a presupposition of the challenge the poor put to the rich that the latter do prefer, and intend, to work less hard if the tax goes up, and in speaking of what is "worth their while" the rich can only be reminding the poor of those preferences and intentions: they cannot mean, for example, that they are paid nothing, or paid badly, if they work hard at a 60 percent rate of tax.

So the burden of the rhetorically presented justificatory move is that a typical poor person would behave just as the rich, on the whole, do. But there is something that the poor person can say in reply: "Neither of us really knows how I would behave. Not all rich people market-maximize as a matter of course, and I hope that, if I were rich, I would not belong to the vast majority that do, especially if I retained a lively sense of what it is like to be in the condition I am now actually in." (A slave need not be impressed when a master says: "Had you been born into the slave-holder class, you too would have lived well and treated your slaves like slaves." Such counterfactual predictions do not show that what people at a certain social level typically choose to do is justifiable.)[32]

Suppose now that the rich abandon the vivid but problematic "you'd do the same in my shoes" style of justification. Suppose they just say (this being the content of the text to note 31, without its rhetorical cast) that, even when desert and entitlement are set aside, only an extreme moral rigorist could deny that *every person has a right to pursue self-interest to some reasonable extent* (even when that makes things worse than they need be for badly off people).

I do not wish to reject the italicized principle, which affirms what Samuel Scheffler has called an "agent-centred prerogative."[33] But a modest right of self-interest seems insufficient to justify the range of inequality, the extremes of wealth and poverty, that actually obtain in the society under discussion. Entitlement or desert might justify vast differences between rich and poor: no limit to the inequality they might endorse is inscribed in them. This is particularly clear in the case of the entitlement principle that I am absolute owner of my own labor power. When my

32. I have always thought that the right reply to a white South African who says to an anti-apartheid advocate, "You would see things differently if you were in my position," is: "Quite: I'm sure it does blind one's vision."
33. See his *Rejection of Consequentialism*.

power to produce is conceived as fully private property, I may do with it as I will and demand what I may for its use. A proportionately greater attention to one's own interest, as opposed to that of others, is more limited in its justificatory reach, and it seems unlikely to justify the existing contrast of luxury and want.

Now it might be objected that, in characterizing the position of the less well off as one of deprivation or want, I am unfairly tilting the balance against the incentives argument. To such an objection I have three replies.

First, I am in this chapter concerned (albeit *inter alia*) with a real political use of the incentives argument. Reference to real circumstances is therefore entirely appropriate.

Second, the incentives argument is quite general. It should therefore apply no matter how badly off the badly off are, both absolutely and relatively to the well off. Accordingly, it is methodologically proper to evaluate it in particularly dramatic cases of its application.

And it is precisely when the condition of the badly off is especially wretched that the *major* premise of the incentives argument can pass as compelling. Where the worst off are not too badly off, it looks more fanatical to assign absolute priority to their claims. But the stronger the case for ameliorating the situation of the badly off is, the more discreditable (if I am right) the incentives argument is on the lips of the rich. So the argument is most shameful where, at first sight, it is most apt.

Now a society that implements John Rawls's two principles of justice will not display the degree of inequality that characterizes contemporary Britain. Accordingly, the foregoing attempt to neutralize the agent-prerogative defense of the incentives argument in its common use will not serve to defeat it as a defense of the Rawlsian use of the argument, and more will be said about that later.[34]

34. (Added, 2008) In the section that ends here I countenance a personal prerogative that, so I argue (and see, further, in relation specifically to Rawls, pp. 71–72), does not vindicate the incentives argument, but that permits individuals in the right sorts of cases to provide less benefit to the worst off than strict adherence to the difference principle would command. As it stands in the original text of this chapter, this move might be judged to be a mere ad hoc concession. I hope that the elaboration of the point at section 5 of the Introduction renders it less ad hoc, and more circumspectly theorized. (For further reflections on the prerogative, see section 4 of the General Appendix.)

9. *The Incentives Argument and Bad Faith*

The resolve of talented rich people to produce less if tax rises makes the factual premise of the incentives argument true and ensures that the poor are poorer than they otherwise would be. I have argued that, within the restriction of naked use of the incentives argument, the rich cannot justify making its factual premise true. There is consequently an impression of incoherence when they employ the argument in defense of low taxes on top salaries: for the more disposed they are to affirm its normative premise, the less disposed they should be to make its factual premise true.[35] The argument stands up only because the agents mentioned in its minor premise do not act as one would expect people who put forward its major premise to act. If they did so act, they would not make the minor premise of the argument true, it would then not be true, and the argument would collapse.

For an analogy to the bad faith that comes when the rich themselves propound the argument, think of kidnappers who say that, since the safety of the hostage should be of paramount concern, her loved ones should pay for her release. That structurally similar—and risible—posture is portrayed in the film *Ruthless People,* in which frustrated kidnappers express outrage against the husband of the unwanted wife whom they hold hostage, when they become apprised of that husband's blithe lack of desire to pay for his wife's release. Or think of a crowd of recently munching strollers who complain about the failure of the city's street cleaning service as they toss their Big Mac containers into the gutter. There is similar incongruity when talented rich people indignantly condemn parties of the Left for a supposed lack of concern for the poor supposedly shown by the Left's policy of taxing the rich heavily. They can say that such political parties are stupid in light of the terms of coopera-

35. This claim, that affirmation of the major premise of the argument by the talented rich *does not cohere* with their disposition to make its minor premise true is not identical with (though it is related to) the claim labored above, to wit, that the talented rich *cannot justify* making the minor premise true, when the incentives argument is used nakedly. The incoherence claim depends on what the major premise says, and goes with certain formulations of it only. If the kidnapper changes the major premise of his argument from "children should be with their parents" to "parents should pay to retrieve kidnapped children," the claim about his minor premise survives, but the incoherence claim goes. Analogous results obtain if the rich employ as major premise: "the poor should vote for whatever enhances their interests."

tion to which they, the rich, are themselves resolved to stick, but although that may be true, it is not a reason for *them* to display indignation against those parties.

10. Should the Poor Reject the Incentives Argument?

The incentive rationale might convince the poor that they should vote to maintain low taxes. But it does not show them why the rich have made it true that they might be well advised to vote like that. And the poor might refuse to vote that way. They might support Labour and press for higher taxation on high incomes, and not because they do not accept the minor, factual, premise of the incentives argument. On the contrary: they might believe that the minor premise is true, they might notice that its truth reflects the insistence of the rich on an unusually high standard of life and work, and they might want not to condone that insistence but to resist it, even at the cost of their own material self-interest. They would then reject the major premise of the incentives argument. They would say that inequalities that enhance their own position are not justified when the reason why they enhance it is the one that features in the minor premise of the argument.

The poor have *a* reason to respond as the rich suggest, since if they do they prosper better materially, and they might care enough about that to play ball with the rich. But it would not necessarily be irrational for the poor to reject what the rich suggest and forgo the promised material gain. It is not necessarily irrational (and it is sometimes felt to be morally imperative) to refuse to deal with a person who wields power unjustifiably even if, should you accede to the proposal he makes, you would be materially better off. That is not necessarily irrational both because how well off you are is not a matter of your material situation alone, and because how well off you are is not the only matter it is rational for you to care about. (That low-income people sometimes care about other things, such as retaining their self-respect and not collaborating with what they think unfair, is shown in their frequent willingness to hold out on strike for higher wages beyond the point where that could be thought rational in expected-income-maximizing terms.)

Still, the indignant poor might, as I said, care enough about prospective extra income to fall in with what the rich propose. They could think: we want to improve our modest lot, so it is entirely reasonable for us to accept the enhanced-incentives proposal. But they could not say to the rich: yes, your proposal is entirely reasonable. If the rich could claim that they *need* extra money to perform better or that without superior pay a superior performance would mean that they live bleak lives, then the poor could accede to the proposal of the rich in the dimension of I-thou interaction. In the case that I am envisaging (that is, in the Standard Case of the Table), resisting their proposal is one way of treating the rich as a set of thous, rather than as a powerful opaque force. If the rich could be regarded as external things like machines, or bits of nature, it would then be irrational for the poor not to accept their proposal. It is irrational to be angry with a lofty mountain, to think "I'm damned if I'm going to climb you or walk around you to get where I want to go," since, unless you are an animist, your relationship to a mountain properly takes an I-it form. But the poor know that the rich are persons, and they may regard them as fellow members of a community who can be asked, face to face, for justification. And then rejection by the poor of the proposal made by the rich is not necessarily irrational: uncooperative anger is one rational response to what the rich say. (To be sure, they can respond so even in the absence of community, but the response takes a sharper form when a norm of community is ostensibly in place.)

11. First Persons and Third Persons

The incentives argument is not problematic (in the particular way that I say it is) when it is thought acceptable to view the rich as outside the community to which the poor belong. But sometimes, in Britain anyway, many of the rich themselves are eager to invoke community, when, for example, they react with (real or fake) horror to militant agitation among the poor. (Maybe some of the rich think that "belong to the same community as" denotes a nonsymmetrical relation).

Of course, particular talented people can affirm the incentives argument without difficulty by declaring that they personally lack the disposition attributed to members of their class in the argument. But if the argument is going to pass muster as a justification of unequal reward within community, then putting it forward in the first person, and without such disavowal, should be unproblematic.

In the third person, the minor premise of the argument just predicts how the rich will behave, and it can show misunderstanding of the speaker's message to demand a justification of that behavior: the speaker is not responsible for it, and he might himself be disposed to condemn it.

But to affirm the minor premise of the argument with full first-person force is to declare, or, what suffices for present purposes, to manifest, an intention, and a demand for justification is therefore in order. Observe the difference between these two interchanges, each of which follows assertion of the minor premise of the argument to a poor person, in the first case *by* a poor person, or by some third party.

> *Poor person:* But they, the rich, should not demand so much.
> *Reply:* That has nothing to do with me. The fact is that they do.

That is a valid reply to the poor person's lament. But now consider an analogous interchange following a first-person presentation of the premise:

> *Poor person:* But you, the rich, should not demand so much.
> *Reply:* That has nothing to do with me. The fact is that we (I, and the others) do.

Here the very incoherence of the reply confirms the aptness of the challenge against which it strains.

Finding it difficult to provide a convincing reply, the rich may represent their own optional attitudes and decisions as given facts. They might say to the poor, "Look, we all have to accept the reality of the situation." Yet it is not an exogenous reality that they are asking the poor to recognize. In this rhetoric of the rich, a declaration of intention masquerades as a description of something beyond choice: the rich present *themselves* in third-personal terms, in alienation from their own agency.[36]

For an analogous self-misrepresentation, consider how absurd it would be for the kidnapper to say: "Gee, I'm sorry, but the fact is that unless you pay I will not release your child." If he says that in factual style, and not as a piece of macabre humor, his remark expresses an estrangement from his own intention, which means that he is crazy.

And I believe that there is also something weird going on when the will of a class is depicted by its members as just a sociological fact. The rich man sits in his living room and he explains, in a detached style that

36. This is not a rerun of the inability claim, which we left behind at the end of section 7. That claim acknowledges that the rich form and execute a set of intentions, but denies that they could form and/or execute certain alternative ones. In the motif of alienation, the very fact of intentional agency is concealed, or at least obscured.

says his choices have nothing to do with the matter, why the poor should vote against higher taxes on the rich. Here, too, there is alienation, but because it is less obvious than the alienation of the single kidnapper that I just portrayed, you do not have to be completely crazy to slip into it. It is easy to slip into this alienation because each rich person's individual choice lacks salience, lost as it is among the millions of similar choices typical of members of his class: he participates in a practice so familiar that it gets treated as part of, or on a par with, the course of nature. In a reflective moment he might be appalled by the situation of the badly off, but he reifies the intentions of rich people (his own included), which frustrates their claim to priority, into hard data that social policy must take as parametric. He is unalive to the fact that his own decisions contribute to the condition he describes, a condition that is the upshot of a vast number of personal choices, but that he describes in the impersonal discourse of sociology or economics.

Recall the crazy kidnapper who says, "Gee, I'm sorry." The child's parents might display a corresponding craziness. They do so if they treat the kidnapper's intention as an objective fact not only for them but even for him. And then they think of his demand as simply what they happen to have to pay to get their child back, and maybe one of them says to the kidnapper, as to a possibly sympathetic bystander: "Well, £5000 *is* a lot of money, as I'm sure you'll agree, but it's less, after all, than what it cost to have Sally's adenoids removed, and, as you've pointed out, it is her *life* that's at stake."

And these reflections also have a bearing on the incentives argument. I have said that the incapacity of that argument to serve as a justification of inequality when the rich present it to the poor shows that the argument presupposes a lack of community between them. And I have just now also said that when the rich deliver it in a certain cast or tone, they imply that they do not qualify as choosing human agents. In considering that second point, it may be instructive to contemplate a presentation of the incentives argument that we have not yet considered, one in which a poor person addresses a set of rich ones. Now the minor premise will say: if the top tax rises to 60 percent, you will work less hard, and we shall consequently be worse off. If the poor speaker says that in an objective tone of voice, his rich listeners might, as a result, feel the weirdness that comes when someone predicts your behavior as though you have no control over it. Some of the listeners might even protest: "Hey, wait a minute. We would like at least to *try* not to work less if the tax rises."

And the poor speaker might counter: "You're not likely to stick to that resolution. So: *please* vote against the tax rise." In his insistence on the truth of the incentives argument's minor premise, this poor person would be setting his face against community, or against the capacity for agency of his listeners, or against both.

III: Incentives and the Difference Principle

12. *Strict and Lax Readings of the Difference Principle*

I have thus far scrutinized a defense of the inequalities of an actually existing capitalist society (Great Britain) that occurs in ordinary political discourse. I now leave that vernacular context and turn to a text-based examination of John Rawls's difference principle. It is certain that Rawls would not endorse the particular inequalities that prevail in Britain. But his own defense of inequality has significant elements in common with the case for Lawson's tax cut, and much of my criticism of the latter also bears against Rawls's views.

It is usually supposed, and it is evidently supposed by Rawls himself, that his affirmation of the difference principle is consistent with his endorsement of the inequalities that come with special incentives to people of talent. But I shall argue that, when true to itself, Rawlsian justice condemns such incentives, and that no society whose members are themselves unambivalently committed to the difference principle need use special incentives to motivate talented producers.[37]

In this chapter I have been concerned to distinguish between inequalities that are necessary, apart from human choice, to make the worst off better off, and inequalities that are necessary to that end only given what some people's intentions are. And this distinction, between, as one might say, intention-relative and intention-independent necessities, generates a question about how we are to take the word "necessary" in John Rawls's difference principle. When he says that inequalities are just if they are necessary to improve the position of the worst off,[38] does he

37. (Added, 2008) I should now have to add, following excellent criticism by David Estlund, to which I respond in section 4 of the General Appendix, "save within the terms of the personal prerogative discussed in section 8 above."

38. That is one part of the difference principle. Another part says that inequalities are unjust if they worsen the position of the worst off, and, on the generous interpretation of the principle (see p. 29 above), a third part says that they are (not un)just if they have no effect on the worst off.

countenance only inequalities that are necessary (to achieve the stated end) apart from people's intentions, or also, and more liberally (in more than one sense of that term), inequalities such as those that are necessary when talented people lack a certain sort of commitment to equality and are set to act accordingly? We confront here two readings of the difference principle: in its strict reading, it counts inequalities as necessary only when they are, strictly, necessary, necessary, that is, apart from people's chosen intentions. In its lax reading, it countenances intention-relative necessities as well. So, for example, if an inequality is needed to make the badly off better off but only given that talented producers operate as self-interested market maximizers, then that inequality is endorsed by the lax, but not by the strict, reading of the difference principle.

I shall argue that each of these incompatible readings of the principle is nourished by material in Rawls's writings, so that he has in effect two positions on the matter. His comments on the spirit in which people in a just society affirm the difference principle point to the strict, "intention-independent" reading of it: that reading goes with his remarks about "full compliance," the dignity of the badly off, and fraternity. Yet, by endorsing incentives, Rawls treats inequalities whose necessity is relative to the intentions of talented people as acceptable to the difference principle: he proceeds as though he affirms the principle in its lax interpretation.

13. Why Just People Must Practice the Strict Difference Principle

Before turning to Rawls's texts, I want to argue that the strict interpretation of the difference principle is mandatory if we suppose that the people in the society in which it is applied are themselves attached to the idea of justice that the principle articulates and are motivated by it in their daily lives. In other words, if we begin with an uninterpreted statement of the principle, where it is ambiguous across strict and lax interpretations, and we suppose that all of the people in the society it governs comply wholeheartedly with it, by which I mean that they are concerned to ensure that their own conduct is just in the sense defined by the principle, then what they comply with is the principle in its strict interpretation.

In such a society, the difference principle affects the motivation of citizens in economic life. It controls their expectations about remuneration, that is, what they will regard as acceptable pay for the posts they are invited to fill. It is generally thought that the difference principle would be used by government to modify the effect of choices that are not themselves influenced by the principle, but, so I claim, in a society of wholehearted commitment to the principle, there cannot be so stark a contrast between public and private choice. Instead, citizens want their own economic behavior to satisfy the principle,[39] and they help to sustain a moral climate in which others want the same. I show in the next section that much of what Rawls says commits him to such an understanding of the difference principle, even though his approval of incentives embodies a rejection of that understanding, since approving of incentives means accepting the difference principle in its lax form, and in that form it can be satisfied in a society where it has no direct influence on economic motivation.

Suppose I am a doctor contemplating a hospital post that I know I could obtain at, say, £100,000 a year.[40] I also believe that, if—and only if—I took something in the region of £50,000 for filling it, then any difference between my reward and what the less-well-paid get would be justified by what I strictly need to do the job, and/or by its special burdens, and/or by my legitimate personal prerogative. Then how can I say, with a straight face, that justice forbids inequalities that are detrimental to the badly off and be resolved to act justly in my own life, unless, should I indeed go for this particular job, I offer myself at £50,000 and thereby release £50,000 for socially beneficial use?[41]

I might say: "Look, I *am* concerned about the less well off, but I do

39. (Added, 2008) Once again—see the final paragraph of section 8 above—as properly constrained by a legitimate personal prerogative: I won't always add this qualification.

40. (Added, 2008) My use of the doctor example gives the false impression that the principal effect of an egalitarian ethos would be to induce agents to forgo what they can get on the market. Such an ethos would indeed in certain circumstances have that effect, but a more important relevant effect of an egalitarian ethos is to induce agents to accept very high rates of taxation. See section 1 of the General Appendix.

41. People who favor a lax interpretation of the difference principle have suggested that I could say that my giving up the £25,000 would deliver little benefit to any particular person. Yet that need not be so: if it be required that my sacrifice make a palpable difference to some particular person or particular people, then channels that do not fragment its impact could be devised. But the requirement is anyhow misconceived. For one could argue, by the same token, against those who support the difference principle in its lax interpretation, that it is pointless to collect income tax from one person in particular, since that too makes no significant difference to any individual.

not have to devote my whole life to them. It is right for government to serve their interests by taxing me, but I should also be allowed to pursue my own *self*-interest, and that is why I feel justified in taking the salary that hospitals have to offer to attract physicians like me."

But this reply is not sustainable here.

First, notice that I cannot mean the reply in a spirit of apologetic self-criticism, for I am here, *ex hypothesi,* resolved to act justly. Under that hypothesis, I must show that my behavior is not unjust, not that it is an understandable compromise between justice and self-interest. I have to show that the inequalities caused by what I and other professionals choose to do are not unjust, even though they make the lot of the badly off worse than it needs to be. Consequently, I am claiming that some inequality is just because it reflects legitimate pursuit of self-interest on the part of people with a fortunate endowment of talent. I am saying that justice is itself a compromise or balance between self-interest and the claims of equality.

As I indicated earlier (see the text to note 33 of this chapter), I do not aim to impugn the integrity of a conception of justice that allows the agent a certain self-regarding prerogative. But the doctor's reply is meant not merely to articulate a defensible conception of justice, but to reconcile his claim to be wholeheartedly committed to the difference principle's idea of economic justice with his lax reading of that principle. We must ask whether his reply accomplishes that result.

Now Rawls does not speak of distributive justice as a compromise of the contemplated sort,[42] but our question is whether he might, whether, that is, he could vindicate the lax difference principle along the lines of the doctor's reply. And I do not think that he could, since the reply turns

And this is anyhow not the central issue here. For the appropriate question here is not: what, irrespective of the character of the society in which he finds himself, is the moral obligation of a talented individual who believes in Rawlsian justice? The right question is: what would a *society* that is just by the lights of the difference principle be like? How, among other things, would talented people in general behave in such society? If, as I am claiming, they would in general take jobs for modest post-tax salaries, then each could reflect that, together with others, he or she is making a massive difference to (what would otherwise be) badly off people.

42. It would be a mistake to think that the priority of liberty over the difference principle makes for such a compromise. Among the reasons why it does not do so is that we are not here concerned with coercive restrictions, in the name of justice, on the doctor's liberty, but with what would count as a just use of his liberty. (Much more is said about this in section 3 of Chapter 5 below).

on what is here the wrong distinction. The reply defends a limit on the amount of assistance that must be supplied to the badly off: that amount must be moderated by appropriate consideration of the interests of the better off. But the government, pursuing the lax difference principle, might tax me more, or less, than whatever amount is supposed to represent a reasonable compromise between self-interest and service. If it taxed me more than that, I would, according to the reply, have reason of legitimate self-interest to object. So, far from vindicating the difference principle, the reply represents that principle as (at times) too demanding, even in its lax form. And if government taxed me less than what a reasonable compromise would dictate, then I could not say that the laxness in the principle I affirm was justified on compromise grounds, for on those grounds it would then be too lax.[43]

In short, the compromise idea will not in general draw the same line as the difference principle does. Defended along compromise lines, the lax difference principle is at best an imperfect proxy for a just balance and not, what it is supposed to be, a fundamental principle of justice. The compromise idea is, simply, different from the idea that inequalities are justified if they are necessary to benefit the badly off, given that agents are (or might be) self-regarding maximizers on the market. Accordingly, the lax difference principle cannot be what agents committed to difference principle justice affirm: from their point of view, it draws an arbitrary line between serving oneself and serving others.

We are left with the strict difference principle,[44] which government

43. With a certain distribution of talent, the inequalities allowed by the lax difference principle could be quite large, of a size that is intuitively incongruent with the central Rawlsian idea that the gifted owe their special powers to mere good fortune. How can they be thoroughly just people, think themselves merely lucky to have the assets they do, and nevertheless take as much advantage of them as they can on the market? Of course, there are also distributions of talent under which the inequalities might be quite small. But they are not small as a matter of principle, and it is no defense of a supposed fundamental principle, when its consistency with certain consequences generates criticism, to show that it lacks those consequences in practice. So defended, the principle is not, as intended, fundamental, but warranted because, given the facts, it serves more fundamental aims. (That motif is explored at length in Chapters 6 and 7 below.)

44. I do not mean that there is no other game in town, but just that there is no third way of playing the difference principle game. (A further alternative would be the strict difference principle constrained by an agent-centered prerogative. But the added constraint modifies—it does not interpret—the difference principle: see, further, section 4 of the General Appendix below.)

cannot implement by itself. For the strict difference principle to prevail, there needs to be an ethos informed by the principle in society at large. Therefore, a society (as opposed to its government) does not qualify as committed to the difference principle unless it is indeed informed by a certain ethos or culture of justice. Ethoses are, of course, beyond the immediate control of legislation, but I believe that a just society is normally impossible[45] without one, and Rawls himself requires that there be a nurturance and cultivation of appropriate attitude in the just society that he describes.

In a culture of justice shaped by the difference principle, talented people would not expect (what they usually have the power to obtain) the high salaries whose level reflects high demand for their talent (as opposed to the special needs or special burdens of their jobs). It follows that the difference principle in a society of just people would not induce the inequality it is usually thought (e.g., by Rawls) to produce, and it would not, in particular, justify incentive payments in the "standard" sense of that phrase (see Table 1.1 in section 8 above), that is, payments not to compensate for unusually arduous work, but to draw talent to jobs that are not in general especially grueling. In a just society, where justice is defined by the difference principle in its pre-interpreted form, the difference principle will prevail in its strict interpretation.

(It is not true that, in the society I have in mind, a person would have to worry about unfortunate people every time he made an economic decision. Liberals would regard that as oppressive,[46] and whether or not they are right, one function of the egalitarian ethos is to make conscious focus on the worst off unnecessary. What rather happens is that people internalize, and—in the normal case—unreflectively live by, principles that restrain the pursuit of self-interest and whose point is that the less fortunate gain when conduct is directed by them.)

---

45. For example, because of problems of asymmetrical information and incentive compatibility familiar to economists, and that are crudely illustrated by the propensity of the productive to withdraw labor when taxes rise too high. Under abnormal conditions, justice might be consistent with universal self-interested maximizing: if, for example, talents and utility functions are identical, then initial equality of tangible assets might be considered sufficient for justice. (On a Dworkinian view that would be so even with different utility functions.)

46. See, e.g., Thomas Nagel, "Libertarianism without Foundations," pp. 199–200. And, see, in criticism of Nagel, my *If You're an Egalitarian, How Come You're So Rich?*, pp. 168–174, and also the closing paragraphs of section 3 of of Chapter 5 below.

14. The Difference Principle and "Daily Life"

On the lax interpretation of what the difference principle demands, it is satisfied when everyone gets what she can through self-seeking behavior in a market whose rewards are so structured by taxation and other regulation that the worst off are as well off as any scheme of taxed and regulated market rewards can make them. On my view of what it means for a society to institute the principle, people would mention norms of equality when asked to explain why they and those like them are willing to work for the pay they get. This strict interpretation conflicts with Rawls's unqualified endorsement of unequalizing incentives. Yet, as I now propose to show, the strict interpretation of the principle coheres with a number of significant general characterizations of justice to be found in Rawls's work.

It is very important in the present connection that Rawls's theory describes what he calls a well-ordered society, that is, one whose citizens display full and willing compliance with the demands of justice. In a well-ordered society each person acts out of a sense of justice informed by the principles of justice not merely at the ballot box but as he goes about his daily business.

So much is clear from many passages in Rawls's writings. We are told not only that "everyone accepts, and knows that others likewise accept, the same first principles of right and justice," which might, by itself, be consistent with a ballot box view of their commitment, but also that the parties "in everyday life . . . affirm and act from [those] first principles of justice."[47] Full compliance with the principles means that they act *from* them, in everyday life, "in the course," as Rawls also puts it, "of their daily lives."[48] And their "full autonomy is achieved" partly through "acting *from* these principles as their sense of justice dictates."[49] Citizens are strongly committed to acting that way. They "have a highest-order desire, their sense of justice, to *act* from the principles of justice."[50] They "have a desire to express their nature as free and equal moral persons, and this they do most adequately by acting *from* the principles that they would acknowledge in the original position. When all strive to comply

47. "Kantian Constructivism," p. 308.
48. Ibid., p. 315. Cf. *A Theory of Justice*, pp. 253/222: they "knowingly act on the principles of justice in the ordinary course of events."
49. "Kantian Constructivism," p. 315, emphasis added.
50. Ibid, p. 320, emphasis added.

with these principles and each succeeds, then individually and collectively their nature as moral persons is *most* fully realized, and with it their individual and collective good."[51]

Now such statements seem to me to imply that the economic motivation of Rawlsian citizens is influenced by the difference principle. How could they act like maximizing incentive seekers if in *"their daily lives"* they act *"from"* a principle that directs primary concern for the badly off? Can we say that they act *from* such a principle in their daily lives just because they support taxation that is shaped by the principle and aims to modify the results of their acting *from* maximizing motives? Such support might show that you respect the claim of the principle against you, but it surely does not suffice as proof of your being inspired by it as part of a sense of justice on which you operate in your daily life.[52] How could your "nature as [a] moral person" count as *"most* fully realized" when you go for as much as you can get in your own market choices,[53] and merely endorse application of the principle by the government in imperfect moderation of the inequality that the choices of people like you tend to cause?

Consider this passage from *A Theory of Justice*: ". . . by abstaining from the exploitation of the contingencies of nature and social circumstances within a framework of equal liberty, persons express their re-

51. *A Theory of Justice*, pp. 528/462–463, emphases added, cf. ibid., pp. 572/501: "The desire to act justly and the desire to express our nature as free moral persons turn out to specify what is practically speaking the same desire." Cf. ibid., pp. 574/503.

52. Rawls says that "citizens have a normally effective sense of justice, that is, one that enables them to understand and to apply the principles of justice, and for the most part to act from them as their circumstances require" (*Justice as Fairness*, p. 198). Why would they have to apply the principles themselves to their own circumstances if just behavior consisted in obeying laws designed to effect an implementation of those principles?

53. How does the economic behavior of a maximizer who is committed to the lax difference principle differ from that of a maximizer who is not? It might be said that, unlike the latter, the former is willing to maximize only when and because the principle is in force, that is, employed by government in its economic policy. But that is not necessarily true: people who believe that the lax difference principle should be instituted may have various views about what they should do in a society in which it is not. And even if our believer would indeed behave nonmaximizingly if the principle were not in force, that hardly shows that he "strive[s] to comply with" the difference principle in his "daily life."

spect for one another in the very constitution of their society."[54] If that is so, then it seems to me that in a Rawlsian society there will not be incentive seekers, since they do exploit their contingent talent and social advantages, and the passage says that people who do that show a lack of the respect for other people that the constitution of their society requires. If you deny that the passage has this implication, then you must make one or other of two implausible claims. You must claim either that (1) despite what the passage says, Rawlsianly just talented people might exploit the contingency of their superior talent, or that (2) contrary to what seems evident, talented market-maximizers do not engage in such exploitation.

Think about it this way. On a Rawlsian view, there is no reason of basic principle why the talented should earn more than the untalented. It is merely that things (supposedly) fall out that way when the difference principle is applied. So imagine that we address the talented rich people, and we ask them why they do not give the above-average parts of their incomes to people of below-average income, when, *ex hypothesi*, they would have compliantly accepted the resulting post-giveaway incomes had the difference principle happened to mandate them. What could they say? They certainly could not say that they were abstaining from exploitation of their talent advantages, and we could not say that they live under "a conception of justice that nullifies the accidents of natural endowment and the contingencies of social circumstance as counters in the quest for . . . economic advantage."[55]

15. Dignity, Fraternity, and the Difference Principle

Rawls believes that a just society, on the lax understanding of how it operates, honors the dignity of the worst off, since, so he says, they know that they are caused to be as well off as they could be. But that is an illusion. For they are as well off as they could be only given the self-seekingness of those who are better off, and maybe far better off, than they.

Joshua Cohen is a strong advocate of the difference principle. He draws a contrast between a society ruled by that principle and one whose rule is a basic minimum for all and then laissez-faire. Cohen dis-

---

54. *A Theory of Justice*, pp. 179/156, and see, generally, ibid., pp. 72–75/62–65.
55. *A Theory of Justice*, pp. 15/14.

parages the basic minimum/laissez-faire arrangement because of how weak its "affirmation of [the] worth" of the worst off individuals is. For if I am one of them in such a society, "then I know that I could do better if those who are better off were prepared to forgo some of their advantages. And I know that this loss of advantage to me is not just for a stretch of time but covers the course of my entire life. Others know this, and know that I know it, and so on. Still they accept the advantages."[56] Yet Cohen fails to see that all those things can be said about the less gifted in a society ruled by the lax difference principle, where talented people demand, and get, incentive payments. In such a society, clear-thinking unfortunate people know that they "could do better if those who are better off were prepared to forgo some of their advantages." Cohen describes a badly placed person in a Rawlsian society reflecting with satisfaction that "other citizens act from maximin" (that is, in this context, from the principle of putting the interests of the badly off first) and thereby "display a concern for my good and the good of those to whom I am attached."[57] But the badly placed person can enjoy such a reflection only on my revisionary conception of the character of a Rawlsian society. When the difference principle in its conventional, lax interpretation prevails, it is not in general true that citizens "act from maximin," and the inequalities that come as a result might indeed challenge the sense of self-worth of those who are at the bottom. If they succeed in sustaining that sense, that will not be because of their perception of how the better off regard them.

Joshua Cohen's remarks are in the spirit of the Rawls passage which says that "the least favoured man," here called B, "can accept A's being better off since A's advantages have been gained in ways that improve B's prospects. If A were not allowed his better position, B would be even worse off than he is."[58] The second sentence of this passage does not compel agreement with the first, since, with everything else equal, A could have refrained from seizing the full complement of the advantages he was able to seize, and then B would have been better off than he is. It indicates how little A cares about B's lot that he refuses to improve B's bad prospects without the advantages he gets in the course of doing so.

The mistake in Cohen's comment on the difference principle shows

56. "Democratic Equality," p. 743.
57. Ibid., p. 746.
58. *A Theory of Justice*, p. 103, passage omitted in 1999.

that, given his own lax application of it, Rawls is wrong to represent it as a realization of the value of fraternity, which he glosses as "the idea of not wanting to have greater advantages unless this is to the benefit of others who are less well off . . . Members of a family commonly do not wish to gain unless they can do so in ways that further the interests of the rest. Now wanting to act on the difference principle has precisely this consequence."[59] But "wanting to act on the difference principle" has the stated consequence only if we interpret the principle strictly. For wanting not "to gain unless they can do so in ways that further the interests of the rest" is incompatible with the drive for enrichment motivating market maximizers.[60]

We should note an ambiguity in the phrase "not wanting to have greater advantages unless this is to the benefit of others who are less well off." A person of that description does not want to gain unless others thereby do. Does that mean: unless they gain something (no matter how little)? But that does not satisfy the maximinizing criterion laid down by the difference principle, and it is scarcely enough for fraternity. Or does the phrase mean unless none of my gain means that theirs is less than it need be? But provided that the feasible set is sufficiently ample, that means going for equality.

Let me illustrate this point. Two brothers, A and B, are at benefit levels 6 and 5, respectively, in New York, where they live. If they moved to Chicago, their levels would rise to 10 and 5.1, respectively. If they moved to Boston, they would rise to 8 and 7. Is fraternity, as Rawls means to characterize it, consistent with A proposing that they move to Chicago? If so, it is a thin thing. Or is Rawlsian fraternity strictly maximinizing? In that case, Boston is the choice, and in a feasible set with no bar to redistribution (which would mean, here, that each brother could have 7.55 in Chicago), equality is the result. (Notice that in this last example I do not specify what the numbers denote: whatever metric you choose, the reasoning will go through. And that confirms that there is no metric under which the desired result, a justified inequality, emerges).

Consider, in the present connection, Rawls's statement that "the better endowed (who have a place in the distribution of native endowments

59. *A Theory of Justice*, pp. 105/90.
60. The rest of this section incorporates material that originally appeared in "The Pareto Argument for Inequality" and that has been excised from the reprinting of that article in Chapter 2 below.

they do not morally deserve) are encouraged to acquire still further bene-fits—they are already benefited by their fortunate place in that distri-bution—on condition that they train their native endowments and use them in ways that contribute to the good of the less endowed."[61] Let us test what is said in that passage against the difference principle's require-ment that an inequality in primary goods is justified only if it is necessary to expand the size of the smallest primary goods bundles. Let us focus on the condition described in the quoted passage, to wit, that the talented "train their native endowments and use them in ways that contribute to the good of the less endowed." Let us ask: by how much must that train-ing and use contribute to the good of the less endowed? As far as what we can glean from the quoted passage goes, that amount is at best left open and at worst any amount at all, however little. But, so I shall now argue, the difference principle requires that the badly off gain as much in the currency of primary goods as the talented themselves do:

	The Badly Endowed	The Better Endowed
A No training	5	5
B Training and use (I)	6	9
C Training and use (II)	7	8

On the weak reading of the condition mentioned in the quoted pas-sage, and consistently with everything else in that passage, B, which dis-plays more inequality than C, is acceptable, despite the disadvantage (by comparison with C) to the badly endowed. On the difference principle, B is unacceptable, since C is possible, and its possibility establishes that the inequality in B is greater than is necessary to make the badly off better off. But the feasible set will typically also contain D:

D Training and use (III)	7.5	7.5

For why would it be impossible to divide the expanded product equally, other than because, from an egalitarian point of view, indefensi-bly, the talented would be unwilling to produce that much if it were equally divided? Accordingly, it is D that the difference principle would require: it is very difficult to use that principle to justify inequality.

A society of market-maximizers with taxation and regulation dictated by the lax difference principle is necessarily preferable from the point of

61. *Justice as Fairness*, pp. 76–77.

view of the worst off to a laissez-faire society,[62] but in neither society is the conduct of high fliers consistent with the essentially socialist value of fraternity or with motivation informed by the difference principle. Rawls must give up either his approval of incentives to the exercise of talent or his ideals of dignity, fraternity, and the full realization of persons' moral natures. I think the ideals are worth keeping.[63]

16. The Difference Principle and "Mutual Indifference"

At one point, Rawls comments on the view that

> the greater expectations allowed to entrepreneurs encourages [*sic*] them to do things which raise the long-term prospects of the laboring class.[64]

He does not (quite) endorse that factual claim, but he says that, if, as he shows he believes, it is true, then the difference principle recommends the rewards generating those greater expectations and the "initial inequality in life prospects" associated with them.

There are other passages to relevantly similar effect,[65] and there is no point quoting them all here. But I do want to quote and comment on a remark by Rawls that might be read as an attempt to anticipate and deflect the line of criticism that I have developed.

Following one of his incentives-endorsing passages, Rawls says:

> One might think that ideally individuals should want to serve one another. But since the parties are assumed not to take an interest in one another's in-

---

62. (Added in 2008) Laissez-faire could not be preferable, because if it had been better for the worst off, then the lax difference principle would have selected it.

63. It might be thought that, beyond his commitment to those ideals, Rawls has further reason to reject incentives and the lax difference principle, to wit, that the risk aversiveness that induces the parties in the original position to select the difference principle would also incline them to prefer its strict form. I have not used this argument because I seek to pursue my case against the part of Rawls to which I object by invoking Rawlsian ideas with which I agree, and I agree neither that principles chosen in the original position are ipso facto just nor that its parties would choose a maximin strategy and, therefore, if the foregoing suggestion is sound, the strict difference principle.

64. *A Theory of Justice*, pp. 78/68.

65. See ibid., pp. 151/130–131, 157/135–136, 279/246; Rawls, *Justice as Fairness*, pp. 53, 63; Rawls, "Distributive Justice," p. 139.

terests, their acceptance of those inequalities is only the acceptance of the relations in which men stand in the circumstances of justice. They have no grounds for complaining of one another's motives.[66]

It might be said, on the basis of this passage, that my critique of Rawls displays misunderstanding of the role of principles of justice, as he conceives them. Those principles, it might be said, are rules observed by fair-minded people in their mutually advantageous interaction, fair-minded people who may or may not *care* about one another, but who qualify as just as long as they observe the rules. They go beyond justice if they do care about one another, and in demanding that the difference principle be strict I am demanding more than justice.

But that line of thought seems to me untenable. For it wrongly attributes to people in the achieved, just society the mutual indifference that characterizes the specially tailored persons of Rawls's original position, in which the principles that are to govern the just society are chosen. In the original position mutual indifference is assumed for methodological reasons to derive justice from rational self-interest under a veil of ignorance constraint. But it does not follow that the principles chosen by the mutually indifferent parties of the original position are consistent with mutual indifference when they operate as rules of interaction in a functioning society. And to attribute mutual indifference to people in the realized society is surely to contradict the idea that their relations partake of fraternity, as Rawls describes that condition[67] (see the text to note 59 above). People who, like "members of a family," "do not wish to gain unless they can do so in ways that further the interests of the rest" are not people who take no interest in one another's interests. How could a person who takes no interest in the interests of others want advantages for himself only if his enjoyment of them benefits the less well off (see section 15 above)?

66. *A Theory of Justice*, pp. 151/131. For more on "mutual disinterest," see *Justice as Fairness*, p. 62.
67. Rawls himself distinguishes similarly between people's attitudes to one another in the original position and in society when he writes that "although the parties in the original position take no interest in each other's interests, they know that in society they need to be assured by the esteem of their associates. Their self-respect and their confidence in the value of their own system of ends cannot withstand the indifference . . . of others" (*A Theory of Justice*, pp. 338/295).

17. The Difference Principle and the Unjust Society

Rawls says that "a person in the original position would concede the justice of [the] inequalities [required for incentives]. Indeed, it would be short-sighted of him not to do so."[68]

Now the phrasing of this contention is curious, since we normally think of short-sightedness as poor perception not of justice but of one's own interests.[69] And I point out this infelicity in the formulation, since I believe that it reflects an unresolved tension in the Rawlsian architectonic, one that underlies the difficulties exposed in these lectures. That underlying tension is between a *bargaining* conception and a *community* conception of social relationships. (There are conceptions that fall between those two, with elements of each, but as I read Rawls, both of them appear in his work in their extreme forms.)

But let us ignore the infelicitous phrasing in the passage and concentrate on the implied claim that it would be a mistake not to concede the justice of incentive inequalities. My reply to that claim, a reply that by now is entirely predictable, is that if we are talking within the assumption of full compliance, then we need not and should not concede either that incentive inequalities are required to motivate performance or that they are just. Let us now, however, retire the heady assumptions of full compliance and a widespread sense of justice. Consider instead a society like the United States, where fortunate people learn to expect more than they would get when the difference principle prevails in a comprehensive way. In that case, we might agree that it would be a mistake not to concede incentive inequalities. If we need inequalities to "encourage effective performance,"[70] then it might be folly not to have them, but it does not follow that having them is a requirement of basic justice, where a *basic* principle of justice is one that has application in a society where, as in Rawls's, everyone always acts justly.[71]

68. *A Theory of Justice*, p. 151, passage omitted in 1999.

69. A person in the original position does not, in any case, ask himself what is *just*. He asks himself what, given his ignorance, is the best choice from the point of view of his interests.

70. *A Theory of Justice*, p. 151, passage omitted in 1999.

71. (Added, 2008) Cf. Macleod, "Economic Inequality: Justice and Incentives":

". . . it is about as implausible to suppose that a distribution is just *because* it is benefit-maximizing as it would be to claim that conduct is courageous *because* it serves to maximize the benefit for society as a whole.

Although his primary topic is justice under full compliance, Rawls also treats his principles as standards for assessing actually existing society.[72] In my view, the difference principle, conceived as one that would govern a just society, condemns as unjust those existing inequalities that are necessary to benefit the worst off where that necessity reflects the intentions of the talented rich; but, given that the inequalities are necessary, albeit for the stated reason, to remove them would be reckless. Along with Nikolay Bukharin, I would have said to the kulaks: enrich yourselves!, without supposing (any more than Bukharin did) that I was thereby voicing a demand of justice. If we are concerned about the badly off, then we should sometimes concede incentives, just as we should sometimes satisfy even a kidnapper's demands. We are not then acting on the difference principle in its strict interpretation, in which it is a principle of justice governing a society of just people who are inspired by it. We are acting on the lax version of the difference principle, which endorses incentives and has application in societies of the familiar unjust kind. On the assumption that they are indeed unavoidable, incentive payments may be justified, but it does not follow that no injustice occurs when they are provided. (One might say to a child's guardian: the kidnapper is unjustly threatening the safety of the child, and justice to the child therefore demands that you pay him. And one might say to legislators in a structurally unequal society: the talented are unjustly indifferent to the plight of the poor, and justice to the poor therefore demands that you do not impose very high taxation).

The policy of paying productive people plenty to get them to produce so that badly off people will be better off is rational when productive people are resolved to serve only if they are richly rewarded.

"There is a somewhat similar confusion in Rawls's position when he contrives to represent as just (or not unjust) any incentive-providing inequality that will serve to maximize the benefit to the worst-off. Incentive schemes that measure up to the demanding requirement embedded in Rawls's Difference Principle cannot be said *on that account* to be just. To suppose that they can would be to suppose that we can represent as fair, for example, the exorbitant demands of people who happen to have socially valuable and comparatively rare skills, even where the fact that they press these demands more relentlessly than others with roughly similar competences is principally a reflection of their greater greed or obstinacy in the negotiations that determine the distribution of resources" (p. 186).

72. *Theory*, pp. 245–246/216.

But their stance is then unjust by the very standard that the difference principle itself sets. Accordingly, on a strict view of Rawlsian justice, the difference principle in its lax interpretation, which does mandate the incentives policy, is not a basic principle of justice but a principle for handling people's injustice. It is not a basic principle of justice, since it confers benefit on market maximizers who offend against justice. We might call it a principle of damage limitation in the field of justice.[73]

When doing so limits the damage, it is wise to run society on lax difference principle lines, but it is also wise to recognize that society is not then based on justice. A related and more general point is that one should not suppose that, as Rawls says in *A Theory of Justice*, "justice is *the* first virtue of social institutions," where that means that "laws and institutions . . . must be reformed or abolished if they are unjust."[74] For sometimes justice is unattainable, and we do well to settle for something else. When there is no way to get the child back without paying, when a just outcome is not to be had, then paying, which makes all (kidnapper, parents, child) better off than refusing to pay, is almost certainly preferable, although in some cases, with less at stake, we might prefer to forgo the Pareto improvement, in order not to accede to an unjust demand.

Similarly, and according to an ancient Marxist wisdom, justice is not the first virtue of institutions in conditions of scarcity. Under those conditions a just distribution may be impossible to achieve, since powerful people will block it. In that case striving for justice may make everyone worse off, and unjust laws and institutions should not be "reformed or abolished." And scarcity in the Marxist sense is not poverty of supply, but the wider circumstance that, to secure what might be a quite reasonable supply, most people must spend most of their time engaged in labor that interferes with self-realization.

Under such a condition, and it is a huge and difficult question whether we are still in it, it might be right to tolerate, and even, sometimes, to nourish, incentive motivation, despite the fact that it contradicts justice. Sometimes the difference principle in its lax interpretation can be recommended as a first virtue of social institutions, because we cannot

73. Or, in a phrase of ibid., pp. 246/216, a "principle for meeting injustice."
74. Ibid., pp. 3/3, my emphasis.

get justice, and the injustice that goes with incentives is the best injustice we can get.[75]

My principal contention about Rawls is that high fliers would forgo incentives properly so-called in a full compliance society governed by the difference principle and characterized by fraternity and universal dignity. I have not rejected the difference principle in its lax reading as a principle of public policy:[76] I do not doubt that there are contexts where it is right to apply it. What I have questioned is its description as a *basic* principle of justice, and I have deplored Rawls's willingness to describe those at the top end of a society governed by it as undergoing the fullest possible realization of their moral natures. My own socialist-egalitarian position was nicely articulated by John Stuart Mill in his *Principles of Political Economy*. Contrasting equal payment with incentive-style payment according to product ("work done"), Mill said that the first

> appeals to a higher standard of justice, and is adapted to a much higher moral condition of human nature. The proportioning of remuneration to work done is really just, only in so far as the more or less of the work is a matter of choice; when it depends on natural difference of strength or capacity, this principle of remuneration is in itself an injustice: it is giving to those who have; assigning most to those who are already most favoured by nature. Considered however, as a compromise with the selfish type of character formed by the present standard of morality, and fostered by the existing social institutions, it is highly expedient; and until education shall have been entirely regenerated, is far more likely to prove immediately successful, than an attempt at a higher ideal.[77]

75. I express more doubt about the characterization of justice as the first virtue of institutions in Chapter 7, section 4 below.

76. (Added, 2008) Nor have I denied that it can be optimal from the point of view of distributive justice (in the absence of an egalitarian ethos).

77. *Principles of Political Economy*, Book II, Chapter I, section 4, p. 210. In Chapter V of his *Utilitarianism* Mill argues, at great length, that justice is a species of expediency. But here the self-same principle of remuneration is, under the stated conditions, both "highly expedient" and "an injustice." It is a nice question whether that conjunction of designations is compatible with everything that Mill says in *Utilitarianism*.

Rawls's lax application of his difference principle means "giving to those who have." He presents the incentive policy as a feature of the just society, whereas it is in fact, and as Mill says, just "highly expedient" in society as we know it, a sober "compromise with the selfish type of character" formed by capitalism.[78] Philosophers in search of justice should not be content with an expedient compromise. To call expediency *justice* goes against the regeneration to which Mill looked forward at the end of this fine passage.

78. For sapient criticism of Rawls along these lines, see Allen Buchanan, *Marx and Justice*, pp. 127–128.

According to Mill, "the deep-rooted selfishness which forms the general character of the existing state of society is so deeply rooted only because the whole course of the existing institutions tends to foster it." *Autobiography,* pp. 168–169, and see, for further pertinent references, Richard Ashcraft, "Class Conflict and Constitutionalism in J. S. Mill's Thought," pp. 117–18.

2

THE PARETO ARGUMENT

1. Introduction

Some ways of defending inequality against the charge that it is unjust require premises that egalitarians find it easy to dismiss, statements, for example, about the contrasting deserts and/or entitlements of unequally placed people. But a defense of inequality suggested by John Rawls and elaborated by Brian Barry[1] (who themselves reject the premises that egalitarians[2] dismiss) has often proved irresistible even to people of egalitarian outlook. The persuasive power of this defense of inequality has helped to drive authentic egalitarianism, of an old-fashioned, uncompromising kind, out of contemporary political philosophy. The present essay is part of an attempt to bring it back in.

In his *Theories of Justice*, Barry devotes some fifteen pages to sympathetic reconstruction of the Rawlsian argument that I have in mind. He resolves it into two stages. In the first stage, which Barry calls "From Equal Opportunity to Equality," "Rawls establishes equality as the only *prima facie* just basis of distribution." In the second stage ("From Equality to the Difference Principle") there is an "argument for a move from an equal distribution to a[n unequal] distribution governed by the difference principle,"[3] to, that is, a Pareto-superior[4] unequal distribution in

---

1. See John Rawls, *A Theory of Justice*, sections 10–17; and Brian Barry, *Theories of Justice*, pp. 213–234.
2. Whether they should themselves be styled "egalitarians" is not a matter that needs to be addressed here.
3. Barry, *Theories of Justice*, p. 217.
4. Definitions: State A is *strongly Pareto-superior* to state B if everyone is better off in A than in B, and *weakly Pareto-superior* if at least one person is better off and no one is worse off. If state A is Pareto-superior to state B, then state B is *Pareto-inferior*

which all people, and therefore, in particular, the people now at the bottom, are better off than they were in the initial state of equality. The difference principle is (at least) logically compatible with an equal distribution of goods, for it says that inequality is justified if (and only if) it renders the worst off better off than they would otherwise be: the principle itself does not say when, if ever, that condition on the justifiability of inequality is satisfied, as a matter of social fact. But Rawls believes that it generally is satisfied, that "deep inequalities" in initial life prospects are "inevitable" in any modern society, and that the difference principle tells us *which* inequalities of that deep type are justifiable.[5] In the present exercise I challenge neither the difference principle nor the Pareto principle, that Pareto-superior distributions are always to be preferred. My object is to show that the two-stage argument does not establish the justice of the inequalities that Rawls thinks are just.

Now as Barry recognizes, the two-stage argument, which I shall call the Pareto argument, is not Rawls's official argument for difference principle inequality, since the Pareto argument dispenses with the device of the original position. And Barry has interesting things to say about the relationship between the Pareto argument and the official, contractual one, which, unlike Rawls, Barry thinks less good.[6] Because, moreover, the Pareto argument is avowedly a product of Barry's reconstruction, one may doubt whether Rawls would endorse all of its moves, as Barry sets them out. But whatever role the argument is supposed to play, or does play, in Rawls's writings, it manifestly serves to advance the Rawlsian purpose, which is, here, to reconcile certain inequalities with justice, and many, like Barry, have found the argument convincing. So it is worth scrutinizing.

---

to state A. State A is *Pareto-inferior (tout court)* if some state is Pareto-superior to A. State A is *Pareto-optimal* if no state is Pareto-superior to A: it is *strongly* Pareto-optimal if no state is weakly Pareto-superior to it and *weakly* Pareto-optimal if no state is strongly Pareto-superior to it. States A and B are *Pareto-incomparable* if neither is (even weakly) Pareto-superior to the other. A change is a *weak Pareto-improvement* if it benefits some and harms none, and a *strong Pareto-improvement* if it benefits everyone. The *Pareto principle* mandates a Pareto-improvement whenever one is feasible: the strong Pareto Principle mandates (even) weak Pareto improvements, and the weak one only strong Pareto improvements.

5. *A Theory of Justice*, pp. 7/7. Cf. Rawls, *Political Liberalism*, p. 80, "Reply to Alexander and Mugrave," p. 246: "inequalities are assumed to exist."

6. See Barry, *Theories of Justice*, pp. 213–215, and see Rawls, *A Theory of Justice*, pp. 104/89.

Before looking at the argument in detail, I shall summarize its course, as we find it in Barry, and outline my reasons for rejecting it.

The starting point of the argument is not the Pareto principle but the ideal of equality of opportunity, and there are essentially two thoughts in the argument's first stage. The first thought is that true equality of opportunity is achieved only when all morally arbitrary causes of inequality are eliminated, where, so I take it, a cause of inequality is "morally arbitrary" if it does not justify that inequality because of the kind of cause of inequality that it is. (To get what I mean by that, reflect that non-Rawlsians think that causes of inequality that are appropriately associated with desert or entitlement do justify the inequality that they cause.) And the second thought in the argument's first stage is that there exist no causes of inequality that are not arbitrary in the specified sense. Accordingly, so Barry claims, true equality of opportunity "amounts to equality of outcome,"[7] which is therefore designated as "*prima facie* just."[8]

But full equality of opportunity, or, equivalently, equality of outcome, is only prima facie just, since although no *cause* of inequality can make it just, it might yet be true that an inequality could be just in virtue of its consequences. And that brings us to the second stage of the argument, which pleads that inequality is indeed just when and because it has the particular consequence that it causes everyone to be better off, including, of course, those who end up least better off, the worst off in the new dispensation, who are so placed that, if anyone has the right to complain about inequality, they do. The two thoughts in the second stage of the argument are, first, that it is irrational to insist on equality when it is a Pareto-inferior state of affairs (why would anyone, and, in particular, the worst off, prefer equality to an inequality in which everyone is better off?); and, second, that sometimes, and indeed typically, equality *is* Pareto inferior.

The essence of my objection to the argument is that consistent adherence to the rationale of its first move puts its second move in question: I shall argue that anyone who believes that, because the possible sources of inequality are morally arbitrary, an initial equality is prima facie just has no reason to believe that the recommended Pareto improvement pre-

---

7. Barry, *Theories of Justice*, p. 224. That may seem to be a strange thing to say. On pp. 92–93 below I try to make it seem less strange.
8. Ibid., p. 226.

serves justice, even if that improvement should be accepted on other grounds.[9] The set of possible social worlds will, moreover, usually contain a Pareto-optimal equal distribution that is also Pareto-superior to the initial equality, and that must be preferred to the recommended unequal distribution, on pain of abandoning the rationale of the initial equality. As Rawls says, "it is obvious . . . that there are indefinitely many ways in which all may be advantaged when the initial arrangement of equality is taken as a benchmark."[10] I claim that the particular type of Pareto improvement picked by Rawls contradicts the rationale of the original move from equality of opportunity to equality.

Although I am in sympathy with the first part of the Pareto argument and hostile to the second, I do not have to endorse or reject either part to prosecute the present critique. For my critical contention is that the two parts of the argument are inconsistent with each other, that those who, like Rawls and Barry, make the second move after making the first have failed to see how far-reachingly egalitarian the argument's first move is. Someone who agrees with my criticism could respond by rejecting the argument for an initial equality, rather than, as I would, by rejecting (at least) the argument for abandoning it.[11]

There is an argument for inequality that is simpler than the one I shall criticize and that I do not address here. This simpler argument is easy to confuse with the one I shall focus on. It runs as follows: the distribution of goods must be either equal or unequal. But the best feasible equal distribution is Pareto-inferior to some feasible unequal distribution. An unequal distribution is, therefore, always to be preferred. In this different argument, equality and inequality are symmetrically placed. Equality is not a privileged starting point dictated by justice from which we are asked to pass on to inequality. Accordingly, the simpler argument pro-

---

9. The claim that the Pareto-improving unequalizing move might be accepted on grounds other than justice, that, indeed, Rawls's own case for it is not really one of justice, was persuasively made by David Lyons in his "Nature and Soundness of the Contract and Coherence Arguments," pp. 152–153.

10. *A Theory of Justice*, pp. 65/56.

11. Although, as I have said, I am in sympathy with the first part of the argument, I also have reservations about it. Rawls's use of the motif of moral arbitrariness is subject to (as yet) largely unanswered searching criticism by Robert Nozick in his *Anarchy, State, and Utopia*, pp. 213–227. See, further, Chapter 4, sections 3 and 5.

vides no reason for starting with equality that a critic could press as a reason for not departing from it. But Rawls says that

> *since* the parties regard themselves as [free and equal moral] persons,—the obvious starting point is for them to suppose that all social primary goods, including income and wealth, should be equal: everyone should have an equal share.[12]

Rawls lays out a rationale for starting with equality, and its detailed development, expounded below, impugns, so I shall argue, the subsequent case for abandoning equality. The simpler argument could not be Rawls's, for it does not mandate difference-principle inequality in particular, as what I call the Pareto argument does. It is, indeed, the considerations that motivate the difference principle in particular that tell against replacing the initial equality by an unequal distribution.

The two-stage argument stakes out a middle ground between laissez-faire libertarianism and radical egalitarianism. Such ground may be tenable, but not, if I am right, in the way that it is staked out here. One theme in Chapter 1, which I continue to pursue here, is that the sort of inequality that Rawls tolerates, and indeed encourages, requires for its defense the very notions of desert and entitlement that he wants to reject. Accordingly, if I am right, there should be more polarization in political philosophy between left and right positions. If there is to be a middle position, it cannot be defended in Rawls's way.

2. The Argument Expounded

The first part of the Pareto argument takes its departure from equality of opportunity as that conception is understood by laissez-faire libertarians: opportunity is, for them, equal when there is no legal bar, such as exists under slavery or serfdom, to anyone's economic or social self-advancement. In this conception, the unequalizing effect on opportunity of "natural and social contingencies"[13] (of birth, upbringing, and so forth) is tolerated, and the conception is consequently untrue to the ideal of equal opportunity that it purports to advance: its "most obvious injus-

12. "The Basic Structure as Subject," in *Political Liberalism*, p. 281 (emphasis added); and see "A Kantian Conception of Equality," p. 262.
13. Rawls, *A Theory of Justice*, pp. 72/62.

tice . . . is that it permits distributive shares to be improperly influenced by these factors [that is, "natural and social contingencies"] so arbitrary from a moral point of view."[14]

A few remarks on the character, and the limits, of this rejection of laissez-faire. To be convicted of infidelity to his own principle of equality of opportunity, the proponent of laissez-faire must reject feudal and other status barriers for a particular reason, to wit, just because they defeat equality of opportunity and not, for example, because a society without status barriers is optimific in a utilitarian sense (although he may, of course, believe that as well). If he were against feudalism for utilitarian reasons and in favor of equal opportunity for those reasons alone, he would not be vulnerable to the charge that the opportunity he favors is not truly equal, since he would not have to claim that it is; and he could also not be accused of trafficking in the morally arbitrary.[15] And he would also be immune to the present argument if he affirmed laissez-faire because he considered it to be the social structure answering to the principle of self-ownership: that is the position of most contemporary philosophical libertarians. The target libertarian, who cannot be a very clear thinker, and who is statistically rare,[16] must say that he supports laissez-faire *because* he believes in equality of opportunity, and that he believes in the latter because he thinks it unfair for people's progress to be differentially impeded and promoted by restrictions and advantages for which they are in no way responsible. Then, and only then, is he exposed to the indicated immanent criticism.

Having rejected laissez-faire, Rawls and Barry move on to a conception of equality of opportunity that seeks to remove (not merely legal but also) social barriers to advancement: it says for example, that children from deprived backgrounds should not have less good education than what privileged children get. In this substage "equal opportunity" is identified "with the elimination of all [unequalizing] factors except that of genetic endowment."[17] But Rawls maintains that the "natural distribution of abilities" is quite as "arbitrary from a moral perspective"[18] as

14. Ibid., pp. 72/63.

15. Thomas Nagel's defense of utilitarianism against Rawls is relevant here: see his "Equality," p. 119.

16. As I indicate in n. 19 below, I do not believe that Rawls construes libertarianism in the suggested strained fashion.

17. Barry, *Theories of Justice*, p. 222.

18. *A Theory of Justice*, p. 64.

is that distribution modified by unequal social prospects. Accordingly, we pass on to, and come to rest with, a truly complete equality of opportunity, in which neither natural nor social advantages contribute to inequality of well-being.[19]

Barry says that this radical interpretation of equal opportunity, as "nothing other than equal prospects of success for all," "amounts to equality of outcome."[20] Now that might be thought a strange identification, so let me explain what I take Barry to mean. To put his point in the form of a familiar image, he means that, in a perfectly handicapped race, everyone crosses the finishing line at the same time: equality of outcome is the test of equality of opportunity.

That conveys Barry's meaning well enough for the special case where one good is at stake, and all are assumed to want it equally. To express his point more generally, we can say that, in the dispensation under discussion, such differences in outcome as may obtain are due not to differences in opportunity or ability but to differences of taste or choice, and for that reason, and in that sense, no such difference in outcome counts as an inequality. If you can reach only the oranges, and I can reach both them and the apples, and I get two oranges and two apples,

---

19. In the foregoing paragraphs I present the movement from natural liberty to equality as an entirely immanent one, each of its first two substages yielding to its successor because the latter is more faithful to its predecessor substage's rationale. I believe, without being certain, that Barry intends to ascribe precisely such an argument to Rawls, but I am certain that the structure of the argument that Rawls himself presents (See *A Theory of Justice*, sections 12 and 13) is in one way different from the structure of the one that I have constructed, which is based on pp. 218–220 of Barry's *Theories of Justice*.

Rawls proceeds as follows. He cites the principles of "natural liberty," "liberal equality" and "democratic equality" as affording three readings of the ideal of equality of opportunity. Natural liberty is rejected because of its complacency about the influence of natural and social luck on shares. Because liberal equality aims to suppress social luck, it is commended, but it is then criticized on the ground that there is no difference between social and natural luck that would justify exclusive preoccupation with the former.

Accordingly, the movement from liberal equality to democratic equality is indeed an immanent one, but the movement from natural liberty to liberal equality is not. Natural liberty is not rejected by Rawls because of any internal incoherence of the sort at which Barry gestures: it is rejected because it fails to resist the morally arbitrary.

20. *Theories of Justice*, p. 224.

and you get only two oranges, then you are on the down side of an inequality between us. But if we can each reach both, and I end up with oranges and you with apples, or even if I end up with more of each than you do (because you care less than I do for fruit), then no relevant inequality of distribution holds (unless, what I here assume to be false, the menu was rigged to suit my tastes). It does not matter whether the outcome, in which there is no inequality that reflects unequal opportunity, can or should be called *equality, tout court,* as opposed to *justified* (on egalitarian grounds) *inequality.* What matters is that the outcome is a distribution that egalitarians would endorse,[21] and one that functions here, whatever its name should be, as the initial stage in the Rawls/Barry argument construction. Following Barry, I shall call it "equality" here.[22]

So much, then, on how we arrive at the initial equality. Let me now display some texts in which Rawls defends the second movement, from equality to inequality. I shall then (in section 3 below) ask some disambiguating questions about the character of the first, equality, stage.

Rawls frequently remarks that inequality of primary[23] goods is justi-

---

21. Different egalitarians believe that different things should be equalized, so they would endorse and condemn different outcomes, but that does not matter here: the phrase "outcome that egalitarians would endorse," as it applies to the initial stage, can be treated as a variable here, since the argument we shall examine is for inequality no matter what conception of equality is embraced.

22. If, as Barry says, true equality of opportunity amounts to equality of outcome, then stage two of the Pareto argument, in asking us to abandon equality, also asks us to abandon true equality of opportunity. I doubt that Barry was fully alive to this aspect of his position, which implies that "the *most* just society" (*Theories of Justice,* p. 217, my emphasis, and cf. p. 234) lacks equality of opportunity.

23. Strictly, of *social* primary goods, but as Rawls himself does, I shall abbreviate to "primary goods" where misunderstanding is unlikely. Primary goods are "things that every rational man is presumed to want" since they "normally have a use whatever a person's rational plan of life." The "social primary goods" are the primary goods "at the disposition of society," to wit, "rights and liberties, powers and opportunities, income and wealth," and the social bases of self-respect. "Other primary goods such as health and vigor, intelligence and imagination, are natural goods; although their possession is influenced by the basic structure, they are not so directly under its control" (*A Theory of Justice,* pp. 62/54). Will Kymlicka argues that Rawls has no good reason for restricting his index of well-being to the social primary goods: see his *Contemporary Political Philosophy,* pp. 70–73. Thomas Pogge's defense, in his *Realizing Rawls,* of what he calls Rawls's *"semi-consequentialism"* supports Rawls's restriction of the purview of justice to social primary goods.

fied when and because it represents a Pareto-superior alternative to an equal share-out. For example:

> . . . the parties start with a principle establishing equal liberty for all, including equality of opportunity, as well as an equal distribution of income and wealth. But there is no reason why this acknowledgement should be final. If there are inequalities in the basic structure that work to make everyone better off in comparison with the benchmark of initial equality, then why not permit them? The immediate gain[24] which a greater equality might allow can be regarded as intelligently invested in view of its future return.[25]

Again, and more compendiously:

> an equal division of all primary goods is irrational in view of the possibility of bettering everyone's circumstances by accepting certain inequalities.[26]

And then, in a passage that, more explicitly than others, separates the two stages in fictional time:

> Imagine . . . a hypothetical initial arrangement in which all the social primary goods are equally distributed: everyone has similar rights and duties, and income and wealth are evenly shared. This state of affairs provides a benchmark for judging improvements. If certain inequalities of wealth and organizational powers would make everyone better off than in this hypothetical starting situation, then they accord with the general conception,

according to which,

> all social values—liberty and opportunity, income and wealth, and the bases of self-respect—are to be distributed equally unless an unequal distribution of any, or all, of these values is to everyone's advantage.[27]

24. To, that is, the worst off; better off people gain immediately from *in*equality. The idea is that we withhold from the poor to give more to the rich and, as a result, the poor end up better off, later.
25. *A Theory of Justice*, p. 151. On pp. 130–131 of the 1999 version, the quoted text is extensively revised, but not materially to my present interpretation and use of it.
26. Ibid., p. 546. This sentence and the one that precedes it are dropped at the corresponding page (478) of the 1999 edition. But there is no doubt that Rawls continued to believe the proposition expressed by the sentence that I have quoted.
27. Ibid., pp. 62/54–55.

It is clear from other passages that, in the inequality recommended in those exhibited above, the people who do better than others are those with more productive talent. They get more primary goods than do their less gifted fellow citizens. And as I have indicated, Rawls invites (even) egalitarians to endorse that result, on pain of displaying irrationality.

Now as we have seen, Rawls emphasizes that greater talent is good fortune, which means both that it is a good for those who have it and that it is sheer luck that they have it. And the fact that their possession of talent is mere good luck is treated as a reason why they should not have further advantages except on terms that also benefit those who lack their initial advantages: because they are already better off, they should not have more primary goods than others do unless, as a result, the less fortunate have more primary goods than they would otherwise have had. "Those who have been favored by nature . . . may gain from their good fortune only on terms that improve the situation of those who have lost out."[28]

Consider the following characteristic passage:

the better endowed (who have a place in the distribution of native endow-ments they do not morally deserve) are encouraged to acquire still further benefits—they are already benefited by their fortunate place in that distri-bution—on condition that they train their native endowments and use them in ways that contribute to the good of the less endowed (who have a less fortunate place in the distribution [of native endowments—G.A.C.] they also do not morally deserve).[29]

28. Ibid., pp. 101/87, and see ibid, pp. 75/64–65, 102/87, 179/156, and, decisively in favor of the interpretation of Rawls given in the present paragraph, "A Kantian Con-ception of Equality," pp. 263–264.

29. *Justice as Fairness*, pp. 76–77.

In my interpretation of the passages cited in this and the previous footnote, the constraint placed on how far ahead the talented may get depends on its being good for them that they have more talent. In a suggested counter-interpretation, Rawls says that talent endowments are morally arbitrary, so no one may benefit from them as a matter of desert, but, if the well endowed benefit from their talent in ways that also help the untalented, then the benefit redounding to the former is acceptable. In the counter-interpretation, it is immaterial to Rawls's argument that, as he mentions, talent is a good thing.

The counter-interpretation argument may be both coherent and Rawlsian (for there is more than one argument in Rawls), but, for two reasons, I rest with my own interpretation of the cited passages. First, the counter-interpretation does not ac-count for the rhetorically strategic placement of the repeated reminder that talent is

Now what exactly does Rawls mean by *"still further* benefits"? It appears that what the well endowed already have counts as benefit in virtue of a comparison of their endowment with that of others: it is a matter of "their fortunate *place* in [the] distribution" of endowment. One may then infer that the "further benefits" they "are encouraged to acquire" means still further differential advantage, that is, larger additions to their stock of primary goods than the ill endowed get. The phrase can hardly mean primary goods as such (conceived as a benefit beyond that of having talent), for they already have some primary goods (and if they did not, then, on the suggested interpretation, and given the rest of what is said, *"still further* benefits" would imply that the talented should starve to death unless the terms on which they survive benefit the untalented!). Someone might question my confidence that the meaning I discern in them can be wrung out of this particular trio of words (*"still further* benefits"). But no one can doubt that, in the recommended Pareto-superior inequality, the talented have typically more primary goods than the untalented. Rawls makes it abundantly clear that the inequality of reward serves as an encouragement to the talented in particular.

3. The Argument Challenged

So we start with equality in social primary goods and inequality in the (nonsocial primary) good of talent, a state of affairs that I shall label D1;

---

beneficial. Second, and perhaps more importantly, Rawls is in my interpretation readily seen to be addressing an intuitively grounded protest against superior emolument to the talented, a protest that such emolument follows the notion that "to them that hath shall be given": see the Mill citation in the following footnote. Rawls is naturally interpreted as replying: that is fine, provided that those that hath *not* also benefit.

As I pointed out in n. 6 of Chapter 1, there is ambiguity in Rawls with respect to which inequalities are permitted. Many texts, such as those cited above, permit only inequalities that help the worst off. Other texts, those, for example, in which the leximin principle is affirmed, also permit inequalities that do not harm them. The counter-interpretation argument corresponds to the less egalitarian leximin principle. Unlike my interpretation, it does not explain why maximin might take a restrictive form, and that is the form in which maximin appears in the cited passages.

See, further, section 5 of Chapter 4 below: "What is the Moral Arbitrariness of Talent Differences Supposed to Show?"

and we move to a Pareto-superior alternative state, D2, in which the talented enjoy not only their original advantage but the further one of a larger social primary goods bundle. Notice, then, that in the movement away from D1, inequality of talent is reinforced (and not, for example, counterbalanced) by an inequality in social primary goods. We might find it surprising that the talented in particular should end up with more, since a principal insistence of the first part of the argument, which took us to D1, was that the circumstance of their greater talent justifies no distributive effect. And egalitarians might regret this "giving [more] to those who have"[30] than to those who have not.

With such thoughts in mind, I now begin to scrutinize Rawls's irrationality thesis (the thesis that it is irrational not to replace D1 by an unequal state of affairs).

The first thing to notice is that the baseline situation, D1, is significantly underdescribed. We lack information about D1 that we require for a comprehensive assessment of the recommendation that it should give way to D2, and, so I believe, the underdescription, the lack of information, makes the glide from D1 to D2 smoother than it otherwise would be. D1, the "initial equality," "provides a benchmark for judging improvements." We cannot say whether, and how, D2 improves on D1 until we know more than Rawls tells us about what D1 comprises.

In D1 "all the social primary goods are equally distributed: everyone has similar rights and duties, and income and wealth are evenly shared."[31] But the baseline is thereby underdescribed in the following respects, among others. First, since we know only about social primary goods, we do not know what labor inputs talented and untalented people supply in D1.[32] We know neither how much time they spend working nor how toilsome that time is.[33] And we also do not know what the

30. John Stuart Mill so describes higher reward to the talented on p. 210 of section 4 of Chapter I of Book II of his *Principles of Political Economy*. For an adverse contrast between Rawls and Mill on this issue, see the final page of Chapter 1 above.
31. *A Theory of Justice,* pp. 62/55.
32. For related points, see Ronald Dworkin, "Equality of Resources," pp. 116–117.
33. As Michael Lessnoff pointed out, it was inconsistent with Rawls's understanding of justice as a matter of "the proper distribution of the benefits *and burdens* of social cooperation" (*A Theory of Justice,* pp. 5/5, emphasis added) that he omitted labor burdens from the index of social primary goods ("Capitalism, Socialism and Justice," p. 143).

initial equality of primary goods is, precisely, in one crucial dimension, an equality of. Consider the goods of income and wealth. We can suppose that wealth holdings are intended to be strictly equal in economic value (that is, therefore, that *each* of income and wealth is equal: it is not [merely] the value of some function of the two that is equal). Unearned incomes are consequently equal in a straightforward sense. But equality of earned income (henceforth, for simplicity: income) is more problematic. Is it, here, an equality of wage rate (that is, of income per period of time worked), with, consequently, possibly different weekly or annual incomes, or an equality of weekly or annual income, with possibly different wage rates, or something else again? Finally, and more globally, at what level is the equality of income and wealth in D1 pitched, and why is it not postulated to be higher, or lower, than whatever that level is?

I have no view about what Barry (or Rawls) intended by way of answers to those surely relevant questions. But what matters is not what

---

Later, Rawls contemplated including leisure time among primary goods: see his "Reply to Alexander and Musgrave," p. 253, and "The Priority of Right and Ideas of the Good," p. 455. And Thomas Pogge is quite definite: "the index must also include *leisure time* as a distinct social primary good. This good can be defined simply as the inverse of time worked, which is a burden of social cooperation" (*Realizing Rawls*, p. 198). This is not entirely satisfactory since, if "time worked" is a burden, it is one that varies importantly in size with the character of the job and the makeup of the person (cf. John Baker, "An Egalitarian Case for Basic Income," p. 125, n. 4). And it makes matters more difficult still that some people find their fulfillment in their work. Is it a *burden* of social cooperation for them too?

Nineteen years after the publication of "Reply to Alexander and Musgrave," Rawls sustains his noncommitment on the matter of whether leisure should be included among the primary goods (see *Political Liberalism*, pp. 181–182). I believe that this fence-sitting reflects the fact that labor is a burden (and, sometimes, benefit!) of social cooperation (so it should be a primary good) that fails the test of public checkability (see *A Theory of Justice*, pp. 95/81) laid down for primary goods (so it should not be one).

Henceforth, when I speak of "labor burden," I mean to refer not only to the quantity of a person's labor but also to its character in the sense of how burdensome or oppressive it is. Notice that, even if *A Theory of Justice* had included leisure time as a primary social good (or labor time as a primary social bad), we should still have been in the dark not only about the character but also about the mere quantity of people's labor inputs in D1.

I return to the theme of labor burden in the metric of advantage in sections 5 and 6 below, and also in section 3 of Chapter 5.

was intended but whether the questions admit of natural answers that preserve the initial persuasiveness of the recommendation that D1 be abandoned in favor of an unequal distribution of goods.

Now, setting aside the questions about the toilsomeness of labor and about the level of income and wealth in D1—to both of which I shall return—let us suppose, so that we have something sufficiently determinate to think about, that the D1 income equality is of wage per hour (called the D1 wage rate W); that talented and untalented people work the same number of hours and apply themselves with the same degree of effort: this is a plausible partial reading of the stipulation that their "duties" are "similar"[34]; and that, being more talented, and putting in the same effort, the talented consequently produce more than the untalented do, although *ex hypothesi* they get no more income as a result. Many would regard that as unfair, but the greater output of the more able is here to be regarded as due to the morally arbitrary circumstance of their lucky talent endowment, which is among the factors whose effects are to be discounted in the argument for an initial equality.

Now on the foregoing assumptions about D1, we can infer that at D2 both talented and untalented enjoy wage rates higher than W, here labeled, respectively, as Wt and Wu. We also know that Wt is greater than Wu; that it is the extra productivity (over what they supply at W) supplied by the talented when they receive Wt that enables the untalented to be paid Wu; and that the difference between Wu and W is thought by Rawls to be necessary to justify the difference between Wt and Wu. Let us also further suppose, for simplicity, and to improve the case for the inequality that will here be opposed, that the untalented produce no more in D2 than they do in D1.

Of course, that is just one way of filling in some of the spaces left blank by Rawls and Barry. But it is quite a natural way, and I am in any case confident that the result of reflecting on the issue when the baseline is thus specified will be robust, that other acceptable specifications would generate similar conclusions.

Consider now a logically possible distribution, D3, which may or may not be practically feasible, in which the same amount is produced as in D2 but which differs from D2 in that in D3 wages are equal, at a rate labeled We, where We exceeds W and Wu but is less than Wt (so $Wt > We > Wu > W$). D3 is Pareto-superior to D1 but, unlike D2 (with which

---

34. *A Theory of Justice*, pp. 62/54–55: see the text to n. 31 above.

it is Pareto-incomparable[35]), D3 preserves equality, and the untalented are better off in D3 than they are in D2, while the talented are less well off in D3 than in D2, and both are better off in D3 than they are in D1[36]. If D3 is feasible *and* talented people are willing to produce at *We* what they do at *Wt*, then Rawls's claim about the irrationality of insisting on equality in the face of the possibility of a Pareto-superior inequality would lose its force, since a Pareto-improving *equality-preserving*[37] move, in which no one is as badly off as some are in D2, would now also be available. We can suppose that if D3 is indeed feasible, then the additional product, vis-à-vis D1, is, once again, wholly due to the greater productivity of talented people. But, wage rates being equal in D3, the talented do not in D3 gain differentially from the increase in product, as they do in D2.

4. The Argument Rejected

Let us now ask: what might explain and/or justify replacing D1 by D2, rather than by D3?

The first answer to be considered is that, by contrast with D2, D3 would be unfair to talented people, who produce in D3 more than others do and yet get no more than others do by way of reward. But that was

---

35. See n. 4 above. D2 and D3 are Pareto-incomparable because in each some are better off than they are in the other.

36. For some readers, the following tabular presentation of the above array of comparisons may be helpful:

	D1		D2		D3
Talented	W	$<$	Wt	$>$	We
	$=$		$>$		$=$
Untalented	W	$<$	Wu	$>$	We

$<$ means "is less than," $>$ means "is greater than," and $=$ signifies equality

37. (Added, 2008) It preserves, that is, equality of wages, and thereby serves the difference principle when its metric is income alone. If, however, the talented work harder in D2 than they do in D1, then equal wages are unjustified from an egalitarian point of view, if a defensible metric is adopted, and the example would have to be perturbed slightly, but to no substantive effect. (See sections 5 and 6 below, on competing metrics of equality.)

already true of, but because of Rawls's egalitarian argument, no objection to D1, so it cannot, in all consistency, be pressed against D3.

A second answer is that D3 is objectively unfeasible, where "objectively" means that the unfeasibility is not a matter of human will. This answer says that D3 is unfeasible because, with all the will in the world, the talented *could* not produce at *We* as much as they do at *Wt*. But that is hardly likely, for realistic assignments of *Wt* and *We*.[38] It might be true under special circumstances, in which case the Pareto argument for inequality works, but only (on this showing) in special circumstances.[39] In normal circumstances nothing but the unwillingness (be it justified or not) of the talented to share equally the greater product produced in D2 could make D3 impossible when D2 is possible.

Next there is the answer that D3, although objectively feasible, is indeed ruled out by the attitude of talented people: they are not willing to work at *We* as long and/or as hard as they do at *Wt*. There are three pertinently different subvariants of this case, each of which calls for separate comment, and which I shall label the bad (or "rent," or "bluff") case, the good (or "special burden") case, and the standard case: it is the standard case that represents the site of my disagreement with Rawls.[40]

The bad case: if their wage rate were *fated* to be *We*, then the talented would happily produce at *We* precisely what they do at *Wt*,[41] but they refuse for strategic reasons to produce that much when offered *We*, since their refusal induces an offer of *Wt*. But this answer sullies the recommendation of D2. It is not irrational, here, in the sense Rawls intended, even if it is quixotic, in the face of the power of the talented, to express a preference for the equality-preserving D3.

By contrast with what holds for the bad case, in both the good and the standard cases talented people prefer, and are resolved, to produce less at *We* than at *Wt*, and that is why D3 is unfeasible (although it is not objectively so). In the good variant of that, the work of the talented in D2 is more arduous than that of the untalented, sufficiently more so to justify

38. See Chapter 1, section 7, for an extended discussion of, in effect, this issue.
39. Such as those that are provided by the Van Parijs examples in section 6 of Chapter 7.
40. The alternative names in the parentheses were introduced on p. 57ff. of Chapter 1.
41. Which is to say that their labor supply curve is in the relevant region vertical. It could also be backward-bending, in which case they would produce more at *We* than they do at *Wt*.

the difference between Wt and Wu. (Notice that, to acknowledge this possibility, I need not say how such judgments of arduousness, and of what would compensate for it, are to be reached.) In that case paying everybody We would be unfair, *from an egalitarian point of view*: in the good case the talented carry a special burden that any reasonable egalitarian must think should be compensated. Thus suppose, to take a different sort of example from the one that confronts us here, that although people are of equal talent, circumstantial constraints mean that some work more hours than others, that all other things (including people's utility functions) are equal, and that utility is a decreasing function of labor time. Then no clearheaded egalitarian would approve of equal total weekly payment, whether or not—this would depend on further features of the case—he should insist on (precisely) equal payment per hour.

The egalitarian principle that greater burden justifies greater compensating reward operates in our context in favor of D2 and against D3 in the good case. Where work is specially arduous, or stressful, higher remuneration is a counterbalancing equalizer, on a sensible view of how to judge whether or not things are equal. Accordingly, and because we are examining a supposed justification of inequality, the good or special burden case poses no problem for us, for what we get when special burden is invoked is not a justification of an inequality, all things considered, but a denial that there is an inequality, all things considered.

Now in what I have called the standard case, the work of talented people is not distinctively burdensome but, on the contrary, characteristically more congenial than the work of others is.[42] It is untrue in the standard case that high pay compensates the talented for specially arduous toil. Suppose then that we are in the standard case, in which Wt in particular is not required to compensate the talented for a special burden, and that there is, more generally, no special burden case against paying everyone We. Then although talented people may, as in the bad case, successfully hold out for Wt as a condition of producing more than what they do in D1, and thereby make D3 impossible, it is hard to see why an egalitarian should be expected to regard what they then do as acceptable, even if nothing can be done about it. In explaining her refusal to endorse the justice of D2, the egalitarian can draw on the notions used

42. It might therefore be suggested that they be paid less than others. But I shall not pursue that suggestion here: I am rebutting an argument for inequality, not sketching a complete egalitarian theory.

by Rawls to pass from equality of opportunity to D1. She can say that, in knocking D3 out of the feasible set, talented people are violating

> a conception of justice that nullifies the accidents of natural endowment and the contingencies of social circumstance as counters in the quest for . . . economic advantage. . .[43]

Instead, they are operating in conformity with a conception of justice that, in significant degree (albeit, to be sure, not in the same degree as laissez-faire does)

> weight[s] men's share in the benefits and burdens of social cooperation according to their social fortune or their luck in the natural lottery.[44]

At one point Rawls says that the Pareto-improving inequalities might work by "set[ting] up various incentives which succeed in eliciting more productive efforts,"[45] and another passage suggests that this is the principal form of Pareto-improving inequality that he contemplates.[46] This means that talented people require an unequalizing incentive to produce more than they do at D1: it is because they are in a position to take more than what the untalented could then have that D3 falls out of the feasible set. Now it is entirely reasonable for the talented to get more than the W they get in D1 when they produce more, as they do in D2, but they do get more than W when they get We in D3. What is startling is that Rawls recommends a rate of pay, $Wt,$ that is higher than that of others, a rate they secure by virtue of the disposition of the market to reward superior talent, when that superior talent was originally, in the construction of D1, said to justify no superior reward. If the talented had objected to the equality of D1 on the ground that they produce more than others do in D1, they would have been told that they were seeking to exploit morally arbitrary advantages. They can be told the same thing when they reject D3 in favor of D2. We can ask: why was the original equality not pitched at D3, instead of at D1, when D3 is Pareto-superior to D1 (at least on the present assumption, to wit, that the labor of the talented is not spe-

43. *A Theory of Justice,* pp. 15/14, which changes "nullifies" to "prevents the use of."
44. Ibid., pp. 75/65.
45. Ibid., p. 151, passage omitted in 1999.
46. Ibid., pp. 78/68.

cially burdensome)? Had we begun with D3, D2 would have been seen for what it is: an unjustifiable (on the assumptions that lead to D1) alternative to an objectively feasible equal condition, namely, D3.

Note that the Rawlsian argument is not that the talented carry a special labor burden in 2 for which they need to be compensated. If they were to get more money because of such a burden, then this would not be an argument for *in*equality, but the application of a principle of equality that reasonably takes into account not only money, but also how oppressive a person's labor is. And we can now, therefore, state the following dilemma for the Pareto argument. Either the talented carry, in D2, a special burden that is compensated for by the difference between *Wt* and *Wu*, in which case *it is a mistake to represent movement from D1 to D2 as issuing in an inequality;*[47] or *Wt* is not required to compensate for any burden, in which case *there is no reason for an egalitarian to regard D2 as acceptable, and every reason for him to recommend D3.* In other words: either the extra money that the talented get in D2 makes them no better off, all things (including labor burden) considered, than the untalented, or it does make them better off than the untalented, all things considered. In the first alternative there is no justified *inequality,* all things considered, because there is no inequality, all things considered; in the second, there is no *justified* inequality, or at any rate the inequality that obtains still awaits its justification, *and it is difficult to see how it*

47. This holds whether or not D1 itself turns out, after further required specification, to be an equal distribution: that would partly depend on comparative labor burdens in D1, which were not specified on p. 100 above.

Note that, had we specified earned income equality in D1 as wage per unit output (as opposed to, as we did, as wage per unit time), we should then have been unable to represent D1 as a state of equality without stipulating that the talented carry special labor burdens, since, for morally arbitrary reasons, they would then have been earning more per hour than the untalented. By stipulating equal wage per hour, we concealed, up to now, the labor burden issue.

Ex hypothesi, the talented get the same primary goods as others at D1. If leisure is a primary good, then they work as many hours as others, therefore produce more, but get the same income. If leisure is not a primary good, and payment is per unit output, then they get more leisure and/or more primary goods, and not, in general, the same basket of primary goods, thus specified, but just the same rate of primary goods per unit output. It would be hollow to call that a society of equality, as Rawls's own (curiously unconsummated—see n. 33 above) inclination to acknowledge leisure as a primary good betrays. If talented people should not get more just because they are talented, they should not get more leisure in the initial equality.

could be justified by anyone who approves of the first Rawlsian move, from equality of opportunity to equality. So neither way does a justified (all things considered) inequality emerge. Only when the issue of labor burden is obscured can it be made to seem that a justified inequality emerges.

5. Labor Burden in the Metric of Equality

I must now defend my description of the first horn (see the first italicized clause in the foregoing paragraph) of this dilemma. That description might be thought inadmissible, since it employs a metric for equality in which things (that is, labor burdens) other than social primary goods count, and those are the only goods that figure (officially) in Rawls's metric. The description of the special burden (or "good case") variant of D2 as consistent with equality fails when social primary goods alone constitute the metric, for there is, *ex hypothesi,* an inequality of such goods in D2. Accordingly, the reference to special labor burdens looks out of order, given what Rawls means by "equality" and "inequality" here.

My first defense of mention of labor burdens is that it is flatly absurd, when assessing distributions from an egalitarian point of view, to bracket off that significant aspect of a person's social condition.[48] But I can also supply a defense of the contested procedure that is less dogmatic, because founded on ideas that Rawls himself affirms.

Recall that Rawls regards it as normatively relevant that the natively well endowed are, as such, more fortunate than others. That inequality, *which is not a matter of social primary goods,* is given as a reason in distributive justice why the talented should not benefit further from their already greater fortune except on terms that benefit the less fortunate.

---

48. (Added, 2008) Had I written the article that is the substance of the present chapter after I had reached the distinction drawn in Chapter 6 between fundamental principles and rules of regulation, I would have said that labor burdens must come into assessments of fundamental justice, however difficult it may be to represent them, even by proxy, within rules of regulation. (Welfarist considerations that have regard to the nonresource benefits and burdens of life, are quite generally difficult to cater for within rules of regulation, but they are not wholly unmanageable. Dispensers of public housing, for example, rightly take into account the different degrees of distress that those who occupy poor housing experience, and not just how big the dwellings they now occupy are.)

Since Rawls thereby treats something other than an existing social primary goods distribution as a proper constraint on further distribution of social primary goods, he could not say that labor burden is distributively inconsequential on the entirely general ground that it involves no deficiency/surplus in social primary goods.

But one can mount an even stronger tu quoque claim. Let us ask: why is it (as Rawls says it is) a piece of good fortune to be talented? Part of the reason is that talent enables people to get things that they want, including, notably, income. That is why Rawls classifies talent as a primary good: not, of course, a social one, but a "natural" one.[49] But here we must abstract from the power of talent to generate income, since Rawls represents the parties as benefiting from their talent in the first stage of his construction, what I called D1, when no income benefits have as yet accrued. The income-generating aspect being set aside, it is surely a large part of the answer to the question heading this paragraph that the exercise of talent is inherently rewarding. But that is a consideration relating to labor (benefit and) burden. Accordingly, Rawls could not consistently protest against my reference to such considerations. (Notice that, since Rawls strongly emphasizes the intrinsic rewards attached to the exercise of talent,[50] it is the second horn of the dilemma described in the final paragraph of section 4 above, the "standard case" horn, which is most likely to apply: it is hard for Rawls to claim that the work of high fliers is [income aside] less rewarding than that of the less well off.)

6. Inconsistent Metrics

So much in defense of reference to labor burdens in the statement of the dilemma that refutes the Pareto argument. I now want to show that it is

---

49. See *A Theory of Justice*, pp. 62/54.

50. He does so in his affirmation of the Aristotelian Principle: "other things equal, human beings enjoy the exercise of their realized capacities (their innate or trained abilities), and this enjoyment increases the more the capacity is realized, or the greater its complexity" (ibid., pp. 426–427/374). It is the final phrase, much emphasized in the rest of the paragraph that this statement of the principle introduces, that matters in our inquiry. (Anthony Skillen noted that the Aristotelian Principle is hard to combine with Rawls's endorsement of incentives for people of talent. Rawls "assumes . . . that the very minority who can enjoy stretching their capacities, the entrepreneurs, will need great wealth and prestige to motivate their activity" [*Ruling Illusions*, p. 47].)

not necessary, in order to refute that argument (as opposed to: in order at the same time to suggest what the positive truth of the matter is), to put labor burden within the metric of advantage. For the Rawlsian argument is persuasive only when we equivocate across metrics that do and do not include labor burden. Accordingly, we do not have to favor either metric to dismiss the argument.

The official metric of the argument is that of primary goods. Expressed within that metric, the argument runs as follows: there is no reason for primary goods to be unequally distributed (first stage of the argument), unless an unequal distribution benefits everyone (second stage). But that, we saw, cannot justify the move from D1 to D2, since, where D2 is possible, so, standardly, is D3, and, relative to D3, D2 is *not* an unequal distribution that benefits everyone: the worst off do better in D3 than they do in D2.

Now some people, reading the above paragraph, will feel that it proceeds too smoothly, that the refutation is too quick, that a piece of the argument under comment has been left out. And I think that something like the following, enriched, version of the argument underlies their resistance: "Originally everything was equal. Now everything remains as before, except that the talented are working harder and producing more. Accordingly, they should have more of that extra product than the untalented do, since they are the ones that are working harder." But that way of presenting the argument requires inconsistent metrics: since the original equality was one of primary goods, why, suddenly, is labor burden relevant? We cannot have one metric for judging whether the baseline is just and another for judging the justice of departures from it.

Suppose, then, that our metric does admit labor burden, and that we pronounce D1 to be a state of equality only after we have taken that burden into account: equality of primary goods is no longer sufficient (or necessary) for equality. We cannot then count D2 as a state of *in*equality unless we think that in D2 the talented are, unequalizingly, *over-* (or *under-*) compensated for their pains. D2 is *ex hypothesi* an unequal distribution of primary goods, but in a metric that includes labor burden, that inequality is insufficient for inequality as such.

In short, if we use a primary goods metric, then D2 indeed exhibits an inequality, but one that lacks justification: D3 being feasible, how can D2 be justified, with the assumptions that led to D1 still in place? If, on the other hand, we use a metric that includes labor burden, then it is unclear whether D2 exhibits an inequality, since it is specified in terms of primary goods alone. But if it does involve an inequality, then it is an inequality that lacks justification, because it does not give the talented the right amount of compensation (if it did, there would be no inequality, judged by this metric).

A justified inequality appears to emerge only when, quite inconsistently, we use the primary goods metric to establish that D2 is an unequal distribution, and we look to labor burden to justify that inequality.[51]

7. Raising the Baseline

As I acknowledged in section 3, there are ways other than the one I there elected of filling in the spaces left blank in the Rawls/Barry description of D1, but, so I claimed, my argument is essentially independent of the particular specifications that I laid down. I also remarked (page 99) that Rawls and Barry say nothing about the *level* of income and wealth in D1, and I did not myself pitch them at a particular level.

Now, an impatient friend of the Pareto argument might have long since wished to protest that the equality with which it evidently makes sense to begin is the highest possible one, and the suggestion embodied in that protest could be thought to have intuitive recommendation. However that may be, the Pareto argument is not thereby made safe against my criticism of it, which can readily be redeployed. The same problems as before will appear once we press, as before, and as we still can, the question *what,* exactly, the posited equality is an equality *of.* Suppose that we have a plausible answer to that question under which the proposed starting point is the highest possible equality: call it D3 to tie it in with the foregoing discussion. Then the objections given above raise up the suggestion that there is no reason to think that a Pareto-improving D4 is possible.[52]

51. For more discussion of Rawls's misguided affirmation of the metric of primary goods, see p. 200ff. of Chapter 5 below.

The next section is numbered "7" here, and not, as in the original article version of this chapter, VIII. I have omitted the original section VII, which repeats material in Chapter 1 above, and which also contains non–Chapter 1 material that has now been relocated in section 15 of Chapter 1.

52. Or, more strictly, such a D4 will be possible only in virtue of those few inequalities, at which I nodded on p. 102 above, which do not depend on the will. There will then be much less inequality than Rawls and Barry think can be justified.

8. *Impartiality and Mutual Advantage*

Income differences may reflect not differential productive power, but different income/leisure preferences.[53] But, as we saw, the income differences defended by Rawls do reflect differences of ability: it is the talented who make more money, on condition that, when they do, the less talented make more money than they otherwise would.

Someone who finds it unsurprising that a talent-favoring inequality supervenes in D2 may be thinking of the terms on which self-seeking talented people would be willing to cooperate for mutual advantage with untalented ones: they can be expected to rule out the equal wages (*We*) terms inscribed in D3 (it is not because the less talented prefer D2 to D3 that D3 fails to obtain!). And it is, indeed, the contractarian (in the Gauthier rather than the Scanlon sense[54]) strain in Rawls's political philosophy that accounts for the fact, and the form, of D2's inequality. Being contractarian, the rationale of that familiar inequality is at odds with the opening argument for an initial equality, which says that inequality cannot be justified from a rigorously impartial point of view, a view (this being what is here meant by "impartial") that ignores the happenstance bargaining advantages and disadvantages of differently situated people. If a rigorously contractarian approach, purged of all elements of impartiality, in the stated sense, had been adopted at the outset, then D1 would not have withstood scrutiny: the talented people who make D3 impossible by insisting on D2 would hardly have agreed to the initial equality in D1.

The foregoing paragraph employs a distinction central to Brian Barry's *Theories of Justice,* the distinction, that is, between the standpoint of impartiality as he defines that and the contractarian standpoint of mutual advantage.[55] To see, quickly, the difference between those stand-

53. Compare the defense of Barry's use of the phrase "equality of outcome" on pp. 93–94 above. There could be a feasible set of collections of apples and oranges, the same for all takers, and we could think of income and leisure on the model of apples and oranges.

54. For Gauthier's contractarianism, see his *Morals by Agreement,* especially Chapter 6, and for Scanlon's see his "Contractualism and Utilitarianism," and *What We Owe to Each Other,* Chapter 5.

55. See Barry, *Theories of Justice,* pp. 7–8, and passim, using index entry on "impartiality." On p. 266ff. of his "Constructing Justice," Allan Gibbard sketches a possible third conception, "justice as fair reciprocity," which would be intermediate be-

points, consider the case of an infirm person who cannot contribute anything to the social product. From a contractarian point of view, no one owes him anything: he cannot enter relations of mutual advantage. From an impartial point of view, his plight warrants our assistance.

Given his justified insistence on the distinction of standpoints, his astute criticism of Rawls for conflating the two, and his robust endorsement of the standpoint of impartiality, it is surprising that Barry is content with the second move in the Pareto argument, which makes sense in contractarian, but not in impartiality, terms. Barry realizes that the difference principle is too strongly egalitarian when judged from the perspective of mutual advantage,[56] but he does not see that the application of the difference principle in the second stage of the Pareto argument is too *in*egalitarian, when judged within the perspective of impartiality, as he himself interprets the latter's demands.

When the Pareto argument is expounded, whether by Rawls or by Barry, too little is said in explanation why, to use my nomenclature, D2 rather than D3 presents itself as the improving alternative. We are shown curves, which, to simplify their message, give us a choice between D1 and D2, curves that are drawn and commented upon as though they represented natural facts.[57] But the curves do not depict purely objective feasibility sets: they reflect the expectations and insistences of talented people. In this chapter I have asked whether those expectations and insistences are defensible within the scope of the egalitarian premises that lead to D1.

---

tween Barry's two. Gibbard is uncertain that it is truly distinct and coherent. Rawls (*Political Liberalism,* p. 17) commends Gibbard for successfully identifying what he, Rawls, is after, but he does not address Gibbard's reservations about the notion, and, at ibid., pp. 17 and 50, he mischaracterizes "mutual advantage" so as to lose contact with Barry's notion.

In my view, Gibbard's "justice as fair reciprocity" is only superficially distinct if we press for its rationale, its hybrid character becomes apparent, a fork opens, and we have to choose, again, between mutual advantage and impartiality.

See Barry, *Justice as Impartiality,* pp. 48–50 for a critique of Gibbard, and p. 60 for critical comment on the *Political Liberalism* passage that I criticized in this footnote.

56. See, e.g., *Theories of Justice,* p. 213.

57. The curves are presented on pp. 76–77/66–67 of *A Theory of Justice* and p. 62 of *Justice as Fairness,* and they are discussed by Barry on p. 229ff of *Theories of Justice.*

Barry summarizes the argument for an initial equality as follows:

> Fundamental to the case for the difference principle is the case for the *prima facie* justice of equality. On Rawls's conception of the morally arbitrary, all differences in achievement are based on morally arbitrary factors. Perhaps the most plausible presentation would be to talk of three lotteries: there is the natural lottery, which distributes genetic endowments; there is the social lottery, which distributes more or less favourable home and school environments; and then there is what Hobbes called "the secret working of God, which men call Good Luck"—the lottery that distributes illnesses, accidents, and the chance of being in the right place at the right time. Let us now add the principle that what is morally arbitrary should make no difference to how well people do in terms of primary goods. Then there is no case *at the most basic level* of justification for anything except equality in the distribution of primary goods.[58]

Now let me (as you might think, belatedly) confess that I do not find these occurrences of *"prima facie"* and "at the most basic level" easy to construe.[59] Why should the various lotteries "make no difference" "at the most basic level of justification," whatever that may be, yet legitimately make a difference higher up?[60] Why is a protest by the more productive that they should have more pay than others do disallowed at D1, but certified when they reject D3 in favor of D2?

In a case where people of middle income stand to lose from a change that would benefit both best and worst off, Barry has the worst off defending the change as follows:

> . . . the extra amount that those people are getting at that point [i.e., prior to the mooted change] over what we are getting derives from morally arbitrary advantages. They cannot therefore reasonably keep all of those gains if by giving up some of them we could be made better off.[61]

58. *Theories of Justice*, p. 226, my emphases.

59. Rawls himself does not say that the initial equality is *prima facie* just. But he is seeking to justify a principle of justice, and he regards equality as the correct starting point in such an exercise, because citizens are "free and equal" (see p. 91 above). The obscurity surrounding *"prima facie* just" attaches, similarly, to the idea of the correct starting point.

60. One may distinguish (see p. 89 above) between justification by causes and justification by consequences, but the fact that causes come first in the causal order does not mean that they figure at a more basic level in the order of justification.

61. *Theories of Justice*, p. 232.

Barry endorses this statement, but he fails to note that it applies against "the extra amount" that the best off get in D2. Why is it all right for the highest fliers to keep their gains? Why does the inference carried by the word "therefore" in the above argument fail in the case of the best off? How does the (admittedly) special context of the quoted statement prejudice the generality of its argument?

9. Inequality: A Necessary Evil?

Barry characterizes "inequality" "as at best a necessary evil"[62]: that is a deliverance of the first stage of the Pareto argument. But he falls into incoherence in calling it an "evil," and he slurs over an important distinction in calling it "necessary."

The incoherence in Barry's designation of inequality as "evil" nicely compresses the inconsistency in the structure of the Pareto argument that I have striven to expose. For, one can and must ask, *in what terms* is the recommended inequality an evil? *Ex hypothesi*, it is not an evil as far as anyone's welfare is concerned, for it represents a Pareto improvement. But since, *ex hypothesi*, it is for the sake of justice, it is hard to see how it can be an evil in terms of justice, that is, an injustice, and Barry indeed denies that that is the type of evil it is.[63] How could adding an injustice to what is "*prima facie* just" (whatever that means) produce an improvement in the calculus of justice? The first part of the Pareto argument implies that inequality is an evil, but the second part implies that it is not.

I turn from "evil" to "necessary." According to Barry, the paramount importance, morally, of the position of the worst off reflects

> the crucial role that is played by the idea that what is fundamentally just is equality and that departures from it reward features that are morally arbitrary. Critics of that idea will, of course go on to criticize the difference principle [for being too egalitarian]. But if one accepts the premise (at least for the sake of argument) then it seems to me quite reasonable to say that in justifying inequality all that matters is to justify it to the worst off. And the best justification is that they could not be any better off.[64] (Recall that "the

62. Ibid., p. 234.
63. Ibid.
64. Strictly, that is the wrong thing to say here, and for reasons that have nothing to do with the criticism of this kind of formulation that dominates the present essay. For, as Barry recognizes elsewhere, one may "not ascribe a fixed identity to the worst

worst off" are a large group with a single representative.) Those who are better off than the worst-off group have no moral standing for any complaint on the ground that they might under alternative arrangements be even better off. For the only reason for their being permitted to be better off than some others at all is that this is *necessary* in order to benefit the worst off.[65]

Let us focus on the final sentence of this excerpt, and let us distinguish between inequalities that are necessary, apart from human choice, to benefit the worst off, and inequalities that are indeed necessary to that end, but only given what some people's intentions are. If there exist inequalities of the first kind, the D2 inequality is not one of them. It is not necessary, *tout court,* to make the badly off better off, but necessary only given that talented producers operate as self-interested maximizers. Now Barry says that "all that matters is to justify the inequality to the worst off." How then might the better off reply to worst off people who ask them to justify the D2 inequality? They could not say, "The inequality that we defend is necessary to make you better off," since it is they who make it necessary, and the question the worst off put asks, in effect: what is your justification for making it necessary?

The well off cannot invoke their own deserts and entitlements: that strategy of justification is repudiated by both Rawls and Barry. Nor can they point to the specially grueling character of their labor: that idea was given its due in section 4 above. But there remain things that they can say, which have to do with freedom of choice of occupation, and with a certain notion of the slavery of the talented. Those are serious considerations, and I address them in Chapter 5.

---

off group" (ibid., p. 216). Yet he does just that here; and again on p. 233, where he says: "The worst off gain as much as they possibly can from inequality, so they have no reasonable complaint"; and again on p. 242, where he says that "the reply to one who does badly is that if others did not do better he would be even worse off." The right reply, in line with p. 216, is not that he but that *someone* would be even worse off than he now is, be that someone he or somebody else.

The recurrent violation of the stricture that Barry lays down on p. 216 is a not uninteresting slip. In this slip the contractarian motif, which requires fixed identities, replaces the framework of impartiality, in which identities are dissolved.

For criticism of Rawls's significant equivocation across fixed and variable reference in his uses of the phrase "the worst off," see Derek Parfit, *Reasons and Persons,* Appendix H; and G. A. Cohen, *Self-Ownership,* p. 88.

65. Ibid., p. 233, emphasis added.

10. Conclusion

I have contended that the two parts of the Pareto argument are inconsistent with each other. The grounds given in its first part for choosing equality as a just starting point contradict the grounds given in its second part for endorsing a departure from equality as just. For all that the Pareto argument shows, departure from equality is necessary only if and because the behavior of talented people violates the demands of the conception of justice that supplies the grounds for starting with equality. The final recommendation of the Pareto argument accedes to injustice in its account of what justice is.

The Pareto argument proposes a dilemma: you cannot have both (1) equality and (2) Pareto optimality within the normal functioning of an economy. I have argued that, strictly speaking, the Pareto principle does not require inequality; and that, unstrictly speaking—taking the behavior of the talented as given—the inequality it requires is unjust.

Thereby, so I believe, the Pareto argument is demolished. But in line with what was said in the closing sentence of section 9, I acknowledge that a refurbished form of the Pareto argument must also be addressed. The refurbished form of the argument replaces the dilemma described above with a trilemma: you cannot have all of (1) equality, (2) Pareto optimality, and (3) freedom of occupational choice. That, too, I believe to be mistaken, and I shall strive to show why in Chapter 5.

3

THE BASIC STRUCTURE OBJECTION

> Only when the actual, individual man has taken back into himself the abstract citizen and in his everyday life, his individual work, and his individual relationships has become a *species-being*, only when he has recognized and organized his own powers as *social* powers so that social power is no longer separated from him as *political* power, only then is human emancipation complete.
>
> —*Karl Marx, "On the Jewish Question,"*
> *p. 241 (translation slightly amended)*

1. *"The Personal Is Political"*

In this chapter I defend a claim that can be expressed in the words of a now familiar slogan: *the personal is political*. That slogan, as it stands, is vague, but I mean something reasonably precise by it here, to wit, that principles of distributive justice, principles, that is, about the just distribution of benefits and burdens in society, apply, wherever else they do, to people's legally unconstrained choices. Those principles, so I claim, apply to the choices that people make within the legally coercive structures to which, so everyone would agree, principles of justice (also) apply. (In speaking of the choices that people make within coercive structures, I do not include the choice whether or not to comply with the rules of such structures [to which choice, once again, so everyone would agree, principles of justice (also) apply], but the choices left open by those rules because neither enjoined nor forbidden by them.)

The italicized slogan that I have appropriated here is widely used by feminists.[1] More importantly, however, the idea itself, which I have here used the slogan to formulate and which I have tried to explicate above, is a feminist idea. Notice, however, that, in briefly explaining the idea that I shall defend, I have not mentioned relations between men and women in particular, or the issue of sexism. We can distinguish between the substance and the form of the feminist critique of standard ideas about justice, and it is the form of it that is of prime concern to me here,[2] even though I also endorse its substance.

The substance of the feminist critique is that standard liberal theory of justice, and the theory of Rawls in particular, unjustifiably ignore an unjust division of labor and unjust power relations within families (whose legal structure may show no sexism at all). That is the key point of the feminist critique, from a political point of view. But the (often merely implicit) form of the feminist critique, which we get when we abstract from its gender-centered content, is that choices not regulated by the law fall within the primary purview of justice, and that is the key lesson of the critique from a theoretical point of view.

Because I believe that the personal is political, in the specified sense, I reject Rawls's view that principles of justice apply only to what he calls the "basic structure" of society. Feminists have noticed that Rawls wobbles, across the course of his writings, on the matter of whether or not the family belongs to the basic structure of society and is therefore, in his view, a site at which principles of justice apply. I shall argue that Rawls's wobble on this matter is not a case of mere indecision, which could readily be resolved in favor of inclusion of the family within the basic structure: that was the view of Susan Okin,[3] and, in my opinion, she was wrong about that. I shall show (in section 5) that Rawls cannot admit the family into the basic structure of society without abandoning his insistence that it is to the basic structure only that principles of distributive

---

1. But it was apparently used by Christian liberation theologians before it was used by feminists: see Denys Turner "Religion: Illusions and Liberation," p. 334.

2. Or, more precisely, that which distinguishes its form. (Insofar as the feminist critique targets government legislation and policy, there is nothing distinctive about its form.)

3. Okin was singularly alert to Rawls's ambivalence about admitting or excluding the family from the basic structure: see, e.g., her "Political Liberalism, Justice, and Gender," pp. 23–24, and, more generally, her *Justice, Gender and the Family*. But so far as I can tell, she was unaware of the wider consequences, for Rawls's view of justice in general, of the set of ambiguities of which this one is an instance.

justice apply. In supposing that he could include family relations, Okin showed failure to grasp the *form* of the feminist critique of Rawls.

2. Incentives and the Difference Principle: A Review of the Argument

I reach the conclusion announced above at the end of a trail of argument that runs as follows. Here in section 2 I restate a criticism that I have made elsewhere of John Rawls's application of his difference principle,[4] to wit, that he does not apply it in censure of the self-seeking choices of high-flying marketeers, which induce an inequality that, so I claim, is harmful to the badly off. In section 3 I present an objection to my criticism of Rawls. The objection says that the difference principle is, by stipulation and design, a principle that applies only to social institutions (to those, in particular, that compose the basic structure of society), and therefore not one that applies to the choices, such as those of self-seeking high fliers, that people make within such institutions.

Sections 4 and 5 offer independent replies to that basic structure objection. I show in section 4 that the objection is inconsistent with many statements that Rawls made about the role of principles of justice in a just society. I then allow that the discordant statements might be dropped from the Rawlsian canon, and in section 5 I reply afresh to the basic structure objection, by showing that no defensible account of what the basic structure is allows Rawls to insist that the principles that apply to it do not apply to choices within it. I conclude that my original criticism of Rawls stands vindicated, against the particular objection at issue here. (Section 6 comments on the implications of my position for the moral blameability of individuals whose choices violate principles of justice. Section 7 explores the distinction between coercive and noncoercive institutions, which plays a key role in the argument of section 5.)

Appendix I adduces further puzzles, beyond those canvassed in the chapter proper, regarding the question whether the basic structure can be identified with the state-coercive part of society, and Appendix II explains why the basic structure is called "a structure."

My criticism of Rawls is of his application of the difference principle. That principle says, in one of its formulations,[5] that inequalities are just

4. See the preceding chapters, passim.
5. See n. 6 of Chapter 1 for four possible formulations of the difference principle, all of which, arguably, find support in *A Theory of Justice*. The argument of the present chapter is, I believe, robust across those variant formulations of the principle.

if and only if they are necessary to make the worst off people in society better off than they would otherwise be. I have no quarrel here with the difference principle itself,[6] but I disagree sharply with Rawls on the matter of which inequalities pass the test for justifying inequality that it sets and, therefore, about how much inequality passes that test. In my view, there is hardly any serious inequality that satisfies the requirement set by the difference principle, when it is conceived, as Rawls himself proposes to conceive it,[7] as regulating the affairs of a society whose members themselves accept that principle. If I am right, affirmation of the difference principle implies that justice requires (virtually)[8] unqualified equality itself, as opposed to the "deep inequalities" in initial life chances with which Rawls thinks justice to be consistent.[9]

It is commonly thought, for example by Rawls, that the difference principle licenses an argument for inequality that centers on the device of material incentives. The idea is that talented people will produce more than they otherwise would if, and only if, they are paid more than an ordinary wage, and some of the extra that they will then produce can be recruited on behalf of the worst off.[10] The inequality consequent on differential material incentives is said to be justified within the terms of the difference principle, for, so it is said, that inequality benefits the worst off people: the inequality is necessary for them to be positioned as well as they are, however paltry their position may nevertheless be.

Now before I mount my criticism of this argument, a caveat is necessary with respect to the terms in which it is expressed. The argument focuses on a choice enjoyed by well-placed people who command a high salary in a market economy: they can choose to work more or less hard,

6. I do have reservations about the principle that I express elsewhere, but they are irrelevant to the present argument. I agree, for example, with Ronald Dworkin's criticism of the "ambition-insensitivity" of the difference principle: see his "Equality of Resources," pp. 116–117. And see, too, n. 7 of Chapter 1, and sections 1–5 of Chapter 4.

7. "Proposes to conceive it": I use that somewhat precious phrase because part of the present criticism of Rawls is that he does not succeed in so conceiving it—he does not, that is, recognize the implications of so conceiving it.

8. The qualification is that, so I believe, each person has a right to pursue her own self-interest to some reasonable extent. But that is a quite different justification of inequality from the incentives justification: see Chapter 1, p. 61.

9. *A Theory of Justice,* pp. 7/8.

10. This is just the simplest causal story connecting superior payment to the better off with benefit to the worst off. I adopt it here for simplicity of exposition.

and also to work at this occupation rather than that one, and for this employer rather than that one, in accordance with how well they are remunerated. These well-placed people, in the foregoing standard presentation of the argument, are designated as "the talented," and, for reasons to be given presently, I shall so designate them throughout my criticism of the argument. Even so, these fortunate people need not (all) be thought to be talented, in any sense of that word that implies something more than a capacity for high market earnings, for the argument to possess whatever force it has. All that need be true of them is that *they are so positioned that, happily, for them, they do command a high salary and they can vary their productivity according to exactly how high it is.* But as far as the incentives argument is concerned, their happy position could be due to circumstances that are entirely accidental, relative to whatever kind of natural or even socially induced endowment they posses. One need not think that the average dishwasher's endowment of strength, flair, ingenuity and so forth falls below that of the average chief executive to accept the argument's message. One no doubt does need to think some such thing to agree with the different argument that justifies rewards to well-placed people in whole or in part as a fair return to exercise of unusual ability, but Rawls's theory is built around his rejection of such desert considerations. Nor does Rawls believe that the enhanced rewards are justified because extra contribution warrants extra reward on grounds of proper reciprocity. They are justified, in his view, purely because they elicit more productive performance.

I nevertheless persist in designating the relevant individuals as "the talented," because to object that they are not actually especially talented anyway is to enter an empirical claim that is both contentious and, in context, misleading, since it would give the impression that it should matter to our assessment of the incentives argument whether or not well-placed people merit the contestable designation. The particular criticism of the incentives argument that I shall develop is best understood in its specificity when the apparently concessive word "talented" is used: it does not indicate a concession on the factual question of how top people in a market society get to be where they are. My use of the argument's own terms shows the strength of my critique of it: that critique stands even if we make generous assumptions about how well-placed people secured their powerful market positions. It is, moreover, especially appropriate to make such assumptions here, since the Rawlsian difference principle is lexically secondary to his principle that fair equality of op-

portunity has been enforced with respect to the attainment of desired positions: if anything ensures that those who occupy them possess superior
creative endowment, that does. (Which is not to say that it indeed ensures that: it is consistent with fair equality of opportunity that what
principally distinguishes top people is superior cunning and/or prodigious aggressivity, and nothing more admirable.)

Now for the following reasons, I believe that the incentives argument
for inequality represents a distorted application of the difference principle, even though it is its most familiar and perhaps even its most persuasive application. Either the relevant talented people themselves affirm
the difference principle or they do not, that is, either they themselves believe that inequalities are unjust if they are not necessary to make the
badly off better off, or they do not believe that to be a dictate of justice.
If they do not believe it, then their society is not just in the appropriate
Rawlsian sense, for a society is just, according to Rawls, only if its members themselves affirm and uphold the correct principles of justice. The
difference principle might be appealed to in justification of a government's toleration, or promotion, of inequality in a society in which the
talented do not themselves accept it, but it then justifies a public policy
of inequality in a society some members of which—the talented—do not
share community with the rest[11]: their behavior is then taken as fixed or
parametric, a datum vis-à-vis a principle applied to it from without,
rather than as itself answerable to that principle. That is not how principles of justice operate in a just society, as Rawls specifies that concept:
within his terms, one may distinguish between a just society and a just
government, one, that is, that applies just principles to a society whose
members may not themselves accept those principles.

So we turn to the second and only remaining possibility, which is that
the talented people do affirm the difference principle, that, as Rawls
says, they apply the principles of justice in their daily life and achieve a
sense of their own justice in doing so.[12] But they can then be asked why,
in the light of their own belief in the principle, they require more pay

11. They do not, more precisely, share *justificatory community* with the rest in the
sense of the italicized phrase that I specified on p. 43 of Chapter 1.
12. "Citizens in everyday life . . . affirm and act from the first principles of justice."
They act "from these principles as their sense of justice dictates" and thereby "their
nature as moral persons is most fully realized." (Quotations drawn from, respectively, "Kantian Constructivism," pp, 308, 315, and *A Theory of Justice,* pp. 528/
463.)

than the untalented get, for work that may indeed demand special talent but that is not specially unpleasant (for no such consideration enters the Rawlsian justification of incentives-derived inequality). The talented can be asked whether the extra they get is necessary to enhance the position of the worst off, which is the only thing, according to the difference principle, that could justify it. Is it necessary *tout court,* that is, independently of human will, so that, with all the will in the world, removal of inequality would make everyone worse off? Or is it necessary only insofar as the talented would *decide* to produce less than they now do, or to not take up posts where they are in special demand, if inequality were removed (by, for example, income taxation that redistributes to fully egalitarian effect[13])?

Talented people who affirm the difference principle would find those questions hard to handle. For they could not claim, in self-justification, at the bar of the difference principle, that their high rewards are necessary to enhance the position of the worst off, since, in the standard case,[14] it is they themselves who make those rewards necessary, through their own unwillingness to work for ordinary rewards as productively as they do for exceptionally high ones, an unwillingness which ensures that the untalented get less than they otherwise would. Those rewards are, therefore, necessary only because the choices of talented people are not appropriately influenced by the difference principle.[15]

Apart then from the very special cases in which the talented literally could not, as opposed to the normal case where they (merely) would not, perform as productively as they do without superior remuneration, the

13. That way of achieving equality seeks to preserve the information function of the market while extinguishing its motivational function: see Joseph Carens, *Equality, Moral Incentives, and the Market*, passim, and p. 189ff. of Chapter 5.

14. For precisely what I mean by "the standard case," see section 8 of Chapter 1.

15. Rawls allows the talented to say that their high rewards are justified because they are needed to make the low rewards of the badly off no worse than they already are. But as I argued in sections 7 through 11 of Chapter 1, that may serve as a justification of their high rewards when the talented are referred to in the third person, but, crucially, not when they are themselves offering it to the poor. Analogously, I do have good reason to pay a kidnapper who has taken my child, but he cannot, on that basis, justify his demand for payment from me: he cannot say that he is justified in demanding it because only if I meet that demand will I get my kid back. The talented rich are not, of course, at any rate as such, as bad as kidnappers, but the justification they give collapses as much as his does when it is cast in I–thou terms: as I said above, the justification of incentives to them works only if they are conceived as alien to the society in question.

difference principle can justify inequality only in a society where not everyone accepts that very principle. It therefore cannot justify inequality in the appropriate Rawlsian way.

Now this conclusion about what it means to accept and implement the difference principle implies that the justice of a society is not exclusively a function of its legislative structure, of its legally imperative rules, but also of the choices people make within those rules. The standard (and, in my view, misguided) Rawlsian application of the difference principle can be modeled as follows. There is a market economy all agents in which seek to maximize their own gains, and there is a Rawlsian state that selects a tax function on income that maximizes the income return to the worst off people, within the constraint that, because of the self-seeking motivation of the talented, a fully equalizing taxation system would make everyone worse off than one that is less than fully equalizing. But this double-minded modeling of the implementation of the difference principle, with citizens inspired by justice endorsing a state policy that plays a tax game against (some of) them in their manifestation as self-seeking economic agents, is wholly out of accord with the (sound) Rawlsian requirement on a just society that its citizens themselves willingly submit to the standard of justice embodied in the difference principle. A society that is just within the terms of the difference principle, so we may conclude, requires not simply just coercive *rules,* but also an *ethos* of justice that informs individual choices. In the absence of such an ethos, inequalities will obtain that are not necessary to enhance the condition of the worst off: the required ethos promotes a distribution more just than what the rules of the economic game by themselves can secure. And what is required is indeed an ethos, a structure of response lodged in the motivations that inform everyday life, not only because it is impossible to design rules of egalitarian economic choice conformity with which can always be checked,[16] but also because it would severely compromise liberty if people were required forever to consult such rules, even supposing that appropriate applicable rules could be formulated. The indeterminacy of egalitarian duty is its saving grace.[17]

To be sure, one might imagine, in the abstract, a set of coercive rules

16. A major reason why no such "public" rules could be designed is that it is not always possible to tell, even for the person in question, whether or not her demand for more money as a condition of moving to a socially more desirable job is justified as compensation for "special burden," and is therefore permissible within the frame of equality, all things considered. For (much) more on publicity, see Chapter 8.

17. See the last three paragraphs of section 4 of Chapter 8.

so finely tuned that universally self-interested choices within them would raise the worst off to as high a position as any other pattern of choices would produce. Where coercive rules had and were known to have such a character, agents could choose self-interestedly in confidence that the results of their choices would satisfy an appropriately uncompromising interpretation of the difference principle. In that (imaginary) case the only ethos necessary for difference principle justice would be willing obedience to the relevant rules, which is an ethos that Rawls (perforce) expressly requires. But the vast economics literature on incentive compatibility teaches that rules of the contemplated perfect kind cannot be designed. Accordingly, as things actually are, the required ethos must, as I have argued, guide choice within the rules, and not merely direct agents to obey them. (I should emphasize that this is not so because it is in general true that the point of the rules governing an activity must be aimed at when agents pursue that activity in good faith: every competitive sport represents a counterexample to that generalization. But my argument for the conclusion stated above did not rest on that false generalization.)

3. The Basic Structure Objection

There is an objection that friends of Rawls's *Theory of Justice* would press against my argument in criticism of his application of the difference principle. The objection is that my focus on the posture of talented producers in daily economic life is inappropriate, since their behavior occurs within, and does not determine, the basic structure of society, and it is only to the latter that the difference principle applies.[18] Whatever people's choices within it may be, the basic structure is just provided that it satisfies the two principles of justice. To be sure, so Rawls acknowledges, people's choices can themselves be assessed as just or unjust, from a number of points of view. Thus, for example, capriciously appointing candidate A rather than candidate B to a given post might be judged unjust, even when it occurs within the rules of a just basic structure (since those rules could not feasibly be designed to outlaw the variety of caprice in question).[19] But such injustice in choice is not the sort of

18. For a typical statement of this restriction, see Rawls, *Political Liberalism*, pp. 282–283.
19. See the first sentence of section 2 of *A Theory of Justice* ("The Subject of Justice"): "Many different kinds of things are said to be just and unjust: not only laws, institutions, and social systems, but also particular actions of many kinds, including

injustice that the Rawlsian principles are designed to condemn. For, *ex hypothesi*, that choice occurs within an established basic structure: it therefore cannot affect the justice of the basic structure itself, which is what, according to Rawls, the two principles govern. Nor, similarly, should the choices with respect to work and remuneration that talented people make be submitted for judgment at the bar of the difference principle. So to judge those choices is to apply that principle at the wrong point. The difference principle is a principle of justice for institutions. It governs the choice of institutions, not the choices made within them. Accordingly, the development of the second horn of the dilemma argument on p. 121ff. misconstrues the Rawlsian requirement that citizens in a just society uphold the principles that make it just: by virtue of the stipulated scope of the difference principle, talented people do count as faithfully upholding it, as long as they conform to the prevailing economic rules because that principle requires those rules.

Call that "the basic structure objection." Now before I develop it further, and then reply to it, I want to point out that there is an important ambiguity in the concept of the basic structure, as that is wielded by Rawlsians. The ambiguity turns on whether the Rawlsian basic structure includes only coercive aspects of the social order or also conventions and usages that are deeply entrenched but not legally or literally coercive. I shall return to that ambiguity in section 5, and I shall show that it shipwrecks not only the basic structure objection but also the whole approach to justice that Rawls has taught so many to pursue. But, for the time being, I shall ignore the fatal ambiguity, and I shall take the phrase "basic structure" as it appears in the basic structure objection as denoting some sort of structure, be it legally coercive or not, but whose key feature, for the purposes of the objection, is that it is indeed a structure, that is, a framework of rules within which choices are made, as opposed to a set of choices and/or actions. Accordingly, my Rawlsian critic would say, whatever structure, precisely, the basic structure is, the objection stands that my criticism of the incentives argument misapplies principles devised for a structure to individual choices and actions.

In further clarification of the polemical position, let me make a background point about the difference between Rawls and me with respect to

decisions, judgments, and imputations" (ibid., pp. 7/6). But Rawls excludes examples such as the one given in the text above from his purview, because "our topic . . . is that of social justice. For us the primary subject of justice is the basic structure of society" (ibid.).

the site or sites at which principles of justice apply. My own fundamental concern is neither the basic structure of society, in any sense, nor people's individual choices, but the pattern of benefits and burdens in society: that is neither a structure in which choice occurs nor a set of choices, but the upshot of structure and choices alike. My concern is distributive justice, by which I uneccentrically mean justice (and its lack) in the distribution of benefits and burdens to individuals. My root belief is that there is injustice in distribution when inequality of goods reflects not such things as differences in the arduousness of different people's labors, or people's different preferences and choices with respect to income and leisure, but myriad forms of lucky and unlucky circumstance. Such differences of advantage are a function of the structure *and* of people's choices within it, so I am concerned, secondarily, with *both* of those.

Now Rawls could say that his concern, too, is distributive justice, in the specified sense, but that for him distributive justice obtains just in case the allocation of benefits and burdens in society results from actions that display full conformity with the rules of a just basic structure.[20] When full compliance with the rules of a just basic structure obtains, it follows, on Rawls's view, that there is no scope for (further) personal justice and injustice that affects *distributive* justice, whether it be by enhancing it or by reducing it. There is, Rawls would of course readily agree, scope within a just structure for distribution-affecting meanness and generosity,[21] but generosity, though it would alter the distribution, and might make it more equal than it would otherwise be, could not make it more just than it would otherwise be, for it would then be doing the impossible, to wit, enhancing the justice of what is already estab-

20. *A Theory of Justice*, pp. 274–275/242–243: "The principles of justice apply to the basic structure . . . The social system is to be designed so that the resulting distribution is just however things turn out." Cf. ibid., pp. 545/478: "the distribution of material means is left to take care of itself in accordance with the idea of pure procedural justice." Cf. "Constitutional Liberty and the Concept of Justice," p. 89, n. 5, and "Distributive Justice: Some Addenda," p. 157. The Rawlsian formulations show that David Estlund and Joshua Cohen are, if Rawlsians, then revisionist Rawlsians, since they believe that justice is prejudiced by choices within the rules that display certain sorts of motives. See, respectively, their "Taking People as They Are" and "Liberalism, Equality, and Fraternity," and see section 4 of the General Appendix below.

21. This is a different point from the one made at the outset of this section, to wit, that there is scope within a just structure for justice and injustice in choice in a "nonprimary" sense of "justice."

lished as a (perfectly) just distribution[22] by virtue merely of the just structure in conformity with which it is produced. But as I have indicated, I believe there is scope for relevant (relevant, that is, because it affects justice in distribution) personal justice and injustice within a just structure, and, indeed, that it is not possible to achieve distributive justice by purely structural means.

In discussion of my claim (see the penultimate paragraph of section 2) that social justice requires a social ethos that inspires uncoerced equality-supporting choice, Ronald Dworkin suggested[23] that a Rawlsian government might be thought to be charged with a duty, under the difference principle, of promoting such an ethos. Dworkin's suggestion was intended to support Rawls, against me, by diminishing the difference between Rawls's position and my own, and thereby reducing the reach of my criticism of him. I do not know what Rawls's response to Dworkin's proposal would have been, but one thing is clear: Rawls could not have said that, to the extent that the indicated ethos-promoting policy failed, society would as a result be less just than if the policy had been more successful. Accordingly, if Dworkin is right that Rawlsian justice requires government to promote an ethos friendly to equality, it could not be for the sake of making society more distributively just that it was doing so, even though it would be for the sake of making its distribution more equal. The following threefold conjunction, which is an inescapable consequence of Rawls's position, on Dworkin's not unnatural interpretation of it, is strikingly incongruous: (1) the difference principle is an egalitarian principle of distributive justice; (2) it imposes on government a duty to promote an egalitarian ethos; (3) it is not for the sake of enhancing distributive justice in society that the principle requires government to promote that ethos. Dworkin's attempt to reduce the distance between Rawls's position and my own threatens to render the former incoherent.

Now before I mount my two replies to the basic structure objection, a brief conceptual digression is required in clarification of the relationship

---

22. (Added, 2008) Or, at any rate, as a distribution perfectly free of injustice: "the principles of justice define the constraints which institutions and joint activities must satisfy if persons engaging in them are to have no complaint against them. If these constraints are satisfied, the resulting distribution, whatever it is, may be accepted as just (or at least as not unjust)" ("Constitutional Liberty and the Concept of Justice," p. 77). What unofficial thought prompted Rawls to add the weaker parenthetical alternative? In my view it was a partial return of the repressed egalitarianism.

23. At a seminar in Oxford, in Hilary Term of 1994.

between a just *society,* in Rawls's (and my own) understanding of that idea (see p. 121) and a just *distribution,* in my (non-Rawlsian) understanding of that different idea (see pp. 125–126). A just society, here, is one whose citizens affirm and act upon the correct principles of justice, but justice in distribution, as here defined, consists in a certain egalitarian profile of rewards. It follows that a just distribution might obtain in a society that is not itself just.

To illustrate this possibility, imagine a society whose ethos, though not inspired by a belief in equality, nevertheless induces an equal distribution. An example of such an ethos would be an intense Protestant ethic, which is indifferent to equality (on earth) as such, but whose stress on self-denial, hard work, and investment of assets surplus to needs somehow (despite the asceticism in it) makes the worst off as well off as it is possible for them to be. Such an ethos achieves difference principle justice in distribution, but agents informed by it would not be motivated by the difference principle, and they could not, therefore, themselves be accounted just, within the terms of that principle.[24] Under the specifications that were introduced here, this Protestant society would not be just, despite the fact that it displays a just distribution. We might say of the society that it is accidentally, but not constitutively, just. But, whatever phrasings we may prefer, the important thing is to distinguish "society" and "distribution" as candidate subjects of the predicate "just." (And it bears mentioning that, in contemporary practice, an ethos that achieves difference principle equality would almost certainly have to be equality-inspired: the accident of a non-equality-inspired ethos producing the right result is, at least in modern times, highly unlikely. The Protestantism that I described in this paragraph is utterly fantastic, at least for our day.)

Less arresting is the opposite case, in which people strive to govern their behavior by (what are in fact) just principles, but ignorance, or the obduracy of wholly external circumstance, or collective action problems, or self-defeatingness of the kinds studied by Derek Parfit,[25] or something else that I have not thought of, frustrates their intention, so that the distribution remains unjust. It would perhaps be peculiar to call

24. It might, moreover, be true of the society in question that, because of its traditions, which control its citizens' motivational structures, attempts to make its ethos just, as opposed to Protestant, would be unavailing; and to the limited extent that they were successful, they might induce less justice in distribution than the Protestantism figured above does.

25. See Chapter 4 of his *Reasons and Persons.*

such a society *just*, and neither Rawls nor I need do so: justice in citizens was put, above, as a necessary condition of a just society.

However we resolve the secondary, and largely verbal, complications raised in this digression, the point will stand[26] that an ethos informing choice within just rules is necessary in a society that shows a commitment to the difference principle. My argument for that conclusion did not rely on any contentious rulings about how and where to apply the term "just": it was an argument about what such a commitment must involve, and, in particular, whether it can be present in the absence of the stated ethos. The basic structure objection represents a challenge on that particular score.

4. The Basic Structure Objection: A Preliminary Reply

I now present a preliminary reply to the basic structure objection. It is preliminary in that it precedes my interrogation, in section 5, of what the phrase "basic structure" denotes, and also in that, by contrast with the fundamental reply that follows that interrogation, there is a certain way out for Rawls in face of the preliminary reply. That way out is not costless for him, but it does exist.

Although Rawls says often enough that the two principles of justice govern only justice in basic structure, he also says three things that tell against that restriction. This means that in each case he must either uphold the restriction and repudiate the comment in question or maintain the comment and drop the restriction.[27]

---

26. If, that is, my argument survives the basic structure objection, to which I reply in sections 4 and 5.

27. Because of these tensions in Rawls, people have resisted my incentives critique of him in two opposite ways. Those convinced that his primary concern is the basic structure object in the fashion set out in section 3. But others do not realize how important that concern is to him: they accept my (as I see it, anti-Rawlsian) view that the difference principle should condemn incentives, but they believe that Rawls would also accept it, since they think his commitment to that principle is relevantly uncompromising. They therefore do not regard what I say about incentives as a criticism of Rawls.

Those who respond in that second fashion seem not to realize that Rawls's liberalism is jeopardized if he takes the route that they think open to him. He then becomes a radical egalitarian socialist, whose outlook is very different from that of a liberal who holds that "deep inequalities" are "inevitable in the basic structure of any society" (*A Theory of Justice*, pp. 7/7).

First, Rawls says that, when the difference principle is satisfied, society displays *fraternity*, in a particularly strong sense: its citizens do not want

> to have greater advantages unless this is to the benefit of others who are less well off . . . Members of a family commonly do not wish to gain unless they can do so in ways that further the interests of the rest. Now wanting to act on the difference principle has precisely this consequence.[28]

But fraternity of that strong kind is not realized when all the justice delivered by the difference principle comes from the basic structure, and, therefore, whatever people's motivations in economic interaction may be. Wanting not "to gain unless they can do so in ways that further the interests of the rest" is incompatible with the self-interested motivation of market maximizers, which the difference principle, in its purely structural interpretation, does not condemn.[29]

Second, Rawls says that the worst off in a society governed by the difference principle can bear their inferior position with dignity, since they know that no improvement of it is possible, that they would lose under any less unequal dispensation. Yet that is false, if justice relates to structure alone, since it might then be necessary for the worst off to occupy their relatively low place only because the choices of the better off tend strongly against equality. Why should the fact that no purely structurally induced improvement in their position is possible suffice to guarantee the dignity of the worst off, when their position might be very inferior indeed because of unlimited self-seekingness in the economic choices of

28. (Expanded, 2008). *A Theory of Justice*, pp. 105/90. Compare the unreserved endorsement of a very strong Millian formulations of fraternity on p. 172 of "Distributive Justice: Some Addenda." "This state of mind, if perfect, makes an individual 'never think of, or desire, any beneficial condition for himself, in the benefits of which they are not included.' One of the individual's natural wants is that 'there should be harmony between his feelings and aims and those of his fellow creatures.' He desires to know that 'his real aim and theirs do not conflict; that he is not opposing himself to what they really wish for, namely their own good, but is, on the contrary, promoting it.' Now the desire Mill characterizes here is a desire to act upon the difference principle . . ."

29. See, further, Chapter 1, p. 77ff.: note that I do not here deny that there is more fraternity when high earners willingly submit to taxation shaped by the difference principle than when they insist *on laissez-faire*. For a good discussion of my claims regarding fraternity and Rawls, see Michael Titelbaum, "What Would a Rawlsian Ethos of Justice Look Like?" pp. 28–32.

well-placed people?[30] Suppose, for example, that, as politicians now routinely claim, raising rates of income taxation with a view to enhancing benefits for the badly off would be counterproductive, since the higher rates would induce severe disincentive effects on the productivity of the better off. Would awareness of that truth contribute to a sense of dignity on the part of the badly off?

Third, Rawls says that people in a just society act with a sense of justice *from* the principles of justice in their daily lives: they strive to apply those principles in their own choices. And they do so because they

> have a desire to express their nature as free and equal moral persons, and this they do most adequately by acting *from* the principles that they would acknowledge in the original position. When all strive to comply with these principles and each succeeds, then individually and collectively their nature as moral persons is most fully realized, and with it their individual and collective good.[31]

But why do they have to act *from* the principles of justice, and "apply" them "as their circumstances require"[32] if it suffices for justice that they choose as they please within a structure designed to effect an implementation of those principles? And how can they, without a redolence of hypocrisy, celebrate the full realization of their natures as moral persons when they know they are out for the most they can get in the market?

Now as I said, these inconsistencies are not decisive against Rawls. For in each case he could stand pat on his restriction of justice to basic structure and give up, or weaken, the remark that produces the inconsistency. And that is indeed what he is disposed to do at least with respect to the third inconsistency that I have noted. He said[33] that *A Theory of Justice* erred in some respects by treating the two principles as defining a comprehensive conception of justice[34]: he would, accordingly, now drop the high-pitched homily that constitutes the text to footnote 31. But this accommodation carries a cost: it means that the ideals of dignity, frater-

30. See, further, Chapter 2, section 4.
31. *A Theory of Justice,* pp. 528/462–463, my emphasis. See, further, n. 12.
32. *Justice as Fairness,* p. 199.
33. In reply to a lecture that I gave at Harvard in March 1993, which became Chapter 2 of this book.
34. That is, as (part of) a complete moral theory, as opposed to a purely political one: see, for explication of that distinction, *Political Liberalism,* passim, and, in particular, pp. xv–xvii, xliii–xlvii.

nity, and full realization of people's moral natures can no longer be said to be delivered by Rawlsian justice.

5. The Basic Structure Objection: A More Fundamental Reply

I now provide a more fundamental reply to the basic structure objection. It is more fundamental in that it shows, decisively, that justice requires an ethos governing daily choice that goes beyond one of obedience to just rules,[35] on grounds that do not, as the preliminary reply did, exploit things that Rawls says in apparent contradiction of his stipulation that justice applies to the basic structure of society alone. The fundamental reply interrogates, and refutes, that stipulation itself.

A major fault line in the Rawlsian architectonic not only wrecks the basic structure objection but also produces a dilemma for Rawls's view of the subject[36] of justice from which I can imagine no way out. The fault line exposes itself when we ask the apparently simple question: what (exactly) is the basic structure? For there is a fatal ambiguity in Rawls's specification of the basic structure, and an associated discrepancy between his criterion for what justice judges and his desire to exclude the effects of structure-consistent personal choice from the purview of its judgment.

The basic structure, the primary subject of justice, is always said by Rawls to be a set of institutions, and, so he infers, the principles of justice do not judge the actions of people within (just) institutions whose rules they observe. But it is seriously unclear which institutions are supposed to qualify as part of the basic structure. Sometimes it appears that coercive (in the legal sense) institutions exhaust it, or, better, that institutions belong to it only insofar as they are (legally) coercive.[37] In this

---

35. Though not necessarily an ethos embodying the very principles that the rules formulate: see the last four paragraphs of section 3. Justice will be shown to require an ethos, and the basic structure objection will thereby be refuted, but it will be a contingent question whether the ethos required by justice can be discerned in the content of the just principles themselves. Still, as I suggested on p. 128, the answer to that question is almost certainly yes.

36. That is, the subject matter that principles of justice judge. I follow Rawls's usage here (e.g., in the title of Lecture VII of *Political Liberalism*: "The Basic Structure as Subject," and cf. n. 19).

37. Throughout the rest of this chapter, I shall use "coercive," "coercion," etc. to mean "legally coercive," etc.

widespread interpretation of what Rawls intends by the "basic structure" of a society, that structure is legible in the provisions of its constitution, in such specific legislation as may be required to implement those provisions, and in further legislation and policy that are of central importance but that resist formulation in the constitution itself.[38] The basic structure, in this first understanding of it, is, so one might say, the *broad coercive outline* of society,[39] which determines in a relatively fixed and general way what people may and must do, in advance of legislation that is optional, relative to the principles of justice, and irrespective of the constraints and opportunities created and destroyed by the choices that people make within the given basic structure, so understood.

Yet it is quite unclear that the basic structure is always to be so understood, in exclusively coercive terms, within the Rawlsian texts. For Rawls often says that the basic structure consists of the major social institutions, and he does not put a particular accent on coercion when he announces that specification of the basic structure.[40] In this second reading

38. Thus, the difference principle, though pursued through (coercively sustained) state policy, cannot, so Rawls came to think, be aptly inscribed in a society's constitution: see *Political Liberalism,* pp. 227–230.

39. (Added, 2008) This interpretation appears to be mandated by a statement in *A Theory of Justice* (pp. 236/207) that I overlooked when I wrote the above: "the law defines the basic structure within which the pursuit of all other activities takes place."

40. Consider, for example, the passage at pp. 7–8/6–7 of *A Theory of Justice* in which the concept of the basic structure is introduced: "Our topic . . . is that of social justice. For us the primary subject of justice is the basic structure of society, or more exactly, the way in which the major social institutions distribute fundamental rights and duties and determine the division of advantages from social cooperation. By major institutions I understand the political constitution and the principal economic and social arrangements. Thus the legal protection of freedom of thought and liberty of conscience, competitive markets, private property in the means of production, and the monogamous family are examples of major social institutions . . . I shall not consider the justice of institutions and social practices generally . . . [The two principles of justice] may not work for the rules and practices of private associations or for those of less comprehensive social groups. They may be irrelevant for the various informal conventions and customs of everyday life; they may not elucidate the justice, or perhaps better, the fairness of voluntary cooperative arrangements or procedures for making contractual agreements."

I cannot tell from those statements what is to be included in, and what excluded from, the basic structure, nor, more particularly, whether coercion is the touchstone of inclusion. Take, for example, the case of the monogamous family. Is it simply its

of what it is, institutions belong to the basic structure whose structuring can depend far less on law than on convention, usage, and expectation: a signal example is the family, which Rawls sometimes includes in the basic structure and sometimes does not.[41] But once the line is crossed, from coercive ordering to the noncoercive ordering of society by rules and conventions of accepted practice, then the ambit of justice can no longer exclude chosen behavior, since, at least in certain cases, the prescriptions that constitute informal structure (think, again, of the family) are bound up with the choices that people customarily make.

"Bound up with" is vague, so let me explain how I mean it here. One can certainly speak of the structure of the family, and it is not identical with the choices that people customarily make within it; but it is nevertheless impossible to claim that the principles of justice that apply to

---

"legal protection" that is a major social institution, in line with a coercive definition of the basic structure (if not, perhaps, with the syntax of the relevant sentence)? Or is the monogamous family itself part of that structure? And, in that case, are its typical usages part of it? They certainly constitute a "principal social arrangement," yet they may also count as "practices of private associations or . . . of less comprehensive social groups," and they are heavily informed by the "conventions and customs of everyday life." (Section 5 of Rawls's "The Idea of Public Reason Revisited" offers an exceedingly interesting account of the family as a component of the basic structure. It does not, however, expressly address the question whether it is only in virtue of the coercive rules that govern it that the family belongs to that structure: but I think that it tends, on the whole, to answer that question in the negative.)

Puzzlement with respect to the bounds of the basic structure is not relieved by examination of the relevant pages of *Political Liberalism,* to wit, 11, 68, 201–2, 229, 258, 268, 271–72, 282–83, and 301. Some formulations on those pages lean toward a coercive specification of the basic structure. Others do not. (The rest of this footnote was added in 2008.) And I cannot make out what Rawls says the basic structure is in the text of "The Idea of Public Reason Revisited": see Susan Okin, "Justice and Gender: An Unfinished Debate," pp. 1563–1567, on the obscurity and incoherence of its message.

Kok-chor Tan's confidence ("Justice and Personal Pursuits," p. 346) that the basic-structural aspect of society is its legal-coercive aspect seems to me not reconcilable with everything that Rawls says. Tan's conclusion that there is no "fatal ambiguity" (see the relevant claim, two paragraphs back in the text above) in Rawls's specification of the basic structure ignores the nuances in Rawls's texts and in any case leaves unaddressed the more important claim that each of the disambiguations is unsatisfactory. That would hold for what Rawls says even if it is, as Tan thinks, univocally on the coercive side.

41. See the final paragraph of section 1.

family structure do not apply to day-to-day choices within it. For consider the following contrast. The coercive structure, let us provisionally accept,[42] arises independently of people's quotidian choices: it is formed by those specialized choices that legislate the law of the land. But the noncoercive structure of the family has the character it does only because of the choices that its members routinely make. The constraints and pressures that sustain the noncoercive structure reside in the dispositions of agents that are actualized as and when those agents choose to act in a constraining or pressuring way. With respect to coercive structure, one may perhaps[43] fairly readily distinguish the choices that institute and sustain a structure from the choices that occur within it. But with respect to informal structure, that distinction, though conceptually intelligible, is compromised extensionally: when A chooses to conform to the prevailing usages, the pressure on B to do so is reinforced, and no such pressure exists, the very usages themselves do not exist, in the absence of conformity to them. Structure and choice remain distinguishable, but not from the point of view of the applicability to them of principles of justice (at any rate when, as is *ex hypothesi* the case here, they are thought to apply because of the fateful consequences of that to which they apply: you cannot bring the informal norm within the compass of justice for that reason without also bringing within its compass the actions that give the norm substance and that account for much, if not most, of its effect[44]). Just as you can ask whether legislators act justly when they create a certain coercive structure, so you can assess for their justice the deliberate daily sustaining acts of the informal structure in which its participants engage.

Now since that is so, since appropriately conforming behavior is, at least in the case of the informal structure, subject to the same judgments of justice that apply to that structure itself, it follows that the only way of maintaining the basic structure objection against my claim that the difference principle condemns maximizing economic behavior (and, more generally, of sustaining the restriction of justice to the basic structure against the insistence that the personal, too, is political) is by hold-

---

42. I severely qualify this acceptance in section 7, and I thereby strengthen the present reply to the basic structure objection.

43. I pursue the question further in section 7.

44. (Added, 2008) For excellent comments on the difference between the effects of a norm as such and the effects of the actions that conform to it, see Joshua Flaherty, *The Autonomy of the Political*, p. 5ff.

ing fast to a purely coercive specification of the basic structure. But that way out is not open to Rawls because of a further characterization that he offers of the basic structure: this is where the discrepancy adverted to in the second paragraph of this section appears. For Rawls says that "the basic structure is the primary subject of justice because its effects are so profound and present from the start."[45] Nor is that further characterization of the basic structure optional: it is needed to explain why it is primary, as far as justice is concerned. Yet it is false that only the coercive structure causes profound effects, as the example of the family once again reminds us[46]: if the "values [that] govern the basic [political] framework of social life" thereby govern "the very groundwork of our existence,"[47] so too do the values that govern our nurture and conduct in the family. Accordingly, if Rawls retreats to coercive structure, he contradicts his own criterion for what justice judges, and he lands himself with an arbitrarily narrow definition of his subject matter. So he must let other structure in, and that means, as we have seen, letting chosen behavior in. What is more, even if behavior did not, as I claim it does, partly constitute the noncoercive structure, it will come in by direct appeal to the profundity-of-effect criterion for what justice governs. So, for example, we need not decide whether or not a regular practice of favoring sons over daughters in the matter of providing higher education forms part of the structure of the family to condemn it as unjust, under that criterion.[48]

45. A Theory of Justice, pp. 7/7. "Present from the start" means, here, "present from birth": see ibid., pp. 96/82. But what matters, surely, is the asserted profundity of effect, whether or not it is "present from birth."

46. Or consider access to that primary good that Rawls calls "the social basis of self-respect." While the law may play a large role in securing that good to people vulnerable to racism, legally unregulable racist attitudes also have an enormous negative impact on how much of that primary good they get. See, further, sections 3 and 7 of Chapter 8 on the significance of racism as a counterexample to restrictive claims about the "site" of justice.

47. Political Liberalism, p. 139.

48. Note that one can condemn the said practice without condemning those who engage in it. For there might be a collective action problem here, which weighs heavily on poor families in particular. If, in addition to discrimination in education, there is discrimination in employment, then a poor family might sacrifice a great deal through choosing evenhandedly across the sexes with whatever resources it can devote to its children's education. This illustrates the important distinction between condemning injustice and condemning the people whose actions perpetuate it: see, further, section 6.

Given, then, his stated rationale[49] for exclusive focus on the basic structure—and what other rationale could there be for calling it the *primary* subject of justice?—Rawls is in a dilemma. For he must either admit application of the principles of justice to (legally optional) social practices, and, indeed, to patterns of personal choice that are not legally prescribed, both because they are the substance of those practices, and because they are similarly profound in effect, in which case the restriction of justice to structure, in any sense, collapses; or, if he restricts his concern to the coercive structure only, then he saddles himself with a purely arbitrary delineation of his subject matter. I now illustrate this dilemma by reference to the two items that have already figured in the present chapter: the family, and the market economy.

Family structure is fateful for the benefits and burdens that redound to different people, and in particular to people of different sexes, where "family structure" includes the socially constructed expectations that lie on husband and wife. And such expectations are sexist and unjust if, for example, they direct the woman in a family where both spouses work outside the home to carry a greater burden of domestic tasks. Yet such expectations need not be supported by the law for them to possess informal coercive force: sexist family structure is consistent with sex-neutral family law. Here, then, is a circumstance, outside the basic structure, as that would be coercively defined, which profoundly affects people's life chances, *through the choices people make in response to the stated expectations, which are, in turn, sustained by those choices.*[50] Yet Rawls must say, on pain of giving up the basic structure objection, that (legally uncoerced) family structure and behavior have no implications for justice in the sense of "justice" in which the basic structure has implications for justice, since they are not a consequence of the formal coercive order. But that implication of the stated position is perfectly incredible: no such differentiating sense is available.

John Stuart Mill taught us to recognize that informal social pressure can restrict liberty as much as formal coercive law does. And the family example shows that informal pressure is as relevant to distributive justice as it is to liberty. One reason why the rules of the basic structure, when it is coercively defined, do not by themselves determine the jus-

---

49. See the text to n. 45.

50. Hugo Adam Bedau noticed that the family falls outside the basic structure, under the coercive specification of it often favored by Rawls, though he did not notice the connection between noncoercive structure and choice that I emphasize in the above sentence: see his "Social Justice and Social Institutions," p. 171.

tice of the distributive upshot is that, by virtue of circumstances that are relevantly independent of coercive rules, some people have much more power than others to determine what happens within those rules.

The second illustration of discrepancy between what coercive structure commands and what profoundly affects the distribution of benefits and burdens is my own point about incentives. Maximinizing legislation,[51] and, hence, a coercive basic structure that is just as far as the difference principle is concerned, are consistent with a maximizing ethos across society that, under many conditions, will produce severe inequalities and a meager level of provision for the worst off, yet both have to be declared just by Rawls, if he stays with a coercive conception of what justice judges. And that implication is, surely, entirely implausible.

Rawls cannot deny the difference between the coercively defined basic structure and that which produces major distributive consequences: the coercively defined basic structure is only an instance of the latter. Yet he must, to retain his position on justice and personal choice, restrict the ambit of justice to what a coercive basic structure produces. But, so I have (by implication) asked: why should we care so disproportionately about the coercive basic structure, when the major reason for caring about it, its impact on people's lives, is also a reason for caring about informal structure and patterns of personal choice? To the extent that we care about coercive structure because it is fateful with regard to benefits and burdens, we must care equally about the ethos that sustains gender inequality and inegalitarian incentives. And the similarity of our reasons for caring about these contrasting matters will make it lame to say: ah, but only the caring about coercive structure is a caring about justice, in a certain distinguishable sense. That thought is, I submit, incapable of coherent elaboration.[52]

*   *   *

51. That is, legislation that maximizes the size of the primary goods bundle held by the worst off people, given whatever is correctly expected to be the pattern in the choices made by economic agents.

52. (Added, 2008) As Liam Murphy points out in his "Institutions and the Demands of Justice," Rawls's institutionally focused structure is utterly implausible for the case where institutions are unjust. On Rawls's institutionally focused approach, the only duty of justice that then falls on individuals is to promote just institutions (rather than to comply with them, since they do not obtain). But the worst off might be better served in an unjust society through direct philanthropic assistance, rather than through a possibly fruitless, or less productive, attempt to improve the justice of institutions.

My response to the basic structure objection is now fully laid out, but before proceeding, in the sections that remain, to matters arising, it will be useful to rehearse, in compressed form, the arguments that were presented in the present chapter.

My original criticism of the incentives argument ran, in brief, as follows:

(1) Citizens in a just society adhere to its principles of justice.

But

(2) They do not adhere to the difference principle if they are acquisitive maximizers in daily life.

Therefore

(3) In a society that is governed by the difference principle, citizens lack the acquisitiveness that the incentives argument attributes to them.

The reply to that criticism provided by the basic structure objection is of this form:

(4) The principles of justice govern only the basic structure of a just society.

Therefore

(5) Citizens in a just society may adhere to the difference principle whatever their choices may be within the structure it determines, and, in particular, even if their economic choices are entirely acquisitive.

Therefore

(6) Proposition (2) lacks justification.

My preliminary reply to the basic structure objection says:

(7) Proposition (5) is inconsistent with many Rawlsian statements about the relationship between citizens and principles of justice in a just society.

And my fundamental reply to the basic structure objection says:

(8) Proposition (4) is unsustainable.

Let me emphasize that my rebuttal of the basic structure objection does not itself establish that the difference principle properly evaluates not only state policy but everyday economic choice. The argument for that conclusion was given in Chapter 1 and summarized in section 2 of this chapter. I do not say that *because* everyday choice cannot be, as the basic structure objection says it is, beyond the reach of justice (simply because it *is* everyday choice), it then follows that everyday economic choice is indeed within its reach: that would be a non sequitur. I say, rather, that it is no objection to my argument for the claim that justice evaluates everyday economic choice that everyday choice is (in general) beyond the reach of justice, since it is not.

This point about the structure of my argument is easily missed, so let me explain it in a different way. I have not tried to show, what is false, that a robust structure/choice distinction cannot be sustained in the case of the economy. What I argued is that choices within the economic structure cannot be placed outside the primary purview of justice on the ground that the only thing (quite generally) that is within its primary purview is structure. The family case refutes that argument. That refutation doesn't, I would agree, exclude treating economic choices like the choices of a game player who obeys the rules (and therefore plays not unjustly), while trying to score as many points as he can.[53] What excludes that, what defeats that analogy, is the argument summarized in section 2 above.

6. Who Is to Blame?

So the personal is indeed political: personal choices to which the writ of the law is indifferent are fateful for social justice.

But that raises a huge question with respect to blame. The injustice in distribution that reflects personal choices within a just coercive structure can plainly not be blamed on that structure itself, nor, therefore, on whoever legislated that structure. Must it, then, be blamed, in our two examples, on men[54] and on acquisitive people, respectively?

I shall presently address, and answer, that question about blame, but before I do so, I wish to explain why I could remain silent in the face of it, why, that is, my argument in criticism of Rawls's restricted application of the principles of justice requires no judgment about blaming individual choosers. The conclusion of my argument is that the principles of justice apply not only to coercive rules but also to the pattern in people's (legally) uncoerced choices. Now if we judge a certain set of rules to be just or unjust, we need not add, as pendant to that judgment, that those who legislated the rules in question, and thus produced some justice or injustice, should be praised or blamed for what they did.[55] And something analogous applies when we come to see that the ambit of justice

---

53. See the parenthesized remarks at the end of section 2.
54. We can here set aside the fact that women often subscribe to, and inculcate, male-dominative practices.
55. We can distinguish between how unjust past practices (e.g., slavery) were and how unjust those who protected and benefited from those unjust practices were.

covers the pattern of daily choices in a society. We can believe whatever we are inclined to about how responsible and/or culpable people are for their choices, and that includes believing that they are not responsible and/or culpable for them at all, while holding that on which I insist: that the pattern in such choices is relevant to how just or unjust a society is.

That said, let me now face the question of how blamable individuals are. It would be inappropriate to answer it here by first declaring my position, if indeed I have one, on the philosophical problem of the freedom of the will. Instead, I shall answer the question about blame on the pre-philosophical assumptions that inform our ordinary judgments about when, and how much, blame is appropriate. Working within those assumptions, we should avoid two opposite mistakes about how culpable chauvinistic men and self-seeking high fliers are. One is the mistake of saying that there is no ground for blaming these people *as* individuals, for they simply participate in an accepted social practice, however tawdry or awful that practice may be. That is a mistake, since people do have choices: it is, indeed, only their choices that reproduce social practices; and some, moreover, choose against the grain of nurture, habit, social pressure, and self-interest. But one also must not say: look how each of these people shamefully decides to behave so badly. That, too, is unbalanced, since although there exists personal choice, there is heavy social conditioning behind it and it can cost individuals a lot to depart from the prescribed and/or permitted ways. If we care about social justice, we have to look at four things: the coercive structure, other structures, the social ethos, and the choices of individuals, and judgment on

---

Most of us (rightly) do not so strongly condemn Lincoln for his (conditional) willingness to tolerate slavery as we would a statesman who did the same in 2008, but the slavery institution itself was, I believe, as unjust in Lincoln's time as it would be today.

What made slavery unjust in, say, ancient Greece is exactly what would make slavery (with, of course, the very same rules of subordination) unjust today, to wit, the content of its rules. But sound judgments about the justice and injustice of people are much more contextual: they must take into account the institutions under which they live, the prevailing level of intellectual and moral development, collective action problems such as the one delineated in n. 48, and so forth. The morally best slaveholder might deserve admiration. The morally best form of slavery would not. (Of some relevance here is the brilliant discussion of "how far our rejection of [ancient slavery] . . . depends on modern conceptions that were not available in the ancient world" (p. 106) in Chapter 5 of Bernard Williams's *Shame and Necessity*.)

the last of those must be informed by awareness of the power of the others. So, for example, a properly sensitive appreciation of these matters allows one to hold that an acquisitive ethos is profoundly unjust in its effects, without holding that those who are gripped by it are commensurately unjust. It is essential to apply principles of justice to dominant patterns in social behavior—that, as it were, is where the action is—but it doesn't follow that we should have a persecuting attitude to the people who engage in that behavior. We might have good reason to exonerate the perpetrators of injustice, but we should not deny or apologize for the injustice itself.[56]

On an extreme view, which I do not accept but need not reject, a typical husband in a thoroughly sexist society, one in which families in their overwhelming majority display an unjust division of domestic labor, is literally incapable of revising his behavior, or capable of revising it only at the cost of cracking up, to nobody's benefit. But even if that is true of typical husbands, we know it to be false of husbands in general. It is a plain empirical fact that some husbands are capable of revising their behavior, since some husbands have done so, in response to feminist criticism. These husbands, we could say, were moral pioneers. They made a path that becomes easier and easier to follow as more and more people follow it, until social pressures are so altered that it becomes harder to stick to sexist ways than to abandon them. That is a central way in which a social ethos changes. Or, for another example, consider the recent rise in ecological consciousness. At first only people who appear to be freaky because they do so bother to save and recycle their paper, plastic, and so forth. Then more do that, and, finally, it becomes not only difficult not to do it but easy to do it. It is pretty easy to discharge burdens that have become part of the normal round of everybody's life. Expectations determine behavior, behavior determines expectations, which determine behavior, and so on.

Are there circumstances in which a similar incremental process could occur with respect to economic behavior? I do not know. But I do know that universal maximizing is by no means a necessary feature of a market economy. For all that much of its industry was state-owned, the United Kingdom from 1945 to 1951 had a market economy. But salary differentials were nothing like as great as they were to become, or as they were then in the United States. Yet, so I hazard, when British executives mak-

56. See the immediately preceding footnote, and see Joshua Flaherty, pp. 217 ff.

ing five times what their workers did met American counterparts making fifteen times what their (anyhow better-paid) workers did, many of the British executives would not have felt: *we* should press for more. For there was a social ethos of reconstruction after war, an ethos of common project, that restrained desire for personal gain. It is not for a philosopher to delimit the conditions under which such, and even more egalitarian ethoses, can prevail. But a philosopher can say that a maximizing ethos is not a necessary feature of society, or even of a market society, and that, to the extent that such an ethos prevails, satisfaction of the difference principle is prejudiced.

In 1988 the ratio of top executive salaries to production worker wages was 6.5 to 1 in West Germany and 17.5 to 1 in the United States.[57] Since it is not plausible to think that Germany's lesser inequality was a disincentive to productivity, since it is plausible to think that an ethos that was relatively friendly to equality[58] protected German productivity in the face of relatively modest material incentives, we can conclude that the said ethos caused the worst paid to be better paid than they would have been under a different culture of reward. It follows, on my view of the matter, that the difference principle was better realized in Germany in 1988 than it would have been if its culture of reward had been more similar to that of the United States.[59] But Rawls cannot say that, since the smaller inequality that benefited the less well off in Germany was not a matter of law but of ethos. I think that Rawls's inability to regard Germany as having done comparatively well with respect to the difference principle is a grave defect in his conception of the site of distributive justice.

57. See Mishel and Frankel, *The State of Working America,* p. 122. The contrast is probably much bigger now.
58. That ethos need not have been a (relatively) egalitarian one. For present purposes it could have been an ethos that disendorses acquisitiveness as such (see n. 35 and the digression at the end of section 3), other than on behalf of the worst off. (I have here supposed that the stated difference in salary ratios was not due, or not wholly due, to social legislation that raised the wages of German workers, and/or other features of Germany's coercive basic structure. If that supposition is false, the example can be treated as invented: it would still make the required point.)
59. And note how implausible it would be to say that Germany's (relatively speaking) equality-friendly ethos reduced the liberty of the German better off. I make this point in disparagement of the objection that my extension of the difference principle to everyday life violates the first principle of Rawlsian justice.

7. Coercive and Noncoercive Social Structures

I want now to modify the distinction drawn in section 5 between coercive and other social structure and, thereby, to strengthen my argument against the basic structure objection.

The legally coercive structure of society functions in two ways. It prevents people from doing things by erecting insurmountable barriers (fences, police lines, prison walls, etc.), and it deters people from doing things by ensuring that certain forms of unprevented behavior carry an (appreciable risk of) penalty.[60] The second (deterrent) aspect of coercive structure may be described counterfactually, in terms of what would or might happen to someone who elects the forbidden behavior: knowledge of the relevant counterfactual truths motivates the complying citizen's choices.

Not much pure prevention goes on within the informal structure of society: not none, but not much. (Locking errant teenagers in their rooms would represent an instance of pure prevention, which, if predictable for determinate behavior, would count as part of a society's informal structure: it would be a rule in accordance with which that society operates.) That being set aside, informal structure manifests itself in predictable sanctions such as criticism, disapproval, anger, refusal of future cooperation, ostracism, beating (of, for example, spouses who refuse sexual service), and so on.

Finally, to complete this conceptual review, the ethos of a society is the set of sentiments and attitudes in virtue of which its normal practices and informal pressures are what they are.

Now the pressures that sustain the informal structure lack force save insofar as there is a normal practice of compliance with the rules they enforce. That is especially true of that great majority of those pressures (beating does not belong to that majority) that have a moral coloring: criticism and disapproval are ineffective when they come from the mouths of those who ask others not to do what they do themselves. To be sure, that is not a conceptual truth, but a social-psychological one. Even so, it enables us to say that what people ordinarily do supports the informal structure of society in such a way that it makes no sense to pass

---

60. The distinction given above corresponds to that between the difficulty and the cost of actions, which is elaborated on pp. 258–259 of my *If You're an Egalitarian, How Come You're So Rich?*

judgments of justice on that structure while withholding such judgment from the behavior that supports it: that point is crucial to the anti-Rawlsian inference on page 134.[61] Informal structure is not a behavioral pattern but a set of rules, yet the two are so closely related that, so one might say, they are merely categorially different. Accordingly, so I argued, to include (as one must) informal structure within the basic structure is to countenance behavior, too, as a primary object of judgments of justice.

Now two truths about legally coercive structure might be thought to cast doubt on the contrast that I allowed between it and informal structure in section 5. First, although the legally coercive structure of society is indeed discernible in the ordinances of society's political constitution and law, those ordinances count as delineating it only on condition that they enjoy a broad measure of compliance.[62] And, second, legally coercive structure achieves its intended social effect only in and through the actions that constitute compliance with its rules.

In light of those truths, it might be thought that the dilemma I posed for Rawls (see page 137), and by means of which I sought to defeat his claim that justice judges structure as opposed to the actions of agents, was misframed. For I said, against that claim, that the required opposition between structure and actions works for coercive structure only, with respect to which a relevantly strong distinction can be drawn between structure-sustaining and structure-conforming action, but that coercive structure could not reasonably be thought to exhaust the structure falling within the purview of justice: accordingly, so I concluded, justice must also judge (at least some) everyday actions.

The truths rehearsed two paragraphs back challenge that articulation of the distinction between coercive structure and action within it. They thereby also challenge the contrast drawn in section 5 between two relationships, that between coercive structure and action and that between informal structure and action. And to the extent that the first relationship is more like the second, the first horn of the dilemma that I posed

61. See the sentence beginning "But once" on that page.
62. It does not follow that they are not laws unless they enjoy such compliance: perhaps they are nevertheless laws, if they "satisfy a test set out in a Hartian rule of recognition, even if they are themselves neither complied with nor accepted" (Joshua Cohen, private communication). But such laws (or "laws") are not plausibly represented as part of the basic structure of society, so the statement in the text can stand as it is.

for Rawls becomes sharper than it was: it is sharp not only for the reason that I gave, namely, the consideration about "profound effect," but also for the same reason that the second horn is sharp, namely, that everyday behavior is too germane to the very existence of (even) coercive structure to be immune to the principles of justice that apply to the coercive structure.

The distinction, vis-à-vis action, between coercive and informal structure, so I judge, is more blurred than section 5 allowed, not, of course, because informal structure is more separable from action than I originally claimed, but because coercive structure is less separable from it than I originally allowed. Accordingly, even if the dilemma constructed on page 137 was for the stated reasons misframed, the upshot would hardly be congenial to Rawls's position, that justice judges structure rather than actions, but, rather, congenial to my own rejection of that position. But I want to emphasize that this putative strengthening of my argument is not essential: in my opinion, it was strong enough already.

Appendix I: More on Coercion and the Basic Structure (Added, 2008)

We saw in section 5 that Rawls provides no single answer to the question whether the basic structure, which he considers to be the site of justice, is defined as such by its coercive character. That ambivalence serves his theory's ends: as a liberal, Rawls is inclined to make coercion criterial for the bounds of justice, so that, once the state has done its work, and people comply with its laws, individuals in civil society are free of the demands of justice, but he also wants to claim that he sites justice as he does because of the "profound effect" of what occurs there: that's what's supposed to justify the restriction of the ambit of justice to the basic structure. I argued that the two propositions are not co-tenable: matters that lie beyond the coercive domain also have a profound effect, and are therefore of interest from the point of view of justice.

I now want to identify a further respect in which Rawls assigns a centrality to coercion that cannot, in the end, be sustained, given other things that he says. Consider the central place that coercion occupies in the general question to which political liberalism is supposed to be the answer, the question that is so central to the book *Political Liberalism* that it appears on its dust jacket:

We assume that a diversity of reasonable religious, philosophical, and moral doctrines found in democratic societies is a permanent feature of the public culture and not a mere historical condition soon to pass away. Granted all this, we ask: when may citizens by their vote properly exercise their coercive political power over one another when fundamental questions are at stake?

Now Rawls says that in the well-ordered society "everyone accepts and knows that the others accept the same principles of justice,"[63] and "accept" here implies a disposition, which everyone knows that everyone has, to act on those principles. Why then is any coercion necessary? Perhaps for incidental reasons: the statement taken from *Theory* is an idealization, since there is bound to be in the real world a sprinkling of psychopaths and other deviants who require the rod. But that consideration of realism would not appear to justify the central position assigned to coercion in *Political Liberalism*'s flagship statement. Voters would not in general be "exercising . . . coercive political power *over one another*" (emphases added) when they pass laws that the bulk of them obey for reasons that have nothing to do with any coercive backing that the laws possess. To be sure, one can envisage a set of citizens all of whom are willing to obey the law without coercion, if others do, but who need the background of coercion to be sure that others, too, will obey. But if, as Rawls says, the citizens of his just society all know that everyone is motivated by justice, then why should coercion be required even for that secondary, assurance, reason?

But it could be said that a characterization of full compliance whose only blemish is a sprinkling of deviants remains too idealized. People know that people in general are not saints, so they may accept, without contradicting full compliance, that the rod will be relevant not only to keeping outright miscreants on the straight and narrow. Rawls writes:

> It is reasonable to assume that even in a well-ordered society the coercive powers of government are to some degree necessary for the stability of social cooperation. For although men know that they share a common sense of justice and that each wants to adhere to the existing arrangements, they may nevertheless lack full confidence in one another. They may suspect that some are not doing their part, and so they may be tempted not to do theirs. For this reason alone, a coercive sovereign is presumably always necessary, even though in a well-ordered society sanctions are not severe and may

63. *A Theory of Justice*, pp. 4/4.

never need to be imposed. Rather, the existence of effective penal machinery serves as men's security to one another.[64]

All know that all are genuinely motivated by justice, but they also all know that all are subject to temptation. This does make coercion more important, but it still seems to me not to make the prospect of possible coercion essential to what justice is. One may think that whatever justice is, it may have to be enforced, if necessary, but we don't learn what justice fundamentally is by focusing on what it is permissible to coerce, if coercion is necessary only for deviance or assurance reasons. Perhaps one could argue that the question of what it would be right to coerce, if necessary, is the appropriate question to ask in determining what justice is even if, in the achieved society, nothing needs to be coerced either for miscreant or for assurance reasons. We might say that justice is what warrants coercive imposition where coercion is necessary for it to be observed. That would be a stronger and more principled reason for putting coercion at the center of the matter, and perhaps it operated in the thought behind *Political Liberalism*'s dust-jacket formulation.

Finally, I note the description of the *Political Liberalism* question on page xviii of the book: "How is it possible that there may exist over time a stable and just society of free and equal citizens profoundly divided by reasonable though incompatible religious, philosophical, and moral doctrines?" There is no special emphasis on coercion here, and that seems to me manifestly more appropriate.[65]

The quoted question is, however, not really a question about justice but one about legitimacy.[66] And the Rawlsian answer is that the citizens may strive to operate under principles that are endorsed by an overlapping consensus. But, once again, such a consensus may not only secure stability but make coercion unnecessary: the considerations adduced above also affect the relationship between coercion and the legitimacy that an overlapping consensus is supposed to supply.

64. *A Theory of Justice*, pp. 240/211. Cf. pp. 268–269/237, 315/277, and 336/296.
65. For a compelling interpretation of Rawls in which the question what principles can be coercively imposed is replaced by the question what principles are democratic in the sense that they are acceptable to everyone, see Paul Flaherty's excellent critique of Charles Larmore's coercion-centered treatment of the relevant issues on pp. 188–194 of Flaherty's *The Autonomy of the Political*.
66. See, further, the discussion at subsection (iii) of section 3 of Chapter 7.

Appendix II: The Basic Structure Is a Structure (Added, 2008)

I comment here on a common misdescription of my criticism of Rawls's restriction of justice to the basic structure. A prominent case of that misdescription is provided by Andrew Williams's (consequent) misdescription of my reply to the basic structure objection.[67]

Williams quotes one of my statements in support of the misdescription that I shall presently describe:

> As Cohen explains, "once the line is crossed, from coercive ordering to the non-coercive ordering of society by rules and conventions of accepted practice, then the ambit of justice can no longer exclude chosen behaviour, since the usages which constitute informal structure (think, again, of the family) are bound up with the customary actions of people."[68]

On the basis of this passage, Williams attributes to me the conclusion that the customary actions of people are "an informal part of . . . [the basic] structure."[69] But my conclusion is the different one that the said actions, *despite being no part of the basic structure of society,* are nevertheless assessable at the bar of justice, by the same principles (whatever they may be) by reference to which justice judges that basic structure.

Actions are, in general, no part of the basic structure, because a structure, in the present sense of the term, is a set of rules,[70] and actions are

67. Since the concept of the basic structure plays no substantial role in his criticism of that reply, the misdescription is inconsequential as far as our dispute is concerned: see section 2 of Chapter 8.

68. Williams, "Incentives, Inequality, and Publicity," p. 231, n. 19, quoting "Where the Action Is," p. 20, which is reproduced on p. 134 of the present chapter.

69. Ibid., p. 231. The same misattribution occurs on p. 229 and p. 241. The misattribution is somewhat curious because Williams quotes a passage of the cited article in n. 17 of his p. 230, which proves that it is a misattribution.

There is, on the other hand, a formulation in the article Williams criticizes that encourages the misattribution that I am canvassing. For I say on p. 20 that "behaviour is *constitutive* of *non*-coercive structure," and the most natural reading of that statement, when it is disconnected from the text that surrounds it, favors Williams's misattribution. I have, accordingly, revised the errant sentence: see the first sentence of the second paragraph on p. 135.

70. Rawls characterizes the basic structure as a set of institutions (passim), and he says that he will "understand" "by an institution" "a public system of rules" (*Theory,* pp. 55/47–48). I am partial to those stipulations, but the paragraph in which Rawls makes the second one proceeds also to identify institutions as possible or ac-

not members of sets of rules. So the relevant customary actions, even though they are (as I argued) subject to the same judgments of justice as the rules that they sustain are (see section 5 above), are nevertheless not themselves a set of rules. My point is not that daily behavior, including "individual market behaviour" (p. 229), is part of the basic structure, but that it is so closely related to what must on pain of arbitrariness be included in the basic structure, to wit, the informal structure demanded by justice, that it too, that is, daily behavior, comes under the same principles of justice that judge structural properties of society.[71] That conclusion, that justice applies to chosen behavior, would imply that behavior is (therefore) part of the basic structure only on the premise that whatever justice applies to is part of the basic structure. But, as I conceptualize my case, that is exactly what I deny.

---

tual patterns of conduct ("expressed by a system of rules"): that further formulation leans toward Williams's understanding of institutional structures, but I prefer the paragraph's initial and more straightforward characterization.

71. See p. 134ff.

4

THE DIFFERENCE PRINCIPLE

---

1. Introduction

In the present chapter I take my campaign against the Rawlsian paradigm deeper into its own territory. Section 2 (*Reconsidering the Difference Principle*) proposes that some of the considerations adduced in earlier chapters tell against the difference principle itself, and not merely against the lax Rawlsian application of it. Section 3 maintains that *The Moral Arbitrariness Case for the Difference Principle Contradicts Its Content*. It depicts a radical tension between the Rawlsian case for the difference principle, which includes an affirmation of relational egalitarianism, that is, an egalitarianism that is fundamentally sensitive to comparisons between people, and the content of the difference principle, which makes that principle blind to comparisons between people, in the relevant sense. Section 4 addresses a recent Pareto-like argument that is due to Thomas Nagel, which describes a Rawlsian movement from "negative equality of opportunity" to "fair equality of opportunity" to the difference principle as throughout manifesting "the same reasoning." I show that the relevant reasoning is not "the same," but that, like the Pareto argument that was dissected in Chapter 2, though not precisely in the same way, the Nagel replay of the Rawlsian argument is split down its middle. I also have occasion to comment here on an associated Rawlsian unclarity regarding just how lexical the lexical priority of fair equality of opportunity over the difference principle is supposed to be. Section 5 addresses a specifically *Contractarian Argument for the Difference Principle*. In section 6 (*What Is the Moral Arbitrariness of Talent Differences Supposed to Show?*), I confront an objection that denies my claim that Rawls holds that the arbitrariness of talent differences justifies beginning with equality. In the objector's counter-interpretation, Rawls

151

holds merely that, because of that arbitrariness, talent differences do not justify inequality. Section 7 *(Chamberlain and Pareto)* compares and contrasts the Pareto argument for inequality with Robert Nozick's well-known and so-called Wilt Chamberlain argument for inequality. I argue that, despite the differences between the arguments, a familiar criticism of the Nozick argument, one that Rawlsians are disposed to affirm, also applies against the Rawlsian Pareto argument. And in section 8 *("Can't" or "Won't")*, I contrast different reasons why citizens who sincerely profess the difference principle, and applaud the state's adherence to it, might nevertheless not live by that principle. The discussion proceeds to comment on key ideas in the thought of James Meade and of Karl Marx. Finally, in section 9, I comment on the relationship in Rawls's thought between *Human Nature and Constructivism.*

2. Reconsidering the Difference Principle

I was at pains to emphasize, in the prepublished chapters that precede the present one, that my criticism of Rawls was of what I considered to be his unjustifiably restricted application (to acts of government) of his difference principle, rather than of that principle itself. Yet despite several such prominently placed disavowals,[1] and despite the actual shape of my argument, people commonly mounted replies to what I said in which they said that they were addressing "Cohen's critique of the difference principle" (itself). For a long time, I put that down to mere carelessness, or to an unconcern about looseness of formulation, but I have belatedly come to see that the description in question, while technically incorrect, has a certain justification. The materials for a critique of the difference principle itself are there in the relevant chapters[2]: I just failed expressly to deploy them to that end.

The point can be made by reference to my critique of the Pareto argument in Chapter 2, which, recall, was an argument in justification not, precisely, of the difference principle itself but of the incentives inequality that the principle is used to justify. My main objection to the Pareto argument was that the cause of the inequality that the Pareto argument ends by endorsing might be, and standardly is, the exploitation by the

1. See, for example, Chapter 1, p. 00, and Chapter 3, p. 00.
2. See, in particular, the following parts of Chapter 2: the first part of the "Challenge" to the Pareto argument in section 3; the dilemma posed for the Pareto argument in the last paragraph of section 4, with the two horns representing presence and absence of "special burden"; and section 9 generally, read in a certain possible way.

talented of the morally arbitrary talent differential whose morally arbitrary character led to the provisional affirmation of equality at the outset of the argument. The argument is, therefore, so I claimed, and claim, split down its middle. Similarly, in Chapter 1, I claimed that anyone who affirms the difference principle should judge incentives-generated inequality to be unjust, since it helps the worst off only because the better off disrespect the principle that is supposed to justify that very inequality.

The arguments of Chapters 1 and 2 provide reasons for denying that unequalizing incentives are justified by the difference principle, not, explicitly, reasons for denying the difference principle itself. The arguments depend on the claim of fact that those who demand or accept unequalizing incentives, despite their own professed commitment to the difference principle, are quite able to supply high quality (and not particularly oppressive) labor without those incentives. That is why I confronted Samuel Scheffler's doubts about that assessment of their capacity,[3] and I dealt with those doubts by arguing that they could not extinguish the full force of my argument. But I accepted throughout that if high fliers truly could not work so hard as the strict difference principle would require without high rewards, then there would be no consequent stain of injustice on the resultant society. I accepted the major premise that an insurmountable inability could not be a cause of injustice.

I thereby failed to see that, even if Scheffler were right and the better off could not produce prodigiously without unequalizing incentives, so that they could not be blamed for the inequality that incentives bring, that inequality, though now indeed justified according to the difference

---

3. See p. 51ff. of Chapter 1. To prevent misunderstanding, recall that Scheffler's "inability" claim is not the claim, which I accept, that the unqualified strict difference principle is inconsistent with a Scheffler-like "personal prerogative." The difference between the inability claim and the prerogative claim is easy to overlook, because they can be presented in similar vocabulary. Each claim might, for example, be phrased as follows: "You're asking too much." But in inability discourse, "too much" means "more than I *can* give," whereas, in prerogative discourse, it means "more than I can reasonably be *required* to give."

I regret James Griffin's attempt to diminish the significance of the stated contrast. The section of his *Value Judgment* (Oxford: Oxford University Press, 1996, pp. 87–92) in which he does so is (mis)called "The limits of the will." That title misnames, because going beyond what I can reasonably be required to do breaches no such limits, unless one contrasts the limits of the will with limits on the will, but that is the contrast that Griffin seeks to blur: he treats unwillingness as a limit on what one could will.

principle, would remain unjust, because of its source in morally arbitrary causes. The incapacity of the talented would explain, but not supply a morally nonarbitrary justification of, incentives inequality. And that puts a taint on the difference principle itself: the principle permits inequalities that are morally arbitrary.

In a word, I had failed to note that the final inequality is unjust simply because it is caused by something arbitrary,[4] and, therefore, whether or not the relevant agents stand condemned of violating the principle they profess by deliberately exploiting a morally arbitrary advantage. Accordingly, so I now believe, my past posture was too concessive. Suppose we are disposed to think that pay should be sensitive to labor burden but not to productivity, because that arrangement shows freedom from the influence of the morally arbitrary. And so, being thereby moved by Rawls's most basic thought, we incline toward the strict difference principle, but we might now pause to determine whether people could live up to it, or whether, instead, to expect them to do so would "strain their commitment" to the breaking point. If there were every other reason for thinking that justice abhors the morally arbitrary, why should our inability to live by that precept make us begin to doubt it, as opposed to the quality of our own moral fiber?

Let me try to drive the point home. Suppose, once again, that we are inclined to believe that inequalities are justified only if they are strictly necessary to benefit the worst off but we find, to our dismay, that we simply cannot work hard without unequalizing incentives. Would we not think that the distribution was becoming more just if and as we became more able (let us hypothesize that, for whatever reason, we were to become so) to work hard with less unequalizing reward, and, therefore, to the greater benefit of the worst off? If so, we cannot think that satisfying the difference principle suffices for distributive justice, pure and simple, because it *was* satisfied at the earlier stage, yet now that things have become *more* just. Nor can we think that, as Scheffler and I were supposing, the bounds of possibility contain the bounds of justice.[5]

4. Where the inequality caused by that morally arbitrary cause does not happen, by extraordinary coincidence, to coincide with what would have been brought about by choice if the morally arbitrary cause had not overridden any influence that choice might have had: this and cognate qualifications will always be understood to obtain in what follows.

5. See, further, the discussion of '"ought" implies "can"' in section 13 of Chapter 6, and my comment on Rawls's claim that a conception of justice is unacceptable if humans cannot practice it, in the penultimate paragraph of section 8 of Chapter 7.

Suppose, differently from thus far, that it is not possible to run an economy efficiently, nor, therefore, to the benefit of the worst off, without assigning high rewards to well-placed people, but now for purely informational/organizational reasons,[6] rather than for the motivational reasons that have occupied us hitherto. Such inequalities would then be strictly necessary to benefit the worst off. But the hypothesized impossibility would not render the inequality that it recommends just, because that inequality would, once again, have a morally arbitrary cause: it would be the mere good luck of its beneficiaries that they stand at the receiving end of the unequalizing process. On the anti-moral-arbitrariness conception of justice, the stated impossibility claim supports the conclusion that injustice is good for the worst off. For even an unavoidable inequality remains unjust, on the view that justifies equality as a starting point on the Rawlsian ground that the standard causes of inequality are morally arbitrary.

Since writing the articles that form the three opening chapters of this book, I have moved toward the view that justice is justice, whether or not it is possible to achieve it, and that to conform our conception of justice[7] to what is achievable creates distortions in our thought and also in our practice. But further distinctions are, as always, pertinent. For although I consider a society unjust to the extent that the morally arbitrary, even unavoidably, prevails in it, the nature of the causal source of the unavoidable constraint must affect our judgment of the justice of the people in the society. If, as lately conjectured, inequality is unavoidable for purely organizational reasons, then no stain of injustice attaches to the citizens. If, however, the unavoidability is due to insurmountable cupidity, then we may say that, although they cannot be blamed for this, their very makeup is unjust: they cannot help being unjust.[8] But the impossibility of justice, whether or not it is due to a flaw in human nature, is insufficient for the justice of the possible.

There are, in sum, three cases that Rawls thinks illustrate justice that I think display an injustice. First, and this is the case that dominates the previous chapters, there is the case of the incentives-generated inequality that is not strictly necessary, because productive people have the capacity to supply the same labor without an unequalizing incentive. Rawls

6. Such as those laid out by Philippe Van Parijs and reported in subsection (ii) of section 6 of Chapter 7.
7. As opposed to our conception of achievable justice!
8. For questions that raises about "'ought' implies 'can,'" see, again, section 13 of Chapter 6.

thinks the difference principle endorses that case as just, but I counter-claim that the principle condemns it as unjust. Second, there is the case where the productive strictly need the unequalizing incentive: that case is indeed just under the difference principle, but I regard its implication that this second case is just as a reason for rejecting the principle. And, finally, there is the case, lately contemplated, in which the inequality is again nec-essary, but not for incentives reasons, and the Rawls/Cohen judgments on that case show the same disagreement as they do in the second case.

3. The Moral Arbitrariness Case for the Difference Principle Contradicts Its Content

Recall the point made in section 6 of the Introduction, that conflicting values in our liberal democratic political culture find their expression in tensions within the total set of Rawlsian theses.[9] A signal illustration of that: Rawls affirms, on the one hand, the moral arbitrariness claim, which conjoins a post-medieval principle that none should fare worse than others through no fault of their own and modern sociological so-phistication about the actual sources of how people fare: the moral arbi-trariness claim puts accidentally caused inequality under a cloud, as far as justice is concerned. But, on the other hand, Rawls feels and wields the force of the Pareto principle, which welcomes inequality that benefits everyone whatever, including sheer accident, may be its cause.

In the upshot we have the peculiar result that the moral arbitrariness claim, which looms large in the intuitive case for the difference principle, contradicts the content of that very principle, when it is conceived, as Rawls, of course, conceives it, as a principle of (unqualified) justice. The idea that motivates the Rawlsian starting point of equality (which then gives way to the difference principle, which condemns Pareto-inferior equalities), the idea that justice opposes differences of fortune between people that are due to morally arbitrary causes, because they are un-fair, presupposes or implies that justice has (at least some) regard to the relation between what different people get. But the difference princi-ple is blind to comparisons between people, in the relevant, fundamental sense, and therefore permits that unfairness without any ado.

The specifically lexical, and canonical, version of the difference prin-

9. For a different coverage of some of the points in this section, see the Appendix to Derek Parfit's "Equality and Priority," which anticipates some of what is said here, but with which I am not in full agreement. For one disagreement, see section 5.

ciple[10] represents distribution 5, 10 as unambiguously superior to distribution 5, 8: it is not even *a* point, against the former distribution, that it displays greater inequality. There is nothing especially privileged about equality, on the canonical view: faced with the task of judging a distribution, a proponent of the lexical principle is entirely indifferent to whether or not it displays an inequality and, if so, how much. But a valuation of equality as such persists unofficially in the repeated tendency of Rawls and Rawlsians to express the difference principle in one of its uncanonical forms, in which it says that inequalities are forbidden unless they render the worst off better off. They say it that way even though it is, strictly, incorrect, because of the special normative punch that the formulation carries,[11] which is owed to a relational intuition that is entirely foreign to the lexical difference principle.[12] The lexical difference principle is, moreover, inconsistent with the claim that "wanting to act on the difference principle" implies "not wanting to have greater advantages unless this is to the benefit of others who are less well off."[13] That desire is served by acting on the uncanonical difference principle only, and thereby refusing gains that don't harm but also don't help the worst off.

The two articulations of the difference principle, familiar and canonical/lexical, have different rationales. The thought behind the insistence in the familiar form of the principle that inequality must positively benefit the worst off[14] is that inequality is (at least prima facie) unfair, specifically to

10. See *A Theory of Justice,* pp. 83/72.

11. Some might suggest that they say it that way because they believe that the conditions of "chain connection" and "close-knitness" always obtain: under those conditions, what satisfies the uncanonical principle also satisfies the lexical principle. (See *A Theory of Justice,* pp. 80–83/69–72). But that alternative explanation is both inherently implausible and incongruent with the detailed contours of the uncanonical discourse.

12. Speaking about the difference principle before he has introduced its lexical variant, and referring to it, therefore, in its familiar, uncanonical, form, Rawls himself says (*Theory,* pp. 80/69) that equality plays no essential role in the application of the difference principle. But he is wrong about that: equality is a sufficient condition of satisfaction of the principle, in its uncanonical form. Rawls would have been right had he applied the stated comment to the lexical version of the principle.

13. *A Theory of Justice,* pp. 105/90.

14. See, for example, the statement on p. 135 of "Justice as Fairness," which is hard to reconcile with the lexical version of the difference principle: "an inequality is allowed only if there is reason to believe that the practice with the inequality, or resulting in it, will work for the advantage of *every* party engaging in it. Here it is important to stress that *every* party must gain from the inequality." (Emphases in original.)

those at the bottom of the inequality, but that it would be absurd to let a concern for those people dictate a prohibition on an inequality from which they benefit. The thought is that inequality exhibits a taint at the bar of justice, a taint that is removed (if it can indeed be thought to be only a prima facie taint), or sufficiently counterbalanced by, the Pareto improvement.

But there is no comparable case for endorsing the improvements to the better off that merely do not harm the worst off and that are enjoined by the lexical difference principle. The further inequality that the lexical principle allows and requires does not compensate for, or remove a taint of injustice: it is justified on the different basis that, if something is good for some and bad for none, then it is to be endorsed.[15] The unfairness of arbitrarily caused inequality is the starting point of a chain of reasoning that ends in affirmation of the lexical difference principle, but that principle shows no trace of the commitment to fairness that justifies that starting point.[16]

Note that, in its canonical form, the difference principle implies that *equalities* are unjust unless they render the worst off better off.[17] But Rawls never expressly drew that conclusion, and his indisposition to put it that way shows the persistence of the repressed egalitarianism that is expressly there in the familiar noncanonical statement of the difference principle. If Rawls happily says that inequality is unjust unless it does not harm the badly off, but doesn't happily say that equality is unjust unless it does not harm them, despite the fact that the latter statement is also implied by the lexical difference principle, then that can only be because inequality faces a case to answer that equality does not face. And

15. That is the strong Pareto principle, which mandates all weak Pareto improvements and that was introduced in n. 4 of Chapter 2.

16. As Robert Nozick noticed: "such a staggered principle does not embody a presumption in favour of equality of the sort used by Rawls." (*Anarchy, State, and Utopia*, pp. 229–30).

17. In its uncanonical form, the difference principle is silent about equalities, because its formulation presupposes, what Rawls believes, that inequalities are inevitable: "Social and economic inequalities are to be arranged so that they are . . . to the greatest expected benefit of the least advantaged" (*A Theory of Justice*, pp. 83/72). But unlike the canonical principle, it therefore does not condemn suboptimal equalities: and it is often stated in a fashion that implies that any equality, even one Pareto-inferior to another equality, is all right as far as justice is concerned.

that is inconsistent with the theory of distributive justice that identifies distributive justice with the lexical difference principle.

Why would one think that inequalities are unjust unless they benefit (or, indeed, don't harm) the worst off? Surely because inequalities that fail to satisfy the stated proviso are unfair. But why should the fact that it improves the lot of the worst off render an inequality *fair*? Why is 10, 6, however otherwise superior it may be to 5, 5, more fair than 5, 5, even if the worst off person's improvement from 5 to 6 *compensates* for the unfairness of widening the gap? If we contemplate a 10, 6 distribution, and we think it unjust because nothing about the parties justifies the disparity between them, our thought is not that the inequality renders the worse off person worse off than she needs to be. So when we discover that 10, 6 actually benefits the worse off person, our reason for thinking 10, 6 unjust stands, whether or not we are willing to countenance it as a beneficial injustice.

To be sure, it is possible to hold that, while inequality is always unfair and to that extent unjust, weak Pareto improvements on it are always, all things considered, preferable to it,[18] even from the point of view of justice. But no such position is consistent with Rawls's unnuanced endorsement of the lexical difference principle. The stated position notices the persisting unfairness in the inequality: the lexical difference principle, conceived as the whole simple truth about distributive justice, does not.

The moral arbitrariness claim plays a central role in the intuitive case (that is, not the original position case)[19] for the difference principle. But the moral arbitrariness claim is also part of the underlay of the authority of the original position itself as a device for choosing principles,[20] because the authority of that position presupposes a rejection of principles of desert and entitlement that are defeated by the moral arbitrariness claim. Thus Robert Nozick rightly protests that no believer in entitlement need respect the original position as a criterion of just principle, precisely because it foreseeably excludes the entitlement point of view.[21] But the original position also excludes a concern for how much one per-

18. See Parfit, *Equality or Priority?*, pp. 29–33.

19. See Barry, *Theories of Justice*, pp. 213–216, for the distinction that I am invoking here.

20. Another part of the motivation of the original position is the status of persons, or citizens, as "free and equal." That is supposedly modeled by the veil of ignorance.

21. *Anarchy, State, and Utopia*, pp. 198–204, 207–209.

son gets compared with somebody else: what I get by comparison with others finds no representation within that position, and believers in the claim to justice of relational equality should therefore be as wary of the original position, as a criterion of justice, as Nozick is. The original position gives no shrift to the motivating relational egalitarian thought that differences of fortune between people who are beyond their control represent the triumph of the "morally arbitrary." Since its denizens lack the very concept of justice, comparative rewards could matter within the original position only if those denizens were envious or spiteful, and so forth: being insensitive to justice, as such, they could care fundamentally about the fortunes of other people only from such lousy points of view. In fact, however, they are, *ex hypothesi,* mutually disinterested: nobody cares what others get, as such. The interpersonal-fairness aspect of justice, which motivated the whole enterprise, is thereby dropped at the front door, and there is no back door by which the equality favored by fairness might be reintroduced.[22] What we have is a striking discrepancy between the motivating thought about justice that precedes recommendation of the original position and the character of that position. And because the denizens of the original position are entirely insensitive to inequality as such, they elect the difference principle in its canonical, lexical form, which permits increases in inequality that do not benefit the worst off (as long as they do not harm them), and which, as we have seen, gives no weight to equality at all.

It might seem that the relational aspect of justice finds some proper representation within the output of the original position, not, indeed, in the difference principle but in the principles of equal liberty and of fair equality of opportunity. But the liberty principle is only superficially egalitarian: the liberty it confers is something that is owed to each person, whether or not others have it. By contrast, the fair equality of opportunity principle is indeed interpersonal, but partly for that reason, it is improperly derived: it is difficult to see why the denizens of the original position would be motivated to choose it. Why care, fundamentally,[23] about how much opportunity the other fellow has?[24] (I am not, of

---

22. Contrast the familiar "back-door" utilitarian derivation of equality from the premise that marginal utility declines as resources rise. Utilitarianism is fundamentally unrelational, but it thereby yields an egalitarian upshot.

23. That is, as opposed to because of its effect on how much opportunity I have.

24. For further discussion of the problematic position of fair equality of opportunity in the Rawlsian structure of principles, see the final paragraph of this section.

course, conceding that, by contrast, the first principle is properly derived: the question whether it is properly derived doesn't arise here, since it is not essentially egalitarian in its content.)

4. A Recent Argument for the Difference Principle

The disposition to double vision, in the construction of the case for the difference principle, expresses itself in a complex way in the following argument for that principle:

> ... the principle of negative equality of opportunity, which excludes deliberate discrimination, depends on the belief that the social system should not assign benefits or disadvantages solely on the basis of differences between people for which they are not responsible and which they have done nothing to deserve ...
>
> Yet a system which guarantees only negative equality of opportunity permits class inequalities [which are equally undeserved] to develop ... It must [therefore] be supplemented by positive provision of the resources that will permit each potential competitor to develop his natural abilities and therefore to be in a position to take advantage of his opportunities. That is what Rawls means by fair equality of opportunity.
>
> *The same reasoning* leads him further. Even under a regime of fair equality of opportunity, undeserved inequalities would continue to arise ... people are not equal in natural ability, and their natural or genetic differences will continue to affect the benefits they gain from interaction with the social and economic order. Yet this too is morally arbitrary, for people are no more responsible for their genetic endowment than for their race or the economic status of their parents. Consequently a just society will counter these undeserved differences in benefit to the extent that it can do so without hurting the very people whose arbitrary penalization it is most concerned to rectify, namely, those who come in last in the socioeconomic race. Hence, the difference principle.[25]

I ask: is Nagel right to characterize the reasoning in the step to the difference principle as "the same reasoning" as that which governs the argument's earlier steps? I discern a striking disparity of treatment: while social disadvantages are to be fully counterbalanced, or counterbalanced as much as possible, in the name of removing morally arbitrary inequal-

25. Thomas Nagel, "Rawls and Liberalism," in Samuel Freeman (ed.), *The Cambridge Companion to Rawls*, pp. 78–79: passages in brackets, and italics, added.

ity, disadvantages that are due to differences in natural ability are not similarly counterbalanced but regulated by the disequalizing difference principle.

What explains this disparity of treatment? Natural assets are, of course, untransferable, and compensation for natural asset deficits cannot, therefore, proceed by direct redistribution. But many social assets, such as a cultured family background, are also untransferable, yet that does not extinguish the aspiration to equality at the stage of the argument at which fair equality of opportunity is derived. Instead, compensation for social disadvantages proceeds through substitute resources. Why not proceed similarly at the end of the argument, with respect to natural disadvantages? Whether or not one should do so, would not that proceeding have better, indeed, exclusive, title to be called "the same reasoning"?

It might be said, in Nagel's defense, that sufficient ground for the disparity of treatment is indicated by the "to the extent that it can do so without hurting" clause: the reasoning to the difference principle is the same as before, but further governed by that surely sensible Pareto consideration. But the answer to that defense of the designation "same reasoning" is that there was the same case for that consideration earlier, where it nevertheless went unhonored. Why should not a similar clause be attached to the middle sentence of the middle paragraph of the exhibited passage? Why, in opting for fair equality of opportunity, are we allowed to "hurt the very people" whose morally arbitrary plight we are concerned to rectify?

Let me add some comments on the following *Theory* passage, whose burden is related to the Nagel argument that I am criticizing:

> No one deserves his greater natural capacity nor merits a more favorable starting place in society. But, of course, this is no reason to ignore, much less to eliminate these distinctions. Instead, the basic structure can be arranged so that these contingencies work for the good of the least fortunate.[26]

My first comment is that, once again, the relevant egalitarian counterproposal is not to "eliminate" or "ignore" the distinctions but to com-

26. *A Theory of Justice*, 1999, p. 87. In the original 1971 edition, the parallel passage on p. 102 lacks the middle sentence of the excerpt and has, instead, this pair of sentences: "But it does not follow that one should eliminate these distinctions. There is another way to deal with them."

pensate for them, where they would otherwise induce undeserved inequality.[27]

My second comment is that the passage lacks the disparity of treatment of natural and social inequalities for which I criticized Nagel. But that is because, so far as I can see, the passage[28] contradicts Fair Equality of Opportunity in favor of a more comprehensively maximinizing posture. For Rawls here allows unequal starting places in society, provided that the worst off benefit as a result. For this and other reasons, one wonders about the strength of Rawls's commitment to the lexical priority of Fair Equality of Opportunity.[29] (Gustav Arrhenius points out[30] that capitalism, which systematically induces unequal starting places in society, is inconsistent with Rawlsian fair equality of opportunity. Given that fair equality of opportunity is lexically prior to the difference principle, how then can the difference principle be neutral, as Rawls claims it is, between capitalism and socialism? Under the officially stated lexicality, the difference principle comes too late for capitalism to be allowed. But, of course, it is allowed.)

5. A Contractarian Argument for the Difference Principle

Parfit writes:

> ... An objection to natural inequality is, I have suggested, one of the foundations of Rawls's theory. And Rawls himself claims that, in an account of

27. That is the grand strategy of Otsuka's *Libertarianism Without Inequality*: see, especially, its first chapter.
28. That is, as it appears in both editions of *Theory*.
29. Compare *Justice as Fairness*, p. 163, n. 44: "Some think that the lexical priority of fair equality of opportunity over the difference principle is too strong, and that either a weaker priority or a weaker form of the opportunity principle would be better, and indeed more in accord with fundamental ideas of justice as fairness itself. At present I do not know what is best here and simply register my uncertainty. How to specify and weight the opportunity principle is a matter of great difficulty and some such alternative may well be better." Compare, too, *A Theory of Justice*, pp. 74/64, which seems to say that the achievement of fair equality of opportunity is impossible. See, also, Arneson, "Against Rawlsian Equality of Opportunity," pp.77–112, for a compelling case against the lexical priority of Rawlsian fair equality of opportunity. As Arneson remarks: "According to Rawls's principles of justice, possession of native talent entitles one to special advantages to which the untalented are not entitled, advantages which constrain the commitment of justice to helping the disadvantaged, under certain circumstances" (p. 85).
30. Private Communication.

justice, equal division is the natural first step, and provides the benchmark by reference to which we can defend our final principles.

As Barry notes, this suggests a different way to defend Rawls's Difference Principle. First we argue for equality, by appealing to the arbitrariness of the natural lottery. Then we allow departures from equality provided that these are not worse for those who are worst-off. This explains why, in Rawls's phrase, the worst-off have the veto, so that benefits to them should have absolute priority.[31]

In Rawls's own words: "Because they start from equal shares, those who benefit least (taking equal division as the benchmark) have, so to speak, a veto.[32] And thus the parties arrive at the difference principle."[33] Here's the thinking: justice gives no one the right to more than anybody else. So we start with equality, and everyone has the right to insist on it. But it would be irrational to insist on it when an inequality would benefit all: nobody has reason to veto that inequality. Hence the difference principle applies.

I have two replies to this further attempt to reconcile the difference principle with its egalitarian background. The first reply, which occupies the next two paragraphs,[34] exposes a discrepancy between the reason why the worst off have a veto and the content of the principles that their veto is said to lead them to select. The discrepancy is greater in the case of the lexical difference principle, with which I begin. Suppose the initial equality is 5,5,5. Then A, the first person in that sequence, can forbid a move to 4,6,6. But why can he not also forbid a move to 5,6,6? Why should the veto take this particular form, in which *A* can veto all and

---

31. "Equality or Priority," p. 39, citing Barry, *Theories of Justice*, Chapter 6.

32. Is that supposed to mean that those who benefit more have no such veto? But why shouldn't everybody, including the prospective greater gainers, have a veto? To be sure there is no reason, Rawls supposes, to expect greater gainers to use their veto, but that must also hold for the lesser gainers, if the argument is to work.

33. *Political Liberalism*, p. 282. The characterization of the persons in question as "parties" might suggest that the veto introduced here is part of the apparatus of the original position. But it is not. Rawls is here reviewing "intuitive considerations" (ibid., p. 282) that bear on the question, "By what principle can free and equal moral persons accept the fact that social and economic inequalities are deeply influenced by social fortune, and natural and historical happenstance?" (ibid., p. 281). Cf. *Theory*, 1999, p. 131, where the same veto is within the original position. (The relevant passage did not appear in the 1971 edition of *Theory*.)

34. And which is the fruit of discussion with Michael Otsuka.

only changes that would make him less well off in absolute terms than he would be under equality? Why, in other words, may he not also veto those weak Pareto improvements that do not benefit him (and thereby block the emergence of the lexical difference principle)? If the case for equality spoke directly in favor of people being at the particular absolute level that they would be at under equality, then it might make sense to grant people a veto specifically against falling below that absolute level. But the case for equality is not, except indirectly, a case for being at the particular absolute level at which equality obtains. Rather, the exclusive focus of the case for equality is the badness (the unfairness) of being relatively deprived—of being worse off than others, however well off or badly off in absolute terms one is. A veto merely against falling below the absolute level of equality is insensitive to the relational badness of equality. Such a veto offers no compensation to the worst off for the unfairness to them that a weak Pareto-improvement induces.

Consider now the familiar noncanonical difference principle, which permits only Pareto improvements over equality that benefit the worst off. The popular principle offers some compensation to those who end up worst off for the unfairness that falls upon them, since they are rendered better off in absolute terms than they would be under equality. But that compensation remains insensitive to the magnitude of the unfairness to which the weak Pareto improvement gives rise. The size of the gap that the improvement opens up between the worst off and those who are better off has no effect on the degree to which the worst off must benefit for the gap to be acceptable: any improvement whatsoever to the worst off will always do.

In further reply: whoever has a veto has it because the initial distribution is endorsed by justice. It does not follow that a unanimously agreed change in that distribution could then not also be endorsed by justice, but what would be the reason for saying that it was? One might think that what unanimity incontrovertibly does is to render the inequality that it endorses legitimate, but why just?[35] How can the principle that unanimity is here said to favor be declared, quite simply, just, given the standard of justice that made the initial distribution a demand of justice?

If it legitimates at all, then unanimity legitimates anything that it en-

---

35. For more on the relevant distinction, see subsection (iii) of section 3 of Chapter 7.

dorses.[36] Why would unanimity not render legitimate even a distribution under which the worst off were worse off than anybody needed to be? But no one could think that such a distribution was therefore through-and-through just. In a perspicuous (counter-Rawlsian) representation of the attitude of the non-veto-using worst off, they say, "This unequal distribution is unfair to us: there is no good reason why we should have less than others. But since we get more (or at any rate, not less) in this distribution than we do under equality, we won't oppose it."

6. What Is the Moral Arbitrariness of Talent Differences Supposed to Show?

Some say that it is a misinterpretation of Rawls to attribute to him the view that distribution ought not to be sensitive to talent-explained differences in productivity. They think that the texts that might appear to say so in fact merely deny that distribution ought to be sensitive to talent.[37] They then infer that D2's unequal distribution does not, as Chapter 2 claims, contradict Rawls's foundational egalitarian idea. On the stated counter-interpretation, Rawls is saying that it does not justify giving more to the talented that they produce more (by virtue of their morally arbitrary superior talent), but he is not saying that the morally arbitrary character of what causes them to produce more is a reason for them not to get more product than others do.

My first response to the counter-interpretation is that Rawls's text sometimes flatly contradicts it (and certainly never expressly affirms it). Consider, for example, his criticism of "the liberal interpretation of the two principles of justice":

> While the liberal conception seems clearly preferable to the system of natural liberty, intuitively it still appears defective. For one thing, even if it works to perfection in eliminating the influence of social contingencies, it still *permits* the distribution of wealth and income to be determined by the natural distribution of abilities and talents.[38]

This implies that the income distribution should not be determined by the talent distribution, and not merely that the fact that an income distribution reflects the talent distribution does not justify it.

36. See my "Fairness and Legitimacy in Justice."
37. See, e.g., Samuel Scheffler, "What Is Egalitarianism?" especially pp. 25–26.
38. *A Theory of Justice*, pp. 73–74/63–64, emphasis added.

My second response to the counter-interpretation is not hostage to textual nuances. It is that if Rawls did not hold that talent differences shouldn't determine distribution, he would have no argument for the proposition that we are to begin with the equal distribution, D1. For it does not justify beginning with equality that talent differences do not justify inequality. As Derek Parfit pointed out, if talent differences do not justify inequality, one might as well begin with utility maximization as with equality.[39]

Let us consider more closely the two rival interpretations of the significance of the claim (henceforth, the "moral arbitrariness claim") that differences of contribution are caused by morally arbitrary talent differences. So far as I can see, neither my interpretation nor that of my critics delivers what is needed to render the case for the difference principle coherent.

Take the critics' interpretation first. Their interpretation does not, as I said, justify beginning with equality (or, indeed, with anything in particular). On the critics' interpretation, Rawls is saying that there is no desert or entitlement justification for inequality, but it does not follow that inequality faces a case to answer, with the second stage of the Pareto argument providing that answer. The supposed second stage would then just be an argument for inequality based on Pareto, not something that overturns a presumption of equality, and not, therefore, what I dubbed "*the* Pareto argument for inequality."[40] There is no initial presumption of equality, on my critics' view of the significance of the moral arbitrariness claim.

On my different view, that claim is indeed given as a reason for beginning with equality. But why merely for *beginning* with it? How does the moral arbitrariness of inequality cease to be *a* reason for equality because the Pareto consideration provides *a* reason against it?

In sum: My critic says that Rawls bases the starting point of equality on the proposition that (1) talent differences do *not* justify inequality, *rather than* on the proposition that (2) the arbitrariness of talent differences in some way justifies an initial equality—and (1) is consistent with the move to D2. I reply that (1) is indeed consistent with the move to an unequalizing D2, but that, by the same token, (1) does not motivate beginning with equality, that is, with D1. So either the case for the starting

39. "*Equality or Priority?* p. 12.
40. See the reference in the penultimate paragraph of section 1 of Chapter 2 to a "simpler" argument for inequality: that is the different argument that we confront on the critics' interpretation of the force of the moral arbitrariness claim.

point of the Pareto argument is inadequate or the case for its starting point imperils its inference.

On my view of the significance of the moral arbitrariness claim, the two-step structure of the Pareto argument is unjustified, and what one may justifiably say, if moved by the moral arbitrariness claim, is the following: "Let us see what may be said for and against an incentivizing inequality that benefits the worst off. How does it fare at the bar of fairness? Badly, because of moral arbitrariness. How does it fare at the bar of Pareto? Well. So there is one consideration in its favour and one against." Fairness fanatics will then eliminate the inequality, and sensible folk, like me, will tolerate it, while judging it to be unfair.[41]

The Pareto argument gains credence from its two-step structure, but, there is no justification for the sequencing, on either interpretation of the significance of the moral arbitrariness claim. What really happens is that Pareto is suspended when we focus on moral arbitrarinass and moral arbitrariness is suspended when we focus on Pareto. Clashing considerations in our political culture are misrepresented as appropriate to different stages of an argument. When we don't break our thinking up into these two myopic steps, when we properly contemplate both considerations at once, then the most that we can say in justification of inequality, on the basis of the claims that are here in play, is what I said in the foregoing paragraph, and that doesn't amount to a demonstration of the justice, without qualification, of inequality.

The inconsistencies in Rawls are there because they are in the normative culture, our liberal-democratic-social-democratic normative culture, that his thought embodies so well. *Of course* there is a case for equality. But *of course* there is also a case for departures from equality that benefit all, for no matter what (possibly "lax") reason. The problem is how to negotiate the inconsistency between those two "of courses." I don't think assigning one step in the argument to the equality norm and a second to Pareto addresses the inconsistency problem. The reason we begin with equality is the moral arbitrariness of the standard causes of inequality. We are then told that, if everyone can be made better off, there is no reason to stay with equality. But there is a (nonconclusive) reason to stay with it, to wit, the reason that we had to begin with it.[42]

41. See the final paragraph of subsection (i) of section 6 of Chapter 7.
42. For an interesting discussion of the force of Rawls's moral arbitrariness claim that is largely orthogonal to my own, see Nozick, *Anarchy, State, and Utopia*, pp. 213–227.

7. Chamberlain and Pareto

Initiated readers may have guessed that the names I use in Chapter 2 (D1 and D2) to designate equal and unequal distributions are drawn from Robert Nozick's exposition of his Wilt Chamberlain argument.[43] Nozick's D1 satisfies a principle of equality[44] chosen by an imaginary opponent: D1 is, therefore, *ex hypothesi* (*ex,* that is, Nozick's opponent's *hypothesi*) just. In the Pareto argument D1 is not *ex hypothesi* but prima facie just: its justice is affirmed by the proponent of that argument, with whatever qualification "prima facie" is supposed to signify.[45] So that is a significant difference between the two constructions. But there are also relevant similarities. Thus, in each case, D2 is to be endorsed because it is, supposedly, reached by unimpeachable steps from D1 as a starting point: D2, albeit in different ways in the two cases, is supposed to *inherit* or *preserve* the justice of D1. And another similarity, so I shall suggest, is that the two arguments are liable to similar sorts of objection.

One might think it a large difference between the two constructions that in Nozick the transformation of D1 into D2 depends on ideas of liberty and/or[46] justice, whereas the Rawlsian argument invokes nothing but the Pareto principle to turn D1 into D2. That is, indeed, the outward appearance, but there are some less manifest goings-on that diminish the stated contrast. For Nozick insinuates a Paretian[47] justification of the move to D2 when he urges that Wilt and his fans choose to transact as they do and therefore gain from their transaction, and that third parties do not lose from it, and therefore could object to it only out of (discreditable) envy. And Rawls's worst off man in D2 "would," similarly, "hesitate to agree to these differences only if he would be dejected by the bare knowledge or perception that others were better situated; and I have assumed that the parties decide as if they are not moved by envy."[48]

---

43. *Anarchy, State, and Utopia,* pp. 160ff.

44. Or, indeed, some other non-historical-entitlement principle, but we can here ignore the greater generality of Nozick's D1.

45. For puzzlement about that, see p. 112 of Chapter 2.

46. "And/or" because Nozick is somewhat unclear about the respective roles of liberty and justice in his Chamberlain story. See my "Robert Nozick and Wilt Chamberlain," *Self-Ownership,* pp. 19–20.

47. Despite his (in my view, entirely misguided from his point of view) approval of Amartya Sen's (in my view, mistaken) critique of the Pareto principle: see *Anarchy, State, and Utopia,* pp. 164–166. See Chapter 5, pp. 187–188 for why I think Sen is mistaken.

48. *A Theory of Justice,* pp. 151/131. The quotation that I present here is an amal-

And just as there is more Pareto than first meets the eye in Nozick's construction, so there is a subtextual appeal to freedom in the (surface-wise) more purely Paretian Rawlsian argument. I believe that I have demolished the manifest Rawlsian argument, which relies for its un-equalizing transformation on Pareto alone, but, as we shall see in Chapter 5, there is a way of refurbishing the Pareto argument by adding a premise about freedom of choice of occupation, and, once it is added, the Paretian Rawlsian argument moves closer to Nozick's D1/D2 argument.

Now several criticisms may be made of Nozick's argument, but one that is common in the literature,[49] and that Rawlsians are disposed to affirm, says that he fails to see that the principles that enjoin D1 also prohibit the move to D2: Nozick takes D1 as established, and he succeeds in disestablishing it only because he ignores what established it. And that objection is similar in shape to the one that I leveled in Chapter 2 against the Pareto argument. You cannot begin with equality because all inequalities are morally arbitrary in origin, and therefore unjust, and then treat an unequalizing Pareto-improvement as lacking all stain of injustice. Even if, contrary to the argument of Chapter 2, no Pareto-optimal equality is feasible, the Pareto consideration does not nullify the reason for regarding the inequality that it validates as a compromise against (at least one form of) justice.

8. "Can't" or "Won't"

When someone professes a principle that she appears not to practice, two questions that are distinct, but easy to confuse with each other, arise.[50] One question asks (1) whether the practice that appears to be out

---

gam of the 1971 and 1990 formulations. The 1971 had "regularities," which was corrected to "differences" in 1990, but the words "hesitate to" were mistakenly dropped in 1990, and the result contradicted what Rawls intended to say.

49. See, for example, Thomas Nagel, "Libertarianism without Foundations," in J. Paul, ed., *Reading Nozick*, pp. 201–202; G. A. Cohen, *Self-Ownership*, p. 28.

50. The distinction between the questions is related to points made on pp. 155–158 of *If You're an Egalitarian, How Come You're So Rich?* The title question of that book, as I intended it, allowed that its addressee's profession of egalitarianism was sincere, and asked: "*Given* your sincere belief, how do you justify your apparently discrepant behaviour?" Here I am asking, differently, how could your egalitarian be-

of line with the principle is really out of line with it. And if the answer to that question is yes, one may then ask, distinctly, (2) whether the person's profession of the principle is sincere, whether she really subscribes to it. If the answer to (1) is yes, then the person's adherence to the principle is, in a plain sense, not wholehearted, but can she nevertheless be wholeminded in her affirmation of it? That is, is it possible, nevertheless, that she really believes it?

We can, more particularly, distinguish these specific versions of questions (1) and (2): (3) Does someone who professes a belief in the difference principle but who goes for a disequalizing salary thereby act in contradiction of the principle she professes? (4) If so, can she really believe in the difference principle?

You will know that my answer to question (3) is yes: maximizing behavior contradicts maximinizing principle. But I have not expressly addressed (4), and it merits independent consideration. It would not merit much if philosophers like Richard Hare were right that appropriately conforming behavior is a necessary condition of principled conviction, but I reject that view.[51] The only way that Hare could say no to the (1)-type question and yes to the corresponding (2)-type question is by debiting the relevant agent with an incapacity to act on the principle she professes. Applied to questions (3) and (4), this might amount to adopting an extreme form of the Schefflerian position,[52] and claiming that the folk in question are not able to work at an ordinary wage, not, at any rate, when an extraordinary one is placed within reach. They can applaud government policy with full sincerity because it follows the difference principle yet not follow it in their own lives, because they can't.

On sensible non-Hareian assumptions, another answer to (4) is possible, according to which the maximizer allows that she could behave otherwise but expresses regret that she won't. She is nevertheless glad that government does as much as it can to promote the difference principle. She doesn't find it difficult[53] to vote for economic redistribution in the

---

lief be sincere? which is equivalent to: how can you really hold the egalitarian belief that you profess? (Despite the surface structure of the relevant utterances, sincerity is a property not of beliefs—there is no such thing as an insincere belief—but of its expressions.)

51. See *If*, pp. 155–156.

52. See Chapter 1, p. 51ff.

53. For relevant remarks on cost and difficulty, see *If*, pp. 171–174, and Chapter 5, pp. 203–204.

way that she would find it difficult to work productively for ordinary wages. Her desire to rein in selfishness, including her own, by coercive taxation is perfectly sincere. Such market maximizers say: "We indeed endorse the difference principle, but we know that we lack the will to work hard regardless of the incentives that are before us. So we call upon the state to do what it can."

These speakers are avowing a weakness in their moral character with respect to what they are disposed to choose to do. And because that is so, the non-Hareian non-Schefflerian reply to question (4), the "we could but won't apply the difference principle in our daily lives" reply, for all its realism, and because of its realism, differs from the Scheffler hypothesis in showing no prospect of vindicating the incentives argument at the bar of comprehensive justification: the "wouldn't" hypothesis has the talented confessing to motivation that violates the strict difference principle, as opposed to pleading an incapacity to live by it.

On either the Schefflerian or the non-Schefflerian hypothesis about human capacity and behavior, it is unrealistic to expect the strict difference principle to govern society. But it makes some difference whether the inappropriateness of the strict difference principle's reflects (à la Scheffler) deficient human ability or deficient human will. If we take it in the latter, and, in my view, more plausible way; that is, if they believe but are indisposed to practice a conception of justice that respects the root point that one should not benefit from what is morally arbitrary when others get less as a result, then so much the worse for them (or, er, for us), judged at the bar of justice, rather than for the intuitive idea (which, for all I'm saying here, might of course be challengeable on grounds other than the spurious one that people will not live by it)[54] that justice abhors the morally arbitrary. Earlier (see page 154) I suggested that if there were every other reason for thinking that justice abhors the morally arbitrary, then our inability to live by that statement could not make it false. Now I suggest, in parallel, that if there were every other reason for thinking that justice abhors the morally arbitrary, our unwillingness to live up to that statement could not make it false.

54. This would be an objection to it *as a rule of regulation*. For such rules, "ought" implies not only "can" but (at least typically) "will." If it is a reason not to adopt a rule that nobody can follow it, it is also a reason not to adopt it that nobody will follow it. These considerations lay bare the utter normative nonultimacy of rules of regulation. (For a fuller exposition of the present point, see pp. 253–254 of section 13 of Chapter 6).

Lest it be thought that I am being too severely moralistic here, let me emphasize that I am not saying that any particular quantum of blame should attach to high fliers.[55] I am aware that the flesh is weak, in both the "can't" and the "won't" senses, and that, since the flesh is weak, it is ordinary and normal for people to seek what they can get. What excites my criticism is not human frailty but a strategy of argument—the incentives argument—that purports to justify self-seeking behavior or to put it beyond the scope of justification. The flesh may be weak, but one should not make a principle out of that.

People who know and regret, for Schefflerian or non-Schefflerian reasons, that their own choices are bound not to serve the difference principle take their own infirmity into account when they seek to implement their principles at the political level to the (perforce limited) extent that law and policy can implement those principles. As Daniel Weinstock (mostly) aptly remarks:

> Many liberals have recognized that one of the reasons that institutions are required to constrain individual choice is that individuals are truly conflicted about social justice. Roughly speaking, they want to want to help, but they often find themselves wanting not to help. Institutions which make it easier for people to act on the basis of what they want to want, rather than on the basis of what they often in all-too-human fashion want . . . are a way out of this predicament . . . Thus, by dropping Rawls' requirement of well-orderedness from our picture of the just society, we might be able to resist Cohen's very ambitious claim that only a society in which people *choose* justly can hope to be truly just.[56]

It is not hard to agree that if a just society can consist of unjust people, if it does not need to be well ordered to be truly just, then it might count as truly just even if it is not well ordered. But this hardly shows that there can be a "truly just" society in which people shun justice in their daily lives, any more than dropping the requirement on pianos that they have keys might enable us to say that there exist keyless pianos. As Weinstock recognizes, the society he is describing is not just by *Rawls's* lights, since it violates a Rawlsian requirement of a just society, to wit, well-orderedness. But that is by no means an arbitrary requirement on "just society," one that we can "drop" without dropping satisfaction

55. See, further, section 6 of Chapter 3.
56. Review of *If,* p. 407.

of the predicate "is a just society" itself. I question the idea that a society can be described as "truly just" simply because its unjust people bind themselves, with full sincerity, against (some of) the consequences of their own disposition to injustice, by legislating, in the light of and against that injustice, which is a state of character that, *ex hypothesi*, goes on needing to be legislated against. Note "(some of)": the state cannot deliver as much justice as could be achieved if Weinstock's citizens wanted what they want to want.

Although Weinstock calls his society "truly just," he recognizes a substantial flaw in it. Not so James Meade, who proposes a similar construct but describes it as an "ideal" society, in which "each citizen develop[s] a real split personality, acting selfishly in the market place and altruistically at the ballot box": Meade thereby makes an ideal of the double-mindedness (or, better, double-heartedness) that induces others to raise skeptical questions about the liberal moral division of labor.

I agree with Meade that it is "perfectly possible for a rich . . . man to arrange his affairs" self-interestedly yet "to urge through the political process a change in the law which will work to [his own] disadvantage"; that he can "work politically for a system of taxation which will affect adversely all rich men and will result in a more equal distribution of wealth . . . or . . . for a legislative change which will impose a new charge on all the firms (including his own) in some competitive industry which is causing a problem of pollution."[57] But the characterization of that as an "ideal" arrangement strikes me as hasty. For Meade fails to register a relevant difference between the taxation case and the pollution case. In the pollution case, at least part of the effect of the contemplated legislation is to overcome a prisoners' dilemma. If a single firm stops polluting, on its own, it might go bust because it has to raise the prices of its products. Its more polluting rivals would then pick up its custom, and pollution would not be reduced. But if a market maximizer would prefer not to maximize, he does not always face the danger from acting solo that the reluctant polluter faces. When an individual talented person forgoes what market power would give him, or cheerfully pays high tax in a socially conscientious spirit, there can be measurable gains for badly off people without any consequent catastrophe, or even any independent and further disadvantage for the person himself. Why should what deserves to be called the "social *ideal*" lack such nonmaximizing behavior?

57. *Theory of Economic Eternalities*, p. 52.

I oppose Meade's description of selfish behavior within an altruistically designed structure as a social ideal, for a real-life society of people with different tastes and talents. But, in the absence of such differences, my resistance to Meade retires. Let me explain. Suppose that all citizens have the same tastes and talents, or at any rate that no differences among their tastes and talents would prevent an initial state-enforced equality of resources from reproducing itself under subsequent market-maximizing behavior.[58] Here the Meadian prescription would be sound, from a purely egalitarian point of view (as opposed to from the point of view of an egalitarianism enriched by a principle of community)[59]. But the required conditions will never obtain. Selfish market behavior in any real and therefore heterogeneous society will induce inequality of reward, and state intervention could mitigate but not (consistently with efficiency) reverse that tendency. That being so, an ideal egalitarian society is not Meade's but one in which citizens act altruistically at the ballot box *and* with some self-restraint in everyday life, for example, when they face high taxation that tempts them to withdraw labor: there needs to be an egalitarian ethos within civil society because the state cannot eliminate as much inequality that is adverse to the worst off as the state together with the citizenry can.

Our topic is not what an individual might be expected to do, no matter what others do,[60] but the nature of a just society. I might find it unbearable not to send my child to a good private school when private education is available, even though I believe that its availability contradicts educational justice. So I might vote with full conviction to outlaw private education, yet have defensible reasons for educating my own child privately.[61] But if it is my view that there should not be private education, then how should I regard a society whose ethos is so hostile to the

---

58. Selfish market behavior might be necessary on the stated assumptions, to preserve the initial equality (see the final paragraph of section 2 of Chapter 3): that fact forms part of the basis of Michael Otsuka's criticism of Ronald Dworkin's equality of resources scheme in Otsuka's "Liberty, Equality, Envy and Abstraction." It is also possible, under the right circumstances, to get justice from mere physics: see the queuing example discussed in the final paragraphs of section 3 of Chapter 5.

59. See my "Why Not Socialism?" section 2, pp. 60–67.

60. That is the topic of Chapter 10 of my *If You're an Egalitarian, How Come You're So Rich?*

61. For a brilliant discussion of the problem, see Adam Swift's *How Not to Be a Hypocrite.*

private option that hardly anyone takes it? Must I not think that such an ethos contributes to justice? And if it is for some reason impossible to prohibit private schooling by legislation alone, must I not conclude that such an ethos is required for there to be justice with respect to educational provision?

Permit me to complete this section by offering a brief excursus on the kinship between the pessimism about human nature carried by both the Schefflerian "can't" and the non-Schefflerian "won't" answers to the sincerity question and the (historically qualified) pessimism about human nature that lies at the heart of Karl Marx's historical materialism.[62] That pessimism explains his claim that only capitalism, and only, therefore, an unjust society, can develop the productive forces to a high level,[63] which implies that they cannot be developed to that level by co-operative relations of production: below a certain high level of productive power, so Marx was convinced, cooperative relations, communism, would not be stable.[64]

Marxist pessimism is consistent with both "won't" and "can't" explanations of why humanity must pass through the capitalist vale of tears. Nor does the Marxist thesis that scarcity renders an unjust society inevitable presuppose either hard determinism or soft determinism or their disjunction or anything else by way of an answer to "the free will question."[65] Historical materialism is a theory about what explains what in

62. It was, in my view, "because he was needlessly pessimistic about the social consequences of anything less than limitless abundance that Marx needed to be so optimistic about the possibility of that abundance. A pessimism about social possibility helped to generate an optimism about material possibility" (*Self-Ownership*, p. 132). And Marx's particular pessimism about social possibility can have been grounded only in pessimism about human nature.

63. Some think that the stated claim puts Marxists in the embarrassing position that they must endorse capitalist exploitation because it alone can create the resources that make communism possible: see, e.g., Peter Mew, "G. A. Cohen on Freedom, Justice, and Capitalism," pp. 311–312. I propose a resolution of the tension between the Marxist commitment to advancement of productive power and the Marxist commitment to those at whose expense that advancement occurs in section 5 of "Peter Mew on Justice and Capitalism," which uses materials assembled at *History, Labour, and Freedom*, pp. 303–304.

64. See my "Marxism after the Collapse of the Soviet Union," *Karl Marx's Theory of History*, Chapter 15.

65. I here oppose the teaching of Isaiah Berlin's *Historical Inevitability*. See, further, my *History, Labour, and Freedom*, p. 81.

history, not a theory about *how* it explains it in the sense of that question in which a full answer to it requires a stance on a deep metaphysical issue. We can all agree that, if Etna erupts, it is inevitable that people will run away, even if some of us think that the inevitability is purely causal, while others of us think that it manifests predictable but "contra-causal" human *choice,* and still others of us think still other things.[66] So, similarly, the historical materialist thesis that a cooperative structure that is highly productive is infeasible in advance of abundance can be spelled out, at the level of individual motivation, either à la Scheffler or otherwise (or, of course, drawing on both Scheffler-like and non-Scheffler-like considerations), and also in conjunction with any metaphysics of the will that passes muster.

9. Human Nature and Constructivism

I should like to remark on a change of formulation by Rawls, across two otherwise substantially identical texts, a change that is of some interest in relation to our disagreement about incentives.

In "Justice as Fairness," which first appeared in 1958, Rawls wrote:

> If, as is quite likely, these inequalities work as incentives to draw out better efforts, *the members of this society may look upon them as concessions to human nature:* they, like us, may think that people ideally should want to serve one another. But, as they are mutually self-interested, their acceptance of these inequalities is merely the acceptance of the relations in which they actually stand, and a recognition of the motives which lead them to engage in their common practices.[67]

There are, in my view, a number of obscurities and infelicities in this passage, and further ones in the paragraph from which it is drawn.[68] But I am at present concerned only to remark on the interesting fact that Rawls deleted the 1958 clause that I have italicized when, thirteen years later, he published a reworked version of the relevant paragraph in *A Theory of Justice.* Note in particular the contrast between the first sen-

66. See *History, Labour and Freedom,* pp. 72–75 for a reconciliation between the thesis of historical inevitability and sanguine claims about the opportunities and powers of human choice.
67. "Justice as Fairness," p. 140 (emphases added).
68. See section 16 of Chapter 1 above.

tence in the *Theory* passage that corresponds to the first sentence in the passage above:

> If, for example, these inequalities set up various incentives which succeed in eliciting more productive efforts, a person in the original position may look upon them as *necessary* to cover the costs of training and to encourage effective performance. One might think that ideally individuals should want to serve one another. But since the parties are assumed not to take an interest in one another's interests, their acceptance of these inequalities is only the acceptance of the relations in which men stand in the circumstances of justice.[69]

No explanation was given in 1971 of why the incentives are necessary to the stated ends, but it follows from my argument against Rawls's position on incentives that, if unequalizing incentives[70] are truly necessary from the point of view of the interests of the badly off, then they are necessary only because of an infirmity in human nature, to wit, a certain unjust selfishness, that is more or less acknowledged in the "Justice as Fairness" passage but that gains no mention, as such, in the corresponding *Theory* passage.[71]

69. *Theory*, 1971, p. 151 (emphasis added)/131 (in part): in the 1999 edition of *Theory*, no reason is given why inequalities might be productive. In the paragraph on p. 131 of the 1975 version that more or less reproduces the relevant p. 151 (1971) paragraph, the sentence from 1971 quoted above that seeks to illustrate how inequalities can help is deleted, and replaced by nothing (nor, needless to say, is there any reversion in 1999 to the 1958 "Justice as Fairness" remark about "concessions to human nature").

I do not know when Rawls made the indicated 1958/1971 change. "Justice as Reciprocity," which appeared, like *Theory*, in 1971, preserves the 1958 "concessions to human nature" formulation. It was published as part of a collection (Samuel Gorovitz, ed., *John Stuart Mill*), and collections often have long gestation periods. So I conjecture that it was completed before the *Theory* text was finalized.

70. Note that, unlike incentives to encourage effective performance, money required "to cover the costs of training" is not merely a matter of agents' motivations: the two considerations that Rawls brackets together here (and that he juxtaposes even more casually on p. 82 of his *Collected Papers*) are, in my view, of a very different order from the point of view of egalitarian justice: see the discussion of the contrast between them in subsection (ii) of section 6 of Chapter 7.

71. I by no means agree that (prerogative-exceeding) unequalizing incentives are necessary. I believe that this selfishness, and, too, our equanimity about it, are precipitates of centuries of capitalist civilization. (First capitalism destroys community. Then its defenders say that material incentives are necessary because communal ones

It is as though both the Rawls of 1958 and the Rawls of 1971 agree with Bernard Mandeville (and with Adam Smith) that what Mandeville called "private vices" make for what he called "publick benefits,"[72] that, in other words, human selfishness can be made to benefit everyone, but that the Rawls of 1971 is unwilling to acknowledge that it is indeed vices that are in question. I agree with Mandeville, and against *A Theory of Justice,* that that's what they are.

Rawls's 1958 position contrasts with his 1971 position along the lines of two contrasting rationales for the social-democratic position that recommends a capitalist market alongside a strong welfare state, a position that forgoes the more rigorous equality demanded by communists. The two points of view yield contrasting ways of characterizing the supposed need to offer unequalizing incentives to the better off as a means of benefiting the worst off. The first view, in affinity with the Rawls of 1958, says that the incentives-granting society, though imperfectly just, is the best that can be realized in the light of ineradicable human moral weakness; the second view, closer to the Rawls of 1971, says that incentives are morally warranted, because the talented have the right to refuse highly productive work in their absence. On one view, communism would be ideal, but it is more than what the poor dough of human nature can be made to rise to. On the other, communism would not be the ideal, because it represses the just demands of human nature. It seems that Rawls moved over time from more or less the first view to more or less the second.

Why did Rawls make this big change? I conjecture that it might be thought justified by the constructivism that he self-consciously embraced in *Theory* and that is not so apparent in "Justice as Fairness."[73] According to that constructivism, justice consists of the rules on which we would agree in a privileged choosing situation, in the light, *inter alia,* of

---

aren't powerful enough.) But those claims are not at issue here. And Rawls might have more circumspectly described the relevant concession as one not to human nature as such but to human nature as it manifests itself in the advanced market society that he always holds in view. One need not saddle him with the proposition that even people in small-scale hunter-gatherer societies display an unwillingness to serve one another.

72. *Private Vices, Publick Benefits* is the subtitle of Mandeville's *Fable of the Bees.*

73. Note, for example the constructivist recasting in 1971 of the significance of the fact that people fail to satisfy the "ideal" that is also mentioned in 1958. From being a comment on people's "motives" as such, it becomes an "assumption" about the parties.

(what are taken to be given) facts of human nature. Since justice is constructed with facts of human nature as assumptions that the search for justice presupposes, since "basic psychological principles . . . are known to the persons in the original position and relied upon by them in making their decisions,"[74] it seems impossible for constructivism to regard any such facts as manifesting a "vice" of injustice in human nature.[75] Perhaps, then, the 1958 sentence was dropped because it makes no sense within Rawlsian constructivism, according to which justice simply *is* the set of principles that an ideal choosing procedure says we should live by, all things considered, including the consideration of what people are like. It is difficult, within such a constructivist perspective, to acknowledge that a (supposed)[76] fact of human nature like selfishness shows people to be unjust. And that acknowledgment becomes still more difficult when constructivism comes to be understood specifically politically, in the late Rawlsian sense, as Rawls himself suggested, in a passage that broadly confirms my understanding of the development of his thought:

> a political conception must be practicable, fall under the art of the possible. This contrasts with a moral conception that is not political: a moral conception may condemn the world and human nature as too corrupt to be moved by its precepts and ideals.[77]

In a certain sense Rawls and I have the same picture of the trajectory of his thought, but I believe that the restrictions that Rawls imposes to reach his austerely political conception of justice leave the very concept of justice behind: that is one upshot of what is argued in Chapter 7 of this book.

---

74. *A Theory of Justice*, pp. 456/399.

75. This is not to say that Rawls must think it impossible that human beings are by nature incapable of justice: he might say that they are by nature incapable of it if they are unable to comply with any principles that would emerge from an appropriate constructive procedure. And Rawls thinks that they might indeed be unable to do so: see *Political Liberalism*, p. lxii. But that is different from saying that people might by nature be unjust, let alone that they might by nature be unjust for the reason that Rawls came close to accepting in 1958.

76. Whether or not people are indeed by nature selfish is here beside the point. See n. 71.

77. *Justice as Fairness*, p. 185. Note that "moral conception," in its second occurrence above, must be interpreted as "moral conception that is not political," for consistency with Rawls's view that justice as fairness is itself a moral conception, but one that is not not political: see Rawls, "Reply to Habermas," p. 406.

5

THE FREEDOM OBJECTION

---

1. Introduction

Egalitarians like me think that justice is fully served only if people's access to desirable conditions of life is equal, within the constraint of a reasonable personal prerogative, *deference to which informs the whole of the following discussion.* One consequence of our position is the idea that the only thing about people's labor that would validate the justice of a difference in the income that they get for it[1] is a difference in the burden of that labor, broadly construed (so that it encompasses the burden [if any] of acquiring the skill needed to perform it). If, being more talented and having suffered nothing special to acquire her talent, A produces more widgets per hour of comparably repugnant (or unrepugnant) toil than B, then justice forbids paying A at a higher rate per hour. If, then, A uses her capacity to control how hard she works to secure a higher rate of pay by refusing to produce as many widgets per hour as she could (working no more arduously than B) except at that higher rate, then she strikes a posture that sets her against just egalitarian principle. (And that is so even if her refusal is not strategic, even if she genuinely prefers to produce fewer widgets than she readily could: unless anything is said to the contrary, I have the standard case, not the bad case,[2] in view throughout.)

The egalitarian position's implication sketched in the foregoing paragraph is more immediately palatable than another one that I must now bring to the fore. The implication drawn above is comparatively palat-

---

1. That income excludes income received in consideration not of labor expended but of dependents, special needs, etc.
2. See Chapter 1, p. 57ff., and Chapter 2, p. 122ff.

able because, by hypothesis, the only difference between A and B is that A is more productive than B *within the same line of work*. Different types of work do not come into the foregoing example, and there is therefore no question of asking A to provide a type of work (as opposed to a quantity of effort and product) that she is unwilling to offer at the ordinary rate: we're just asking her to provide greater product than others at the ordinary rate, because she's more able than others and will consequently be as well off as they are (even) if she does so.

With freedom of choice of occupation, individuals choose not only how much toil to apply, as it was contemplated that A might do in the widget example, but also what line to work at, at the given rates of pay. And expecting people to use their freedom of choice in an egalitarian fashion seems more demanding in the case of work type: after all, people may strongly prefer not to do the job to which egalitarian policy assigns them, for no higher pay. In the widgets example there is only one type of job, which is equally a drag or a joy for everyone, but once we contemplate people's preferences across jobs, then, many would say, to demand equality is to be overdemanding: to demand an egalitarian policy in the face of the vagaries of preference appears more radical than to demand it merely in the face of people's different productivities, where their preferences do not differ.

The present chapter is devoted to discussing how radical the egalitarian demand really is, but I want to note before I proceed that the Pareto justification of unequal reward that was studied in Chapter 2 works, if it works at all, as much in the quantitative (choice of amount of labor effort per unit time) as in the qualitative (choice of type of job) case. The Pareto argument is so spare in its premises that it would apply to a world in which there was only one type of work and in which all that distinguished people was their power to produce in that one type of work. So the problem of asking people to choose, for no enhanced reward, a type of work, or a number of hours of work, that they disprefer cannot vindicate the Pareto argument in the entirely general form in which it is actually presented, even if it suggests that the Pareto argument is potent in a more restricted form, that is, in the presence of different types of work. (That is, of course, the real world, but that the Pareto justification recommends what it does for the unreal and simpler one-type-of-work world nevertheless illuminates, and discredits, it.)

In section 2 of this chapter I expound the "trilemma claim," which is that equality, freedom of choice, and Pareto are not co-achievable. I reply that they are indeed co-achievable if people believe in equality, and I defend that reply against various objections, including the objection that such a belief itself constrains freedom of choice, and the objection that the stated reply has a facile character. Section 3 addresses a specifically Rawlsian formulation of the trilemma argument, and I defend the proposition that my reply to the argument, which is substantially similar to the one I mount in section 1 to its not-specifically Rawlsian variant, is consistent with my reply to the basic structure argument in Chapter 2. I proceed to relate the present disagreement with the Rawlsians to the Rawlsian preference for a primary goods metric that excludes welfarist considerations, and I compare the freedom-reducing potential of Rawlsian maximinizing legislation on the one hand and Cohen-type moral inspiration on the other.

In section 4 a new trilemma is introduced, in which freedom of choice of occupation is replaced by freedom, that is, self-realization, within an occupation. I subject the new trilemma argument to a dilemma, which runs as follows. Either self-realization is a good on a par with others, in which case it readily enters the egalitarian calculus; or it is incommensurable with other goods and enjoys a certain lexical priority over them, in which case it is peculiar to use its sacrifice as a basis for claiming extra income. The section ends by exposing an important ambiguity in the idea that it is oppressive to ask a person to work at an occupation that she disprefers. Section 5 criticizes the "unequal income inference," which runs from the premise that it is impermissible to force a person to choose a dispreferred job to the conclusion that she may demand an unequalizing salary to perform that job. The final section explores parallels between selling one's labor and selling blood, kidneys, and sex.

2. Equality, Pareto, and Freedom of Choice of Occupation

Let me now take stock. The Pareto argument for inequality says that justice requires (or at least permits) movement from a properly favored initial state of equality, D1, to D2, an unequal state[3] in which everyone is better off than in D1. I replied that when D2 is possible, then so, standardly, is D3, a Pareto-optimal state of equality that is Pareto-superior to D1 and Pareto-incomparable with D2, but that is to be preferred to D2, if the basis for favoring the initial state, D1, is sound.

Now it is a corollary of the Pareto argument for inequality that the

---

3. Whose degree of inequality exceeds that which would be justified by a defensible personal prerogative: see the first sentence of this chapter.

strict egalitarian must either give up his commitment to equality or forbid Pareto improvements. If the argument is right, the Pareto principle dictates abandonment of equality (whether or not, as the Pareto argument also claims, that abandonment is required or permitted by justice). But if my reply to the Pareto argument in Chapter 2 is correct, then the argument fails, and that corollary dilemma is escaped: we do not have to choose between equality and Pareto.

But if the egalitarian does not face a dilemma, he may nevertheless face a trilemma, and that is the topic of the present section. Equality might be consistent with Pareto, but inconsistency might yet break out when we add freedom of occupational choice to equality and Pareto: the three, it is widely thought, cannot be realized together. And the trilemma proponent indeed claims that, although any two of (1) equality (2) Pareto-optimality and (3) freedom of occupational choice might co-obtain, we cannot have all three together, even if the equality component takes this weakish form: the relevant equality might be only that no one is *substantially* better off than others are with respect to *both* income and job satisfaction, better off, that is, on a scale that exceeds what a personal prerogative might justify. The relevant Pareto requirement is the (weak) one[4] that condemns preserving a state of affairs in which everybody can be made better off. And the freedom requirement is that people not be coerced into particular jobs, whether by direct state order or by something else that also deserves to be called "coercive."

To see the apparent inconsistency of (1) through (3), think of a talented person, the doctor-gardener, who is capable of each pursuit and prefers gardening at £20,000 a year to doctoring at £20,000 a year. She comes to prefer doctoring to gardening (at £20,000 a year) only when the reward for doctoring rises to £50,000. Now her doctoring at £20,000 would, unlike her gardening at £20,000, greatly benefit badly off people, and if she doctored at £20,000 she would have a much better life than most people have (even though a less good one than she would have gardening at that salary: what is peculiar about her is not how much she hates doctoring, for she does not hate it at all, but how much she loves gardening).[5] Then, on the egalitarian view, she conforms with proper principle only if she forswears gardening for doctoring, at the modest £20,000 salary, and therefore takes less pay than what would induce her actually to

4. See Chapter 2, n. 4.
5. It follows from these stipulations that the doctor-gardener illustrates the "standard case." See the end of the first paragraph of this chapter.

prefer doctoring, in the face of her unusually attractive alternative gardening option.

Here is A's preference ordering across the three relevant job-and-income packages that enter our consideration:

  a. A doctor's at £50,000: she is much better off than most people are in both job satisfaction and income.
  b. A gardener's at £20,000: she is much better off than most people are in job satisfaction (even more than she was in a) but not better off in income.
  c. A doctor's at £20,000: she is still much better off than most in job satisfaction, but she is not better off in income.

I further stipulate that the community preference ordering across the exhibited alternatives is c, a, b: it is worth at least £30,000 to the community for the doctor-gardener to give up gardening for doctoring.

The trilemma that the egalitarian is said to face runs as follows. If, in deference to equality and freedom, we freeze salaries at £20,000 and allow the doctor-gardener to choose her job, she will garden, and then both she and the rest of the community will be worse off than they could be: Pareto will be violated. With pay equal, and freedom of choice of occupation, we get the Pareto-disaster that consumers have no say in what gets produced (in this case, some package of gardening and doctoring services). But if, in deference to freedom and Pareto, we offer the doctor-gardener £50,000 for doctoring, then equality goes. And if, finally, in deference to equality and Pareto, she is forced to doctor at £20,000, then freedom of occupational choice is lost.

Let me make the general point without use of the doctor/gardener allegory. Unless consumer preference determines what is produced, Pareto optimality is breached. But consumer preference prevails only if labor shifts occupation in response to it. And short of allocating labor by command, and thereby violating freedom, the only way to induce the desired shifts is by overpricing (relative to equality of reward) what would otherwise be underfilled jobs, and thereby violating equality.

The argument associated with the trilemma—*the trilemma argument*—says that equality is unacceptable, because, realistically speaking,[6] it can be purchased only at the expense of at least one of human welfare and human freedom. And if it is true that (1) through (3) consti-

---

6. See p. 189 below for some explanation of the force of that proviso.

tute a trilemma, if one of the three stated desiderata must indeed be abandoned, then my solution in Chapter 2 to the original dilemma (one must choose between equality and Pareto) works only if and because it overrides freedom of occupational choice. If the trilemma obtains, the only way to get D3 (see the final paragraph of section 3 of Chapter 2) is by denying that freedom to the talented.

Although the trilemma thesis allows that each pair of the three states (1) through (3) conjoins compatible states, it need not be thought to imply that each pair of states is possible, since, taken individually, one or both members of a given pair might be impossible. (Perpetual motion is impossible, but in the available sense of "compatible" that I intend, it is perfectly compatible with perpetual bliss, whether or not that, too, is impossible.) So the trilemma thesis does not require that it be possible to force the doctor-gardener to doctor (well) against her will at £20,000 by, for example, forbidding people to hire her as a gardener. It might be that such forcing is impossible, because a shirking response to the force might be impossible to detect. But in the present understanding of the trilemma claim, and in my response to it, I shall proceed as though each pair of the three states of affairs is possible, in order to deal with the trilemma problem proper.[7]

What is the egalitarian to do? He cannot sacrifice equality without giving up his egalitarianism. So his choice appears to be between rejecting freedom or declaring against Pareto.

Old-style Stalinistically inclined egalitarians might have responded by setting their faces against freedom of choice of occupation. They might have bitten the bullet (they bit, after all, many comparable bullets) and declared that, if people have to be coerced into equality, then so be it. But my own inclinations are more liberal, so that way out is not for me. (In

---

7. The structure of the trilemma is not reproduced if we replace equality by maximin: there is no perfectly analogous (4) maximin/(2)Pareto/(3)freedom of occupational choice trilemma. For while it might indeed be claimed that (4), (2), and (3) form an incompatible set, that could not be claimed by someone who also believes that any two of them are compatible (in the way that each pair drawn from (1), (2), and (3) is presented as compatible in the original trilemma argument). For if (4) and (3) are compatible, then so are all three, for the simple reason that (4) entails (2). (Strictly speaking, maximin [when not interpreted as leximin] entails weak Pareto optimality, and leximin entails strong Pareto optimality. But there obtains the indicated structural contrast between the (1)/(2)/(3) and (4)/(2)/(3) trilemmas no matter how we interpret the maximin and Pareto principles.)

section 4 I study the implications of the stated piece of anti-Stalinist liberalism.)

There may be some egalitarians who would be willing to reject Pareto, but, again, not me. Let me therefore comment on Amartya Sen's claim that Pareto should anyway be rejected (quite apart from whether it conflicts with equality) since, so he says, it is inconsistent with the merest liberalism.

Sen's claim is embodied, *inter alia,* in his commentary on his celebrated Prude/Lewd example.[8] There exists a pornographic book that might be read by one or other, or neither (but not both), of Prude and Lewd. Lewd has two relevant desires: he likes to read pornographic books, and he would like Prude to read one, because he thinks doing so would corrupt Prude into liking pornography. So strong is that desire that Lewd would prefer Prude to read the book, rather than read it himself: his desire to corrupt exceeds his desire to enjoy his own corruption. For his part, Prude dislikes reading pornographic books, and he also dislikes Lewd reading them: he wants no one to read them, but he prefers reading the book himself to Lewd reading it: that way, he thinks, less danger lies. In light of the strengths of their preferences, Prude and Lewd agree that Prude (alone) will read the book. That is their joint first preference, and so it is required by the Pareto principle. Sen claims that the principle thereby endorses an illiberal result.

But that is a serious misdescription of the outcome. While Sen's result is undoubtedly interesting, I do not think it possesses the particular interest that he claims for it: I do not think that it demonstrates the "impossibility of a Paretian liberal." Let me express my dissent within the terms of Sen's Prude/Lewd example. When those characters sign their Pareto-optimizing contract, they do not sacrifice, or even waive, their liberal rights to decide whether or not to read the pornographic book: they simply use their rights in an unexpected way, because circumstances are rather special. Liberalism does not require that you exercise the sovereignty it grants in accordance with your other-things-equal first preferences, and without regard to what you might lose by doing so when other things aren't equal. The liberal right to decide what to read does not require me to read what I initially prefer to read, in advance of considering the full consequences of my doing so. There is no such restriction in the usual understanding of a liberal right. The Pareto solu-

8. See his *Collective Choice and Social Welfare,* pp. 79–81, 87–88.

tion to the Lewd/Prude problem reflects particular exercises of liberal rights, rather than their violation, and Pareto is inconsistent not with liberalism, in the sense of "liberalism" in which John Rawls and Ronald Dworkin (and I) are liberals, but with certain rather distinctive autonomist perfectionist values.[9] What Sen really shows is that, within the structures of possibility that liberal rights create, you cannot both be loyal to certain values and get what you would prefer (not all things considered, but) if you prescinded from those particular values.

Sen's result does not, then, justify a rejection of the Pareto principle, and I, for one, see no other reason for rejecting the Pareto policy: I am an egalitarian who would worry about institutionalizing equality (even though I would still consider it a requirement of justice[10]) if it made us all losers (other than in respect of gaining the equality value). But, since I am also unwilling to reject freedom of choice of occupation, it seems that I am driven to abandon equality, at the policy level. But I shall not abandon equality. I shall instead try to show that the trilemma is misconstructed, because of lack of clarity in the description of its freedom element.

If the supposed trilemma is truly trilemmatic, then we shall face trilemmas in many similar contexts. There will also be, for example, what I shall call the Titmuss trilemma. Let me display that trilemma, and an apparent solution to it, which suggests a solution to the trilemma that is the topic of the present section.

Richard Titmuss favored a system of blood donation with no payment for giving blood and no forcing of anyone to give blood. And he also favored an adequate supply of blood. So Titmuss wanted three things: (4) No payment for giving blood; (5) an adequate supply of blood; and (6)

9. On p. 217 of his "Liberty, Unanimity, and Rights," Sen formulates the liberal principle as follows: "Acceptance of personal liberty: there are certain personal matters in which each person should be free to decide what should happen, and in choices over these things whatever he or she thinks is better must be taken to be better for the society as a whole, no matter what others think." But when Prude and Lewd conclude their agreement, they have not sacrificed their "freedom to decide what should happen" any more than people generally do when they bind themselves contractually, and the agreement between Prude and Lewd therefore does not violate liberalism. Each "thinks it better" that Prude reads the book.

10. I don't have to give up the claim that justice requires equality, where that means that, for there to be justice, there must be equality, rather than that there must (unconditionally) be equality, because of the (unoverridable and always implementable) requirements of justice.

freedom to choose whether or not to give blood. (4), (5), and (6) correspond, respectively, to (1), (2), and (3) in the statement of the freedom of occupational choice trilemma (see page 184 above).

Now a trilemmatic critic of Titmuss would say: what if people are unwilling in sufficient numbers to give blood gratis, but willing to give blood if paid? Then not all three desiderata can be satisfied. You must then pay (at least some) blood donors, or put up with an inadequate supply of blood when you could have an adequate one, or forcibly conscript blood.

How should Titmuss have responded to that trilemma? By expressing confidence that a sufficient number of people might be moved (and, when Titmuss wrote, were in fact moved, in Britain) to give, through some combination of principled commitment and fellow feeling. Unless a person who gives for such reasons counts as giving unfreely, the trilemma is dissolved—and it is not plausible to say that willing donors give unfreely. I shall call that the "ethical solution" to the Titmuss trilemma, but that's just a name. To the extent that fellow feeling plays a role in the explanation of donors' motivation, some, who wish to use "ethical" narrowly, would think "ethical" an inappropriate label for the stated solution, and I need not quarrel with them.

Different trilemma claims should not be confused with one another. The trilemma claim with which I am concerned says that it is impossible, *under realistic conditions*, to have all three of freedom of occupational choice, equality, and Pareto. (It does not say that it is impossible to have all three under *all* conditions: it does not, for example, exclude that all three might co-occur by wildly improbable fluke.) A weaker trilemma claim, that it is not always possible to have all three, does not concern me. Titmuss did not have to claim that there would have been enough blood, right away, if, for example, the United States—which, when he wrote, paid blood donors—were to have switched immediately to a British system, and egalitarians do not have to claim that you can always have both freedom and Pareto with equality, regardless of the inherited political culture.

I suggest that an analogous ethical solution dissolves the egalitarian trilemma, that we may get all three of equality, freedom, and Pareto if the doctor-gardener chooses the stethoscope against his preference for the hoe as a result of some combination, as in the Titmuss solution, of principled commitment and fellow-feeling.

In his *Equality, Moral Incentives, and the Market* Joseph Carens

mounts an attempt at describing the nuts and bolts, the institutional realization, of such an ethical solution. Carens depicts a society in which
what looks like a standard capitalist market organizes economic activity,
but the tax system cancels the disequalizing result of that market by re-
distributing income to complete equality. There are pre-tax-profit-maxi-
mizing capitalists and workers who own no capital, but people acknowledge an obligation to serve others, and they therefore submit to the
taxation that effects a fully egalitarian posttax distribution of income.
Producers aim in an immediate sense at cash results, but they do not
keep the money that accrues, and they seek it out of a desire to contribute to society.

In the proposal of Carens, everyone ends up with the same income, regardless of his or her own labor contribution, but people nevertheless
gravitate to investment opportunities and jobs that are socially useful.
They know which opportunities and jobs are socially useful because of
the money "reward" associated with them, which is market-set, according to what consumers are prepared to pay for goods and services from
their posttax equal incomes. Pretax incomes are like Monopoly money,
since they are all taxed away by the government, which then provides an
identical stipend for everyone. People play this game because they believe in equality.[11]

In the Carens realization of the ethical solution people believe in
equality, so the talented, in particular, disbelieve that anything, including
their fortunate productive endowments, entitles them to better rewards
or better conditions of life. A, being one of them, consequently takes a
doctoring job at (posttax) £20,000: thereby a key presumption in the
trilemma argument, as I expounded it on pages 184–186, is falsified—it
is not necessarily true that, under the conditions that structure the doctor-gardener example, the doctor will (simply) choose £20,000, and eschew doctoring unless she receives £50,000. If we set aside her desire to
satisfy egalitarian principle and/or her sense of commitment to other
people, then she is unquestionably worse off if she chooses to doctor at
£20,000 than if she holds out for £50,000. But so, with corresponding
set-asides, is the person who chooses regularly to give blood, in comparison with what his condition would be if he did not give blood: it is, we
can suppose, a nuisance to give blood. Yet we do not infer that the

11. I am not endorsing the Carens solution. It has its flaws (see n. 38 of this chapter,
and p. 369 in Chapter 8) but it merits contemplation as a pioneering example of the
ethical solution.

Titmuss blood donor gives unfreely. Why then should that conclusion tempt us in the case of Carens's talented egalitarian?

The trilemma argument says that equality cannot be achieved, consistently with Pareto, unless people act unfreely. But the doctor-gardener does not act unfreely if she acts in an egalitarian way because she thinks it's right to do so, even if she would prefer, other things equal (which they are not, because of her egalitarian conviction) to do otherwise; or, differently, if she does the egalitarian thing because she likes doing the egalitarian thing, as such, even at cost to other things that she likes doing, such as gardening. And those two structures of motivation are plausible possibilities.

Notice that, in the ethical solution, the reason why Pareto counts as preserved is not that A is not worse off under equality: I do not need to deny that A's egalitarian choice makes *her* worse off. The reason why the ethical solution preserves Pareto is that the *others* are better off when A chooses to doctor at £20,000, whatever we want to say about whether A herself is better or worse off in that solution (which depends on how we are to reckon doing what you think is right in the calculus of well-offness, a matter that the proposed ethical solution does not require me to address).

One might doubt the organizational feasibility of Carens's scheme, whether, that is, it could work sufficiently well that both equality and Pareto are reasonably closely satisfied: a great deal of Carens's book is given over to arguing that the scheme's logical and empirical presuppositions can indeed be met, and there has been further work on such schemes by Carens himself and by Martin Wilkinson and Stuart White.[12] If no such scheme is feasible, then the trilemma objection prevails.[13] But the question I am investigating is the prior one whether a successful

12. See Joseph Carens, "Rights and Duties in an Egalitarian Society"; T. M. Wilkinson, *Freedom, Efficiency, and Equality,* especially Chapters 10 and 11; and Stuart White, *The Civic Minimum,* especially Chapters 4 and 5.

13. Nozick claims that liberty upsets an egalitarian pattern unless the following three conditions are satisfied: "(1) that all will most want to maintain the [egalitarian] pattern; (2) that each can gather enough information about his own actions and the ongoing activities of others to discover which of his actions will upset the pattern; (3) that diverse and far-flung persons can coordinate their actions to dovetail into the patterns" (*Anarchy,* p. 63, and see my *Self-Ownership,* pp. 29ff. for discussion). He thinks those conditions un-cosatisfiable, but allows that if they are satisfied then liberty is intact. It seems to follow that he would accept the ethical solution in principle, but doubt both that people could be so inspired and that, if they were, they would know what to do. Carens, Wilkinson, and others address the latter question.

scheme which works by (something like) moral inspiration would *count* as dissolving the trilemma. Does the ethical solution, *if* feasible, really reconcile the three desiderata of the trilemma?

The Carens proposal is that the three desiderata are satisfied when and if for ethical reasons talented people use their freedom to take jobs at (posttax) rates that merely self-regarding preference would have caused them to shun. But is it just rhetorical to call that a way of using their freedom? Should we say that they are, in truth, acting unfreely, because they are constrained by their own moral commitment? Or, perhaps, that they would be constrained by morality itself if morality were thought to include the contested egalitarian duty? But, the objecting questioner continues, we surely don't want morality to *constrain* people, so we cannot think that morality imposes such a duty.

Let me respond to the latter proposal first, by subjecting it to a dilemma made possible by the polyinterpretability of the term "constrain," as it appears in the latter proposal. Either the moral prohibition on murder counts as constraining or it does not. If it does, then it is false that we do not want a morality whose edicts are constraining. But if the no-homicide moral restriction does not constrain, then why should the no-inequality moral restriction be thought to constrain? So either morality doesn't constrain,[14] or it's no objection to occupational obligation being a part of morality that morality would in a certain sense constrain if that obligation were a part of it. In the relevant sense of "constraint," it does not follow from morality's anti-murder "constraint" that I act unfreely when I conscientiously refrain from murdering.

The first suggestion, that one might be constrained (not by morality as such but) by one's own moral commitment, perhaps deserves more consideration. Yet we do not normally think that whoever acts under moral inspiration acts unfreely. Why, then, should we think that someone acts unfreely if his occupational choice reflects a sense of social obligation?

There are a lot of very rich people in our market society who do not particularly relish work and who could get by without working at all,

14. The idea that morality itself might constrain, so Shelly Kagan has persuasively argued, embodies a category mistake, a kind of fetishization of what morality is: people who act morally are no more constrained by the laws of morality than people who get their sums right are by the laws of arithmetic (*The Limits of Morality*, pp. 137–38). For penetrating criticism of these Kagan pages, see Seana Shiffrin, "Moral Autonomy and Agent-Centered Conceptions," pp. 248–254. I am not persuaded that her critique, successful though it may be in other respects, touches the particular use of Kagan's argument that I make here.

but who do choose to work out of a sense of social obligation. We do not judge their decision to honor what they regard as a social obligation as an unfree choice. Why, then, should we so regard the decision of the doctor/gardener who chooses doctoring at standard pay out of a sense of social obligation?

Either the trilemma reflects a more general truth, or there is something about being inspired by egalitarian principle in particular that is supposed to make it hold. The more general truth would be that people do things that benefit other people only if they either benefit from doing so themselves or are forced to do so: that would disqualify the ethical solution. But the mooted general truth is false, for it entails either the falsehood that people never act out of generous or conscientious inspiration, with no prospect of benefit, in the relevant extrinsic sense, or the falsehood that such action is a species of forced action. If we stipulate that a person acts freely when and only when he does what he would most like to do, prescinding from his generosity and in disregard of the norms he endorses, then the trilemma problem is insoluble, but also uninteresting. On the stated stipulation, a morally inspired A then indeed acts unfreely if she agrees to doctor at £20,000. But then doing things for moral reasons always means doing them unfreely, and the initially interesting trilemma becomes a mere consequence of a peculiar account of the character of moral motivation.

If, on the other hand, morally inspired action is not by its nature constrained action, then it is difficult to see why the ethical solution does not work to dissolve the trilemma. Liberty, Pareto, and equality join a happy quartet when we add inspiration by principle and/or fellow feeling to the trio.

I say that the doctor who is willing to be one at ordinary pay because she believes that justice requires that choice is not thereby doctoring in response to pressure and she is therefore not unfree *because* she is pressured.[15] But others think that it remains a reason for rejecting the ethical

15. Compare Rawls, *A Theory of Justice,* p, 515/452: "A person's sense of justice is not a compulsive psychological mechanism cleverly installed by those in authority in order to insure [*sic*] his unswerving compliance with rules designed to advance their interests." In the realized just society "we can say that by acting from these principles persons are acting autonomously: they are acting from principles that they would acknowledge under conditions that best express their nature as free and equal rational beings" (ibid.). The real question is whether a duty not to take advantage of one's superior talent is among the principles of a just society. As I am in course of arguing, one cannot deny that it is on the ground that the duty restricts freedom: all duties restrict freedom, in the pertinent (irrelevant) sense.

solution that anyone who thinks herself morally obliged to forgo personal interest for the sake of equality is mistaken. They say that, since the relevant obligation does not exist, people do not act freely when they act out of (supposed) perception of such an obligation. Maybe you compute freely when you submit yourself to the laws of arithmetic, but you don't when you submit to (what are in fact) false arithmetical principles. According to this line of criticism, the Carensian doctor-gardener puts a restriction on her own choice because she has a false conception of what justice demands, a conception that contradicts her untrammeled right to choose her occupation. A person would be laboring under a comparable and similarly self-confining misconception if she chose to eat, dress, and paint her house in ways that pleased others because she thought that justice demanded *that*. (She would not be mistaken if she did those things out of affection for others, or, at any rate, not mistaken in the same way). The doctor-gardener is mistakenly binding herself, sacrificing her freedom, in not allowing herself to choose not to satisfy the interests of other people.

There might be something in this objection, but it cannot run as it stands, since both its premise (there is no egalitarian obligation) and its inference (it is therefore false that those who forgo higher pay act freely) are inadmissible here. Whether or not there is indeed an egalitarian obligation, it is question begging to deny that as a premise here, since the whole point of the trilemma is to produce an argument against the egalitarian norm, and the present move helps itself at the start to the desired conclusion of that argument. So the mooted move is inadmissible here: it would beg the question, in this debate, to say that a socially conscientious doctor-gardener was mistaken. And apart from the fact that its premise begs the question, the argument's inference is peculiar. For we would not normally think that falsehood in belief makes action conforming to that belief unfree. Rather, such action, if not to be judged unfree for other reasons, qualifies as a mistaken use of one's freedom.

The ethical solution says that freedom is secured by absence of legal obligation, and equality is secured, consistently with Pareto, through moral and/or quasi-moral commitment. But someone might say that although, strictly speaking, and as I have insisted, freedom is indeed secured by absence of legal obligation, and moral obligation does not compromise freedom, there is nevertheless no point or value in a freedom to choose between a and b if a alone is morally permitted. So the trilemma resurrects itself if we replace "freedom" by "valuable freedom."

But it is not true that there is no point in a freedom to choose between *a* and *b* when only *a* is morally permitted. Suppose *b* is letting someone die and *a* is saving her at little expense to me, or suppose *a* is helping an old lady across the street and *b* is not helping her. Then my freedom to choose between such alternatives matters enormously, even though *b* is morally forbidden: the measure of how much the relevant freedom matters is not, as the objection now in view would have it, how weak the relevant duty is, but how outrageous it would be for the state to recruit me to these tasks. The value of freedom lies in the absence of coercion itself, not in the absence of legitimate moral demands that, being legitimate, cannot be absent.

Yet another objection might be put against the ethical solution, to wit, that it is all too easy. Of course, it might be said, freedom, Pareto, and equality co-occur if people decide to put a certain priority on a moral belief in equality. But that would be true whatever may be added as a third desideratum (of a sort that is consistent pairwise with each of freedom and Pareto) to the freedom and Pareto pair.

I have two responses to this objection.

First, if the solution is indeed trivial, why doesn't that show that there was something wrong with the problem, to wit, that it was always easy to solve, and could have been thought otherwise only because of elementary errors, such as a false view of the implications for freedom of ethical inspiration? Why must an acceptable solution to the trilemma imply that the problem that the trilemma formulates is hard to solve?

But in any case, and this is my second response to the "the ethical solution is trivial" objection, it in fact required some argument to solve the trilemma. It needed to be argued that the ethical solution actually works, in the face of various objections (and from the point of view of this book, it is supremely important that it should work, since this book promotes the centrality of ethos within the concerns of political philosophy).

It was useful to discuss the trilemma at least as a means of separating out and disputing claims that are mistakenly thought to lend it force. We can perhaps summarize the position we have reached as follows. Either the people of a society believe in equality or they don't. If they do, the prospect of finding a way of reconciling it with freedom and Pareto seems bright. If they don't, then it is likely that equality can be instituted (if at all) only through some unacceptable combination of force and manipulation (effected, for example, by clever economists). It cannot, in any case, be a reason for people *not* to believe in equality that it requires them to reject at least one of freedom and Pareto: it doesn't. The trilemmist says: "We shouldn't be egalitarians, because equality requires a sacrifice of either Pareto or freedom." To which I reply: "That isn't so, because, if we were egalitarians, we should be sacrificing neither." And that reply isn't trivial. It requires the defense that I have tried to provide.

3. Equality, Pareto, and Rawlsian Liberty

I have thus far been speaking of freedom intuitively, rather than in some specifically Rawlsian sense of the term. I now want to examine a Rawlsian objection to my claim in Chapter 2 that the difference principle selects in favor of D3 and against D2, where those are, respectively, a Pareto-optimal equality and a Pareto-optimal inequality. Within the Rawlsian objection, as it is formulated below, "liberty" is to be understood as the liberty mandated by Rawls's first, and lexically prior, principle of justice.

The Rawlsian challenge runs as follows:

1. The liberty principle is lexically prior to the difference principle: it is forbidden to improve the material condition[16] of the worst off in violation of the liberty principle.
2. The liberty principle mandates freedom of choice of occupation.
3. The move from D1 to D3 denies freedom of choice of occupation.
4. The move to D3 cannot be justified on the basis of Rawls's difference principle.

The second premise of the argument can be questioned. The liberty principle was originally conceived, in *A Theory of Justice*, as a principle of civil and political liberty, and it is quite unclear that freedom of choice of occupation can be regarded as an instance of civil or political liberty. Freedom of occupational choice is not, moreover, mentioned by Rawls himself in canonical statements of the liberty principle,[17] and, while there

---

16. Not their condition *tout court*, for it is thought to be beneficial to the worst off to put liberty first, when society is beyond the condition of severe scarcity. Under the "general conception of justice," nothing is permitted to take precedence over improving the condition, *tout court*, of the worst off.

17. See, e.g., *A Theory of Justice*, p. 61/53, and "The Basic Liberties and Their Priority," p. 5 (= *Political Liberalism*, p. 291).

is an affirmation of freedom of occupational choice elsewhere,[18] it is no-where claimed to be part of the liberty principle itself.[19]

For the most part Rawls lists freedom of choice of occupation dis-jointly from the liberty principle, and, for that reason,[20] one may wonder what, precisely, its warrant is, within the machinery of the original posi-tion. But albeit with some decrement of systemic orderliness, premise 2 could be weakened to mandate freedom of choice of occupation, as such, that is, as it were, on its own. The really problematic premise in the argument is, however, 3. For the ethical solution is consistent with the lexical priority over the difference people of freedom of occupational choice, since that freedom is, for Rawls, legal freedom of occupational choice, and no legal duty to choose a particular occupation is affirmed in the ethical solution. Pace premise 3 of the argument above, then, the move from D1 to D3 does not contradict freedom of choice of occupa-tion in the relevant sense.

It is true that, in the passage on exhibit, Rawls expressly mentions only incentives offered by society as motivators here, and not also the moral convictions and fellow-feeling that operate in the ethical solution, but he could not resist the solution by excluding those motivations. Since he could not, they do not contradict his liberty principle. Apart from the inherent untenability of the idea (see page 192) that a moral duty to act in an egalitarian way is itself restrictive of freedom, no such duty re-stricts freedom in the Rawlsian, basic-structural, sense. Rawls is oppos-ing forced labor, not egalitarian inspiration. It could not plausibly be thought to be a violation of their Rawlsian liberty that people have and are noncoercively induced to act upon a duty to help old ladies cross the street. Why then would it be a violation of their liberty if they had, and

18. See *A Theory of Justice*, p. 272/241 and, in similar vein, the lists in "Social Unity and Primary Goods," in *Collected Papers*, pp. 362, 366, "Kantian Constructivism," p. 526 (= *Collected Papers*, p. 313), and "The Basic Liberties and Their Priority," pp. 22–23 (= *Political Liberalism*, p. 308).

19. For exceptions, see *Justice as Fairness*, p. 64, and *Political Liberalism*, pp. 232, 335. At ibid., p. 228, Rawls appears to associate freedom of occupational choice with fair equality of opportunity rather than with the liberty principle, and at *A The-ory of Justice*, pp. 241–241, it appears to be aligned with both principles, in some sort of amalgam. (I am indebted, here, to a private communication from Samuel Freeman.)

20. And also because of uncertainty as to which principle it is supposed to follow from: see the previous note.

were noncoercively induced to act upon, an egalitarian duty that restrains their market seeking?[21]

The essence of my reply to the argument laid out in the second paragraph of this section is that the Rawlsian principle of freedom of choice of occupation excludes coercion but not morally inspired motivation. But someone might now question the consistency between that reply and my reply to the basic structure objection in Chapter 3. For if I say that the liberty principle, and freedom of choice of occupation, conceived as a part of it, properly apply only to what the state does, how can I insist that the difference principle applies beyond what the state does?[22]

The objection is, however, misplaced. The liberty principle, too, applies beyond the state: it targets unacceptable coercion as such, not just state coercion. So, for example, it forbids citizens to prevent others from speaking, for example, by shouting them down in Union Square or by refusing them access to otherwise readily available halls. In respect of the first principle, people must surely do what the state does: permit and promote the relevant liberty. So, too, I more controversially say, must they do what the state does in respect of what the difference principle proposes: promote the interests of the worst off. (And in each case within the limits of a defensible personal prerogative.)[23]

21. Frank Vandenbroucke offers a powerful ad hominem defense (against the Rawlsians) of what is, in effect, the ethical solution:

> There is a crucial difference between acting out of moral commitment and being forced to act in a certain way. Consider the following example: Rawls stipulates, as one of the "principles for individuals": 'As a rational citizen or legislator, a person should, it seems, support that party (. . .) which best conforms to the two principles of justice. This means that he should vote accordingly, urge others to do likewise, and so on. (Rawls 1971, p. 335).'
>
> This bold prescription is—rightly—not seen as contradicting the political liberties. Rawls can simultaneously assert that the political liberties belong to the basic liberties and assert that justice demand that they be used to support one (his) conception only. Similarly, it would not be inconsistent for a contractualist to affirm that reasonable persons agree both on free occupational choice, as a fundamental liberty, and on moral maxims concerning their use of that liberty . . . if we assume, for the sake of moral argument, that total moral commitment to the aims of justice prevails in daily choices, there is no trilemma between equality, Pareto-efficiency, and freedom of occupational choice. (*Social Justice and Individual Ethics in an Open Society,* pp. 171–172)

22. I called this a "strategic contradiction" in an unpublished note of 1996. For an interesting discussion of whether there is indeed such a contradiction, see Paula Casal, "Mill, Rawls, Cohen."

23. Titelbaum's essay (see Introduction, p. 23) constitutes a powerful challenge to what is said in the present paragraph. I regret that I have not yet had the time to address it.

Consider, too, the principle of "fair equality of opportunity," which Rawlsian citizens seek to implement through legislation. Would it not be inconsistent for them to legislate in favor of that principle and then do whatever they can, within the law, to frustrate the principle, when, as may well be, they are in a position to do so? Racist attitudes contradict fair equality of opportunity,[24] but legislation cannot (thank heaven) penetrate to people's attitudes, or, if it can, it shouldn't, on grounds of freedom. It remains inconsistent for people to legislate against racism so far as they can, and then practice racist choice wherever the law cannot forbid them to do so . If you agree that these are inconsistencies, then why is it not inconsistent for citizens to use the state to pursue equality, or the difference principle, but to set such matters aside in the rest of life?

It is of the nature of liberty that it leaves choices open, and, therefore, it is of the nature of the liberty principle that it should apply to the structure of choice alone and be indifferent to the content of choice. It is not of the nature of distributive justice that it should be silent on the content of choice within the right structure. Accordingly, and as Arnold Zuboff says:

> It can be true that you ought to be free (in the relevant sense: i.e., no state coercion) to do what people ought (nevertheless) to morally reproach you for doing. So the liberty principle could say that you should indeed be free while the difference principle says that we should pressure you.[25]

At an early stage of my work on these matters, I asked a politically progressive academic surgeon whether he thought that surgeons were bastards to hold out for the huge salaries they are able to command or whether, on the contrary, he thought they had a right to hold out for them. His plausible and chastening reply was: "Of course they have a right to hold out for them, and of course they are bastards to do so." He thereby rightly rejected the facile assumption that governed the question I had asked him, to wit, that one could not have a right to do what was wrong.[26] I do not question the right of the talented to decide (that is, their right not to be coerced with respect to) how much they will work at various rates of remuneration. I question whether it is defensible for them to exercise such a right, supposing that they have it, in a

24. And also a just distribution of the social bases of respect: see Chapter 3, n. 46.
25. Private communication: compare the Vandenbroucke passage in n. 21 above.
26. See Jeremy Waldron, "A Right to Do Wrong," and David Enoch, "A Right to Violate One's Duty."

standardly self-seeking way, on the assumptions that motivate the entire Rawlsian enterprise.

Recall the guiding egalitarian idea of the present chapter (see its first paragraph), that both money and quality of work experience matter to people, and that both should therefore enter the egalitarian reckoning. Just as individuals trade the two desiderata off against each other in their intrapersonal comparison of the work/money packages available to them, so egalitarians should bring form and amount of work, as well as income, into their conception of equality and inequality at the level of basic principle. There is, to be sure, a certain vagueness or indeterminacy[27] in that prescription, but it shows its substance in the compelling rough-and-ready judgments that it justifies, such as, "It's true that he's not very well paid, but that seems not so unfair when you consider how enjoyable his work is."

Now it is impossible for Rawls to conceive income and quality of work as things to be balanced against each other in the reckoning of justice. Rawls's endorsement of an inequality-producing use of freedom of choice in occupation reflects no prejudice or oversight: it is inescapable, given that Rawlsian justice is blind to the distribution of everything except social primary goods, which are, by definition, (1) *all-purpose means,* that is, things a person needs to pursue his plan of life, whatever that may be; and which are therefore, so Rawls infers, (2) of *neutral* significance with respect to different plans of life. And they are also, so Rawls maintains, (3) *objectively* measurable.[28] Rawls argues that income

27. Chapter 8 defends the claim that vagueness and indeterminacy can inhabit principles of justice.

28. See *A Theory of Justice,* p. 95, and *Justice as Fairness,* p. 83, for emphasis on the objectivity of judgments about quantities of primary goods, and see sections 5 and 6 of Chapter 2 for a resulting problem about the status of burdens of labor. Rawls's insistence on the objective measurability of the *distribuenda* of justice is in line with the requirement that whether or not principles of justice are satisfied must be publicly ascertainable. Chapter 8 is an extended criticism of that requirement.

This is not the place to question whether all the items on Rawls's list of social primary goods (rights and liberties, opportunities, income and wealth, and the social bases of a sense of self-worth: *see A Theory of Justice,* pp. 92/79) do indeed have the general characteristics enumerated above. The match of list to criteria has been chal-

has all of those features, and it takes some ingenuity to controvert him on that score.[29] By contrast, we must agree, quality of work experience plainly has none of them. It is not an all-purpose means, but, at least for many people, much more an end than it is any kind of means: many care enormously about the quality of their work, even if others look on work mainly as a means of getting money. And unlike his income, the quality of a person's working life is very difficult to gauge.[30]

Now *as long as Rawls excludes quality of work experience from the metric of justice, he needs to put job choice beyond the reach of egalitarian principle in order to prevent the difference principle from enslaving the talented.* For if the difference principle were allowed to govern job choice, within the frame of a resources metric, then the talented (and not only the talented) would have to work as much as they possibly could, at whatever job(s) they were most productive at, and regardless of how repugnant the work was to them, as long as their work increased the goods bundles available to those with the smallest bundles.[31]

I do not think that prescinding from the quality of people's work experience is defensible at the bar of egalitarian justice, whatever obstacles there may be to taking full account of it in practice.[32] Rawls believes

---

lenged: see, for example, the powerful case against the strong Rawlsian contrast between utility and primary goods put by Allen Buchanan in "A Critical Introduction to Rawls's Theory of Justice," p. 29. (In Rawls's later writing, primary goods are no longer all-purpose means of neutral significance *tout court,* but things persons need in virtue of their higher order interests as beings possessed of "the two moral powers." This refinement does not affect the problems that I am raising here.)

29. My mother used to say: "Whether you're rich or you're poor, it's good to have money." There are, nevertheless, good objections to the claimed neutrality of Rawlsian primary goods: see Adina Schwartz, "Moral Neutrality and Primary Goods," and Thomas Nagel, "Rawls on Justice." Will Kymlicka replies to Schwartz and Nagel on pp. 886–893 of his "Liberal Individualism and Liberal Neutrality," and Rawls replies to Nagel in *Political Liberalism,* pp. 196ff.

30. Of course, the same might be said about such things as the social bases of a given person's sense of self-worth, but to pursue that thought would be to indulge in the questioning forsworn in n. 28.

31. J. Roemer and R. Howe assign this consequence to the difference principle, since they do not notice that Rawls avoids it by relegating the principle to a lexically posterior position. See their "Rawlsian Justice as the Core of a Game," section 4.

32. A defense of inclusion of quality of work experience in the metric of advantage is given in sections 5 and 6 of Chapter 2. The problem of the difficulty of gauging the quality of people's work experiences is addressed in Chapter 8.

he has sufficient independent (of the slavery problem) reason to reject nonresources, welfare, metrics. I think ignoring welfare in matters of social justice is ludicrous, and that Rawls's reasons for thinking otherwise are misplaced. The lesson of the present discussion is that the following positions form an inconsistent triad: (1) Rawls-style liberal neutrality (which compares, interpersonally, goods or resources bundles, and ignores the extent to which people's preferences are satisfied) (2) optimizing the condition of the worst off and (3) prohibition on slavery of the talented. Rawls and I both affirm (3). I reject (1). Rawls in effect rejects (2): he countenances income inequalities alternatives to which would make the worst off better off, on any metric.[33]

Let us compare further the Rawlsian and the egalitarian conceptions of job choice, in light of the value of freedom. Suppose that only A can do job *j*—it requires special talent—and job *j* is, moreover, the least disagreeable job that A can do. (A might be a quadriplegic, and the job, like Stephen Hawking's, might essentially involve only the use of one's brain.) Then no special incentive will be required to induce A to do *j*. But suppose that A hates job *j*. The Rawlsian response is: tough. The egalitarian response is that A should receive extra compensation. So once again, it is not egalitarianism but Rawlsianism, through its disparagement of the welfare metric, that threatens a slavery of the talented. To be sure, it will do so only in rather special cases, but the point of principle stands. That point is that Rawlsians cannot accuse an ethos-inclusive egalitarianism of being inherently oppressive, since the same case for oppression might also apply against a Rawlsianly taxed market, and, in any case, egalitarianism can't, unlike Rawlsianism, display equanimity in face of the danger that the talented, or anyone else, will end up with a job that she finds oppressive.

The maximinizing legislation that Rawls mandates itself reduces the freedom of choice of the talented in one relevant sense, namely, with respect to how extensive and favorable their menus of options are. A person's freedom to choose "how hard" to work[34] goes down if tax goes

33. An otherwise identical triad, with (2) replaced by *equality of social primary goods* (e.g., equal wage rates) is consistent, but not when Pareto optimality is added as a fourth requirement. Accordingly, Rawls-style liberal neutrality enforces a rejection of one of equality, Pareto and the slavery prohibition.
34. *Justice as Fairness*, p. 64.

up and his spending obligations don't go down, and it's a wholly contingent question how far that freedom gets reduced by Rawlsian legislation, in particular circumstances. In some circumstances, maximinizing legislation with no Cohen-like ethos will confine people more than maximinizing legislation with a Cohen-like ethos would confine them in other circumstances. And legislation, being enforced, will always confine them, whether more or less, in a stronger sense of "confine." There are no relevant general truths about freedom (in the sense of scope of choice) here so far as I can see.

We are not considering here the case of government telling people which jobs to take: that is excluded by legal freedom of occupational choice. But freedom is effectively confined by law that tracks Rawlsian justice. So how can Rawlsians claim that an egalitarian ethos that goes beyond obedience to law is not required by justice *because* it reduces freedom?[35] Rawls regards a policy as interfering with liberty *in the relevant sense* only if it infringes the basic liberties. For that reason he does not straightaway condemn lump-sum taxation because it is contrary to liberty. "To influence by taxation the trade-off between leisure and income, say"[36] is not in itself, for Rawls, to interfere with liberty. How, then, a fortiori, could an ethos with similar influence count as an interference with liberty? If it is all right to confine freedom by law that tracks justice, why may freedom not also be confined (and, indeed, in a weaker sense of "confined") by an ethos that tracks justice? Suppose that clever economists could so price options that a person's best option was always socially optimific. Would that count as a violation of legitimate freedom? Why should legitimate freedom depend on what economists are able to rig? Rawlsians, at any rate, have no grounds for condemning that rigging. But if such manipulation does not compromise freedom, why should conscientious conviction be thought to do so?

So the question persists: why might an egalitarian ethos be thought to be unacceptably demanding, when maximinizing legislation is not thought to be? Is it because it is particularly oppressive, in deference to that ethos, to have to *decide to do* the egalitarian thing? Is there an unreasonable burden on the will here? A complete reply to that argument

---

35. Compare Murphy, *Moral Demands in Nonideal Theory*, pp. 48, 50, on the relevance to demandingness of what he calls "passive" as well as "active" demands.

36. "Reply to Alexander and Musgrave," p. 253. On pp. 157–158 of *Justice as Fairness*, however, Rawls *does* say that "a head tax would violate the priority of liberty." But he does not explain why he there abandons the more circumspect position he took in "Reply."

could be modeled on the discussion in section 11 of Lecture Ten of my *If You're an Egalitarian, How Come You're So Rich?*, in which I reply to an analogous argument about taxation made by Thomas Nagel. But let me say a few words here about the "burden on the will" argument.

First, if indeed the ethos places an oppressive burden on the will that legislation does not impose, then that is precisely because people are free (in the relevant uncontestable sense) to decide what to do when the ethos, rather than coercive legislation, does the motivating. Nagel's case is a case against the burden that freedom imposes, and it is therefore no reply to my defense of motivation by ethos against the charge that it reduces freedom.

I do not, moreover, concede that motivation by ethos is to be rejected because it is oppressive. Consider the following analogy. Suppose we agree that, ceteris paribus, first-come-first-served is the right principle for distributing certain goods: we call that "the queuing principle." In normal conditions the principle is enforced by the visibility of the queue: queue-jumping is prevented by immediate censure and/or by coercion supplied, for example, by bouncers. Or, equivalently for present purposes, we can imagine an unusual queuing-enforcement mechanism that makes it physically impossible to queue-jump: you enter a one-person box in order to queue, and you physically can't enter any but (what is at the time) the last box.

With all of these we may contrast a system in which you queue by ticket from a machine with a number on it, but certain imperfections in the functioning of the machine make undetectable cheating possible. In that unusual (Gyges-type[37]) case, what is achieved by exogenous regulation in the usual cases can be achieved only by morally inspired self-restraint, and such self-restraint can indeed be a burden. But can anyone doubt that that self-restraint is in order, whatever the cost in "burden on the will" that it imposes? No one would doubt that, and the reason why no one would is that everyone recognizes the justice of the queuing principle.

Accordingly, I conjecture that the reason why people judge otherwise in the case of job choice is that they do not really believe in an egalitarian principle, or a strict difference principle, and therefore find the prospect of complying with such a principle particularly oppressive. It would fol-

37. See Plato's *Republic*, Stephanus 359–360.

low that the consideration of burden on the will cannot be an argument against requiring people to follow that principle.

4. Equality, Pareto, and Freedom in Work

Someone might say that section 2 failed to address the strongest possible version of the equality/Pareto/freedom trilemma. When that trilemma is formulated in its strongest form, she might say, the freedom desideratum is not freedom of choice of occupation but, as it were, freedom *in* one's occupation, the pursuit of an occupation that does not make a person's life oppressive and constraining but that allows her powers to flourish in a natural way. The freedom that is lost when the conscientiously inspired doctor chooses to doctor is not her freedom to choose what to do—the present critic can accept that the ethical solution of section 2 refutes *that* charge—but freedom as a feature of her subsequent life. The doctor may choose to forgo gardening, as freely as the donor chooses to give blood, but what the doctor thereby forgoes is so significant that she then lives an unfree life: the slavery of the talented belongs not to her act of choice but to what she is choosing.[38] The Titmuss donor is not comparably unfree, simply because she forgoes nothing of comparable moment. Consider what we should think, with respect to her freedom, if the Titmuss donor spent three hours every day giving blood.

In this fresh proposal the third element in the trilemma is not freedom in the sense of freedom of choice (of occupation), but freedom as a feature of a person's working activity, the freedom, I shall say, of *self-realization*. Note that neither of these freedoms implies the other. A person could freely choose a high-wage job in preference to one where she would feel, and be, more free, and a person could be placed against her will in a job that engages and develops her powers. Section 2 said, to put its point in Martin Wilkinson's words, that "if people want to act on what they take to be a moral duty, that is a use of their" freedom, "not its denial."[39] But in the new trilemma the claimed unfreedom is not in the choosing of what is chosen, but in what is chosen itself: it is the choice in

38. Something like this was, in effect, Moon's protest against Carens. See Moon, review of Carens, pp. 146–150, and for Carens's revisionary reply, see his "Rights and Duties in an Egalitarian Society." I characterized the Carens proposal on p. 189ff. above with one eye on that revisionary, and improving, reply.
39. *Freedom, Efficiency, and Equality*, p. 147.

the sense of the option, not the choice in the sense of the choosing, that is said to be unfree.

Now, and here I begin my response to the new trilemma claim, freedom in the sense of self-realization comes in different amounts. Accordingly, one cannot say, in the general case, that freedom in the sense of self-realization is sacrificed by the conjunction of equality and Pareto: it is vastly more likely that, under equality and Pareto, some citizens lose some freedom (because they have less self-realization than they otherwise would) and some citizens gain some of that freedom. Accordingly, the trilemma disappears. (While it might be claimed that freedom of choice also comes in amounts, and that freedom of choice might be diminished for the talented but, as a result, enhanced for the untalented, I myself made no such claim. I addressed, and refuted, the section 2 trilemma argument in the binary terms that it itself employs, treating freedom of occupational choice as either present, *tout court*, or absent: but a binary construal is a nonstarter when the freedom in question is not freedom of choice but freedom as self-realization.)

The egalitarian can concede without qualm that a talented person's life is less attractive in an equal society than it is when she is at or near the top of an unequal one. And a diminished work experience may be a central way in which a person's life is less satisfactory than it might have been in a less equal society. But the whole point of restricting the goods in the doctor's life is to enhance the lives of less fortunate others: what the doctor makes herself endure in an egalitarian society, is, *ex hypothesi*, not worse than what others have to accept.[40] And when she endures that, others, *ex hypothesi*, benefit, and in some cases with respect to *their* self-realization. Accordingly, one cannot say that freedom in the sense of self-realization is incompatible with the conjunction of equality and Pareto.

An egalitarian can accept that the burden carried by most people whose services command a high reward would be larger in an egalitarian society, since they—we—benefit greatly by this one's inequality.[41] But

40. Strong support for the position stated here is provided by Richard Arneson in "Property Rights in Persons," pp. 213–214.

41. In an amusing (to me) passage, Jan Narveson refers to "the inequalities which we . . . hold dear, namely inequalities of wealth." Whether "we" hold them dear rather depends on who we are and where we are on the wealth scale. But if Narveson means his (or my) typical readers, then what he says is excusable. (See "A Puzzle About Economic Justice in Rawls' Theory," p. 2.)

that does not mean that equality imposes slavery on the talented. If they suffer slavery, then, it might be thought, so does everybody else: the talented are, after all, *ex hypothesi*, no worse off than anyone else. But in fact none of them can be said to suffer slavery: it's just that they all share equally life's benefits *and* burdens, and many are not as free, in the present sense, as they would be if they lived in an unequal society and were perched at or near the top of it. We should not speak of the "slavery of the talented" *just* because, for the sake of some improvement to the common human lot, the talented are asked to accept a life that is more similar to that lot than the one they now enjoy. (Our judgments about what does and what does not constitute slavery exhibit a certain dependence on our judgments of justice. Would we say that a law that forced slave owners to manumit their slaves effected a slavery of the slave owners?)

It is important to note that the rigor of the egalitarian demand is not unrestrained. The talented person is not asked to settle for a work/pay package that makes her less well off than other people are, all things considered: if she is a slave, then she is a peculiar one, since she is not in a specially unfortunate position. Nor is she asked to produce more than other people do just because she is endowed with ampler productive capacity. And she is also not asked to do something that she does not want to do at any price. The doctor-gardener, for example, has her price, to wit, £50,000, and she is therefore unlike someone who prefers gardening at £20,000 a year to doctoring at any salary. If our doctor-gardener says that it is harsh to expect her to be a doctor at, say, £49,000, since gardening is her heart's desire, we know that her heart has an even bigger desire, to wit, to be a doctor at £50,000. If we were to force her to be a brain surgeon at £49,000 by dropping her gardening wage below, say, £8,000, being a gardener at £20,000 a year is not the strongest desire of hers that we would thereby frustrate.

If the doctor-gardener's plea sounds powerful, that may be because of a confusion. One too readily infers from her preference ordering that it would be terrible for her to be a doctor, but that conclusion has to be false here, since she would then no longer illustrate the standard case: if it is terrible for her to be a doctor, then she would *not* be better off as a well-paid doctor than most people are. Here, *ex hypothesi*, the doctor-gardener is better off as a surgeon at £20,000 than most people are. She prefers gardening to doctoring not because doctoring is so bad for her, but because gardening is so good for her. To preserve the relevance of the example, doctoring for her has to be, by any standards, excellent. She illustrates the standard case only because, for her, being a gardener is super-wonderful.

If she works as a doctor, she will of course suffer regret that she is not a gardener. Some might say that such regret should not enter the egalitarian reckoning. But even if it has standing from an egalitarian point of view, notice that we cannot imagine that her regret amounts to a life-draining pining, since, *ex hypothesi,* she is not asked to endure a condition of life that is less eligible than the norm. She is simply asked to forgo sailing above the norm as much as the bargaining power associated with her (relatively) rare talent would enable her to do.

So when she expresses her regret, we can say: "Many of the rest of us also regret that our lives do not have a different shape. But despite your regret, and taking your regret into account, you remain a well-off person, and we are only asking you to be content with being rather better off than other people, as opposed to rather more than rather better off." Once again the doctor-gardener example appears powerful against my attitude to the standard case only because we think about the example in inconsistent ways: as truly instantiating the standard case, and yet as being a case where it is an especially awful thing for the woman to be a doctor, which is a description that cannot apply to the standard case.

Egalitarians ask more product or service of the talented, but not more sacrifice. It is an aspect of their greater talent that, usually, producing more product or service than others provide does not mean, for them, more sacrifice than others endure. The point is not to get as much as possible out of talented people, but to get out of them the amount of product or service (which is greater than normal) that comes with ordinary amounts of effort and sacrifice. The talented will, as a result, be less well off than they are in the unequal societies with which we are familiar. But it is to be expected that, with more equality, those at the top in an unequal society will be less well off. That does not justify a cry of "slavery," and I sometimes think that philosophers who believe in believing in equality misname it "slavery" only because they recoil (as I do, too: what reasonably well-heeled person with a fulfilling job would not?) at the thought of the lot that they themselves would have in a more equal society.

The old communist slogan, "From each according to his ability, to each according to his need" was at best poorly formulated, because it suggested that the more able should give more of themselves irrespective of the needs that might thereby be fulfilled or frustrated. To avoid unfair burden on the talented, or on anyone else for that matter, the first part of the slogan should, instead, be constrained by its second part: no one should be expected to serve in a fashion that will unduly depress her position, in comparison with others, with respect to what she needs to have to live a fulfilling life.

Now it might be contended that I have dealt too crudely with the revamped trilemma, in my treatment of the good of self-realization as just one good among others, and as therefore trade-offable against other goods, and against the self-realizations of others. Instead, it might be claimed, the good of self-realization is incommensurable with other goods. True, that does not itself forbid reducing one person's self-realization for the sake of enhancing another's. But the opponent might add that the stated incommensurability is associated with a kind of lexical priority that self-realization enjoys in the order of value, which is such that people cannot be obliged to forgo *any* self-realization for the sake of other people. They cannot be expected to settle for less of it than they might get.

The proponent of the revamped trilemma now faces a dilemma. *Either* we treat self-realization, and toil, as just sources of utility and disutility, so that performing a dispreferred job will then be seen as a burden in life commensurable with its other burdens and benefits, something negative that sufficient compensation could make worthwhile: *or,* as suggested in the immediately preceding paragraph, self-realization and, therefore, labor as its prime medium, has some sort of privileged status. And each alternative leads to difficulty for the proponent of the trilemma argument.

Suppose, first, that the trade-off account of the value of desirable labor is correct. Then, as explained above, we simply weigh that value with other things in a general well-being balance, and the talented person who demands more money for doing this job *just* because she prefers that other one is simply insisting on a package that gives her more benefit than others get: from an egalitarian point of view, she is simply being unjustly inegalitarian. If we yield to her, then we indeed lose equality, but we do not gain either freedom in the sense of self-realization or Pareto. There is nothing in the nature of freedom as self-realization that means it is there only if it is unequally distributed, and there is no Paretian benefit when we maintain an unequal Pareto-optimum in preference to an equal one.

To be sure, the Pareto-optimal equality may be unattainable, because the doctor-gardener refuses to doctor for less than £50,000. But it is often the case that Pareto is served only if people are allowed morally unjustified benefits. It frustrates Pareto—everybody loses—if a child's parents refuse to pay a kidnapper a ransom that is the only way of retrieving the child. Pareto is served only if the kidnapper gets his morally unjustifiable reward. So, similarly, we might think that justice requires A to doctor for £20,000, but that if, as a matter of fact, she would choose not to do so, then, since it would be outrageous to apply force to her, we should have to forsake equality for Pareto and pay her £50,000. We then settle for inequality at the level of policy, in the face of our egalitarian convictions.

On the alternative account of the relationship between self-realization and life's other goods, there are barriers to the trade-off reasoning employed hitherto in this section: there is a point at which[42] the value of work gains a certain lexical priority over the value of other goods. Accordingly, the doctor-gardener's life would in some unacceptable way be blighted if she became a doctor. But if one's work matters so much that it is somehow inappropriate to trade its value off against income, then how can it follow that the right thing to do is to lure the gardener into doctoring by offering a compensating amount of money, so that Pareto will be served? If the egalitarian solution to the trilemma threatens self-realization, then so does this opposing attitude. We cannot appeal to self-realization to vindicate the doctor-gardener's moral right to choose gardening, and then use that appeal to justify paying her more to follow an occupation in which she violates her self-realization.

If we affirm a conditional lexical privilege (conditional, for example, as just suggested, on reaching an income that covers basic needs) upon avoiding a job that is dispreferred because it prejudices self-realization, then we cannot also countenance the doctor-gardener's saying that she would doctor if paid enough to do so.[43] That avowal would be inconsistent with her claim that her interest in meaningful work is beyond price. She would be like a Christian greengrocer who protests against being forced to open on Sunday but who declares that, *because* Sunday is a day on which it is repugnant for her to trade, she would open only if she could charge double. Such a grocer could not credibly say: "Since it's

42. Say, somewhere beyond, but not way beyond, the point at which an income that covers basic needs is reached.
43. As in a number of Jewish jokes whose punch lines are variants of "Now you're talking!"

such a matter of anti-commercial principle for me not to open on Sunday, I shall do so only if I am granted the right to charge double if I do so." (Should she be allowed to charge more the deeper her religious conviction is?)[44]

But it can be objected that I have ignored a certain strategic possibility, to wit, that although (paid) labor is a medium of self-realization, it is not the only one. Sylvia yearns to write poetry, and for her that would be a supreme medium of self-realization. But there are no poetry jobs available, only jobs in gardening and in advertising. Sylvia takes the advertising job, at much greater expense to her self-realization than gardening would impose, because only the advertising salary buys for her the leisure time and space that she needs to write poetry. Her demand for a high salary as an advertiser on the ground that advertising goes against self-realization and self-realization is a lexically prior value is unabsurd: in this range of cases, the opponent slides off the second horn of the dilemma.[45]

If you are now inclined to ask, "Why should we pay her more so that she can get poetry when we don't pay him more so that he can get pushpin?" then that is a question that you must put to the proponent of the lexically-prior-self-realization/equality/Pareto trilemma. I have no commitment to distinguishing "higher" and "lower" goods here. Anyone who asks that question in its rhetorical mode is simply returning us to the *first* horn of the anti-trilemma dilemma (see pages 209–210). I have no polemical reason to prefer one horn over the other.

In sum, either we count self-realization in labor as just another element in the calculus of well-being, in which case it lacks a special position as something that no one can be asked to sacrifice. Or, because of lexicalities, self-realization in labor cannot enter such a calculus, and people have some sort of right to self-realization that they can invoke to resist the call on them for socially beneficial service. If, however, they

---

44. Cf. T. M. Wilkinson, *Freedom, Efficiency, and Equality*, p. 154: "Choices which forgo self-realization cannot be supported by appealing to the value of self-realization, whatever other justifications are available. Nor does self-realization support incentives. The point of incentives, of course, is to change people's preferences so that they choose different jobs. Self-realization does not support the payment of incentives when their effect is to lead people to give up self-realization for money."
45. That is not, of course, to say that the anti-egalitarian's case for paying such person a lot to do a dispreferred job is sound, but simply to acknowledge that it doesn't involve the particular incoherence that is spiked by the second horn of the dilemma.

sacrifice that right, then they are not entitled to incentive payments, unless they are used to fund special high-value pursuits, for the point of the right to self-realization is to protect self-realization, not to enrich people at the expense of their self-realization.

The following is a coherent position, in which we get the resultant of the forces of the egalitarian and the lexical self-realization thoughts. (I am not endorsing the position, but exhibiting it simply because of its inherent interest.) The doctor-gardener has a right to occupational choice, which is based on the lexical priority of self-realization and which she can use either to achieve self-realization as a gardener or to perform meritorious social service as a doctor: morality does not forbid her to put social before personal goals. What she may not conscionably do is use her right to occupational choice to enrich herself in a job that denies her self-realization (and does not indirectly promote it, by funding some high-quality leisure pursuit). She may take a job that thwarts her own self-realization, but not for the mere sake of a high income. Quality of work, we are here assuming, has lexical priority over income, and since no increase in income can compensate, we are supposing, for a decrease in the quality of work, we cannot require or expect the doctor-gardener to take a job that reduces the quality of her work experience. But we can readily deny that she has the option, morally speaking[46], of simultaneously sacrificing her own self-realization *and* frustrating equality, and we can therefore criticize her for taking advantage of her right to refuse to doctor *in order* to maximize her income. (If she says, "Don't expect me to doctor [at £20,000]: doctoring frustrates my self-realization," then we should say, "Fine." But we can then be aggrieved if she turns around and bargains her way into a £50,000 medical post.)

The more general form of that thought is: you are not required to sacrifice a certain value, but *if* you do so, then you must do so for restricted reasons, in a certain way, for example, for the sake of another significant value. No one can be required to risk her life by entering a burning building, but if you enter a burning building, then it is not permissible for you to save an endangered parrot instead of an endangered baby.[47] (You do not have to doctor, but if you doctor, you must doctor to serve society, at £20,000, not to make yourself rich, at £50,000.)

Some might take a different line (and I am here offering neither, since I

46. There is no question here of coercively excluding that option.
47. Shelly Kagan's example: see *The Limits of Morality*, pp. 16, 240.

do not myself endorse the lexical priority of self-realization). They might say that there should be a limit to how much self-realization the talented should even *consider* sacrificing for the sake of the mere benefit of the untalented. Perhaps such sacrifice is acceptable, at least in certain ranges, only if what is thereby enhanced is not the income but the self-realization of the untalented. Further questions are thereby raised, but enough has been said, I think, to defeat the trilemma in its revamped form, with freedom understood as self-realization.

Our question has been whether it is an oppressive denial of the doctor-gardener's aspiration to freedom to expect her to become a doctor at unenhanced pay. But there are two strongly contrasting interpretations of that oppression charge. If one finds repugnant the idea of expecting a person to do the job he or she disprefers because egalitarianism favors it, then there are two different reasons why one might find that repugnant.

In its first interpretation, the oppression claim says that it blights a person's life to require her to do a job that she disprefers, sometimes partly because, like the doctor-gardener, she will be oppressed by regret that she forsook a preferred job for no extra compensation. But where that is so, where the appeal is to the severity of the deprivation that the dispreferred job imposes, then no problem for egalitarianism is raised, because egalitarians take into account, when expecting or not expecting a person to do a job, the full costs of doing so for that person (including, if that is judged to be admissible, whatever depth of regret or value forgone there is in not doing some alternative job). Egalitarianism cannot demand that the doctor-gardener live a particularly bleak life (compared with other people's lives).

In its contrasting second interpretation, the foundation of the oppression claim is that a person has an untrammeled moral *right* to choose her occupation: it is *therefore* oppressive to expect her to doctor at no enhanced pay, regardless of the levels of advantage that the different occupations provide for her, by comparison with the enjoyments and burdens of other people. In the first interpretation of the oppressiveness claim, the doctor-gardener has a moral right to be a gardener, or a well-paid doctor *because* it might be oppressive for her to be a doctor at ordinary pay: the asserted danger of oppression is the foundation of the said right. In the second interpretation of the oppression claim, something like the opposite inference is endorsed: it is *because* she has the right to be a gardener that it would be (or, better, *count* as) oppressive to expect her to be a doctor. Egalitarians can endorse the first argument, where it really applies, and they can maintain that, absent further argument, the second argument begs the question against equality[48] by affirming a species of self-ownership that proponents of equality more or less expressly deny. They might conjecture that the oppressiveness claim seems to bring independent weight against egalitarianism only so long as its two interpretations are conflated.

I don't know how much people are inclined to confuse the two arguments that I have tried to distinguish, when they say that it's oppressive to deny a person the right to choose the job she wants. Do they mean that her life becomes an oppressive one, irrespective of whatever rights she may be said to have? Or do they simply mean that it is her *right* not to choose the dispreferred job? Confusion between these two questions makes it hard to focus on the only question that matters, which is the second one, since, as I have explained, if the dispreferred job would be oppressive in a non-rights-presupposing sense, that is, in a sense that does not rely on (but, on the contrary, is supposed to support) the idea that they have a right to choose the job they prefer, then the example poses no problem for egalitarians, because they condemn such oppression.

It has been suggested to me that I deal in inexplicably contrasting ways with the freedom challenge to equality, which I manifestly think warrants a whole chapter, and the self-ownership challenge, which I here summarily dismiss. But, apart from the—-here incidental—-fact that I did devote the better part of a whole book (that is, *Self-Ownership*) to its nonsummary dismissal, the difference is justified as follows. Freedom is a universal value with which egalitarians must make their peace by providing a credible interpretation of it that is consonant with their views. But egalitarians are not similarly required to make their peace with the highly controversial thesis of self-ownership.

5. The Unequal-Income Inference

Let me now review some elements in the foregoing presentation. In section 2 I expounded the equality/Pareto/freedom trilemma, with freedom

---

48. So long as the asserted right exceeds the limits of the personal prerogative by which equality should be constrained.

understood as freedom to choose one's occupation, and I defended what I called the "ethical solution" to that trilemma. Section 3 retained that first understanding of the trilemma and the stated solution to it, in confrontation with specifically Rawlsian formulations. In section 4 I interpreted the freedom component of the trilemma differently, as self-realization in work, and I defeated that new trilemma by posing a dilemma for its proponent: whatever he means by "self-realization," either it can be traded off, without aggregate loss, against income, or it cannot. If self-realization is indeed just one good among others, if it can be traded off, then it simply enters the aggregate egalitarian calculus: in the egalitarian proposal, some people get more freedom (so understood) and some less than they would get under less equalizing arrangements, but neither freedom (*tout court*) nor Pareto is sacrificed to equality. But if, on the contrary, self-realization cannot be traded off, because it has some sort of lexically prior special status, then that might indeed entitle the doctor to garden, but it will not justify luring her toward doctoring with the prospect of enhanced income, for that would prejudice the very value that is given special status in the argument. Finally, at the end of section 4, I exposed an important equivocation in the claim that requiring someone to choose a dispreferred occupation is oppressive.

I remarked on page 186 that an alternative and tougher egalitarian response than my own to trilemma-type arguments would be to accept that egalitarianism implies that the doctor-gardener should be forced to doctor, but to urge that the resulting equality justifies that forcing. I did not take that Stalinist line, and I am not attracted to it. But we have now seen that it does not follow from denying that the doctor-gardener should be forced to doctor that there is nothing wrong in her getting whatever pay she can get for agreeing to be one. The *"unequal income inference,"* which proceeds from the premise that A should not be forced to work as a doctor to the conclusion that anything goes, morally speaking, about the terms she sets for being a doctor, is invalid.[49]

49. For an excellent critical treatment of this inference in its more general form, see Richard Arneson's "Liberalism, Freedom, and Community," which is a long review of Joel Feinberg's *Harmless Wrongdoing*. In its more general form, the inference goes like this: because X should be free to decide whether or not to do A, there is nothing wrong in X's charging whatever she can get to do A. The criminal law violates that inference, since it forbids blackmail (charging for not revealing information) with respect to information that individuals have a right to conceal or reveal. Arneson defends the consistency, in this respect, of the criminal law.

Not only is the stated inference invalid, but some grounds for affirming its "no-forced-occupational-choice" premise are also reasons for rejecting its conclusion: the special importance of self-realization (call it ground (1)) was an example of that. When the deep meaning that work has for people is put as the ground of the premise that one may not be forced into some particular line of work, then the basis for the argument's premise is incongruent with its conclusion. On the lexical self-realization account, so we saw in section 3, a doctor who asks for a premium is misusing the freedom she asks us to grant her: it is wrong for her to use a freedom that is justified on the relevant high-minded grounds to bargain her way into wealth. The lexical self-realizer who affirms the conclusion of the unequal income inference is hoist on her own petard.

Four further putative grounds of the no-forcing premise will be considered here: (2) the principle of self-ownership, (3) equality of opportunity, (4) the right to contribute to society, and (5) my own reasons. It is of interest that in no case shall we find a ground that a Rawlsian in particular can use for the non-forcing premise that *also* permits affirmation of the inference's conclusion. Rawlsians cannot use (2) because they don't believe it, they cannot use (3) because it is not in fact a good ground for the premise, and they cannot use (4) because, whether or not it is a good ground for the no-forcing premise, it kiboshes, as (1) does, the unequal income inference from that premise. And my own reasons ((5)) for shrinking from forcing also fail to justify the Rawlsian conclusion.

(2) For libertarians, the ground of the no-forcing premise is the principle of self-ownership, which says that each person has over herself as a matter of natural right all those rights that a full liberal owner of an object has over that object.[50] When that principle grounds the premise of the unequal income inference, then, so far from contradicting the conclusion of the inference, the ground of the premise represents a more direct basis for that conclusion than the premise itself does. For among the rights of full liberal ownership are those not only to retain and not sell one's services but also to sell them at whatever price one can get. But Rawlsians cannot use this ground for the no-forcing premise, since they acknowledge no such right.

(3) A third candidate rationale for freedom of choice of occupation is

---

50. See my definition of "self-ownership" at *Self-Ownership,* pp. 213ff., and see, now, a definition that improves on mine, in Vallentyne, Steiner, and Otsuka, "Why Left-Libertarianism Is Not Incoherent, Indeterminate, or Irrelevant," p. 204.

equality of opportunity with respect to occupation. But it would be possible to have equality of opportunity to get available jobs without freedom of choice of occupation, provided that (somehow) the freedom was denied equally (maybe by permitting and forbidding the same jobs to everyone). (Note, by the way, that equality of opportunity to get available jobs will not *itself,* that is, other than as a [supposed] justification for freedom of occupational choice, justify unequal rewards.)

(4) Consider, next, John Rawls's "principle of open positions":

> It expresses the conviction that if some places were not open on a basis fair to all, those kept out would be right in feeling unjustly treated even though they benefited from the greater efforts of those who were allowed to hold them. They would be justified in their complaint *not only* because they were excluded from certain external rewards of office, but because they were debarred from experiencing the realization of self which comes from a skillful and devoted exercise of social duties. They would be deprived of one of the main forms of human good.[51]

Now the person with a complaint against a regime that denies the principle of open positions is here said to be fired by two grievances: exclusion from external rewards of office, "such as wealth and privilege,"[52] and exclusion from experiencing a realization of self from "devoted exercise of social duty." But the first grievance seems misplaced: a Rawlsian cannot assert a right to the rewards of office, save when an institutional structure is in place and a person has duly come to occupy an office to which certain rights to rewards are attached. Any such rights are post-institutional and therefore irrelevant when a foundational discussion (like the present one) about how to structure institutions is in place.[53]

51. *A Theory of Justice,* p. 84/73, italics added. For sapient criticism (that serves a different purpose from my own) of this passage see Richard Arneson, "Against Rawlsian Equality of Opportunity," pp. 98–100.

52. The phrase "such as wealth and privilege" followed "office" in the first edition of *Theory,* and although Rawls dropped it, I use it here to illustrate what Rawls had in mind (even when completing the second edition of *Theory*) by "external rewards," since they must have remained (at least) among the external rewards that he had in mind.

53. The fact that Rawls rewrote the passage (see n. 52) but left "not only" as it was strongly suggests that he did not intend "not merely because" in the sense of "not for the mere reason that," when he wrote "not only," both in 1971 and in 1990: on one

The second and more high-minded consideration that Rawls describes in the passage is a bona fide pre-institutional one. But when the point of freedom of choice of occupation is that second high-minded one, then it is a perversion of that freedom to use it to make more money. The stated purpose, here, of freedom of occupational choice is to enable one to contribute to society: yet the more one earns, the less, *pro tanto*, one contributes, the more one is withholding what one could (also) contribute. This Rawlsian ground for protecting labor against conscription therefore sits ill with paying the reluctant doctor a premium to induce her to doctor.

(5) Why would I not myself take the Stalinist plunge and force the doctor to doctor? My thoughts about that have not achieved a finished form, but I report them, for what they are worth, as they currently stand, even though I am not satisfied with them, and I know that they will be subjected to criticism.[54] I offer four reasons for not (trying to) force doctor-gardeners to doctor, reasons that are, severally, and in their full conjunction, consistent with believing that the uncooperative doctor-gardener behaves unjustly. The four reasons concern (i) counterproductive deterrence, (ii) information deficits, (iii) doing things in the right spirit, and (iv) not using a person as a means.

There are many things that we think people are obliged to do, *inter alia* as a matter of justice, that we would not seek to force them to do. Take, for example, the obligation to keep (even) important promises. One reason why we should not enforce noncommercial promises is that the prospect of penalty for nonperformance might deter people from making promises, to the detriment of both promisors and promisees. So, analogously, (i) the possibility of being conscripted to doctoring might deter people from acquiring knowledge and developing skills that might make them vulnerable to such conscription, with adverse consequences for the supply of doctors. Someone, for example, who doesn't want to be a doctor but is fascinated by biology might be deterred from pursuing a

---

interpretation of the former phrase, Rawls would not thereby have asserted, as his actual language makes him do, that the people in question had the distinct complaint, just questioned by me, about being denied external rewards. When I read the 1971 text, I hoped that Rawls had merely meant "merely" when he wrote "only," but my examination of the 1990 text dashed that hope.

54. At least from Michael Otsuka, who proposes to challenge them in an issue of the journal *Ratio* that is devoted to articles about this book and that is provisionally set to appear in December 2008.

university degree in biology and opt for his second, socially less useful, choice of a degree in gardening, if a degree in biology would make him vulnerable to conscription as a doctor. It might be suggested that, to get around this problem of deterrence, the state could conscript people to pursue the education and training that would enable them to contribute maximally usefully, within the constraint that they do not end up hating (more than people in general hate) what they do for a living. But to suppose that the state could know what it would have to know about people's powers and about their propensity to enjoy and disenjoy jobs, in order to run such a conscription scheme fairly, is quite absurd. And that is the second, epistemic, reason, reason (ii), against Stalinist forcing. For whereas it is fairly easy to know who promised what to whom, we cannot tell what people's total situations are exactly, and there is consequently a danger of coercing those whom we wouldn't coerce into a particular job (even if anybody should *ever* be coerced into a job) if we had knowledge about them that we can't have. I believe that the rough-and-ready "everyone must do his or her bit" principle that prevailed in the Britain of World War II was a principle of justice, despite an inevitable uncertainty as to whom it commended and condemned,[55] but it would have been grotesque to try to enforce it coercively, because one person's easy bit is another person's hard bit, and figuring out what's hard for whom is an unmanageable task. We similarly can't tell how much the doctor-gardener dislikes doctoring, or not without an enormously invasive apparatus. (It does not follow that she is as much at a loss as we are with respect to knowing the size of that dislike, and therefore whether her salary demand is defensible from the point of view of egalitarian justice.[56])

Those reasons against a policy of force say, respectively, that it can be counterproductive with respect to achieving its end, and that it can be impossible to apply it in a fair, because appropriately informed, manner. But suppose that we could efficiently force just the right doctor-gardeners to doctor. There would remain two strong reasons for not doing so.

To see the first of these, consider again the promising example, and observe that there is more satisfaction all around when a promise is kept voluntarily. A person wants to keep, and wants to know that he keeps, his promises for high-minded reasons, and it is difficult to achieve such a

55. See p. 353 of Chapter 8.
56. Cf. T. M. Wilkinson, *Freedom, Efficiency, and Equality,* p. 172.

condition of mind when one would be forced to keep one's promise anyway. And that consideration, (iii) that both the agent and people at large have reason to prefer that the right thing be done for the right reason, also applies to the doctor-gardener's choice.

(iv) A fourth consideration is that we should not use a person as a means (which is not to say that she should not, as it were, use herself as a means, in the interests of justice). With respect to the charge that she is being used as a means, both the Rawlsian economic policy that might make the doctor-gardener choose doctoring because of the restrictions that the policy places on her options and the Cohenian ethos that helps to nudge the doctor-gardener toward doctoring contrast with frog-marching her into that profession.

The last three considerations relate to the personal prerogative against which, for Nagelian reasons,[57] people must set their sense of their social obligations. That prerogative falls short of the absolute moral privilege conferred on personal economic decision by the Rawlsian view that market results, in a difference-principle constrained market, bear the stamp of justice as a matter of pure procedural justice. We can affirm a limited prerogative, but also believe that, for several reasons, we cannot say where the limit of the prerogative lies: with regard to that, everyone must make her or his own principled decision.

But does this mean we should prefer fewer doctors *freely* choosing to doctor at an ordinary salary to *more* doctors choosing to doctor, with (at least) some of them being forced to do so? Why should we prefer the first state of affairs, with respect to what is *ex hypothesi* a demand of justice? Because, for the reasons that I have been stating, it is sometimes right not to force people to do what they are obliged, as a matter of justice, freely to choose to do. The World War II "do your own bit" example shows that it's false that, if it's justice, then it's OK to bring it about by force.

The considerations adduced above sustain a rejection of the Rawlsian position that the choices of economic actors who comply with Rawlsian laws are beyond the judgment of justice, without committing those of us who reject that view to endorsing forced labor. And it is worth noting that a Rawlsian liberal could not comfortably refuse to force the doctor-gardener to doctor on the ground that people should do the right thing for the right reason, since he would then have to abandon his conviction that it is all right to get him to doctor by offering him extra money. I re-

57. See section 4 of the Introduction to this book.

ject both Stalinist force and Rawlsian inducement, in favor of an ethos of justice.

It has been objected to the foregoing account of my reasons for not applying coercion to occupational choice that it shows a tenderness toward agents that I would not apply in the case of enforced income taxation. But don't the nonpractical considerations against forcing, that is, reasons (iii) and (iv), apply equally against taxation?

Let us distinguish between ideal theory, which says what transpires in the ideal society, and nonideal theory, which applies to settings in which, among other things, citizens do not affirm and act upon the correct principles of justice. To fix ideas, let the nonideal context be one in which a wholeheartedly egalitarian government rules over a halfheartedly egalitarian electorate that voted for that government because the only alternative to it was a party that sought to promote laissez-faire.

In a truly just society, with full compliance, taxation on behalf of equality would not need to be coerced. But there might still be a state, that is, a central organizing body, that proposes a tax structure of egalitarian inspiration around which people would voluntarily coordinate. Informational problems would prevent the state from similarly (noncoercively) legislating job allocation. But if it could do so, under a properly prerogative-informed egalitarian principle, then I would see nothing wrong with that. And for all the reasons that were presented in section 3, that legislation could not be regarded as especially oppressive. It is worth noting that we think it justifiable to coerce or, what is relevantly analogous here, request, on pain of social disapproval, people to do army service when the threat is sufficiently urgent. So similarly, the more urgent the social need is, the more it weighs against personal preference in the matter of job choice.

In the case of nonideal theory, I do qualmlessly allow coercive taxation. For epistemic and deterrence reasons, coerced labor would remain unacceptable, but would it be acceptable even if there were no practical or epistemic obstacles to it? I think not: the taxation/forced labor contrast would stand even on that extravagant assumption (one so extravagant that it strains even my own extreme tolerance of extreme counterfactual suppositions). Income taxation forces you to give money on the basis of (fairly) readily determined information about your income. It does not assert a control over your behavior that exercises a knowledge of the intimacies of your personality, what pleases you, what bores you, and so forth. That control means manipulation of people on a scale to which only a crazed libertarian could think income tax comparable. Even if (a further extravagant assumption) people did not mind their whole inner economy being known by officials, they would have to be meeker than human to not mind that knowledge being used to tell them what to do.

It does not follow from the case I have presented that the roughly welfarist egalitarian principle that I endorse justifies no coercion. Coercive progressive taxation can be justified on the egalitarian welfarist ground that *on average* welfare is higher the more wealth a person has: we only need confidence in the averages, we need not invade individual psyches, to tax on a welfarist basis.

Suppose one wanted people to work harder, or more hours than they currently choose to do. Then the Stalinist procedure would be to order them to do so. But that rides roughshod over people's preferences, and if, to avoid that, one investigates those preferences individually, to produce a policy that is sensitive to important variations among people, then the "invasion of the inner economy" objection resurfaces. By contrast with both of those policies, so structuring people's options that, in the aggregate, more productive work will be forthcoming is much less destructive of freedom.

The progressive taxation case depended on the assumption that welfare is a monotonic function of resources. But a similar general versus particular targeting point can be made in cases where resource-welfare functions are more chaotic. Consider a library that charges no fee, or the same fee, to all, regardless of the prices of the books that they borrow.[58] One thought behind the policy is a thought to do with egalitarian fairness. We conjecture that people end up more equal, in the coinage that really matters, under the same-fee arrangement than they would under individual pricing. The policy operates coercively: those with cheap library taste are forced to subsidize those with expensive ones. But that coercion, operating as it does on a structure rather than distinctively on each individual, under a knowledge of the intimacies of his psychology, is manifestly less repugnant, and indeed, I would claim, wholly unrepugnant, from the point of view of the value of freedom, with which non-Stalinist egalitarians must come to terms, and which they can honor as much as anyone can.

---

58. For more on this example and its significance for debates about the currency of equality, see my "Expensive Taste Rides Again," p. 11.

6. *Blood, Kidneys, and Sex*

The unequal income inference fails because, in virtue of the kind of good or service that it is, it can be wrong to force X to yield up a good or service, even though X is not entitled to demand a price, or more than a particular (just) price, for that good or service: so if X should not be forced to work in a particular job, it does not follow that it is appropriate for X to ask for just any amount of money for doing that job. And the stronger point, we saw, is that some rationales for forbidding coercion of a service also tell against using the resulting freedom to make money out of that service. When it is said to be important for certain sorts of deep reason for a person to choose the type of work that he does, it is impossible to add that he is entitled to use the freedom being demanded merely to enrich himself. Indeed, the deeper the reason is for preferring job *j*, the less moral sense it may make to require extra money for doing the dispreferred job *k*. There might even be cases where one's willingness to do *k* instead is an inverse function of how well *k* pays: one will sacrifice *j* and do *k* out of duty, but not for monetary reasons. Compare a blood donor who says: "I will take the £10. That compensates me for my inconvenience. But I find it disgusting to be offered £500."

I proceed to further illustrations of the fundamental point. Many are shocked when they learn that indigent third world people have sold their kidneys (that is, one per vendor) for transplanting. They are not *just* shocked at the poverty that makes the kidney sellers do that, for they are not comparably shocked by other things that the same poverty makes them do, such as ride dangerously on the roofs of wobbly railway carriages. Now these shocked people, it goes without saying, would be more shocked still were someone's kidney obtained by coercive threat. So, once again, you can think it impermissible to force a service out of someone without thinking it unproblematic for that service to be an object of purchase and sale. And some reasons for *prohibiting* its coerced transfer are also reasons (even if not of the same strength) for *discouraging* a market in the object. You might, in parallel, think it outrageous to conscript blood, and *for related reasons* you might discourage a market in it.

The shocked people need not think that it is always shocking when someone gives up a kidney. They might not be shocked if someone gave one gratis to a friend or a relative or even to an anonymous kidney deficiency sufferer. They might say: "It is such a grave thing to yield a kidney that, if one does, then the reason for doing so should be correspondingly grave." The kidney vendor's financial condition might be so parlous that it is his best recourse, and one that should not be forbidden, but there is reason to deplore the character of that recourse all the same. Thus those Americans who do not think buying and selling blood is offensive might yet see something offensive in buying and selling kidneys, despite the fact that yielding a kidney is losing much more. They might say that it is precisely because it means losing something so much more significant than a pint of reproducible blood that a kidney should not be exchanged for money.

Consider, now, prostitution. Between this and the kidney case there are differences and similarities. There is the difference that giving up a kidney is under all circumstances *pro tanto* regrettable, while sexual giving is under some circumstances glorious. Yet there is the similarity that we may think prostitution (being paid to give sex) bad for reasons related to why we think rape (being forced to give sex) bad. We may think that in each of rape and prostitution, just as in each of forced kidney extraction and kidney selling, the wanted thing is yielded for the wrong reason.

One might condemn rape solely because it is a species of assault. In that case the condemnation of rape is consistent with indifference toward prostitution. Indeed, if one condemns assault simply because it is a breach of self-ownership, and the principle of self-ownership exhausts one's ethical armory, then, in parallel with the implications of the self-ownership justification (see (2) on page 216) of the unequal income inference, the very basis for condemning rape also confers unlimited license on prostitution. But if one condemns rape because it is forcing something that should be given only in love, or at least in desire, then that reason for condemning rape is also a reason for disapproving of prostitution. (It is a further question what institutionalization, if any, the disapproval of prostitution would help to justify: it would not follow that prostitution should be illegal. Nor would it follow that prostitutes, or their clients, should be condemned. But it would follow that it is a deplorable fact about a society that there is prostitution in it.)

Few think about labor in general in the way that most think about a prostitute's labor: it is much more widely held that one should never be paid for sexual services than that one should never be paid for services generally. In the widespread view, it is all right to sell your labor, though not, perhaps, for absolutely whatever you can get.

But I belong to the stated few.[59] I have some sympathy with the communist slogan that says "From each according to his ability, to each according to his needs." The slogan divorces labor, the exercise of ability, from income, which, it says, should answer strictly to need. In the communist ideal labor is given freely, like noncommercial love (though not, therefore, out of love). But the slogan is uncircumspect, since "from each according to his ability" places no limit on the expectation of service (see, further, pages 208–209). This is indeed the slavery of the talented, and it needs to be scaled down. Correspondingly, we need to say, instead, that in the communist view, labor, like love, should, if given, be given freely.[60] Prohibitions on rape don't justify prostitution.

The communist view has a place within familiar family norms. A relative who does house repairs for a living has a cousin who needs to have some repairs done. Each is reasonably affluent. The relative is busy and can do the work only on a Sunday. We can suppose that, under standard family norms, the relative is not obliged to give up his Sunday leisure and do the work, that it would be unreasonable for his cousin to prevail on him to do so. But the same set of norms may also declare that if the relative does offer to do the work, then he should not ask for payment. Nevertheless, if the relative chooses not to offer, then this might be judged Pareto-suboptimal, because he might well be keen to do it for a fee that the cousin would be keen to pay. But that's not how you treat relatives, and it's not how you treat fellow citizens, in a communist society.

59. Note that the strong position with whose statement I close the present chapter is not required by or for rejection of the unequal income inference.
60. Compare Karl Marx, *Economic and Philosophical Manuscripts*, p. 156: "Prostitution is only a *specific* expression of the *universal* prostitution of the worker, and since prostitution is a relationship which includes both the one who is prostituted and the one who prostitutes (and the latter is much more base), so the capitalist, etc. comes within this category."

II

RESCUING JUSTICE FROM . . .

6

THE FACTS

1. A Statement of My Thesis

This chapter concerns the relationship between facts and normative principles (or, as I shall call them, for short, "principles"). A normative principle, here, is a general directive that tells agents what (they ought, or ought not) to do, and a fact is, or corresponds to, any truth, *other than (if any principles are truths) a principle,* of a kind that someone might reasonably think supports a principle. Most philosophers who provide an answer to the question whether principles are grounded in facts say that (sound) normative principles, as such (and, therefore, all of them), are (at least *inter alia*) grounded in the facts of human nature and of the human situation. John Rawls expresses that belief when he says that "Conceptions of justice must be justified by the conditions of our life as we know it or not at all," for he does not mean thereby to contrast principles of justice with other principles that are not justified by facts about our condition.

The central thesis of this chapter (which is clarified in section 4) denies the stated belief. I argue that a principle can respond to (that is, be grounded in) a fact only because it is also a response to a more ultimate principle that is not a response to a fact: accordingly, if principles respond to facts, then the principles at the summit of our conviction are grounded in no facts whatsoever.

Note that the stipulations provided in the first paragraph above do not exclude that normative principles might themselves be facts in a different sense of "fact" from that which is there stipulated. Principles might, that is, be facts in the broader sense of "fact" in which all truths, including, therefore, true principles (if there are any), represent facts. I myself believe that there exist true normative principles, but the thesis about principles and facts to be defended here is, as I shall explain in section 17, neutral with respect to whether any normative principles are truths.

2. Facts, and Some Meta-Ethical Questions

I shall also explain in section 17 why the very little (almost nothing) that I just said about what constitutes a fact suffices for my demonstrative purposes. I am happy for facts to be whatever my opponents in this debate, whose position I shall describe in section 3, (reasonably) understand them to be: my argument, so I believe, is robust across permissible variations in the meaning of "fact," and it is also neutral across contrasting conceptions of the relationship of fact and value. Nor does my view about facts and principles, or so I argue in section 12, require me to take a position on the famous question of whether an "ought" can follow from an "is." It bears emphasis that the question that my thesis answers is neutral with respect to controversies about the objectivity of principles, the relationship between facts and values, and the "is-ought" question, and, let me add for good measure, the realism/anti-realism/ quasi-realism/a-little-bit-of-realism-here-not-so-much-realism-there controversy. The question pursued here is distinct from those that dominate the meta-ethical literature, and so far as I know, it is hardly discussed in that literature. You will inevitably misunderstand me if you assimilate the thesis that I shall state to one within those familiar controversies.

The independent status of the issue canvassed here in relation to long-standing controversies makes the present discussion less interesting than it otherwise might be, in that it has limited implications for those popular philosophical controversies, but also in one way more interesting than it otherwise might be, in that it addresses a relatively novel and, I think, consequential issue, an issue that philosophers don't argue about much but about which most of them spontaneously, or, when appropriately provoked, display strongly opposed and unargued views, which each side finds *obviously true:* the latter circumstance suggests that there's something of a philosophical problem here, about which most philosophers are at least in part mistaken (because a view is unlikely to be obviously true if a goodly number of reflective thinkers believe it to be obviously false).[1]

---

1. Much philosophy seeks to negotiate a consistent path between inconsistent propositions both or all of which we are inclined to affirm. We are, for example, inclined to affirm *both* that we are responsible for our choices, *and* that science shows that we

3. What Most Philosophers Think about Facts and Principles

The thesis to be defended here contradicts what many people (and, I believe, most moral and political philosophers) are disposed to think, to wit, that our beliefs about matters of normative principle, including our beliefs about the deepest and most general matters of principle, should reflect, or respond to, truths about matters of fact: they should, that is— *this is how I am using "reflect" and "respond to"*—include matters of fact among the grounds for affirming them. So, for example, many find it obvious that our beliefs about principles should reflect facts about human nature, such as the fact that human beings are liable to pain, or the fact that they are capable of sympathy for each other, and also facts about human social organization, such as the tendency for people to encounter collective action problems, or for societies to be composed of individuals who have diverse interests and conflicting opinions. These people believe that all sound principles are, as I shall say, fact-sensitive, by which, once again, I mean neither more nor less than that facts form at least part of the grounds for affirming them.[2] Constructivists about justice[3] believe that,[4] and it was my interest in that constructivism that

aren't; *both* that we know a host of undeniable truths *and* that we can be certain of almost nothing; both that moral judgments are objective, since otherwise they would have no force, and that moral judgments are merely subjective, since there is no way of showing them to be true. There is a certain obviousness on both sides of these antithetical views, and the resistance to resolution of philosophical controversy is no doubt at least partly explained by that. And, in each case, proponents on each side are mistaken when they think that their view not only has, as it were, a certain obviousness, but is just plain obviously true.

2. A principle might be said to be "fact-sensitive" in a different use from mine of the quoted expression, in that, absent certain facts, the principle lacks an intelligible meaning. I believe that ultimate principles are fact-insensitive not only in the sense specified in the text but also in the further sense just specified in this footnote, but I defend only the former claim in the present book.

3. I use the phrase "constructivism about x" here to denote the view that the principles that x affirms gain their validity through being the output of a privileged selection procedure. Some believe that it is a defining feature of constructivism that it identifies the validity of a principle with its being the output of such a procedure. Constructivism as I have just specified it is consistent with both presence and absence of that feature. See, further, section 1 of Chapter 7.

4. Thus Rawls writes: "Conceptions of justice must be justified by the conditions of our life as we know it or not at all," and he does not thereby mean to leave room for

led me to think about, and address, the issue under discussion here. I explore, here, in general terms, the relationship between principles grounded in facts and the facts that ground them. I apply what results to constructivism in Chapter 7. (There is some anticipation of that application in sections 18 and 19.)

4. My Thesis: Ultimate Principles Are Fact-Insensitive; and the Clarity of Mind Requirement

The view that all principles for governing human life are sensitive to facts about human life sounds reasonable, and it seems to many people to be obviously correct, but I believe it to be demonstrably mistaken. I believe that it cannot be true of *all* principles that they are sensitive to fact, and that it is true of *some* principles only because it is false of other, fact-*in*sensitive, principles, which explain why given facts ground fact-*sensitive* principles. In my view—and this is my thesis—*a principle can reflect or respond to a fact only because it is also a response to a principle that is not a response to a fact.* To put the same point differently, principles that reflect facts must, in order to reflect facts, reflect principles that don't reflect facts.[5]

---

the affirmation of principles more ultimate than those of justice that do not depend on such conditions for their justification. (*A Theory of Justice*, pp. 454/398).

But it is not only contructivists who affirm the grounding of ultimate principles in fact. Some nonconstructivist witnesses: John Dupré, "It is . . . a commonplace that no normative political philosophy can get off the ground without making some assumptions about what humans are like." *Human Nature and the Limits of Science*, p. 86. If I understand Dupré aright, I deny the commonplace that he affirms in section 4 below. (I understand him awrong if he agrees with me that, once political philosophy does get off the ground, it leaves the ground of fact behind.) Or consider the testimony of Charles Taylor: It "is true of any normative theory . . . that it is linked with certain explanatory theory or theories . . ." ("Neutrality in Political Science," p. 32). Or, in a different register, that of Allan Gibbard: "Human nature, it seems, must be one of the things we should ponder in any search for broad reflective equilibrium in ethics." (*Wise Choices, Apt Feelings*, p. 25). To be sure, those statements require interpretation, and Rawls alone clearly affirms what I deny. But I judge the non-Rawls statements sufficiently opposed in spirit to the spirit that animates me to warrant their exhibition here.

5. After Amartya Sen, we can call principles that don't reflect facts *basic* principles. See his *Collective Choice and Social Welfare*, which defines a "basic value-judgment" as a value-judgment that remains the same for the judger under any and all assumptions about the facts (p. 59). In my view (which, I have been surprised to

My thesis depends on what it is for a principle to be a principle and, more particularly, on what it is for a fact to ground a principle. The thesis is not restricted in scope to principles that are in some or other sense correct. The thesis applies to anyone's principles, be they correct or not, *so long as she has a clear grasp both of what her principles are and of why she holds them*[6] (where "grasping why she holds them" is short for "knowing what she thinks are the grounds of the principles" rather than for "what causes her to hold them"). It also characterizes (under an appropriate reformulation) whatever (if anything) constitutes the *correct* set of principles.

5. An Illustration of the Thesis

Let me now develop the advertised thesis. First, I proceed abstractly, but what I hope is a helpful illustration follows shortly.

Suppose that proposition *F* states a factual claim and that, in the light of, on the basis of, her belief that F, a person, affirms principle *P*. We may

---

discover, is controversial), there exist basic value-judgments, and I also believe that all value-judgments that are not basic are derived from basic ones, together with statements of fact. An argument modeled on the one to be provided here with respect to principles would establish those claims about value judgments.

I should say that I do not agree with everything in Sen's discussion of basic and nonbasic value judgments in *Collective Choice*. I believe, for example, that his statement that "*no* [particular] *value judgment* [made by some person] *is demonstrably basic* [for that person]" (p. 63) depends upon a standard of proof that is inappropriately stringent in the present context. By that stringent (and, I conjecture, excessively Popper-influenced) standard, and as Sen recognizes, *no* "factual hypothesis" can ever be demonstrated to be true: for the stated recognition, see Sen's "Nature and Classes of Prescriptive Judgments," p. 53. I also think that Sen's *Collective Choice* (p. 59 [13]) remark that "it is not asserted here that both the categories [i.e. basic and non-basic value-judgments—GAC] must be non-empty" betrays needless caution, because I think that the existence of basic value judgments is demonstrable.

6. The italicized requirement constrains what is said here about an individual's principles, but it also serves as a heuristic device for highlighting truths about how normative principles justify and are justified, within a structure of normative principles, and independently of anybody's belief. In speaking of the structure of the principles held by someone who is fully clear about her principled commitment, I am speaking not only, precisely, of that, but also of the structure of a coherent set of principles as such, and, therefore, more particularly, of the structure of the principles that constitute the objective normative truth, *if* there is such a thing.

then ask her *why* she treats F as a reason for affirming P. And if she is able to answer that question, then her answer, so I believe, will feature or imply an affirmation of a more ultimate principle (call it *P1*), a principle that would survive denial of *P* itself, a principle, moreover, that holds whether or not *F* is true and that explains *why F* is a reason for affirming *P*: it is always a further principle that confers on a fact its principle-grounding and reason-providing power. The said principle *P1* is insensitive to whether or not *F* holds, although *P1* may be, as we shall see, sensitive to other facts: I have not yet argued that the original principle *P* presupposes a principle that is insensitive to *all* facts, a principle, that is, which is insensitive not only to *F* but which is *altogether* fact-insensitive.

Let me illustrate what I am in course of claiming. If I am right, what I say about the forthcoming example provides an argument for my thesis, since what I say about it is, I believe, both patently true and patently generalizable.

Suppose someone affirms the principle that *we should keep our promises* (call that *P*) because *only when promises are kept can promisees successfully pursue their projects* (call that *F*). (I am not saying that that is the only basis on which *P* might be affirmed: that it is one plausible basis suffices for my purposes.)Then she will surely agree that she believes that *F* supports *P* because she affirms *P1,* which says, to put it roughly, that *we should help people to pursue their projects*. It is *P1,* here, that makes *F* matter, which makes it support *P,* but the subject's affirmation of *P1,* as opposed to whether or not that affirmation induces her to affirm *P* itself, has nothing to do, essentially, with whether or not she believes that *F.* She would affirm *P1* even if she did not believe the factual statement *F: P1* is not, in her belief system, sensitive to whether or not *F* is true. If she came to think that facing broken promises builds character, and thereby helps to turn people into more effective project pursuers, and that *F* is therefore false, she would have reason to abandon or modify her affirmation of *P* but no reason to abandon *P1.*

6. More Illustration of the Thesis

Although a principle that makes a fact matter, in the indicated fashion, is insensitive to whether or not *that* fact obtains, it may yet be sensitive to (other) facts. To see this, return to the promising example, in which *P1* says that we should help people to pursue their projects. What, we may now ask, supports *P1*? A possible answer is a fresh factual claim (call it *F1*), which says that people can achieve happiness only if they are able to pursue their own projects. But, manifestly, *F1* then supports *P1* only in the light of a yet more ultimate principle, *P2*, which says that, absent other considerations,[7] people's happiness should be promoted: and it is possible that there will be no fact on which that principle, *P2*, is grounded.

Merely "possible," though, if only because some might base *P2* on the (supposed) fact that promoting people's happiness expresses our respect for them. But then they must hold principle *P3*, namely, that we ought to express our respect for people, which, if itself based on fact, is based on the fact that people possess what are thought to be respect-meriting characteristics. The relevant basic fact-free principle *P4* may then be: one ought to respect beings, human or otherwise, who have the relevant characteristics. Note that *P4* is immune to denials that human beings, or any beings, have the relevant characteristics. To be sure, *P4* is inapplicable if no beings have such characteristics, but that certain beings *do* have such characteristics is nevertheless no ground for affirming *P4*.

Many will think that the consideration (*F*) that *only when promises are kept can promisees successfully pursue their projects* is not the right, or at any rate not the only, ground for the principle that we should keep our promises. For many (for example, I) think that breaking promises is wrong because doing so constitutes a violation of trust. Now that ground for the promising principle might be regarded as other than a fact, in which case I need make no comment on it here: nonfactual grounding of principles falls outside the scope of my thesis. But if anyone does want to present the claim that promising violates a trust as a fact, then I would point out that what makes that (putative) fact a ground for the promising principle is the more ultimate principle that one should

---

7. "Absent other considerations" is required because other principles might override the stated principle when it is stated without that rider. To reduce the danger of irritating the reader, I won't in what follows always insert this phrase where it is plainly required. As John Rawls says: "The phrases 'other things equal' and 'all things considered' (and other related expressions) indicate the extent to which a judgment is based upon the whole system of principles. A principle taken alone does not express a universal statement which always suffices to establish how we should act when the conditions of the antecedent are fulfilled. Rather, first principles single out relevant features of moral situations such that the exemplification of these features lends support to, provides a reason for making, a certain ethical judgment" (*A Theory of Justice*, pp. 341/300).

not violate a trust. And that more ultimate principle is either itself fact-insensitive, or, if it is indeed fact-sensitive, you will know by now how I would press beyond it to a fact-insensitive one.

7. The Argument for the Thesis

The argument for my thesis has three premises. The first premise says that whenever a fact F confers support on a principle P, there is an explanation *why* F supports P, an explanation of how, that is, F represents a reason to endorse P. That first premise rests upon the more general claim that there is always an explanation why any ground grounds what it grounds. I have no argument for that more general claim—it strikes me as self-evidently true, under a properly unrestricted understanding of what would qualify as such an explanation.

Note that this first premise places no restriction on the form that the answer to a question about why a ground grounds what it grounds must take. So, for example, it is allowed here to be an explanation (albeit a singularly unsatisfying one) of why p (if it indeed does) supports p that they are the same proposition. A restriction of the form that the answer to the relevant why-question takes in our specific case, that of facts supporting principles, is affirmed not by the first but by the second premise of my argument.

For the second premise says that the explanation whose existence is affirmed by the first premise invokes or implies a more ultimate principle, commitment to which would survive denial of F, a more ultimate principle that explains *why* F supports P, in the fashion illustrated above. For this second premise my defense is simply to challenge anyone who disagrees to provide an example in which a credible and satisfying explanation of why some F supports some P invokes or implies no such more ultimate principle.

(Note that the second premise doesn't say that the pertinent *more* ultimate principle is either ultimate (*tout court*) or fact-insensitive—as opposed to insensitive to the particular fact F. That stronger claim is the forthcoming conclusion of the argument. Note, further, that as I stated the second premise, it presupposes the truth of the first. But for those who like the premises of an argument to be independent of one another, the presupposition can be dropped, through restatement of the second premise in conditional form. It then says that *if* there is an explanation why fact F supports principle P, then it invokes a more ultimate principle that is insensitive to F).

Armed with these premises, we may ask anyone who affirms a principle on the basis of a fact what further and more ultimate principle explains why that fact grounds that principle and, once that more ultimate principle has been stated, whether it, in turn, is based on any fact, and so on, reiteratively, as many times as may be required, until she comes to rest with a principle that reflects no fact, unless the sequence of interrogation proceeds indefinitely. But the third premise of my argument is, simply, a denial that it will so proceed. The case for that premise is three-fold. First, it is just implausible that a credible interrogation of that form might go on indefinitely: if you disagree, try to construct one, one that goes beyond citation of, say, five principles. Second, such an indefinitely continuing sequence would require something like an infinite nesting of principles, and few will think that there exist a relevantly infinite number of principles. Finally, an unending sequence of justifications would run against the requirement (laid down in section 4) that she who affirms *P* has a clear grasp of what her principles are and of why she holds them: for we can surely say that a person who cannot complete the indicated sequence, because she has to go on forever, does not know why she holds the principles she does. To sum up the case for the third premise: the sequence cannot proceed without end because our resources of conviction are finite, and even if they were not, proceeding without end would violate the self-understanding stipulation.

It follows from the stated premises that, as I claimed, every fact-sensitive principle reflects a fact-insensitive principle: that is true both within the structure of the principled beliefs of a given person, as long as she is clear about what she believes and why she believes it, and, by a certain parity of reasoning that I shall not lay out here, within the structure of the objective truth about principles, if there is an objective truth about principles.[8] But, as I indicated in section 2, my thesis about principled beliefs, or "beliefs," holds even if there is no objective truth about principles, and even if what we call "beliefs" about principles are really expressions of endorsement, or universal commands, or non-truth-bearing items of some other kind: see, further, section 17.

I now enter further comment on each of the three stated premises.

7(i). A Defense of the First Premise of the Argument

The first premise does not say that everything, or every principle, must have grounds on which it is based: I am neutral on that claim. The prem-

8. Cf. the heuristic role assigned to the "clarity of mind" stipulation in n. 6.

ise rather insists that there is always an explanation that explains why a ground grounds what it grounds. What initiates the sequence of principles is not a need for justification—that, we may suppose, has already been fulfilled by the cited fact—but a need for explanation (of why a stated justification justifies).[9]

Nor is it a valid objection to, or a truth about, my thesis that it implies that (beliefs about) ultimate principles cannot themselves be justified: my view lacks the stated implication. What rather follows from it is that ultimate principles cannot be justified by facts. My view is neutral on whether they can be justified in some other way. For my argumentative purposes, fact-free principles might be self-evidently true,[10] or they might for some other reason require no grounds or they might need grounds and have grounds of some nonfactual sort (they might, for example, be justified by some methodological principle that is not itself a normative principle but a principle that says how to generate normative principles[11]), or they might need grounds but lack them, or, as we shall see in section 17, they might be judged to be outside the space of grounds because, as some noncognitivists think, they might not be objects of belief at all.

Let me amplify the foregoing clarification of my first premise by explaining why that premise does not say anything like what Lewis Carroll's tortoise said to Achilles.[12] That misguided tortoise said that an

9. Let me clarify the structure of this sequence, which is neither one of explanations nor one of justifications but one that alternates those illocutions: that makes my argument more complex than it might at first appear to be. We begin with "*F* justifies *P*." We then ask: "*Why* does *F* justify *P*?," and the answer takes the form: "Because *P1* makes *F* a justification for *P*." We ask: "But what *justifies P1*?" And the answer will be: "Fact *F1*" or "No facts, but . . ." (The long final sentence in the paragraph that follows in the text above indicates various ways that those dots might be filled in.)

See the pain example in section 8 for a variant sequence, which converges in due course with the sequence just characterized, but in which, initially, other facts explain why a given fact justifies a given principle.

10. As some anti-Humeans think: see section 12.

11. Note that the possibility acknowledged within these parentheses does not imply that such a methodological principle might explain, in the absence of any further normative principle, why a certain fact supports a certain principle. That further supposed possibility contradicts my second premise: see section 7(ii).

12. See "What the Tortoise Said to Achilles," in Lewis Carroll, *Symbolic Logic*, pp. 431–434.

inference is valid only if the principle that validates it is stated as a further premise of the inference. An unmanageable infinite regress ensues, and the take-home lesson is that principles of inferential validity do not function as premises in the arguments they validate.

Lewis Carroll's lesson is no challenge to my first premise because that premise concerns not inferences and what makes them valid but justifying grounds and what makes them justify. What the tortoise says to Achilles is that *"q"* doesn't follow from the conjunction of *"if p then q"* and *"p"* alone: he says the inference fails unless you add *"If 'if p then q'* and *'p,'* then *'q'"* as a further premise. But in my proceedings no inference is ever said to be invalid and therefore needful of a further premise. When someone claims that a fact *grounds* a principle, she affirms a *grounding* relation, not one of deductive inference. And I do not say: no, that fact doesn't ground that principle, unless we add . . . I simply ask nonrhetorically why the fact supports the principle, and I claim that a satisfactory answer will always feature a further principle P1: that is, precisely, a (correct!) claim, not a move demanded by logic. And unlike the sequence generated by the tortoise, the sequence that my claim generates is finite: it comes to an end with the statement of a principle that is fact-insensitive and therefore one to which my sequence-generating question ("Why does this fact support this principle?") doesn't apply.

7(ii). A Defense of the Second Premise of the Argument

I defended my second premise, which affirms the indispensable explanatory role of fact-insensitive principles, by challenging anyone to provide an alternative candidate that fulfills that role. An objector might rise to that challenge. She might grant (my first premise) that there must be an explanation why a fact *F* supports a principle *P*, but deny that the only available type of explanation cites a further normative principle, and thereby deny my second premise. For an alternative explanation why *P* is supported by *F* might be some methodological principle, for example, says the objector,[13] the methodological principle embodied in the design of a constructivist machine, be that machine the original Rawlsian original position, or the late Rawlsian "overlapping consensus," or Scanlon's reasonable rejection test. Within the operation of such machines facts support principles in the light of what is indeed a further principle, but

13. I add that interjection because I do not wish to imply that Rawls regarded the original position device as methodological and not normative.

that further principle is not, as required by the second premise of my argument, a normative one. The contemplated further methodological principle does not tell you (directly) what to do, that is, what action(s) to perform; it rather tells you how to choose principles that tell you what to do. This methodological principle, or meta-principle, so the objection runs, explains why the given facts justify the fact-sensitive normative principles that constitute the output of the constructivist procedure, to the detriment of the second premise of my argument.

It illuminates the objection, and lends it force, to consider the relationship of facts, laws, and methodological principles in natural science. Natural laws are grounded in factual observations, even if there is hot dispute as to the nature of that grounding, with Popperian mere non-falsification at one extreme and Carnapian confirmation at the other. But if we ask why given facts justify a given law-statement, we reach no fact-insensitive law-statement (for there is no such thing) but instead some methodological principle, some sort of inductive (or Popperian) principle. There is indeed a need for an ulterior general principle that explains why certain facts support certain claims of natural law, but that ulterior general principle is not itself a natural law. And the objector to my second premise claims that, *mutatis mutandis,* what holds for the justificatory relationship between facts and laws of nature holds for the justificatory relationship between facts and normative principles. The objector says: yes, something more general than the principle supported by a fact explains why that fact supports that principle, but the required more general principle can be something other than a normative principle itself.

I have two replies to this objection, when it is sustained by reference to Rawls's original position, replies that may serve here as a model for how I would approach the objection in other cases.

First: when the original position machine selects P in the light of a set of factual truths, that is because it would, so I claim, select a fact-free normative principle $P1$ when those factual truths are suspended: and it will not be possible for those who endorse the original position methodology[14] and, therefore, the P that it selects in the light of the facts, to deny $P1$, or its justificatory role.[15]

14. That is, not the ontically challenged denizens of the original position themselves, but we supposed endorsers of that device for generating principles.
15. See, further, the discussion in sections 19 and 20 of Rawls's arguments for the comprehensive dependence of principle on fact.

Second, and more controversially, we have to reckon not only with the principles justified by the original position procedure, but also with the principles that justify that procedure. Procedure is not ultimate: as Rawls says, not everything is constructed.[16] And the reason why the constructive procedure is judged appropriate is, to put the matter simply, that it reflects the "conception" of persons as free and equal. But that way of conceiving them either embodies or presupposes a fact-insensitive normative principle (to the detriment, be it said, of Rawls's claim—see, further, sections 19 and 20—that even the most fundamental principles depend on fact: there is a tension between that claim and Rawls's acknowledgment that not everything is constructed, since there appear to be normative principles among what is not constructed, and I do not see how those particular principles could be thought to rest on fact).

The second reply is challengeable: it is not obvious what the implications of the conception of persons as free and equal are. But the first reply suffices to still the objection.

A distinct objection to my argument's second premise, a distinct proposal in rival explanation of why a fact might support a principle, is illustrated by a certain style of belief in God. This rather specialized objection is addressed in the Appendix to this chapter.

7(iii). A Defense of the Third Premise of the Argument

Someone might raise against the third premise of my argument the objection that it presupposes a controversially foundationalist view of justification. On a contrastingly "holist" or "coherentist" view of justification, so the objection that I here envisage runs, the indefinite sequence of justificatory interrogation that my third premise seeks to exclude can obtain, harmlessly, because, for every statement, there is a set of statements that justify it: on a holistic view, justifications lie not on a line with a beginning and an end, but on a finite beginningless and endless network of (now branching, now converging) lines of justification that runs through a body of belief and along which one may travel for as long as one likes. The coherentist view, so the objection continues, defeats the considerations that I offered in favor of the third premise of my argument: a holistic-justificatory conversation *can* proceed indefinitely, in the absence of an extravagant proliferation of norms, and reliance on a holistically structured justification is consistent with having a grasp of what one's

16. *Political Liberalism,* p. 103 (reply to "a second question").

principles are and of why one holds them. In a word, you *can* go on justifying forever with finite belief resources, and you can do so without prejudice to self-understanding.

I reject both the premise and the inference of the holism objection, but my rejection of its premise has no bearing here.

Let me explain. The premise of the holism objection is holism itself, and I reject it on grounds anticipated by Jonathan Bennett and developed more fully by Jerrold Katz.[17] This is hardly the place and I am not the person to mount an extended treatment of these matters: it must here suffice to state, briefly and starkly, what seems to me to be the key point, which is that the truths that determine the impact that our statements have upon one another, within the full set of our statements, cannot themselves be treated holistically, on pain of infinite regress.[18]

Consider now a position that modifies holism in deference to the Bennett/Katz objection by allowing the presence in a belief-system of a set of long *and unrevisable* statements that disjoin the maneuvers that are possible (in response to recalcitrant evidence) within an otherwise entirely holistic belief system. Call that position *quasi-holism*. Then quasi-holism founds (whether well or badly) precisely the same objection to the third premise of my argument as holism did. And that is why I said that my rejection of holism has no bearing here.

But my substantial reply to the holism objection is that, even if true, holism (and quasi-holism) do not threaten my proceedings. For consider: within an holistic framework, some statements are sensitive to (certain) others only so indirectly as to be virtually independent of the latter. So, for example, even if holism is true, the facts of human psychology remain virtually insensitive to facts about the distance of some far-flung galaxy from some other one. It would require exposition of an enormous network to connect them: no holist would say: "Well, this psychological theory has a certain recommendation, but we'd better see whether it fits with what seem to be the facts of astronomy." It is always a legitimate question, even for a holist, whether there is any substantial influence of one sort of statement on another, for selected statements, and sometimes the answer is no.

Accordingly, I am happy to concede that, if holism is true, then,

17. See Bennett, "Analytic-Synthetic," pp. 163–188; Katz, *Realistic Rationalism,* Chapter 3.
18. Cf. Thomas Nagel, *The Last Word,* p. 65: "Not everything can be revised, because something must be used to determine whether a revision is warranted—even if the proposition at issue is a very fundamental one."

through a veritable mass of connections, facts could affect ultimate principles (just as, on a holistic view, astronomy could affect psychology). But no one affirms the view I am opposing on such a basis: people who think that facts support ultimate principles don't think that they do so in virtue merely of the relationship of mutual support, however exiguous that may be, that obtains among arbitrary sets of accepted statements. My opponents believe in arguments from facts to fundamental principles that do not depend on vast stretches of the total web of belief. They believe in a more "local" sensitivity of principles to facts, and they must, accordingly, press a localized rather than a general holism against me. So, to press a holism objection, they have to claim that the local context under discussion, the context of *facts and the principles they support*, is *itself* holistic. Now I have no reason to deny that fact-insensitive principles themselves form a whole, without priority for some privileged set of them.[19] But I will find the view that they belong to a fuller whole that also embraces facts challenging only if the contemplated opponents are able to provide an illustration of how a change in one's view of a principle can alter one's belief about the sort of fact that they think supports principles. I wager they could not come up with an effective example of that description, an example, that is, whose relevance to present concerns would not be defeated by its peculiar character.[20] And that would

19. Nor need I deny that, to employ Geoffrey Sayre-McCord's description of the "method of reflective equilibrium," "the process of developing an acceptable moral theory is a matter of shifting back and forth among the various moral judgments one is initially inclined to make and the more or less abstract theoretical principles one is examining and attempting to develop, altering the collection of principles to fit better the judgments and adjusting the judgments so as to bring them, as best one can, in line with plausible principles" ("Coherentist Epistemology and Moral Theory," p. 141). What I would deny is an expanded description that adds factual beliefs to the mix: see ibid., p. 142.

20. So, for example, it might be said that the factual claim that Harry is a just man is grounded in a certain principle of justice, together with the fact that Harry obeys it. But whether or not that example should be set aside for other reasons, the Harry fact is not at all the sort of fact that my opponents see as undergirding principles. Such "facts" are not part of "the conditions of our life" (see n. 4), in the relevant sense of that phrase.

Consider also the challenge that says that a change in my principles could lead me to give up the factual belief that a certain person is mentally deranged. As in the previous case, facts about who is and is not deranged are facts of the wrong sort to serve here.

mean that, despite their holistic rhetoric, they could not sustain a ho-lism-inspired objection here.[21]

8. *Still Further Illustration and Defense of the Thesis*

In the hope of consolidating my conclusion, I now offer further illustra-tion and defense of it. (Those who are already convinced, whether or not because they will have thought that what I have made a show of demon-strating is obviously true, may proceed to section 9).

Suppose that F is the factual statement that religion is important in at least some people's lives, and P directs freedom of religious prac-tice. Then whoever believes that F supports P believes the more general principle, *P1*, that if something is important in people's lives, then they should be free to pursue it, and no doubt she believes *P1* because she be-lieves *P2*, that what's important in people's lives merits respect, and, more likely than not, she believes *P2* because she believes somewhere up the line that *(Pn) all* beings merit respect if they have the characteristics that make people merit respect. And, very likely, no facts ground that last normative affirmation, *Pn*.[22]

21. Sarah Moss provides a distinct form of the holism objection. Consider this se-quence, which is formed under the interrogation-procedure with which I developed my third premise:

P: One ought not to go to war.
F: Wars cause chaos.
P1: One ought not to cause chaos.
F1: Chaos causes war.
P:
F:
etc.

This sequence satisfies the first two premises of the argument but not the third, be-cause it *can* go on forever. True, it's plainly crazy: chaos and war cannot take in each other's normative laundry like that, and mutual laundering remains open to a charge of pyramid selling even if the circle is expanded. But Moss's construction neverthe-less demonstrates that it's not logically inconsistent to affirm ultimate principles that are fact-sensitive. Or, perhaps, not exactly ultimate principles, but principles than which none is more ultimate: the example enforces a need to distinguish strong and weak forms of ultimacy.
22. I also hold that *Pn* would continue to deserve affirmation (if it deserves it in the first place) even if as a matter of fact nothing was ever important to any being, or, at

An illustration of slightly different shape from those exhibited thus far: Suppose that *F* says that human beings have nervous systems, and *P* says that their bodies should, absent other considerations,[23] be treated with caution. Then the believer in *P* on the basis of *F* almost certainly believes the further factual claim, *G*, that beings with nervous systems are liable to pain and other malfunction[24]: *G*, we can say, makes *F* a reason for *P*. But the question remains, what confers that potency on *G*? And the answer, manifestly, is a further principle, *P1*, which says that, absent other considerations, *one should avoid causing pain*. And *P1* is probably the relevant end-of-the-line fact-independent principle here. It is equivalent to: *if a being is liable to pain, you ought not to cause it pain*, and, manifestly, affirmation of that principle is not, in particular, grounded in a belief that there are any beings who are sensitive to pain. (If that were a ground for affirming the stated principle, then it would also be a ground for affirming that *if a being is liable to pleasure, you ought not to cause it pleasure*, that there are beings who are sensitive to pleasure.) What other factual belief might ground it?[25]

9. The Clarity of Mind Requirement

I should observe that the clarity of mind requirement (see page 233) is by no means universally satisfied by affirmers of principles: people display contrasting degrees of certainty with respect to why they affirm the principles that they affirm. So, for example, a person might say with assurance that the reason why she affirms that, if a being is vulnerable to suffering, then, absent other considerations, it should be protected against suffering, is (quite simply) that beings should be protected

---

any rate, to any being possessed of the relevant respect-worthy characteristics, or, indeed, if no being was judged to possess respect-worthy characteristics, although someone with such factual beliefs may have had no occasion to consider whether or not the principles sequenced above warrant affirmation: but the stated additional claim requires the further thesis expounded in n. 2, which, so I said, I would not defend here.

23. Other principles, enjoining suspension of caution with respect to a person's body in certain circumstances, might override the stated principle.

24. For simplicity of statement, I omit reference to non-pain malfunction in what follows.

25. For what some may think to be an answer to that question, see the final paragraph of section 17.

against suffering: protection against suffering is, for her, the relevant ultimate norm. But another person who affirms the stated principle may just not know whether that principle is, for her, as it is for the first person (entirely) fact-insensitive, or whether she affirms it (at least also), for example, on the basis of the fact that suffering interferes with projects (including, *inter* very many *alia,* the project of avoiding suffering itself) together with the principle that, absent other considerations, people's projects should be facilitated. And if she affirms the original anti-suffering principle for that further, projects-centered, reason, then she may not know whether she means thereby to endorse human freedom to pursue projects as such, or whether she affirms the project-respecting principle for the reason that not freedom as such but welfare as such is to be promoted, and a person is (usually) better than other people are at discerning the path that leads to her welfare.

A further vagary merits exposure. Sometimes, while a person will suspect that *not-F* might support principles different from those that she affirms on the basis of a fact *F,* she will be uncertain which principles in particular *not-F* does, or even might, support. It is, for example, bewildering to try to say what principles we would affirm for beings who were otherwise like us as we are in our adult state but whose normal life spans occupied only twenty-four hours, beings of the sort that have often been disparaged for dwelling only in philosophers' heads, but that might be produced in biologists' labs before the present millennium is over. Would we think that the freedom, in comparison with the welfare, of these here-today-gone-tomorrow beings matters as much as we think our own does, or would we think that their freedom matters less, in comparison with their welfare? That is a difficult question, but, once again, its difficulty does not diminish the force of the argument that, where a principle *P* is affirmed in the light of certain facts, we can ask for a fact-free principle that explains why *P* is affirmed in the light of those facts. The explanation we get will, however, probably be incomplete in the contemplated case: if we don't know what principle we would affirm for people who live only for a day, we don't thoroughly understand why we believe the principles that we affirm for lives that last decades, because we don't know what it is about decades that makes their normative significance different from that of twenty-four hours.

Another example. As a matter of fact, zygote/fetuses become progressively more babylike as they proceed toward birth. But suppose things were different. Suppose, for example, that they were initially more baby-like, and then regressed to a less and less babylike condition until the day before they are born, when they undergo a spectacular humanization. Then it could not be a reason for not aborting two days before birth that the fetus was already babylike. I think that might throw us into normative turmoil. Our norms are formed under the factual constraint that fetus-age goes with fetus-level-of-development, but since our norms are indeed so formed, we don't know what to say when asked what their ultimate warrant is.

It is true that we don't need to know what that warrant is, for practical purposes, but (in my view) philosophy's role is not to tell us what we need to know (in that sense), but what we want or ought (for non-practical reasons) to know. Not all will agree. Some might attack my philosophical presuppositions as "philosophist." In that spirit, they might accept the three premises of my argument but deny the propriety of the clarity of mind requirement.

10. The Merely Logical Priority of Fact-Insensitive Principles

I have argued that affirmations of fact-insensitive principle are logically prior to affirmations of principle that are made when factual information is brought to bear. But the priority enjoyed by fact-insensitive principles is purely logical, and not temporal or epistemic, or at any rate not epistemic in at least one sense of that term. The priority of fact-insensitive principles is a matter of what utterances of principle commit one to, not of how one comes to believe or know what one says in uttering them. That is why I do not deny (in fact, I would assert) that asking what we think we should do, given these or those factual circumstances, is a fruitful way of determining what our principles are; and sometimes, moreover, responses to actual facts reveal our principles better than our responses to hypothesized facts do, because the actual facts present themselves more vividly to us, and, too, they concentrate the mind better, since they call for actual and not merely hypothetical decisions. But none of those considerations bear on whether commitment to fact-sensitive principles carries with it commitment to fact-insensitive principles.

11. The Conditional Character of the Thesis

My thesis is conditional: it is that *if* any facts support any principles, then there are fact-insensitive principles that account for that relationship of support (and, by the same token, if[26] we have any principles at

26. This "if" falls within the scope of the italicized *if* above.

all, then we have fact-insensitive principles). I also believe the consequents of those conditionals, if only because I believe their antecedents, and I therefore believe that *there are fact-insensitive principles,* but I have not argued for the italicized unconditional thesis as such.

The conditional character of my thesis renders it consistent with the view (with which, independently of the claims of the present paper, I disagree) that there exist cases in which no general principle is required for a fact to justify an action. The thesis is also consistent with the stronger view, defended by different thinkers on various grounds, that reasons for action quite generally do not presuppose principles.[27] The stated consistencies obtain because my thesis concerns what happens if and when facts ground principles, not whether actions can be justified by facts only through principles. Most people think, as I do, that facts do ground principles, and my thesis claims that they are thereby committed to acknowledging the existence of fact–insensitive principles. But my thesis doesn't depend on people being right when they claim that there are principles that respond to facts, or that facts justify actions only through principles. To be sure, my thesis is less interesting if those claims are false, but it is not for that reason less true.

12. On "Is" and "Ought"

Some people think that one can, as the idea is often expressed, " 'go' from an 'is' to an 'ought,'" that, for example, the statement that Harry is in pain entails that Harry ought to be assisted, or that the statement that Harry is innocent entails that it would be an injustice to punish Harry (where "p entails q" says that it would be a contradiction to affirm p and deny $q,$ because of what "p" and "q" mean). David Hume (is widely thought to have) rejected that view, and, on first acquaintance with my thesis about facts and principles, many understand it to be a reissue of Hume's (when Hume is so understood: henceforth I drop that qualification).[28] But that understanding of my thesis is mistaken. I do not say that, *since* (as Hume says) one cannot go from an "is" to an "ought," a person who affirms P on the basis of F must also affirm the truth of some

---

27. See, e.g., Jonathan Dancy, *Moral Reasons,* Chapters 4–6, and John McDowell, "Virtue and Reason," in his *Mind, Value, and Reality,* p. 57ff.

28. No thesis about what Hume himself thought is material to my purpose. If he is thought to have said something different, and more problematic for my purposes, then it would be that different thing that matters (and I would welcome its being aired), but not that Hume said it.

fact-independent normative statement. No such Humean premise was part of my argument. Nor does my conclusion support Hume's view.[29] I believe that I have demonstrated my conclusion, but I cannot claim the remarkable achievement of having proved that one cannot go from an "is" to an "ought."

To see that my argument presupposes no denial that one can go from an "is" to an "ought," observe that, far from rejecting my thesis, someone who thinks that one *can* go from an "is" to an "ought" need not deny my thesis, and she must, indeed, affirm it, *if,* that is, and as I shall now suppose, she believes that facts support principles at all.[30] Suppose, then, that someone who does believe that facts support principles also thinks that you *can* go, by semantically based entailment, from an "is" to an "ought." Like many other people, she affirms the principle that injured people should be assisted, and when asked why, she defends that, as other people do, by reference to the fact that injured people suffer pain and/or other disability: for simplicity, I'll stick to pain. But then she must believe the further principle that *people in pain should be assisted,* and, if asked why she believes that principle, she will say something like this, which now distinguishes her view from that of other people, including David Hume's: that it is a conceptual truth that people in pain should be assisted, that a person doesn't understand what the words "pain" and/or "assist" and/or "should be" (and so on) *mean* if she doesn't think so. But if this anti-Humean is right, then her principle, *if X is in pain, then X ought to be assisted, is* insensitive to fact, since it is an entailment, and entailments, being *a priori,* are insensitive to fact. No change in her beliefs about facts would cause her to doubt the italicized principle.

My view that all fact-sensitive principles presuppose fact-insensitive principles doesn't, then, require that an "ought" can't follow from an "is." My position is neutral with respect to that dispute, and as far as its disputants are concerned, it is not the Humeans but the anti-Humeans (that is, the " 'is' to 'ought'" brigade) who must agree with me.[31]

Unpersuaded by the foregoing paragraphs, one critic argued that I

---

29. How could it, there being nothing about "is-to-ought" in the premises used to reach it? One might say: if you don't include a prohibition on going from "is" to "ought" in the premises, you won't find one in the conclusion.

30. That "if"-clause is enforced by the point about the conditionality of my thesis that was made in section 11.

31. I of course think that Humeans, too, should adopt my position, but only because it is the correct position, not because it follows distinctively from the Humean position. My position follows distinctively only from the anti-Humean position.

must reject the anti-Humean position, since, for anti-Humeans, so he said, there is a set of facts that entail every valid moral principle. But that remark mischaracterizes the anti-Humean position. Anti-Humeans typically believe (as most of us do) that the principle that one ought to try to relieve pain is a valid moral principle *and* they believe (as perhaps most philosophers do not) that the said principle is true by virtue of the meanings of the words used to state it. So it is just false that they think that it is because they are entailed by facts that valid moral principles are valid. What anti-Humeans think is that factual statements (such as "Harry is in pain") entail singular ought-statements (such as "Harry ought to be helped") because of valid moral principles[32] (such as "One ought to help people who are in pain") that are true by virtue of meanings: the principles have to be true by virtue of meanings (and, therefore, to be fact-insensitive) to endow factual statements with the "ought"-entailing power that anti-Humeans attribute to them.[33]

13. On "Ought" and "Can"

Philosophers are substantially divided on whether you can ever get an "ought" from an "is," but they are nearly unanimous that you can always get a "can" from an "ought." Yet while there is no doubt some truth in the "'ought' implies 'can'" thesis, the truth in question lacks the significant implications for the nature of normativity that is typically claimed for it: in a word, and as I shall now argue, what's true in "'ought" implies "can'" does not show that fundamental normative truth is constrained by what it is possible for people to do.

It is convenient to begin my argument indirectly by replying to an "'ought' implies 'can'"–inspired objection to my claim that ultimate principles are not grounded in facts. The objection runs as follows: facts often make a mooted ultimate principle impossible to follow, and, since "ought" implies "can," facts thereby disqualify the mooted principle: they constitute grounds for rejecting it.

I shall complete my answer to that objection in the penultimate para-

---

32. The stipulation in the text to n. 30 remains in force.

33. Note that the foregoing section does not deal with the fact/value question, which some people misidentify with the "is"/"ought" question, and that I have not addressed the claim, which is not, I believe, at stake in the standard fact/value disputes, that values are grounded in facts. Please apply to me should you wish me to send you an unpublished treatment of fact/value in relation to "is"/ "ought."

graph of this section, after visiting related issues on the way. But the first thing to say in reply to the objection is that whether or not the premises and conclusion of its argument are true, they represent no difficulty for my thesis, which is that facts ground principles only in virtue of further principles that are not grounded in facts and that explain why the given facts ground the given principles. The objection lacks application to that thesis, since excluding a principle (because the facts mean it can't be complied with) isn't grounding any principle.

But while that initial reply to the "'ought' implies 'can'" objection saves the letter of my thesis, it also confesses to a restriction on the scope of that thesis that had not been made explicit: the thesis, as stated, allows that facts can refute, that is, provide conclusive grounds against, (supposed) ultimate principles. I have defended no stronger thesis here that forbids what that weaker one allows, but I now proceed to do so.

When a fact of the kind here in question, that is, a fact about human incapacity, is said to exclude a principle because it can't be obeyed, we may then ask what we should say about the putatively excluded principle on the counterfactual hypothesis that it *could* be obeyed. And it is only when we thus clear the decks of facts about capacity and get the answer to that counterfactual question that, it seems evident to me, we reach the normative ultimate. Anyone who rejects "one ought to do A" on the sole ground that it is impossible to do A, anyone, that is, who would otherwise affirm that principle, is committed to this fact-insensitive principle: "One ought to do A if it is possible to do A."

If I am right, the dictum that "'ought' implies 'can'" is misused when it forms part of an attempt to show that feasibility constrains the content of ultimate normative judgment. The following argument, or something like it, will be familiar to many readers:

1. Normative judgments are "ought"-statements.
2. "Ought"-statements imply corresponding "can"-statements.
∴ 3. Normative judgments imply "can"-statements.

Consider the statement-form that I introduced a couple of paragraphs back, that is, "One ought to do A if it is possible to do A." Call it 4. Now either 4 is an "ought"-statement or it is not one. Suppose that 4 is an "ought"-statement. Then premise 2 is false, because 4 entails no relevant "can"-statement. But suppose instead, as some might, that 4 is not an "ought"-statement. Then premise 1 fails, because conditional statements of the form of 4 say something essential (indeed, the whole essential truth)[34] about the normative.

The foregoing point applies to the virtue of justice, with respect to which two inquiries must be distinguished. If we are interested in obeying injunctions that carry the authority of justice, and we have a number of competing injunctions before us, then usually[35] in the course of satisfying the stated practical interest, it is wise to cross out any injunction that fails the '"ought" implies "can"' test. But the result of that procedure does not provide us with a complete picture of the nature of justice itself. Our picture is incomplete unless we can say of rejected injunctions whether they are rejected *solely because* of their infeasibility. And where that is indeed the only reason for rejecting them, then, once again, we find fundamental justice within claims of the form: if it is possible to do A, then you ought to do A. If I am right, *all* fundamental principles of justice, whether or not we call them "ought"-statements, are of that conditional form. We derive unconditional ought-statements from them when reality is plugged in. But reality primarily affects, as it were, the "possible" part, and only thereby the "ought" part, of the statement.

What goes for justice goes for all values that generate injunctions, and even for the "ought" of practical rationality, if there is such a thing, whatever may be the relationship that rationality bears to justice and to other values. For I would argue that the ultimate deliverances of rationality take the form "If it is possible to do A, then you ought (that is, rationality requires you) to do A." We readily say things like, "Even if that course were possible, it would be irrational." This means that we make judgments, however merely implicitly, of the form "If that course were possible, it would be rational." And I claim that when our judgment is fundamental, we judge practical rationality, as we judge justice, and the normative in general, independently of factual possibility, and we therefore at least implicitly affirm principles of the indicated "conditional-possible" form. It makes perfect sense to say that "we ought to eliminate as much injustice as we can." The statement is consistent with the claim that "You ought to do A implies that you can do A," but not with the view that feasibility establishes the bounds of justice. If justice is, as Jus-

34. Note that I need not make that additional and stronger claim in order to reject the exhibited argument.
35. Why not always? The explanation is in the penultimate paragraph of this section.

tinian said, each person getting her due, then justice is her due irrespective of the constraints that might make it impossible to give it to her.

The doctrine that feasibility constrains the normative ultimate is a misapplication of a nearly exceptionless truth about directives addressed to individuals severally, or as such, as in what I shall call *rules of regulation,* to the very different topic of the nature of ultimate norms. (See sections 19 and 20 and section 1 of Chapter 7 for further discussion of the difference between fundamental normative principles and rules of regulation.) It is of course a standard and an almost always decisive reason against adopting a rule that directs doing A that people are unable to do A. (I say "*almost* always decisive" because the rule might nevertheless be adopted for nonstandard reasons, such as to shame people, or to provide an excuse for punishing them, and so on). And one reason why such a rule is not to be adopted is that adopting it would be futile: the standard point of rules is to shape social reality to their demands, and that's impossible when people can't comply with them. But note that a rule is similarly futile when people will not comply with it, even though they could, and rules are often wisely abolished or abandoned when that is or becomes the case. It is indeed a reason not to adopt a rule when and because the fact that no one can follow it makes it futile, but it is equally a reason not to adopt a rule when futility reflects the different fact that no one *will* follow it, even though he can. But one would never say, investing the statement with the sort of importance that attends typical announcements that "ought" implies "can," that "ought" implies "will." And that shows the normative non-ultimacy of the rules of regulation with which, as we shall see in depth in Chapter 7, Rawlsians and others misidentify fundamental justice. The fact that we should not adopt a rule that *can't* be followed no more shows that the principle that "ought" implies "can" controls the normative ultimate than the fact that we should not adopt a rule that *won't* be followed shows, what would be absurd, that the normative ultimate is regulated by "'ought' implies 'will'" (which would mean that nobody ever fails to do what she ought to do).[36]

Facts about agent incapacity are (usually) the end of the matter with

36. Note that the foregoing argument does not rest on the false claim that its futility is the only reason for not adopting a rule that can't be followed. The key point is that it shows the philosophically shallow significance of the "'ought' implies 'can'" thesis, that the futility of unfollowable rules is *a* reason for affirming it, and that is brought out by the fact that followable rules that could, but won't in fact, be followed are equally futile.

respect to rules of regulation, but not with respect to ultimate principles. It's futile to adopt a rule that no one can follow, but to say that it's futile to subscribe to a certain fundamental principle is a category mistake: unlike instituting a rule, subscribing to a principle is not an action but the having of a belief or an attitude, and, not being an action, such subscribing cannot be futile (though it can, of course, be misguided). Accordingly, to return to the objection in the second paragraph of this section, and to complete my answer to it: facts about capacity do not disqualify the principles that are here in dispute, that is, fundamental ones. They disqualify, at most, rules of regulation.

A final word. The Rawlsians, who believe that the constraints of human nature and human practice affect the content of justice, are inclined to regard me as unrealistic and/or utopian in that I believe that justice is unaffected by those mundanities. But it is worth pointing out that they are in one way more Utopian than I. For in believing that justice must be so crafted as to be bottom-line feasible, they believe that it is possible to achieve justice, and I am not so sanguine. It follows from my position that justice is an unachievable (although a nevertheless governing) ideal.

14. Possible Misunderstandings of the Thesis

I claim that all principles that reflect facts reflect facts only because they also reflect principles that don't reflect facts, and that the latter principles form the ultimate foundation of all principles, fact-reflecting principles included. My thesis is readily misunderstood, so I shall here indicate three things that it is not[37]: (15): it's not a causal thesis; (16): it's not a psychological thesis; and (17) although it *is* a meta-ethical thesis, it is noncommittal with respect to what might reasonably be regarded as the central question of meta-ethics.

15. The Thesis Is Not a Causal Thesis

Mine is a thesis about the structure of belief in principles, not about what *causes* people to believe in principles: it is not a thesis about how people come to hold the principles that they do. At least standardly, peo-

---

37. I have already indicated that my thesis is not, in at least one sense of "epistemic," an epistemic one: see section 10.

ple *do* arrive at *all* the principles to which they adhere as a result of their experience of life, which is, as it were, an experience of facts, and of their reflection on that experience. My claim is that what they thereby come to believe includes and depends upon belief in principles that are independent of anything they believed or believe about facts.

Consider a child who does not know that three plus six is nine but who knows (at least roughly) what numbers are, and who therefore also knows how to count. He puts three marbles on the left and six marbles on the right, he counts, and he gets nine. He surmises that three and six make nine, but he wants to check the generality of his experimental result. So he tries it out with other sets of marbles. He is groping through experience to a correct arithmetical belief, yet the belief he will form doesn't depend on any truths about the shape of his experience, however much he may think that it exhibits such a dependence. Three and six will make nine however objects in the world behave. The outcome of the child's experiment (or pseudoexperiment) is predetermined by an *a priori* arithmetical truth, *provided that he conducts the experiment aright.* (Notice that he might be unable to conduct it aright if he used not marbles but mergeable blobs of mercury.)

In a partly parallel way (a merely partial parallel suffices for present purposes), it is, typically, in and through experience that people form and adjust their principles, but facts of experience are nevertheless immaterial to their ultimate principles. Suppose some person, having observed the toils of unwanted parenthood suffered by some of her friends, consequently believes that abortion is morally acceptable, at any rate at early stages of fetal development. She then becomes pregnant herself and comes to think otherwise, and thereby changes her principles. She comes to believe that it is wrong to kill a living human fetus, however young that fetus is. She has come to believe that it is wrong to take human life, as such, and she has come to believe that in the wake of, as a result of, the experience of not being able to take (or direct the taking of) a human life herself. But if she is (perhaps unusually) reflective, she will realize that she has come to believe a principle (do not take lives of creatures with humanlike features) whose authority for her is independent of any facts of experience that she or others might have learned. She must believe that it would have been right for her to accept that principle whether or not she'd had any experience that induced a belief that lives of human beings *in particular* should not be taken, just as it is right for the child to believe that three and six make nine whether or not he has played with marbles and thereby discovered that the stated arithmetical truth is very neatly illustrated by the relevant marbles transactions.

Mine is a claim about the structure of normative beliefs: it is not a claim about their genesis. It is a claim about how a person must, in all reason and clarity, conceive of her own normative beliefs, however she might have arrived at them. But the points about the causation of conviction made above join the related epistemic/logical distinction made in section 10 in helping to diagnose the tendency to resist my claim. People are misled by the truth that it is (of course) in the wake of our experience of life that we adopt the principles that we do into denying my claim that we are committed to some fact-insensitive principle whenever we adopt a principle in the light of, and, therefore, sensitively to, the facts. But my claim is consistent with the stated truth.

16. The Thesis Is Not a Psychological Thesis

Suppose you ask someone why she thinks it's wrong to restrict a person's freedom with respect to a matter that doesn't affect the interests of anybody but that person herself. My thesis says that there is an ultimate fact-free principle (or several such) that will be exposed if you continue that interrogation for as long as may be necessary, and *if* the person knows what her principles are, and why she holds them. The *"if"* clause in the statement of the thesis renders it a nonpsychological one. As I remarked in section 9, a person may not know whether she favors freedom just as such; or, differently, whether she favors freedom because she favors promotion of welfare as such and holds the factual belief that freedom is the route to welfare; or, differently, something else. That person may not know whether her endorsement of freedom is fact-based or not, and *there may not even be an answer to that question,* since the person herself may be radically unclear. No such phenomenon touches my thesis. Being a philosophical thesis, it is immune to the psychological facts.

In a certain central respect it is with my thesis about the structure of normative commitment as it is with theses about the essential nature of rationality, as I, at any rate, understand the latter theses. In my view, we investigate *a priori* what the essential nature of rationality is. It is, for example, an *a priori* question whether rationality requires maximizing, as opposed to satisficing. We may also ask *how* rational human beings actually *are,* by whatever is the right standard, and that question is, of course, *a posteriori*. The question how many people can state ultimate fact-free principles that ground all of their principles is similarly *a posteriori*. But mine is the *a priori* thesis that, if facts ground principles, then fact-free principles are at the foundation of the structure of the belief of anyone who is clear about what he believes and why he believes it, just as it is *a priori* that anyone who is rational maximizes, or satisfices, or whatever.[38]

17. The Thesis Is Neutral with Respect to Central Meta-Ethical Disputes

Finally, although my thesis is undoubtedly meta-ethical, it is neutral with respect to what one may reasonably regard as the central question of meta-ethics. My thesis is meta-ethical, because it is a thesis about principles that is silent about which principles should be accepted and which rejected: it is not a contribution to what is sometimes called substantive, as opposed to meta-ethical, ethics. But my thesis is neutral on that central question of meta-ethics that concerns the objectivity or subjectivity of normative principles, and that asks "What is the status of normative principles?" in the sense of "status" in which objectivists, realists, cognitivists, subjectivists, imperativists, emotivists, expressivists, error theorists, and so on provide variously contrasting and overlapping answers to that question. My claim is that anyone who is entirely clear about what her principles are and why she holds them has principles that are independent of her beliefs about facts, whether or not her affirmations (or "affirmations") of fact-insensitive principles are to be understood as claims about a timeless normative reality, or as expressions of taste, or as emotional commitments, or as universally prescribed imperatives.[39]

To be sure, my thesis would have to be rephrased to suit certain answers to the central question of meta-ethics. Under emotivism, for example, it would have to be stated with eschewal of such phrases as "believes

38. I do not think that it prejudices the *a priori* status of claims about the nature of rationality that we would be inclined to reject a characterization of rationality if it had the consequence that most people were very irrational most of the time.

39. I personally believe in moral objectivity with respect to these matters. But note that it is only if (≠ if and only if) one *adds* something like a thesis of moral objectivity to my denial that facts control morals that one can suppose that my argument has been a rationalist one, one that says that moral norms come *a priori* from *reason*.

principle *P* to be true." Under an emotivist construal of the "affirmation" of the principle that one ought to keep one's promises, the speaker is really saying (or uttering, or otherwise emitting): "Boo to breaking promises!" Now that "Boo!" no doubt reflects her factual beliefs, perhaps, for example, the belief that breaking promises prejudices people's projects. But then, clearly, she is disposed to say (or shout) "Boo to prejudicing people's projects!" and if I am right, she is committed to an ultimate "Boo!," perhaps a rather long "Boooooooo!," that depends on no factual beliefs. (Some would say that emotivists must deny that people have what are, strictly speaking, *principles,* and/or that the facts that people adduce to explain their "affirmations of principle" constitute *grounds* for them. If they are right, that is no threat to my thesis, for that thesis, I remind you [see section 11], is the *conditional* one that, *if* facts support principles, then there are principles that are not supported by any facts. If, on the other hand, emotivism *does* countenance principles and grounds, then the reading of my thesis, *modulo* the emotivist position, is as given in the preparenthetical part of the present paragraph.)

To expose a further stretch of meta-ethical neutrality, let me observe that it is not necessary for me to say what facts *are*,[40] or, for example, whether value-free statements of them are available. Whatever anyone can reasonably consider to be a fact that is not *itself* a principle, ultimate principles will not depend on it. So, for example, suppose that someone insists that it is a *fact* that pain is bad, a fact, moreover, that grounds a principle against causing pain. Then my thesis implies, what I find no difficulty in claiming, that she is committed to a more ultimate and, almost certainly, fact-insensitive principle, to the effect that we ought not to cause bad things to happen. (Of course, those who say that all principles depend on facts mean by "facts" plain ordinary facts, not fancy facts like "pain is bad." It is nevertheless worth pointing out that my argument appears to be robust across unusual understandings of the boundaries of fact.)

18. Some Bad Rawlsian Arguments That Reject My Thesis

I remarked in section 2 that the meta-ethical literature says very little about the question pursued in the present chapter. But a notable excep-

---

40. That is, within the restriction on the extension of "fact" that is stipulated in section 1 above.

tion is the work of John Rawls, who argued that fundamental principles of justice and, indeed, "first principles" in general, are a response to the facts of the human condition. (That is why the principle-choosing denizens of the original position are provided with extensive factual information.) Rawls calls the alternative to that view "rational intuitionism," and he disparages that alternative.[41]

"There is," according to Rawls, "no objection to resting the choice of first principles upon the general facts of economics and psychology." He adds, in illustration of his claim, that the difference principle *"relies* on the idea that in a competitive economy (with or without private ownership) with an open class system *excessive* inequalities will not be the rule."[42]

But the illustration that is here supposed to show the unobjectionability of the dependence of first principles on fact is unequal to its task. For it follows from what Rawls says (note *"relies"*) that, if he appraised the facts differently, he would reject the difference principle, *because it permitted too much inequality.* But it then further follows, in line with the second premise of my argument (see the second paragraph of section 7), that there *is* an unarticulated (within the canonical statement of what the principles of justice are) background principle of equality (something like: "One ought not to cause too much inequality") that explains why the stated fact about a competitive economy supports the difference principle, and, for all that Rawls shows, *that* further principle *either* itself does not depend on any facts, *or* points to a still more ultimate principle behind it that does not do so.[43] Rawls needs to deny what I regard as the evident truth, affirmed in the second and pivotal premise of my argument, that a fact supports a principle only in the light of a further principle, yet the very phrase, "excessive inequalities," that he uses in the example at hand confirms that premise, since it fuses reference to a fact

41. See *A Theory of Justice,* pp. 158–61/137–139; "Kantian Constructivism in Moral Theory," pp. 343–346; and "Themes in Kant's Moral Philosophy," in ibid., p. 510ff.

42. *A Theory of Justice,* p. 158/137, my emphases.

43. "For all that Rawls shows" puts the case mildly: I believe that not much reflection is required to see that "Don't cause too much inequality" is either itself fact-insensitive or immediately dependent on a closely related fact-insensitive principle. Accordingly, Rawls's illustration of the supposed unobjectionability of fact-dependent "first principles" not only fails to illustrate the latter but also illustrates the very opposite of what Rawls seeks to illustrate.

with reference to a principle that renders that fact relevant: excess qualifies as *excess* only in the light of a principle that says how much is *too much*.[44]

But I want to make a further point that cries out to be made here even though it is less relevant to the immediate dispute. And that is that the official two principles of justice do not really exhaust what Rawls thinks justice is. For alongside them, and of no lesser status in his thought, there is, his illustration shows, an independent principle that forbids more than a certain amount of inequality[45] and against which the claims of (at any rate) the difference principle must be traded off.[46] In a more perspicuous presentation of what Rawls really thinks,[47] both "promote equal-

44. See, further, *A Theory of Justice*, pp. 536/470; *Justice as Fairness*, p. 67.

For a partly similar critique of Rawls's reconciliation, *via* sanguine factual assumptions, of the difference principle with a principle of equality, see Chapter 10 of Brian Barry's *Liberal Theory of Justice*, and especially the paragraph overlapping pp. 111 and 112, whose content explains why I call Barry's critique (merely) *partly* similar to my own: he describes the perspective from which I am mounting my own critique of Rawls (a perspective that had not, to my knowledge, received an express defence before Barry wrote the cited book) as "ludicrously extreme" (p. 112). But, in my view, the logic of Barry's critique would have pushed him to a critique identical with my own had he thought that logic through more fully. He complains that Rawls does not go "the whole hog," and Barry's own hog is undoubtedly wholer. But it is not whole enough: Barry does not bring home (all) the bacon.

45. There is a strain in Rawls toward identification of equality with justice, and that is what I sought to rescue in the first part of this book. Cf. Chapter 2, section 9: "Inequality: A Necessary Evil?"

46. The point made above vitiates the contrast that Rawls draws between his own procedure in political philosophy and looser philosophical proceedings that he affects to disprefer: "In everyday life we often content ourselves with enumerating common sense precepts and objectives of policy, adding that on particular questions we have to balance them in the light of the general facts of the situation. While this is sound practical advice, it does not express an articulated conception of justice. One is being told in effect to exercise one's judgment as best one can within the framework of these ends as guidelines . . . By contrast, the difference principle is a relatively precise conception, since it ranks all combinations of objectives according to how well they promote the prospects of the least favored." (*A Theory of Justice*, pp. 317–318/279–280). The plurality and imprecision that other views present up front is behind the scenes in Rawls: I don't think that's an advantage. For a defense (to me unconvincing) of Rawls's procedure, see Samuel Scheffler, "Rawls and Utilitarianism," pp. 442–443.

47. As opposed to what he purports to make himself think, in pursuit of a misguided methodology for identifying "first principles."

ity" and "promote the condition of the worst off" would be fact-free injunctions whose claims are to be balanced against each other.[48]

Despite the curiously mishandled illustration of his position, Rawls says that those, like me, who affirm the rival position that ultimate principles are fact-independent, make

> moral philosophy the study of the ethics of creation: an examination of the reflections an omnipotent deity might entertain in determining which is the best of all possible worlds. Even the general facts of nature are to be chosen.[49]

But it is flatly untrue that the view that ultimate principles are independent of fact commits those who hold it to legislating not only principles but also facts. That would follow only on an assumption *opposite* to what we affirm: that, contrary to what we affirm, all principles must be chosen in the light of facts (so that, having decided to ignore the actual facts, we should have to make up for that by *legislating* facts). The second sentence of the above passage can best be regarded as a slip that should be ignored.[50]

A more apt application of the fact-free-principles-are-only-for-deities motif appears in Rawls's argument that, in the absence of factual input, the parties to the original position will have no idea what to choose:

48. See *Justice as Fairness*, p. 68, n. 36, and the text to that footnote for a sign of the strains that come when one does not frankly accept the conflicts in one's thought. The footnote runs as follows: "Of course, within justice as fairness, we do not have any further criterion to judge whether the ratio [of the shares of the more and less advantaged] is unjust, for all our principles are met. It is simply that the actual ratio may disturb us and make us wonder. It is as if a state of reflective equilibrium is a bit upset. We hope the disparities that do occur fall within a range where we are not thus troubled. I am indebted to Ronald Dworkin for pointing out the need to make this point explicit." Rawls says that there is no "further criterion" in a passage written because he recognizes that there is one: equality. I don't think any point is made particularly "explicit" here.

49. *A Theory of Justice*, pp. 159/137.

50. In his *Lectures on the History of Moral Philosophy* Rawls characterizes Leibniz's "ethics of creation" as one that "specifies principles that lie in God's reason and guide God in selecting the best of all possible worlds" (p. 108, and cf. p. 107). So Rawls perhaps means, in the exhibited curious *Theory* passage, that the *function* of fact-independent principles is to determine what the general facts of nature are to be. The right reply to which, here, is: they might have that function for God, but they need not therefore have that function for us.

How . . . can they possibly make a decision? A problem of choice is well defined only if the alternatives are suitably restricted by natural laws and other constraints, and those deciding already have certain inclinations to choose among them. Without a definite structure of this kind the question posed is indeterminate. For this reason we need have no hesitation in making the choice of the principles of justice presuppose a certain theory of social institutions. Indeed, one cannot avoid assumptions about general facts . . . If these assumptions are true and suitably general, everything is in order, for without these elements the whole scheme would be pointless and empty.[51]

This argument falls before the distinction between logical and epistemic priority that was made in section 10. However difficult it may be to decide on principles, to know what all your normative beliefs are, in the absence of facts, decisions of principle that indeed reflect facts carry a commitment to foundational fact-independent principles, and that is the point at issue between those who affirm and those who reject what Rawls *calls* "rational intuitionism."[52] Because of a perfectly ordinary poverty of imagination, the denizens of the original position, and we ourselves,[53] may need factual information to provoke appropriate reflection, but the result of that reflection does not repose upon that information.[54]

I had earlier occasion to remark (see the final paragraph of section 7(ii)) that Rawls's thesis that first principles rest on fact sits ill with the circumstance that seemingly non-fact-based principles justify the use of the original position machine: it is justified by the "free and equal"

51. *A Theory of Justice*, pp. 159–160/138. There is, in my opinion, a tension between the quoted methodological statement and an element in Rawls's account of reflective equilibrium—see the reference to "all possible descriptions" in ibid., pp. 49/43—but I shall not pursue that difficulty here.

52. I emphasize "calls" because "rational intuitionism" is too specific a name for the wide family of positions about principles each member of which, so I have argued (see section 17), is consistent with denial that facts affect ultimate principles.

53. See the penultimate paragraph of section 7(ii) on the relationship between them and us.

54. As Shelly Kagan reports, "most advocates of the ideal observer approach would agree that the ideal observer should be perfectly rational and in complete possession of all relevant factual information." *Normative Ethics*, p. 273. If so, then the Ideal Observer, too, needs facts only heuristically, because he can't see, directly, the fact-free principles by which he is guided.

standing of members of society, but that standing reflects fact-free principles about the proper treatment of beings of the sort that they are. So, it might be asked, "How much difference would it make if Rawls did not call his two principles 'first principles' but reserved that designation for the principles that justify the original position machine?" The answer depends on the particular intellectual concern that is in play. To our assessment of the desirability of the principles that *A Theory of Justice* tells us to follow it might make no difference at all. But it would manifestly make a massive difference to the thesis of fact sensitivity and the arguments for it scouted in this section, since it would represent the abandonment of both, and it is that thesis, and not its importance within the Rawlsian enterprise, that is immediately at stake here. If the arguments scouted in the present section were sound, then the principles that help to explicate "free and equal" standing could not be fact-free, because the stated arguments deny that there are any fact-free principles.

19. Utilitarianism, and the Difference Between Fundamental Principles and Rules of Regulation

Many object to utilitarianism that it recommends slavery for conditions in which slavery would promote aggregate happiness. Many utilitarians reply that such conditions do not in fact obtain. I close my criticism of Rawls's defense of his thesis that first principles are grounded in fact by examining his endorsement of that utilitarian recourse to fact:

> It is often objected . . . that utilitarianism may allow for slavery and serfdom, and for other infractions of liberty. Whether these institutions are justified is made to *depend upon* whether actuarial calculations show that they yield a higher balance of happiness. To this the utilitarian replies that the nature of society is such that these calculations are normally[55] against such denials of liberty.

> Contract theory [and, therefore, Rawls] agrees . . . with utilitarianism in holding that the fundamental principles of justice quite properly depend upon the natural facts about men and society.[56]

55. In my forthcoming discussion of this passage I shall prescind from the occurrence of this (as I believe it to be) infelicitous modifier until we reach the final paragraph of this section.
56. *A Theory of Justice*, pp. 158–159/137, emphasis added.

Rawls here endorses neither utilitarianism nor its defenders' factual claim about slavery. But he endorses the procedure of invoking "natural facts about men and society" to defend a fundamental principle, such as the supposed natural fact that slavery is not a happiness-maximizing arrangement for human beings.

I hope that the ensuing discussion of the quoted passage will reinforce the case for my view about facts and principles, show that Rawls's contrary view is ill-considered, explain why he makes the mistake that he does, and expose the importance of the present dispute.

The beginning of wisdom in this matter is to mark an ambiguity that Rawls misses in the slavery objection to utilitarianism. The words of the first two sentences of the exhibited passage formulate what are in fact two independent slavery objections to utilitarianism, but Rawls treats the two as variant expressions of a single objection. Objector A and objector B below are differently animated, but what A says is in line with the first sentence of the Rawls passage and what B says is in line with its second:

A: I oppose utilitarianism because if we adopt utilitarianism then we might face circumstances in which (because it maximizes happiness) we should have to institute slavery, and I am against *ever* instituting slavery.

B: I oppose utilitarianism because it says that if circumstances were such that we could maximize utility only by instituting slavery, then we should do so, and I do not think that would be a good reason for instituting slavery.

To see that objectors A and B are differently animated, observe that the stated single reply in Rawls's third sentence to their two objections (to wit: slavery will never in fact be happiness-maximizing) should silence A but should leave B unsatisfied. A was worried that slavery might have to be imposed, in obedience to the utilitarian command. She learns that there is no such danger, so her reason for objecting to utilitarianism is overcome. But that slavery is not in fact optimific should cut no ice with B. B's objection was that whether slavery is justified should not be made to "*depend upon*" an "actuarial calculation." Saying that the result of such a calculation will always be reassuring is no reply to the objection that whether or not we institute slavery *shouldn't depend upon* such a calculation. (Note that while B may, like A, oppose slavery under any circumstances, her objection commits her to no such stance. She might think slavery a just punishment for terrible misdeeds yet remain outraged at the thought that it would be right to impose it if it produced enormous happiness, at whatever cost in unhappiness to innocent slaves.)

Observe that I used the word "adopt" in the statement of *A*'s objection but not in the statement of *B*'s. And that is because of the difference of status that the utilitarian principle enjoys in the different optics of the two objections. *B* attacks utilitarianism not as a rule for regulating our affairs that we might consider adopting, but as a principle that formulates the moral truth or, to speak with more meta-ethical neutrality (see section 17), as a principle that formulates an ultimate conviction or commitment. But *A* attacks utilitarianism as a rule of regulation, that is, as a certain type of social instrument, to be legislated and implemented whether by government itself or within social consciousness and practice. A rule of regulation is "a device for having certain effects,"[57] which we adopt or not, in the light of an evaluation, precisely, of its likely effects, and, therefore, in the light of an understanding of the facts. And we evaluate those effects, and thereby decide which fact-bound principles to adopt, by reference to principles that are not devices for achieving effects but statements of our more ultimate and fact-free convictions.[58]

Rawls fails to distinguish between rules of regulation that we decide whether or not to adopt and (his expression) "first principles" that are not in that way optional. That is why he is able to endorse the utilitarian reply procedure without qualification and that is why he is correspondingly able to believe that even first principles are rooted in fact. As I shall explain at greater length in sections 1 and 2 of the next chapter, it is a fundamental error of *A Theory of Justice* that it identifies the first principles of justice with the principles that we should adopt to regulate society. Rawls rightly says that "the correct regulative principle for anything depends on the nature of that thing"[59]: facts are of course indispensable to the justification of rules of regulation. But rules of regulation[60] neces-

57. Robert Nozick, *The Nature of Rationality*, p. 38.

58. Jeff McMahan's well-drawn distinction between what he calls "the deep morality of war" and what he calls "the laws of war" is a special case of the distinction between fundamental principles and rules of regulation. See "The Ethics of Killing in War," pp. 730–731.

59. *A Theory of Justice*, pp. 29/25.

60. I prefer the coinage "rule of regulation" to Rawls's "regulative principle," be-

sarily lack ultimacy: *they* cannot tell us how to evaluate the effects by reference to which they themselves are to be evaluated. Sociology[61] tells us what the effects of various candidate rules would be, but a normative philosophy that lacks sociological input is needed to evaluate those effects and thereby to determine, jointly with sociology, what rules we should adopt. (Thus, to take an extreme but illuminating case, a rule of regulation might recommend behavior that is the opposite of the behavior that its institution is intended to induce, because, for example, people tend to behave countersuggestibly, in the relevant domain.)

If *A*'s objection were the only objection to adopting utilitarianism, and the factual reply to it were correct, then, for all practical purposes, the utilitarian principle would be fine. But only for all practical purposes, not otherwise, and not in particular for the purpose of formulating our ultimate convictions. Such convictions include a hostility to slavery that is not utilitarianly based, a hostility, be it noted, that is shared by any soi-disant utilitarian who thinks it necessary to cite the facts to silence objector *A*. And that hostility to slavery expresses the fact-free conviction that no beings characterized as human beings happen to be characterized should be in a relationship of slavery to each other (or some more qualified fact-free convictions that allows slavery under special circumstances, such as—see page 265 above—as a means of punishment).

The question, What principles should we adopt? is not the question, What principles formulate our fundamental convictions? And an answer to the first question presupposes an answer to the second: in the sense of "adopt" that governs here, we adopt the principles that we adopt in the light of principles that we don't adopt. The distinction is transparently important, but it is not only not recognized but expressly rejected by Rawls, since he identifies the fundamental principles of justice with the principles that specially designed choosers would adopt for the sake of regulating society. Whatever the merits may be of that design, and whether or not it ensures a sound answer to the question as to what principles should be adopted, that the denizens of the original position ask

---

cause the latter phrase puts one in mind of Kant's "regulative idea," with which rules (or principles) of regulation have nothing in common: if any principles belong with the concept of a regulative idea, it is basic principles and not what Rawls calls "regulative principles."

61. Including armchair sociology, which is sometimes enough, or nearly enough, for the purpose stated here.

and answer *that* question ensures that the output of the original position is not a set of first principles of justice.[62]

The defender of Rawls's view might respond thus: "Fine. I accept your distinction between basic principles and principles of regulation. But why should I care about basic principles? I care about what we should *do,* and the rules of regulation that we adopt in the light of the facts determine that." The response is unsustainable because we necessarily have recourse to basic principles to justify the rules of regulation that we adopt: facts cast normative light only by reflecting the light that fact-free first principles shine on them.

Another way of making the required distinction is by exposing the error or limitation in the following argument:

(1) The essential purpose of principles is to guide practice.

(2) No guide to practice can ignore the facts.

∴ (3) Principles must be sensitive to facts.

Either "principles" here denotes rules of regulation, and not also fundamental principles, or it includes the latter in its designation. If it denotes the first, then (1) is true, but (3) doesn't follow: for there might exist other principles that are not sensitive to facts. And if it denotes the second, then (1) is false. It is not *the* purpose of fundamental principles to guide practice, any more than it is *the* purpose of arithmetic to reach by calculation truths about the empirical world. Arithmetic indeed serves that purpose, when it is yoked to facts about the world, but that purpose is not constitutive of what arithmetic is: if the world were to become too chaotic for arithmetic to be applied to it,[63] arithmetic would remain exactly what it now is. And fundamental principles indeed serve the purpose that (when combined with the facts) they tell us what to do, but their standing, too, lies upstream from their serving practical purposes. So one cannot say "*The* purpose of fundamental principles is to guide practice," even though they of course do so.

The facts determine what questions will arise from (but *only* from) a practical point of view. Joshua Cohen infers that "we do not need to have principles of justice that address" circumstances that will not in fact obtain. So, for example, he continues, "we need not have anything

---

62. See, further, sections 1 and 2 of Chapter 7.

63. I don't think this supposition has to be coherent, for present purposes.

definite to say about what we *would* do if [contrary to fact-based expectation] the satisfaction of the difference principle led to" great inequality[64]. Now it is indeed true that to decide what to do we need say nothing definite, and, in fact, nothing at all, about that. But suppose that, like me, you think that political philosophy is a branch of philosophy, whose output is consequential for practice, but not limited in significance to its consequences for practice. Then you may, as I would, protest that the question for political philosophy is not what we should do but what we should think, even when what we should think makes no practical difference.[65] Given the claim that the world forces no choice between the difference principle and the principle of not having too much inequality, a certain decision about fundamental principle has no practical significance. But fundamental principles retain practical significance even here, because it is by appeal to them, together with the facts, that the maximinizing policy is justified.

I have thus far supposed (see footnote 55) that utilitarians claim that slavery would diminish happiness not just in some given society, but in human society as such. Suppose now that it is true of some societies but not of others that slavery would be unoptimific. Then the person who responds to objector A in the fashion indicated above would have to rescind that response and insist that the utilitarian principle would be correct for some societies but not for others. Yet, in so concluding, the erstwhile responder to A would not be displaying any commitment to relativism. And that shows, once again, that the principles A and his critic are evaluating are not first principles: you cannot think a first principle right for one society but not for another without embracing relativism.

20. The Interest of My Thesis

My thesis, that principles that reflect facts reflect principles that don't reflect facts, is, if correct, of interest for several reasons.

First, it is of interest in itself simply as a piece of neglected, and routinely denied, meta-ethical truth, one, moreover, that answers a meta-

---

64. "Taking People as They Are?," p. 385. Cf. the discussion of the difference principle and "excessive inequality" on pp. 259–260 above.
65. Compare my response to Peffer on p. 306ff. of Chapter 7.

ethical question that is surprisingly distinct from the "is"/"ought" question.

But my thesis is also of interest, so I believe, because the fact-free principles that lie behind our fact-bound principles are not always identified in contexts where they should be identified, partly because neglect of the meta-ethical truth that I believe I have established has meant that there has been insufficient effort to identify them. And identifying our (one's, their) fact-free principles has value both for self-clarification and for clarification of what is at stake in controversy. Sometimes, to be sure, when we expose the unstated fact-insensitive principle that undergirds a fact-sensitive one, it will provoke no surprise. Sometimes, however, it will be unexpected. And it will always be worthwhile to expose it to view.

The thesis also has the merit that, as we saw in section 19, it generates a distinction between ultimate fact-free principles and adopted rules of regulation, a distinction that, we also saw, refutes Rawlsian[66] constructivism as a meta-theory of justice. For Rawlsian constructivism, fundamental principles of justice, for all that they are fundamental, which is to say, not derived from still more fundamental principles, reflect facts. Rawls believes that because he misidentifies the question "What is justice?" with the question "What principles should we adopt to regulate our affairs?" For facts undoubtedly help to decide what rules of regulation should be adopted, that is, legislated and implemented, if only because facts constrain possibilities of implementation and determine defensible trade-offs *(at the level of implementation[67])* among competing principles. But the principles that explain, with the facts, why a given set of principles is the right one to adopt don't reflect facts, and non-exposure of those more ultimate principles means failure to explain why we should adopt the principles that we should adopt.

Failure to distinguish between rules of regulation and the principles that justify them leads to confusion of different questions. Suppose I ask, what is the right thing to do when only the torturing of two or three sus-

---

66. And other, but I won't go into that here, except to note that the task Scanlon sets his moral legislators is, precisely, to discover principles for the "general regulation of behaviour": if he uses those words advisedly, and I believe he does, then a critique similar to that made here of Rawls might apply against Scanlon. I say no more than "might," because there are subtleties that can't be broached here: see Chapter 7, section 3, subsection (ii).

67. For a comment on this phrase, see p. 272.

pects will save the lives of tens of thousands of innocents? Suppose, further, that I am referred, by way of reply, to philosophers who say: we should adopt a rule that forbids torture under any circumstances, but we should break the rule in rare and compelling circumstances of that sort.

The answer might be regarded as fatuous, or incoherent, but it isn't an inappropriate answer to a question that, as it happens, I did not ask. As long as we are talking about what rule merits adoption, the distinction between an exceptionless rule that we sometimes break and a rule that incorporates exceptions is perfectly real, because the contrasting rules involve different strategies of internalization and of inducing dispositions to obey, and the preference across the packages of motivation and principle between which we are to decide is settled (at least in part) by recourse to questions of fact, questions, *inter alia,* of psychological and social-psychological fact.

But the question that I put two paragraphs back is not answered by either of the stated rule proposals, or, if it is answered, it is answered, very indirectly, by what the contrasting proposals have in common, and therefore by neither in particular. I did not want to know what rule to adopt. I was not asking how good the prospects were for socially engineering this or that rule, and how good its effects would be. When I contemplated myself facing the question, I was torn by the independent normative forces of the conflicting considerations: that one should not torture, and that one should save human life. The agony of decision that I contemplated was about what to do, *not* about what would be the right rule to adopt.

I suggest that if we are puzzled by what the philosopher says who recommends adopting exceptionless rules that we should sometimes break, then that is because what she says makes a kind of sense if it is taken in one way, but no sense if it is taken in another. In the land of rules of regulation, her proposal is a contender. But it goes astray when it enters the territory of fundamental principle.

When, to speak more generally, I ask a truly normative question, a would-be respondent does not address my question if she says, for example, that this rule is a wise one to adopt because it is not too demanding, or that that one is an unwise one to adopt because it is hard to bear in mind all the considerations to which its enforcement demands attention. Those facts may justify rulings on rules, but my normative question is not sensitive to those (or any other) facts.

We perforce live by rules: we cannot engage in fundamental normative thought whenever we face a decision. And it is fine to act without reflection on a rule that we know belongs to the set of rules in which we repose confidence. But if something makes us reflect, or even if we perchance reflect, here and now, then we rise above the rule: it is only as a rule that a rule should do its work as a rule.

The distinction between rules of regulation and the principles that justify them helps to illuminate what is at stake in normative controversy. Such controversy is better conducted when the status of the norm under examination—basic or regulative—is clearly specified. For example: Certain recent critiques of the "luck egalitarian" view of justice, while undoubtedly containing some good challenges, are disfigured by failure to distinguish between rejection of the luck egalitarian view as a proposed rule of regulation and rejection of it at the fact-insensitive fundamental level at which the view is properly pitched. Thus much (not all) of Elizabeth Anderson's broadside against the "luck-egalitarian" view of justice[68] highlights the effect of striving to implement the luck-egalitarian principle without compromise, but difficulties of implementation, just as such, do not defeat luck egalitarianism as a conception of justice, since it is not a constraint on a sound conception of justice that it should always be sensible to strive to implement it, whatever the factual circumstances may be.[69] Justice is not the only value that calls for (appropriately bal-

---

68. Elizabeth S. Anderson, "What Is the Point of Equality?." Cf. Samuel Scheffler, "What Is Egalitarianism?"

69. Richard Arneson makes a related point in his reply to Anderson when he contrasts "a set of principles of justice" with "a specification of just institutions or just practices": see his "Luck Egalitarianism and Prioritarianism," p. 345.

To be sure, it might be claimed that the difficulties of implementation that Anderson raises have a special character that makes them a true test of justice, so that it is not merely "difficulties of implementation *just as such*" that she is pressing. If and when someone makes a persuasive case for that claim, I shall respond to it.

Having reviewed John Rawls's objections, at the bar of justice, to inequalities that reflect social and genetic luck, Murphy and Nagel write: "This leaves only people's free choices as a possibly nonarbitrary source of inequality, and Rawls is skeptical that there are feasible institutions that could detect the extent to which people's fortunes are due entirely to their choices. That in turn leads him to support the difference principle, which requires the elimination of all inequalities up to the point where greater equality could only be achieved at the cost of harming the worst off" (p. 55). If Murphy and Nagel are right, then it might be said that Rawls himself identifies justice with the luck-egalitarian principle, but that he supports the difference principle because justice itself (so conceived) is infeasible. See, further, the references to David Lyons and others at n. 9 of Chapter 2 and in the final paragraph of section 3 of Chapter 7.

anced) implementation: other principles, sometimes competing with justice, must also be variously pursued and honored. And the facts help to decide the balance of due deference to competing principles: the facts constitute the feasible set that determines the optimal point(s) on a set of fact-independent indifference curves[70] whose axes display packages of different extents to which competing principles are implemented. (That is why I emphasized "at the level of implementation" on page 269. The trade-off values, the rates at which it would be appropriate to allow reduced implementation of one principle for the sake of increased implementation of another, are *a priori*[71]: the facts determine only which implementation packages are feasible. In other words: How much deviation from principle P is justified for the sake of better compliance with principle Q, across different types of circumstances, is an *a priori* matter, not one sensitive to fact. But how much we actually implement P and Q depends on the factual question: what circumstances are we actually in.)

It is with principles as it is (in the respect to be specified) with preferences. For reasons of economy of reflection, and poverty of imagination, preferences are formed over, and in response to, the feasible set, but the preferences so formed presuppose feasibility-independent ultimate preferences: my favorite ice-cream would be a blend of vanilla and strawberry, but the Häagen-Dazs chemists have told me that it's impossible to produce that. And my ultimate principles are no more hostage to fact than my ultimate preferences are.

Appendix: God

There is a way of construing theistic morality under which it provides an apparent counterexample to the second premise of my argument (see sections 7 and 7(ii)). A believer might say, "I affirm the principle that one ought to be charitable, on the ground—because of the fact—that God commands it." The proponent of the second premise now asks her to explain why that fact supports that principle. Unless she is particularly eccentric, her initial reply will be, "Because one should do whatever God commands." The said premise-proponent now asks what the justifica-

---

70. Just as indifference curves for a pair of commodities are not price-dependent, so the principle-combinations indifference curves are not fact-dependent.
71. That is, non-a-posteriori: see n. 39 above.

tion is for that general principle, and there are then two routes that the believer might take.

The first is to say *what* it is about God that makes His commands worthy of obedience, what general features, possessed by God but not, for example, by Harry, explain the authority of His commands. But then the general principle that the edicts of beings with those features are obedience-worthy, upon which the believer relies, will almost certainly be fact-insensitive, and the counterexample will thereby be retired.

The more promising alternative for the purveyor of the counterexample is to eschew an explanation in terms of God's features, the ones that distinguish Him from Harry, and to say that it is not *what* God is but *who* He is that explains why we should obey Him. But that God *is* God is a fact, and I, the proponent of the second premise, can suggest no further principles that confer upon that fact its principle-justifying power. This theism is a bona fide counterexample to my second premise.

Some might conclude that the thing that makes this style of belief in God provide a counterexample to the second premise of my argument also shows the deep irrationality of this style of belief in Him: it is irrational, they might say, to worship God because of who He is, and not at all because of what He is, His nature. But I forgo that step if only because, as I have explained, I do not regard the second premise as a truth of logic. Accordingly, these believers are at liberty, so far as anything shown here is concerned, to believe what they believe and to reject my argument. But it is to be noted that this reason for rejecting it can provide little encouragement to my Rawlsian adversaries. Few of them would rather embrace God than Cohen. Or, anyway, none of them would want to embrace God in order to reject Cohen.

7

CONSTRUCTIVISM

1. Introduction, and Preliminary Overview

The chapter begins with a preliminary overview, in which the constructivism under criticism here is defined and a sketch of the argument to come is presented. Section 2 *(Fundamental Principles of Justice and Constructivism)* provides that argument, which turns on the distinction, violated by constructivism, between fundamental principles of justice and optimal rules of social regulation. Section 3 addresses *Matters Arising,* questions that the exposition in the first two sections bring to the fore. Section 4 challenges the extensively unexamined Rawlsian claim that *Justice Is the First Virtue of Social Institutions.* Section 5 presents *Two Illustrations* of the contrast pursued in section 2, and section 6 explores the relationship between *Justice and the Pareto Principle.* Sections 7 and 8 oppose the claims of, respectively, *Publicity* and *Stability* as constraints on justice, and section 9 urges the irrelevance of *The "Circumstances of Justice"* to its nature. A brief *Conclusion* ensues, followed by an *Appendix,* which argues that *The Original Position Justification of Principles Is Not Contractarian.*

This chapter rejects the constructivist approach to social justice. In its most general description, constructivism is the view that a principle gains its normative credentials through being the product of a sound selection procedure. But I am not concerned in this book with constructivism in its entirely general form. I am concerned with, precisely, the constructivist approach to social justice in particular, which is constructivism, understood as characterized above, but with respect to fundamental principles of social justice in particular, *and* that proceeds by putting and answering the question "What rules of governance are to be adopted for our common social life?" Unless otherwise indicated, all that is what I shall mean by "constructivism" here.

A leading example of the constructivist procedure, so understood, is Rawls's use of the original position to determine the nature of justice, and that is the constructivism I shall have centrally in view. But the broad outline of my critique of Rawlsian constructivism also applies, *mutatis mutandis,* to Scanlonian contractarianism, to Gauthier's contractarianism, and to Ideal Observer theory, where each is recommended as a procedure for identifying what justice, in particular, is.

I argue in what follows that the constructivist approach to social justice mischaracterizes justice both because it treats justice as sensitive to certain sorts of fact and because it fails to distinguish between justice and other virtues. The two errors reflect the single disfigurement by that constructivism from which I seek to rescue justice, and that is constructivism's identification of principles of justice with the optimal set of principles to live by, all things considered. My objection to that identification is that, simply because they *are* the *all*-things considered best principles to live by, optimal all-things-considered principles are therefore not necessarily the best principles considered from the point of view of justice alone. The present chapter is an extended defense of the claim that the constructivist approach to social justice is, for that particular, and transparently simple, reason, misguided.

Social justice constructivism's misidentification of principles of justice with optimal principles of regulation is dictated by the question that it puts to its privileged selectors of principles. They are not asked to say what justice is: it is we who ask that question, and the constructivist doctrine is that the answer to our question is the answer to the different question that is put to constructivism's specially designed selectors, which is, what are the optimal rules of social regulation? My generative criticism of constructivism is that the answer to that question need not, and could not, be the same as the answer to the question: what is justice?

I should acknowledge, here, a distinction that is of the first importance philosophically but that will have no bearing on my own proceedings. I mean the distinction between the view that what it *is* for a principle to be valid, is that it is a product of some favored constructivist procedure; and a view according to which the constructivist procedure merely makes the principles valid, but that does not say that their-having-been-produced-by-the-favored-procedure is what it *is* for them to be valid.[1] The stated distinction is at the pinnacle of meta-ethics, a pinnacle that my discussion does not reach. My question is whether its being the product of a favored procedure for choosing the general rules for social existence establishes that a principle is one of justice, whether or not those who think so think it because they also think that they are describing what is, in a principle, the very property of validity itself, when they lay out what their favored procedure is.

Finally, let me point out, before I proceed, that the question of the primacy of the basic structure as a site of justice is not to the fore in the present critique of constructivism. The present critique is of *how* constructivism selects principles of justice, and not of what I conceive to be, and argued in Chapter 3 is, an unjustified restriction on their scope. If constructivists were to allow that the principles of justice that their procedure generates apply to government and citizens alike, they would remain open to the challenge that I shall raise in what follows. The present challenge is neutral to that extent[2] with respect to the question whether the basic structure is the sole site at which justice applies.

My critique of constructivism rests upon two distinctions. The first is the exclusive but not exhaustive distinction between (a) fundamental normative principles, that is, normative principles that are not derived from *other* normative principles, and (b) principles of regulation or, as I have preferred to say,[3] *rules* of regulation, whether they be those rules that obtain by order of the state or those that emerge within the milder order of social norm formation: income tax rules are state rules of regulation, and rules about what we owe to each other beyond the realm of state force, such as the rules that govern (or misgovern) the battle of the sexes, are nonstate rules of regulation. (The distinction is not exhaustive because there exist derivative normative principles, some fact-insensitive and some not, that are not rules of regulation.) We *create*, we *adopt*, rules of regulation, to order our affairs: we adopt them in the light of what we expect the effect of adopting them to be. But we do not in the same sense adopt our fundamental principles, any more that we adopt

1. Thomas Scanlon draws the stated distinction on p. 391, n. 21, of *What We Owe to Each Other*, and classifies his own theory as one that says "what it is for an act to be wrong."

2. The qualification is necessary because, if I am right about the scope of principles of justice, then the misidentification of justice with rules of regulation has further erroneous consequences.

3. See sections 13, 19, and 20 of Chapter 6.

our beliefs about matters of fact.[4] Our fundamental principles represent our convictions. They are not things that we *decide* to have and that we consequently work to install or instill and sustain; we do not proceed with them as we do with rules of regulation. We do not decide what to believe, whether about fact or about value and principle, in the light of what we expect the effect of believing it to be. The adoption of rules of regulation is a practical task: the formation of conviction and attitude is not. It is our principled convictions that justify what we do, and that includes the doing that is adopting rules of regulation.

The question "What are the rules of regulation that govern society?" is a sociological question, whereas the question "What rules of regulation ought to govern society?" is a philosophical question, or if you prefer, a question in political theory, because the answer to that second question depends strongly on general social facts. The question "What is justice?" is a philosophical question, and there is no coherent question of the form "What ought justice, or the principles of justice, to be?" The incoherence of that question reflects the status of justice as something that transcends rules of regulation.[5]

Let me now add to the distinction between fundamental principles and rules of regulation a simpler distinction, between justice and other virtues, and, therefore, between (c) principles that express or serve the value of justice and (d) principles that express or serve other values, such as human welfare, or human self-realization, or the promotion of knowledge. (In the senses of the forthcoming italicized words that I intend here, fundamental principles *express* values and justified rules of regulation *serve* them, by serving the principles that express them.)

Now, Rawlsians believe that the correct answer to the question "What is justice?" is identical to the answer that specially designed choosers, the denizens of the Rawlsian original position, would give to the question "What general rules of regulation for society would you choose, in your particular condition of knowledge and ignorance?" Their answer to *that* question is supposed to give us the fundamental principles of justice. But in thus identifying justice with optimal rules of regulation, Rawlsians breach both of the distinctions that were drawn above.

The present charge is not a criticism of the particular device, that is, the original position, that Rawls employs to *answer* the question, namely,

4. Or, indeed, our sentiments: my denial that we adopt our normative principles does not require a cognitivist view of ethics.
5. Its incoherence also explains why I consider Andrew Williams concepts of "constraints on" and "desiderata of" justice to be incoherent: see section 7 of Chapter 8.

what rules should we choose, that the denizens of the original position answer. Mine is not a criticism of the original position device *as* a device for answering *that* question. Instead, I protest against the identification of the answer to *that* question with the answer to the question "What is justice?" The said identification represents a double conflation, of fundamental principles with rules of regulation, and of principles of justice whether they be fundamental ones that express justice, or rules of regulation that serve to realize justice (as much as is possible and reasonable), with principles, whether, again, they be fundamental ones or rules of regulation, that respectively express or serve other values. The upshot is a misidentification of fundamental principles of justice with optimal principles of regulation quite generally.

The two criticisms that I make of the Rawlsian procedure can be presented within a simple two-by-two matrix:

	(a) fundamental principles	(b) rules of regulation
(c) justice	(1) fundamental principles of justice	(3) that serve justice in particular
(d) values in general	(2) fundamental principles generally	(4) that serve fundamental principles generally

The effect of the original position procedure is to identify (1) and (4), and thereby to locate justice both in the wrong column and in the wrong row.

I argued in Chapter 6 that fundamental principles, that is, principles that are not derived from other principles, do not rest on factual grounds. But I have not appealed to that premise in the foregoing presentation. The charge that justice cannot be identified with optimal rules of regulation does not require the claim that justice is wholly fact-insensitive: justice might, for all that the charge is sound, still depend (as I shall later argue that it does not) on the character of basic facts of human nature. So I have not here asked you to agree with my strong view, demonstrable though it is, that no facts control fundamental principles, but only with the weaker and overwhelmingly intuitive claim, that the sorts of facts about practicality and feasibility that control the content of sound rules of regulation do not affect the content of justice itself. The point will be amply illustrated in what follows: see especially the property tax and social insurance examples in section 5.

I end this overview by indicating the relationship between the two rescues that the present book pursues: that of the claim, pursued in Chapters 1 to 5, that equality constitutes distributive justice, and that of the concept of justice itself, which is pursued in the present chapter. The two rescues are connected because each of the two errors in the Rawlsian identification of principles of justice with optimal rules of regulation induces us to disidentify justice and equality. The first error, the placing of justice in the wrong column of the matrix, induces that disidentification because difficulties of obtaining relevant information and other practical problems make equality an infeasible policy goal: one can only approach it, but that is not in my view a reason for identifying justice with whatever workable rule comes closest to equality, as opposed to with what we are trying to approach, that is, equality itself. And the second error, the placing of justice in the wrong row, introduces principles other than that of justice that may rightly compete with equality in various contexts. Accordingly, the rescue of the *concept* of justice serves the end of rescuing the egalitarian thesis about distributive justice.

2. Fundamental Principles of Justice and Constructivism

A *fundamental* principle of justice is here defined as a principle of justice that is not an applied principle of justice. An *applied* principle of justice is a principle of justice that is derived from (= affirmed on the basis of) a principle of justice *together with* something other than a principle of justice, such as a set of empirical facts, or a value other than justice, or a principle that is not a principle of justice. An applied principle of justice applies justice in the light of such non-justice factual information or value or principle.[6]

As a matter of definition, therefore, fundamental principles of justice might be derived from principles that are not principles of justice,

6. Note that a given principle of justice may be applied within the thought of one person but fundamental within the thought of another person. My statements about how a set of principles of justice is structured are intended as true both of their structuring within a given person's thought and of their structuring within whatever (if anything) constitutes the correct set of principles of justice. Compare n. 6 (on "clarity of mind") in Chapter 6.

whether alone or together with other non-justice premises, such as empirical facts; or from empirical facts alone; or they might be underived, or derived from other principles of justice that are themselves underived or derived from other principles of justice that are themselves underived, and so on. To describe the definitional position in other terms, fundamental principles of justice reflect nothing but considerations of justice, or nothing but considerations that are not considerations of justice, but they may not reflect a mixture of justice considerations and other considerations, for principles that reflect such a mixture are applied principles of justice: that is what it is to be an applied principle of justice. To put the matter more crudely, but perhaps more accessibly, applied principles of justice come from justice *and* something else, whereas fundamental principles of justice, *so far as the mere definition of what they are is concerned,* come from nothing but justice or from nothing but something other than justice. If they come from something other than justice, they are in one way not fundamental, since they're derived, but since it is not then justice from which they derive, they are, nevertheless, fundamental *as* principles of justice. (It may sound strange that fundamental principles of justice reflect either nothing but justice or nothing but what isn't justice, but, strange or not, that follows from the reasonable definition of an "applied" principle of justice as reflecting justice *and* something else, together with the reasonable definition of a "fundamental" principle of justice as a principle of justice that is not applied).

This picture formulates the definitional structure articulated above, with the arrows, read upward, signifying "may be derived from."

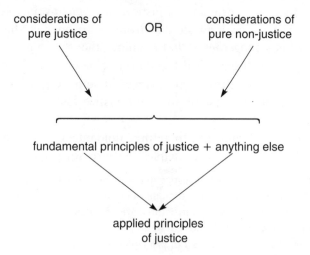

Constructivists delete the top left-hand item (with its arrow), and I delete the top right-hand item (with its arrow). We thereby maintain contrasting substantive *theses* about the source of fundamental principles of justice, each of which is consistent with the *definition* of "fundamental principles of justice" that I have defended here.

All of that is a matter of mere definition; it should generate no quarrel (which is not to claim that it won't). Against the background of the stated definitions, I now state the disagreement that I have with constructivism. According to constructivism, fundamental principles of justice are derived from judgments (that do not themselves reflect principles of justice) about the right procedure for generating principles of justice, together with facts of human nature and human society. That view is not excluded by the definition that I gave of "fundamental principles of justice," but I believe that it is incorrect, that Rawlsians are mistaken when they delete the top left-hand item, with its arrow, in the figure. I believe that, whatever their content may be, fundamental principles of justice are in no way dependent on the character of any facts, or, indeed, and equally importantly for my purposes, on any considerations of value or principle that are not considerations of justice: I delete the top right-hand item, with its arrow, in the footnoted figure. I thereby affirm that constructivists miscast applied principles of justice in the role of fundamental ones.

The stated criticism is intended irrespective of what the correct principles of justice are. My claim is that constructivists are mistaken about the structure of their *own* belief. For as I showed in the previous chapter, whoever affirms any principle, and, therefore, in particular, any principle of justice, that is sensitive to facts of any kind is committed thereby to a fact-insensitive principle, from which, together with the relevant fact or facts, the fact-sensitive principle (for example, of justice) that he affirms is derived. I shall, *moreover*, argue, at the end of this section, that the fact-insensitive principle from which any bona fide fact-*sensitive* principle of justice is derived is *itself* a principle of justice.[7] It may not be evi-

---

7. I emphasize "moreover" because this further claim is not implied by anything demonstrated in Chapter 6. If Chapter 6 is right, then principles of justice that reflect facts reflect principles that don't reflect facts, but nothing shown in Chapter 6 shows that the latter, basic, principles are themselves principles of justice. To show that, one would need to show *either* that in general the basic principles behind a set of fact-sensitive principles articulate the same *value* as they do, *or* that this is so in the particular case of principles of justice and the value of justice. The general claim is no

dent what that background fact-insensitive principle of justice is; it may, indeed, be difficult to identify it. But if I am right that such a principle is presupposed, then constructivists mistake *applied* principles of justice for *fundamental* ones. And the same reasoning applies, *mutatis mutandis,* when justice is tempered by other values. Just as exactly how justice depends on the facts, when it does, is a function of features of justice that don't depend on the facts, so exactly how justice yields to other values is in part a function of features of justice that are wholly independent of those other values.

If I am right that constructivists commit the stated error, then it is not difficult to discern why they make it. They make it because, as I shall now explain, they assign a role to fundamental principles of justice that fundamental principles of justice are not suited to fulfill.

On the constructivist view of justice, fundamental principles of justice are the outcome of an idealized legislative procedure whose task is to elect principles that will regulate our common life. In Rawls's version of constructivism, the legislators, the denizens of the original position, are prospective real-world citizens ignorant of how they in particular would fare under various candidate principles. In a Scanlonian version of constructivism about justice, the legislators are motivated to live by principles that no one could reasonably reject. (I shall, for the most part, be interested, here, in the Rawlsian version of constructivism, although some of my objections to it also apply against Scanlonian and other versions of it.[8]) But however the different versions of constructivist theories of social justice differ, whether in the nature of the selection procedure that they mandate or in the principles that are the output of that procedure, they all assign to principles of justice the same role. That role is de-

---

doubt false, but the specific claim about principles of justice is, I believe, true, and I defend it at the end of this section. (To see that the general claim is false, notice that the ultimate principles behind principles of good town planning are not themselves principles of town planning. So, for example, the principle of town planning that shops be located not too far from homes reflects basic principles that promote human welfare, which no one would classify as principles of town planning. Accordingly my view that, by contrast, the ultimate principles warranting fact-sensitive principles of justice are themselves principles of justice cannot be demonstrated on general grounds, grounds, that is, that apply to all principles.)

8. See, for further discussion of constructivism's versions, section 3(ii), where, among other things, I explain why I call the contemplated version "Scanlonian" rather than "Scanlon's."

termined by the fact that constructivism's legislators are asked to elect *principles that will regulate their common life*: the principles they arrive at are said to qualify as principles of justice because of the special conditions of motivation and information under which principles that are to serve the role of regulating their common life are adopted.

But, and here I state the general ground of my disagreement with the constructivist meta-theory, in any enterprise whose purpose is to select the principles that I have called "rules of regulation," *attention must be paid, either expressly or in effect, to considerations that do not reflect the content of justice itself*: while justice (whatever it may be: the present point holds independently of who is right in disagreements about the *content* of justice) must of course influence the selection of regulating principles, factual contingencies that determine how justice is to be applied, or that make justice infeasible, *and* values and principles that call for a compromise with justice, also have a role to play in generating the principles that regulate social life; and legislators, whether flesh-and-blood or hypothetical, will go astray unless they are influenced one way or another (that is directly, or by virtue of the structure of the constructivist device[9]) by those further considerations. It follows that any procedure that generates the right set of principles to regulate society fails thereby to identify a set of fundamental principles of justice, by virtue of its very success in the former, distinct, exercise. The influence of other values means that the principles in the output of the procedure are not principles of *justice,* and the influence of the factual contingencies means that they are not *fundamental* principles of anything.

The relevant non-justice considerations do indeed affect the outcome of typically favored constructivist procedures. My complaint is not at

---

9. The denizens of Rawls's original position do not, of course, expressly distinguish between considerations of justice and other considerations. They simply choose whatever principle that, given their particular combination of knowledge and ignorance, they see (not as serving justice but) as serving their interests. But in order that they choose principles of regulation well, their choice must in some manner reflect both justice and non-justice considerations.

In partly parallel fashion, the rules of criminal justice, which govern judgments of innocence and guilt, must take into account considerations other than what innocence and guilt *are,* and therefore cannot tell us what innocence and guilt are: they are, on the contrary, fashioned against the background of an antecedent understanding of what guilt and innocence are. See, further, the discussion of loyalty in section 7 of Chapter 8.

all that constructivism fails to take them into account, but precisely that it *does* take them into account, inappropriately, when purporting to identify what justice is. For the influence of alien factors on the output of the constructivist procedure means that what it produces is not fundamental justice, and is sometimes, moreover, as we shall see in section 5 not justice at all. Given its aspiration to produce fundamental principles of justice, constructivism sets its legislators the wrong task, although the precise character and the size of the discrepancy between fundamental justice and the output of a constructivist procedure will, of course, vary across constructivism's variants. That it sets its idealized legislators the wrong task is my principal—and generative—complaint against constructivism as a meta-theory of fundamental justice.[10]

Note that, for all that I am here purporting to show, and as I have acknowledged on pages 277–278, Rawls's original position, or some variant of it, might be the right procedure for generating rules of regulation. I do not happen to believe that, but mostly for uneccentric reasons that have nothing to do with the case being mounted here, and one of which is rehearsed at the end of the present section. I also conjecture that the following case might be made out against the original position as a device for generating rules of regulation: we want those rules to be as just as it is possible and reasonable for them to be, and we are unlikely to achieve that if our reflection does not keep justice, simply as such, in view.

Because it sets its legislators the wrong task, it endows those legislators with cognitive resources that are redundant from the point of view of specifying what justice is. One thing the legislators possess, in the versions of constructivism that exercise me here, is a correct account, or, anyway, the best available account, of the facts of human nature and human society: this helps to determine their selection of principles of justice, and the right principles of justice therefore depend, according to constructivism, on information about human nature and human society.[11] Now we do, of course, need such information when selecting prin-

---

10. If I am right that constructivists miscast fundamental principles of justice in the role of principles of social regulation, what, I may be asked, is the (contrasting and) proper role of fundamental principles of justice? The answer is that they have no proprietary role, apart from the obvious role of spelling out what justice is. Not everything in this world, not even every kind of principle, has the character that it does because of some role that it fulfills. See, further, p. 267 of Chapter 6.

11. See, for example, Rawls, "Kantian Constructivism in Moral Theory," p. 351: ". . . in justice as fairness the first principles of justice depend upon those general be-

ciples of regulation, but, so I am here arguing, facts are irrelevant in the determination of fundamental principles of justice. Facts of human nature and human society of course (1) make a difference to what justice tells us to do in specific terms; they also (2) tell us how much justice we can get; and they (3) bear on how much we should compromise with justice, but, so I believe, they make no difference to the very nature of justice itself.

Importantly, the fact-insensitive principle of justice exposed under appropriate interrogation will sometimes be equivalent to "bring about desideratum J (a form of justice) as much as possible": assumptions about the facts then determine the extent to which J can be brought about. And if a fact F enables more of J to be brought about than *not-F* does, it will then prove true to say that more justice can be achieved if F is true than if *not-F* is true. F and *not-F* will not determine what is (straightforwardly) just in different situations, but how *much* justice can be achieved in different situations. Facts thereby make a difference to what are the right rules of social regulation, rules the effect of whose operation may justifiably deviate from justice itself. This schema will be illustrated in section 5 of the present chapter.

Sometimes, too, the governing principle will not be of the form, as above, "bring about desideratum J (a form of justice) as much as possible," but "bring about desideratum J (a form of justice) to whatever extent is reasonable," since the cost (in sacrifice of other values or principles) of realizing justice as much as possible will, given the facts, be too high. That schema will also be illustrated in section 5.

Three principles that properly influence the selection of rules of regulation but that are not principles of justice, but at most constraints on its implementation, will be discussed in this chapter: the Pareto principle, which mandates improvements on the status quo from which everyone benefits[12] (see section 6); the principle of publicity, which says (roughly) that it should be possible to tell whether or not someone is observing a

---

liefs about human nature and how society works which are allowed to the parties in the original position. First principles are not, in a constructivist view, independent of such beliefs, nor, as some forms of rational intuitionism hold, true in all possible worlds." Compare the discussion in section 18 of Chapter 6.

12. Brian Barry makes the point that choosers in the original position would prefer Pareto to justice. He does not, however, associate the preference for Pareto with the task the choosers are set, but only with the motivations with which they are endowed. See *The Liberal Theory of Justice*, p. 16.

principle (see section 7 and the whole of Chapter 8); and the principle of stability, which says that the principles governing society should be self-reproducing (see section 8). Those principles are standardly honored by constructivists, and there is a case for honoring each of them when selecting rules of regulation, but their intrusion into the constitution of justice distorts the character of that value.

So: justice is not the only virtue that should influence the content of principles of regulation. They need to serve other virtues, such as stability, a healthy respect for Pareto, and certain forms of publicity, about all of which more will be said below. The original position can define neither the nature of justice nor that of any other single virtue, because the legislators are not asked (and are not equipped to say) what any virtue is, but simply what principles they wish to legislate, all things considered.

More generally: if an institution is capable of more than one virtue, then you may properly have regard to each of the virtues of which it is capable in designing it. But the answer to the question What is the right design of the institution? could not, therefore, by itself, tell you the content in general of any one of the virtues, or even the particular distinctive contribution that that virtue makes to the design. You have to understand the content of any given virtue independently of knowing what the rules of the design are to identify the subset of rules that reflect *that* particular virtue.[13] And the point holds for the virtue of justice even if justice is, as I personally do not think it is (see section 4), the first virtue of social institutions, in the sense that Rawls said that it is. For that would not mean that justice is the *only* virtue that would be manifest in an acceptable design. Whether or not justice is the first virtue of institutions, they have, or lack, other virtues, too, and constructivist devices, whether or not they are capable of getting right all the principles that all the virtues of institutions require, cannot tell us which principles are ones of justice and which not. To discriminate principles of justice within the set of constructively selected principles, we need a contentful conception of justice that isn't constructed.

In my opposition to the constructivist view that fundamental principles of justice are fact-sensitive, I have affirmed both a strong thesis and a

---

13. Note, further, that no particular subset need reflect exclusively any particular virtue, as opposed to the resultant of balancing several competing virtues.

weaker thesis. The strong thesis says that constructivism's fact-infested principles of justice presuppose fact-insensitive principles *of justice* which constructivism fails to expose. The weaker thesis, which follows from the general doctrine about facts and principles set out in Chapter 6, drops the italicized words (*"of justice"*). If even the weaker thesis is true, constructivism obscures how the principles it selects are arrived at, whether or not the fact-insensitive principles that it presupposes and fails to expose are properly called "principles of justice," simply because it does not expose those fact-insensitive principles to view.

The strong thesis says that, when the underlying fact-insensitive principles are exposed, we shall recognize them to be the *fundamental* principles of justice that a given constructivism latently affirms: it will be those principles that endow the constructively selected principles with whatever amount of justice they have.

As I said, the weaker thesis is an application of the account of facts and principles that was demonstrated in the preceding chapter. I can offer no similarly formal demonstration of the strong thesis. From the next paragraph on, I defend it against a supposed counterexample to it that turns on the relationship between justice and democracy, and in section 5 I exhibit illustrations that seem to me to support it, drawn from the domains of social insurance and property taxation. But I do not prove the stronger thesis in general terms.

Someone has pressed the following objection to the strong thesis (which says that fact-free principles of *justice* in particular lie behind fact-dependent principles of justice). Consider the right to freedom of speech: the principle conferring that right is one that we would normally regard as being a principle of justice. According to the objector, that right, like the set of democratic rights to which it belongs, is geared to promoting human flourishing. It is justified in the light of a principle that is not a principle of justice and that directs the promotion of human flourishing, together with those facts of human nature and human society that decide what human beings need in order to flourish. (It is consistent with the objection that the principle directing human flourishing be fact-insensitive: the example is not intended to challenge the weak thesis.)

The objection succeeds only if we can sustain in tandem both the view that democratic rights are requirements of justice and the view that the foundation of those rights is that they promote the general welfare (where that promotion is not seen as in turn required by justice). The argument of the objection, in its general form, proceeds as follows:

1. All principles that confer rights are principles of justice.
2. Some principles that confer rights are based on the principle of promoting the general welfare.
3. The general welfare principle is not a principle of justice.
∴ 4. The strong thesis is false.

Consider, then, what the objector says about freedom of speech, in supposed illustration of the stated argument. She says that there is a right to freedom of speech, that it is unjust to deny somebody that right, but that that principle of justice is based on the fact that freedom of speech promotes democracy, to the general benefit, and on the principle that one ought to act for the general benefit, which is not a principle of justice.

I agree that the general welfare principle is not a principle of justice. Some will not, and, unlike me, they will therefore reject the argument by rejecting its third premise. But I shall reject the argument on the different ground that its first and second premises are (effectively) inconsistent.

We can distinguish between two classes of rights. There are *strongly individual* rights, by which I mean rights whose violation gives the violated agent a *special grievance*. So, for example, most people would agree that the right not to be molested is strongly individual: we may *all* have *a* grievance against the molester, but whether or not that is so, his victim's grievance is special and additional to whatever grievance we may have, however that is to be spelled out by a legal system and/or in further moral terms. Contrast rights that are vested in individuals because that vesting serves some general end, like the right of a seller of art to tax relief on the proceeds of the sale of paintings to public institutions. That right is granted *to*, but not especially *for the sake of*, the seller of the art. It is granted so that more art will flow from private to public collections, and if a seller is mischievously impeded in his legitimate quest for the tax relief, then we *all* (he and the rest of us) have, if any, the *same* grievance against that, namely, that it militates against sustaining good public collections. If a society fails, as some do, to legislate against rape, then it violates the rights of (at least) women. If it fails to legislate tax relief on selected sales of art, it does not violate the rights of art owners more than it violates anyone else's rights.

Now it seems apparent to me that anyone who thinks, as our objector must, that promoting the general benefit is not a principle of justice must regard the democratic rights that are justified by that principle as not strongly individual: if the justification is the general interest, then any related grievance is merely general and therefore not a grievance against injustice. To be sure, not everyone will agree that the primacy of the general interest, at either of those conceptual sites (of justification or of grievance), detracts from justice status. But the objector agrees with me that it does at the justification site, and I can't see how he can then regard the general interest as not also primary at the grievance site, and therefore as removing the status of justice from the grievance, and therefore from the associated right.

If freedom of speech is a dictate of justice, then a wrongly silenced would-be speaker has a *special* grievance when he is silenced, one, that is, which goes beyond whatever grievances *everyone* may have when he is silenced (because everyone has a similar interest in the flourishing that democracy brings). The objection is therefore exposed to a dilemma: either the silenced person has a *special* grievance, in which case it is hard to see how the value served by democracy for everyone might explain that grievance; or he lacks a special grievance, in which case the value served by democracy might indeed justify a right to freedom of speech, but not a right that counts as a requirement of *justice*.

In short, the objection is incoherent. Its first two premises are inconsistent.

To restate: Either the foundational democratic values *themselves* embody justice or they do not. If they do not, if (implausibly) democracy itself has nothing to do with justice, then why should the rights that constitute democracy be regarded as a matter of justice? If democracy is justified by the general welfare, then it is surely not an injustice, but a breach of that different value, to fail to institute a right to freedom of speech. (To be sure, if a right to freedom of speech is legally instituted, that will generate legitimate expectations of its exercise, and the violation of those expectations will indeed be unjust, and the same goes for institution of a right to tax relief when selling art to a museum. But consistently with the strong thesis, that will then be an injustice in virtue of a more ultimate principle of justice: that it is unjust to violate legitimate expectations.)

Consider now a distinct attempt to ground rights imposed by justice in some (putatively) non-justice considerations, which begins with the Razian view that a person has a right when an interest of his is a sufficient reason for holding other people to be under a duty.[14] That sug-

14. *The Morality of Freedom*, p. 166. I am not attributing the view that follows to

gests that rights are grounded in the consideration that they promote not, as with premise 2 of the foregoing argument (see page 288), the general welfare but the welfare of whoever has the right in question. Since these rights all pass the "differential grievance" test for strongly individual rights, I have no argument that they are not rights demanded by justice. But the prospects for the contemplated Razian rewrite of the argument remain bleak, precisely because the justification of the right by the interest is so immediate on this different and nonaggregative view that it would seem bizarre to say that honoring the right is a matter of justice but satisfying the interest is not.

I close this section by restating my single objection to constructivism and by contrasting it with a more common line of objection to it. According to constructivism, the principles of justice are those principles that would be chosen by specially designed choosers who are charged with answering the question By what fundamental rules should we regulate our social and political lives? A common line of objection to constructivism is that the design of the choosers is defective, with respect to their capacity to provide an authoritative answer to the stated question, meaning by an "authoritative answer" one that should enjoy authority over flesh-and-blood human beings, such as us. If, for simplicity, we restrict our purview to the constructivism of John Rawls's *Theory of Justice,* then the stated line of criticism asks why the erstwhile denizens of the original position should comply with the principles they have chosen once the veil of ignorance is lifted. So, for example, and here I report or adapt a question raised by Akeel Bilgrami, why should a Muslim who is convinced both that Islam is the true religion and that it is a holy obligation to spread the Muslim word be restrained with respect to the means he or she uses to spread that word by the consideration that *had* she been variously ignorant, *inter alia* of her own identity as a Muslim, and also, therefore, of what she conceives to be the truth of Islam, then she would have legislated a principle of freedom of religious choice that forbade certain forms of proselytizing?[15]

Joseph Raz himself, who cares much less than I do about what does and does not belong to justice. He has, indeed, expressed puzzlement about why I care about it so much.

15. See Bilgrami, "Secular Liberalism."

I am sympathetic to the stated line of criticism of constructivism, and, indeed, to the particular Bilgrami-derived question that I have just formulated. But my line of criticism of constructivism is different. It is not that the Rawlsian choosers are ill-suited to answer the question that faces them, the question, to repeat, by what fundamental rules should we regulate our social and political lives? My criticism is consistent with granting (what, sympathizing with the Bilgrami [and other] criticism, I do not in fact grant) that they are well suited to answer that question, and that they answer it correctly. For my criticism is that the correct answer to *that* question cannot tell us what the correct principles of justice are, and for a spectacularly simple reason, which is that justice is not the only consideration that should affect the answer to the stated question. Sound rules of social regulation must satisfy virtues other than justice, and must defer to factual constraints that do not affect justice itself. Accordingly, my objection is not that the denizens will not answer the question put to them correctly, but that it is the wrong question to put to them if what we want to know is what the fundamental principles of justice are.

I agree with the Socrato-Platonic view that led Socrates to reject illustrations of, for example, just behavior as providing a proper answer to the question "What is Justice?": no list of examples reveals what it is about the examples that makes each an example of justice. Until we unearth the fact-free principle that governs our fact-loaded particular judgments about justice, we don't know why we think what we think just is just. And we have to retreat to (what we consider to be) justice in its purity to figure out how to institute as much justice as possible inside the cave.

The "lovers of sights and sounds" in Book V of Plato's *Republic* think it suffices for saying what justice is to say what counts as just within the world of sights and sounds. They scarcely recognize the question What is justice, *as such*? In a world where the facts are F, they believe that P constitutes justice, and they do not abstract even so far as to see that they believe, independently of the facts, principles of the form *if F then P*. Plato thinks, and I agree, that you need to have a view of what justice *itself* is to recognize that justice dictates P when F is true. That is how justice transcends the facts of the world.

I also happen to agree with Plato that justice is the self-same thing across, and independently of, history. But that extreme anti-relativism is no part of the doctrine here defended that justice is, ultimately, facts-free, within anyone's belief structure, regardless of her position with respect to relativism, and regardless of whether or not relativism is true.

A final point. I have treated the Rawlsian identification of justice with optimal rules of regulation as a methodological claim: it tells you not what justice is but how to determine what it is. But it might be counterclaimed[16] that the stated identification is a normative thesis, so that my disagreement with Rawls is not really a methodological one.

Now I do not think that regarding the identification as a normative thesis is inconsistent with characterizing it as methodological, in the sense of that term that I intended. Yet suppose that it is, that "normative" is the only (of those two) correct way to describe it.[17] Then the important point is that the said normative thesis would, so I claim, lie in contradiction with the concept of justice, because we know, from the sort of concept that justice is, that a correct conception of it excludes the view that its content is the set of optimal rules of regulation.

3. Fundamental Principles of Justice and Constructivism: Matters Arising

In this section I essay answers to questions that may have exercised some readers. The questions are (i) What facts ground the choice of principles in the original position, and what fact-free principles explain why those facts do so? (ii) How do the claims of sections 1 and 2 bear on non-Rawlsian constructivisms? (iii) Does the late Rawlsian "overlapping-consensus" view of justice vindicate the claim that justice depends upon fact? (iv) What happens if we restructure social justice constructivism by purging it of its reliance on fact? (v) How does my critique of Rawls relate to my embrace of what has been called "luck egalitarianism"?

(i) I argued in section 7(ii) of the previous chapter that fact-free principles lie hidden at two sites within the Rawlsian architectonic, although their presence, as fact-free principles, is perforce not acknowledged, because of the fact-idolatry in Rawls's meta-theory of what constitutes principles of justice. First, fact-free principles underlie, they represent unarticulated premises of, the principles chosen in the original position. That first claim has been demonstrated. But they are also hidden within

16. And it was so counterclaimed, by Allan Gibbard.
17. Note that the stated description would disable the defenses of constructivism against my fact-insensitivity thesis in section 7(ii) of Chapter 6 and in section 3(iii) in the present chapter.

the unstated content of the "conception" of human beings as free and equal that justifies the original position itself. I have not tried to demonstrate that second claim, but I think it is plausible.

It might be asked, by someone who accepts the first claim, what *are* the facts on which Rawls's two principles of justice depend, and what *ur*-principles endow those facts with their supportive force? One part of the answer was given in section 18 of Chapter 6: the (supposed) fact that well-regulated market economies can function without "too much inequality" (and, therefore, the principle "One ought not to tolerate too much inequality") underlies choice of the difference principle. Notice next that the lexical order of the two principles depends on absence of severe scarcity: if one relaxes that factual assumption, one regresses to the general conception of justice,[18] according to which *all* primary goods are to be maximinized. The general conception generates no lexical priority for liberty or fair equality of opportunity under severe scarcity, but it does generate such priorities under limited scarcity.

On what factual information does the general conception *itself* (and therefore, too, the two principles) depend? One strategic fact is that there exist goods with which people need to be provided to pursue their life plans.[19] Those help to yield the general conception, together with the unstated fact-insensitive principle that, so far as possible, everyone should be equipped with what, if anything, she needs to pursue her life plan, if she has one, which in turn rests on the principle that *one ought to promote fulfilling lives*. It is quite easy to envisage beings without life plans, but someone might think that it stretches concepts to the breaking point to try to envisage beings with life plans who don't need any such (primary) goods. Yet think of a being with a life plan that is internally fully provided from its inception with everything that it requires for whatever life plan it might choose. To such fantasies some say: what is the point of considering science fiction cases? Answer: in order to expose the center of our principled thought about actual, human, cases, which, in the present case, is *not* focused on the provision of primary goods, but on the facilitation of a fulfilling life. (That disinterment of the indicated italicized fact-insensitive principle is related to Amartya Sen's insistence that capabilities, rather than the primary goods that serve them, are the fundamental concern of justice.)

18. *A Theory of Justice*, pp. 62/54.
19. Ibid.

As things are, primary goods are of course needed to fulfill life plans. But it does not follow that they should constitute the metric of just distribution. That rather follows, for Rawls, because of "the limits of the practicable" (*Political Liberalism*, p. 182, q.v.) and the intractability of alternative metrics of justice, such as the extent of satisfaction of preferences, which is not publicly ascertainable: by contrast, primary goods facilitate publicly visible interpersonal comparison. But we shall in see section 7, and further in Chapter 8, that to rest any claims about fundamental justice on practical obstacles to publicity is a serious error.

Further pertinent supposed facts are that people form, pursue, and revise conceptions of the good, or can do so under benign conditions, that they require self-respect to pursue their idea of the good,[20] that human society is marked by both identity and conflicts of interests,[21] and so on: fact-insensitive principles that are not stated endow each of those facts with normative relevance.

(ii) If I am right, constructivism about justice is mistaken because the procedure that it recommends cannot yield fundamental principles of justice, as opposed to principles that have some other recommendation. The anti-Rawlsian claims set out above also bear, *mutatis mutandis*, on a number of non-Rawlsian constructivisms. Let me now mention some of them.

According to any constructivism about justice that is under criticism here, the right principles of justice are the output of an ideal procedure for legislating rules of regulation. The inputs to the procedure differ across constructivism's several variants, in respect of the *motivation* and of the *information* that they assign to the legislators. In Rawls's constructivism, nonmorally motivated agents choose principles with general knowledge of human nature and human society but in ignorance of anything that distinguishes them (or the principals for whom they act) from other people; in Scanlon's constructivism (or, perhaps, in what is more aptly called a "Scanlonian" constructivism: see the discussion to follow) morally motivated agents, agents, that is, who wish to be able to justify their actions to others, and who therefore seek to cooperate with others under principles that no one could reasonably reject, choose principles in the light of full information about everyone's (includ-

20. That factual claim is subjected to withering criticism by Nir Eyal in his *Distributing Respect*.
21. See *A Theory of Justice*, pp. 4/4.

ing their own) powers, limitations, preferences, and so on; in David Gauthier's constructivism, self-interested agents with similarly full information choose the relevant principles; and in certain forms of "Ideal Observer" theories, factually well-informed and impartially motivated agents choose principles without recruiting any knowledge of their own characteristics to the task. Alongside the stated differences between them, all of these constructivisms agree in endowing the legislator(s) whom they appoint with correct (or the best available) general information about human beings and human society.

I believe that all those constructivisms fall to criticisms analogous to those that I have trained against Rawls: if the procedure works as it is supposed to, then what it delivers can't be *justice* as such. The point may matter differently in different cases: constructivists are differentially invested in the claim that *justice* is the output of the procedures they recommend.

The position of Thomas Scanlon on this count is unclear. To begin with, it is noteworthy that the word "justice" does not appear in the index of *What We Owe to Each Other,* which suggests that justice falls outside its purview. Yet Scanlon says, in a paragraph devoted to taxonomizing these matters,[22] that while he is not discussing morality in the broadest sense, but only a part of it, that part, what we owe to each other, is "broader than justice, which has to do particularly with social institutions": and that implies that justice does fall within his remit. On the other hand, he says that "there are important differences between the subject of Rawls's theory and the one being considered here." He contrasts "assessing the justice of basic social institutions" with determining "what we owe to each other," and he aligns that contrast with a distinction between "principles of justice" and "principles of individual conduct."[23] So there are contrary indications: it is hard to tell whether Scanlon's contractualist formula is intended, *inter alia,* to cover the territory addressed in Rawls's original position.

Now I have serious doubts, based on the position defended in Chapter 3 above, about the cogency of any aspiration that Scanlon may have to distinguish his subject matter from Rawls's, and I believe that the curiously various formulations, quoted above, which tell both in favor of

22. *What We Owe to Each Other,* pp. 6–7. The same taxonomy is suggested on p. 108 of his *Imprints* "Interview."
23. *What We Owe to Each Other,* p. 228.

and against such a demarcation, display a strain in his attempt to do so. (Note that when Scanlon contrasts his subject matter with that of Rawls, he implies, curiously, that the principles that justify the form of social insurance a government may legislate are not principles about what we owe to each other.) But even if I am wrong, and Scanlon has good reason to withhold application of his formula to questions of social justice, and believes in settling them in some other way (about which he gives no hint in *What We Owe to Each Other*), Scanlon's reasonable rejection formula *is* widely seen as an alternative to (and, indeed, as a development of) Rawls's original position, which is, of course, a device for determining the character of justice. If, then, Scanlon does not himself subscribe to constructivism about justice, we can nevertheless speak, as I did above, of a "Scanlonian" constructivism about justice. And that Scanlonian constructivism about justice would be open to substantially the same critique as the one I have made of Rawlsian constructivism: the replacement of the Rawlsian veil of ignorance by a reasonableness requirement makes no difference to my particular critique of constructivism.[24]

(iii) Joshua Cohen has urged, in private discussion, that even if *A Theory of Justice* does not do so, the view of justice that Rawls adopted in his later works shows how fundamental principles of justice can depend on facts. In that later work, principles qualify for adoption[25] by society by virtue of falling within the intersection of an overlapping consensus, where each party to the consensus accedes to the said principles because of certain elements in her reasonable comprehensive doctrine,[26] which is not itself a theory of justice. Cohen plausibly adds that the principles are agreed in the light of a party's reasonable comprehensive doctrine *and* her view of the facts. Accordingly, so he concludes, the chosen principles are *fundamental* principles of justice within the meaning of the act (see page 279ff.), yet they rest on a ground of fact.

On the late Rawlsian hypothesis, as Cohen presents it, there need,

---

24. In a private response (July 17, 2000) to a predecessor-version of the above remarks, Scanlon reaffirms his wish to distinguish between morality and justice, but he allows that he is "if anything more likely to be a constructivist of the kind you are criticizing about justice than about morality."

25. As always, I use this word to denote not the formation of a belief but the social installation (whether by law alone or otherwise) of a norm: see p. 276 above.

26. Or merely because nothing in that doctrine contradicts it—but I set that pregnant alternative aside here.

moreover, be *no* fact-insensitive principles of *justice*. There remains, on Cohen's view, a fact-insensitive meta-principle about the proper source of principles of justice—the overlapping-consensus principle itself[27]— and there might have to be fact-insensitive normative principles within her comprehensive view that explain, for each person, why the fact-sensitive principles in the overlap constitute responses to her view of the facts, but those varying fact-insensitive normative principles do not have to be principles of justice. If Cohen is right, the strong thesis of section 2 falls, whether or not the weak one still stands.

I reject two key claims in Cohen's characterization of the late Rawlsian position. His first key claim is that the principles in the overlapping consensus count as fact-sensitive principles of *justice*. And the second key claim is that the fact-insensitive overlapping consensus principle is not a normative principle, hence not a principle of justice, and hence not a fact-insensitive principle of justice.

I begin with an objection to the first claim. So far as I can see, the principles that fall within the overlapping consensus might or might *not* count as principles of justice: there is no reason to think that it is in the nature of an overlapping consensus that (all) the principles that it favors qualify as principles of justice in particular. The virtue that their pedigree in overlapping consensus bestows upon them is a particular kind of legitimacy: the late Rawlsian *norm* of legitimacy says that we should adopt[28] as principles of regulation ones that lie in the overlap of people's reasonable comprehensive doctrines. Now the principle of legitimacy is a principle of justice, in a certain sense, for it says that we do an injustice to a person if we coerce her on grounds that cannot be endorsed within a reasonable doctrine that she affirms. But legitimacy, while indeed itself a form of justice, does not render the principles that it selects principles of justice, in the relevant sense. For their justice is not, as with Rawls's two principles, a matter of their content. To formulate the position through a semi-stipulative distinction, the legitimated principles are *just principles,* principles that it is just to impose, but they are not necessarily *principles of justice.*

And because the principle of legitimacy is plainly a substantive norm, I also disagree with another premise that Cohen requires, to wit, that

---

27. Compare the objection to the second premise of my facts/principles argument, in section 7(ii) of the preceding chapter.
28. See n. 25.

the overlapping consensus principle is a methodological one. It is not a mere technique for determining what justice is, but a fact-insensitive normative principle that directly prohibits a certain form of injustice. The overlapping consensus principle says that it is a condition of just rule over people whose comprehensive doctrines are reasonable that it be possible to supply them with reasons to obey that they can conscionably endorse.[29]

I am making three claims about the overlapping-consensus legitimacy principle: it is normative, it is fact-insensitive, and it is a principle of justice. To be sure, the consensus principle is not a principle of justice in the sense in which the difference principle is one, because it is not a principle of distributive justice. Nor is it a principle that, like any of Rawls's principles of justice, decides which policies are just by reference to their content. The consensus principle is indeed a principle of justice, but it confers legitimacy rather then justice on what it legitimates. The question of legitimacy is not the question which rules are just, but which *rule*, what sort of ruling *power*, is just. As Rawls himself emphasizes, in his discussion of civil disobedience, it is possible to say: "This law is unjust, but we are bound by it, because it was passed democratically." "Passed democratically" thereby goes to the question of legitimacy or, if you like, that of just rule.

Note that while I disagree with Cohen on two counts, that is, with respect to the status of the principles within the overlap (they are not principles of justice, as such) *and* with respect to the status of the consensus principle itself (it is a principle of justice, not a methodological principle), I need be right on only (either) one of those two counts to deflect the Cohen challenge.

(iv). It is a feature of actually existing constructivism about justice that its authoritative legislators are supplied with (at least the general) facts of human nature and human society.[30] But a revised application of

29. I do not here evaluate that claim, and, speaking more generally, I for the most part ignore late Rawlsian theses about the "politicality" of justice, not because I am out of sympathy with them (although I am), but because my critique of an essentially *Theory*-centered conception of justice is pretty complex as it stands, and it seems wise to set aside the special task of measuring how well that critique also applies to late Rawlsian theses. (See, however, for a pertinent comment, the final paragraph of section 4.)

30. "in justice as fairness the first principles of justice depend upon those general beliefs about human nature and how society works which are allowed to the parties in

constructivism to the determination of the content of justice might be proposed, in which the legislators are not provided with factual information. Such an application of constructivism would make it immune to the criticisms of constructivism about justice, as it is currently conceived, which relate to constructivism's propensity to pollute fundamental justice with fact.

In its generalized description,[31] constructivism about justice is the view that a principle qualifies as one of justice because it is the product of a sound procedure for selecting rules of social regulation. Thus a view remains constructivist if its other elements are retained but selectors are deprived of the information with which actually existing constructivisms about justice endow them. They would then produce rules of regulation for each possible world, or set of assumptions about the facts, that they can reach by formulating principled reactions to merely *hypothesized facts*.[32]

I enter three comments here on the proposed revisionary move, to a constructivism that doesn't feed facts into its favored decision procedure.

First, it makes a considerable difference if the facts aren't brought in. Constructivism about justice is then very differently conceived, and it is clear, from my experience and from commitments in the relevant constructivist writings, that the proponents of constructivism would not be attracted to this revision. For thinkers like Rawls and Scanlon, the appeal to facts is not merely incidental. They believe that it is a profound truth that fundamental principles of justice, and, at least in the case of Rawls, "first principles" in general, are a response to the facts of the human condition. Rawls believes that the alternative to that view is "rational intuitionism," and, as we saw in section 18 of Chapter 6, he disparages "rational intuitionism" and argues against it with vigor.

So one reply to the claim that my criticism of Rawls can be accepted without abandonment of constructivism itself is as follows: even if that

the original position. First principles are not, in a constructivist view, independent of such beliefs, nor, as some forms of rational intuitionism hold, true in all possible worlds" (Rawls, "Kantian Constructivism in Moral Theory," p. 351).

31. One, that is, which generalizes its description by dropping the factual information requirement.

32. See, further, the discussion of Rawls's claim that the parties to the original position cannot possibly make a decision in the absence of factual parameters, on pp. 261–262 of Chapter 6.

is indeed so, leading constructivists, as the Rawls case illustrates, have a huge theoretical investment, albeit, as I have argued, a misguided one, in a specifically fact-sensitive constructivism. Two further points remain to be made.

The first is that, if my criticism is accepted and facts are washed away, then, so I believe, the principles chosen by the denizens of the original position will be of a more purely egalitarian kind, since it is so often the facts that make equality ineligible (as opposed to not identical with justice). So, for example, the "lax" difference principle[33] is, in my view, a principle not of justice but of how to come as close to justice as possible when it is impossible to realize justice fully. In my opinion, Rawls's constructivism, in its appeal to facts, subverts the egalitarianism, manifest in his remarks on the "natural lottery," which is his starting point.

Finally, even a constructivism about justice that is purified of facts generates misteachings about the relationship between justice and other values, such as Pareto, stability and publicity (see sections 6 through 8). And these misteachings, which, once again, deflect principles from egalitarianism, reflect the generative error of constructivism about justice, which survives in a factless constructivism, namely, the identification of principles of justice with the right principles of social regulation: that remains an error even when constructivism's principles about justice are chosen in freedom from factual information, and, therefore, for all possible worlds.

(v) I explain against Susan Hurley in section 7 of the General Appendix that there is no inconsistency between my incentives critique of Rawls and my published embrace of what has been called luck egalitarianism, which is the view that identifies distributive justice with an allocation which extinguishes inequalities that are due to luck rather than to choice. Let me now relate that view to the critique of Rawls that was presented in sections 1 and 2.

There is a big difference between the intellectual project pursued by luck egalitarians and the one pursued by Rawls. Luck egalitarians seek to render precise an intuition about distributive justice, which says, roughly, that inequalities are just if and only if certain facts about responsibility obtain with respect to those inequalities. I believe that Rawls

---

33. The lax difference principle (see section 12 of Chapter 1) is followed by a government in a society whose agents do not themselves respect the difference principle in their economic choices.

also had this intuition, that it governed his remarks about the "morally arbitrary," but that it was not his aim to explore and refine the stated intuition.

Luck egalitarians try to render the intuition in a refined form, try to get to the heart of it, through the entirely appropriate—given what the question is—method of counterexample, revised claim, new counterexample, and so forth. They are not thereby engaged in setting out all-things (i.e., distributive justice *and* other things) considered principles for social life (even though they sometimes mistakenly think that that is what they are about), and for two reasons: First, because it would be insane for the intuition about distributive justice on which they focus to be the only norm to be taken into account in organizing a society, and, second, because even if it *were* the *only* norm to be satisfied, it could not be satisfied in anything except a rough-and-ready way, because of epistemic and other constraints: determining the right effect of those constraints on the principles by which we should live is not part of the task of getting to the bottom of the intuition. Luck egalitarians are interested in the very nature of distributive justice, not in that different question as to what principles, to be influenced by distributive justice *but also by other things,* a society should adopt[34] as its basic ones.

Correspondingly, Rawls's project exhibited a contrary (but unacknowledged) limitation. He was not (really) investigating the nature of justice as such. His project was to establish what the right principles to implement socially are, and at a fundamental level section 1 raised but one objection to him: that he represents the output of that project as a set of principles of *justice* that define the very nature of that virtue. These principles cannot do that, because things other than justice affect what the right social principles should be.

The task of delineating a virtue, in this case distributive justice, is not the same task as that of setting out the design of a society. And—a stronger claim than that so far ventured—the first exercise should influence the second, whereas the second cannot affect the first. That is a stronger claim because it preserves the contrast of enterprises made in the preceding paragraphs but adds a *certain* priority to the first, which proposes to

---

34. See p. 276 above on how "adopt" is to be understood here. Principles that we adopt are adopted in the light of principles that we don't adopt. Rawls operates in the space of principles that we adopt: his view inhabits cell (4) in the matrix on p. 278. Luck egalitarianism operates in the space of principles that we don't adopt: it belongs to cell (1) of the matrix.

say what justice *is,* not how best to realize it under all the constraints of fact and *further* norm that social design must respect.[35]

Some (Brian Barry, David Lyons[36]) have said, in effect, that that priority *is* at bottom respected by Rawls, that his "real" view of justice is that it *is* equality but that we cannot reasonably go with that for the purposes of social design. But others would say, against what I have said thus far, that any intuition of the sort that I see at the heart of a certain conception of justice is just a preliminary prejudice, and one that loses its interest once a full doctrine of principles is at hand. I don't believe that, precisely because I believe that justice is *one* virtue among others that the right principles of regulation should respect, so far as is possible and reasonable.

4. Is Justice the First Virtue of Social Institutions?

Someone might say: for Rawls and the Rawlsians, "justice" is the name of the set of principles that an ideal procedure for choosing rules to regulate our lives prescribes, and it is therefore also the name of whatever are the right principles for regulating society. Accordingly, so it might be objected, the gap that I have sought to expose, between those regulating principles and justice, cannot open, in virtue of the Rawlsian definition of "justice" (or, strictly, by how he uses that word, for Rawls says that he leaves questions of meaning and definition aside).[37]

I disagree with the recommended use of the term "justice" (and I show, moreover, on pages 304–306 that Rawlsians cannot be thought consistently to use the term in that way). I believe, unsayably on the stated use, that justice, whatever its content may be, is only one thing to be taken into account in devising sound rules of social regulation: I don't see how anyone, whatever she thinks justice is, can deny the possibility that certain facts, or other values, might make it inappropriate, or too difficult, or too costly, to produce justice. Given *its* use of "justice," constructivism cannot acknowledge that truth: it is a truth that its very

35. For a highly illuminating contrast between the luck-egalitarian and the Rawlsian projects, with much of which I agree, see pp. 85–87 of T. M. Scanlon, "Justice, Responsibility, and the Demands of Equality."

36. Barry in *The Liberal Theory of Justice* and Lyons in "Nature and Soundness of the Coherence and Contract Arguments," especially pp. 152–153.

37. See *Theory,* pp. 111/95–96, 130–131/112–113, 579/507. Note that it doesn't follow that such questions don't exist, or that they don't raise problems.

definition of justice excludes. Constructivism cannot acknowledge that the right way to choose rules of social regulation is to take into account both justice *and* other considerations, that that is how we reach what is merely *called* "justice," in constructivism's (in my view, neologizing) sense of that word.

Now Rawls famously said that "justice is the first virtue of social institutions, as truth is of systems of thought,"[38] by which I take him to have meant the following: a system of thought may display virtues other than truth, such as economy and coherence, but if it lacks the virtue of truth, then its other virtues do not save the system from unqualified condemnation. So, similarly, an institution may display virtues other than justice, such as economic efficiency and coherent organization, but if it lacks the virtue of justice, then its other virtues do not save the institution from condemnation.

But while there is, undoubtedly, *some* kinship between justice and truth, the particular analogy that Rawls draws between them in his famous statement does not, in my view, hold: the relationship between justice and social institutions is relevantly unlike the relationship between truth and systems of thought. And the disanalogy that I have in mind means that justice is *not* the (sole) first virtue of social institutions.

Truth may be the first virtue of systems of *thought* (which are abstract objects), and it may also be the first virtue of the events or states that are people's thoughts, but it is not also the (sole) first virtue of utterances, and it is utterances, acts of speech, that, so I would claim, are relevantly analogous to social institutions; or, at any rate, the relationship between social institutions and justice is more analogous to the relationship between utterances and truth than it is to the relationship between systems of thought, or people's thoughts, and truth. The stated claim follows from the coherence of the distinction that governs the present chapter: between justice and the right rules of regulation.

Notice that the truth of a statement is neither a necessary nor a sufficient condition of its justifiable utterance. One is not obliged, quite generally, to tell *either* the whole truth *or* nothing but the truth: not *the whole truth,* since some truths are inappropriate to the context of utterance, or too difficult to convey in that context, and sometimes (think of

38. *Theory,* pp. 3/3. Is that famous and widely undiscussed apothegm consistent with the status that Rawls came to assign to (part of) his own system of thought, that it aims not at truth but at reasonable consensus? See, further, the final paragraph of this section.

journalism) the best that one can therefore do, in the very interest of conveying truth itself, is to minimize (without eliminating) falsehood; and not *nothing but the truth,* since it is sometimes justifiable, all things considered, to speak untruthfully, to mislead, or even to lie.

And I believe that, just as not all truth is appropriate to utter, so, similarly, there is some justice that cannot, and some that should not, be implemented institutionally, or indeed, as Shakespeare's Portia knew, at all. Just as truth is not a necessary condition of all justifiable utterance, so it is sometimes justifiable, all things considered, to deviate from justice in the formation of social institutions: these points will be illustrated in sections 5 through 8. Accordingly, as I said, justice is not the first virtue of institutions, as Rawls intended that claim. Institutions have and lack virtues other than justice, such as the general virtue of Pareto efficiency, and the virtues specific to what a particular institution is designed to achieve. Thus educational institutions ought, of course, to be just in the way they distribute educational benefit, but sometimes such justice conflicts with educational productivity itself, and when that is so, justice is not always to be preferred.

Someone might now say: So, if Rawls hadn't called his principles "principles of *justice,*" would you then have no quarrel with him? And what *if* the Rawlsian question, "what rules of regulation should we adopt?" takes us away from justice? Is it not nevertheless a reasonable project to ask what principles should be chosen for regulating society, even if we don't *call* them "principles of justice"? What's in a name?

Determining what the right rules of regulation are is undoubtedly a reasonable project, but what's in the name "justice," what that name denotes, is an elusive virtue discussed for a few thousand years by philosophers who did not conceive themselves to be (primarily) legislators and who consequently had a different project. That different project is too lightly abandoned by those who ask, dismissively, "What's in a name?"

And, indeed, a great deal of the interest of Rawlsianism is that, for all that, under pressure it forswears this very aspiration, it *does* promise to tell us what justice is: constructivism does not, or does not consistently, expressly propose to appropriate the label "justice" to denote what it had not previously denoted. It was because it was thought to offer a new and comprehensive theory of *justice* that the book *A Theory of Justice* was welcomed with such excitement: the excitement was not that Rawls had provided a theory of something, well, *sort* of like justice. And as Rawls himself said, in nearly plain contradiction to his stance elsewhere, "what one wants to know is the way in which [the two] principles complete the sense of justice, and why they are associated with *this* moral concept, and not with some other."[39] Rawls here agrees in effect (and Scanlon does too) that we have strong beliefs about justice *before* we do philosophy, and my argument has been that, whatever the content of those beliefs may be, any procedure for telling us what rules of regulation to adopt, all things considered, will fail to expose and refine those beliefs. What we should do, all things considered, perforce reflects lots of values and (consequently) lots of compromises; but it is a deep truth about our concept of justice that no such compromises affect its content.

If, moreover, and as some of my critics say, "justice" were, for Rawls, merely the name of whatever are the right principles, all things considered, for social regulation, then the statement that "justice is the first virtue of social institutions" would lose the significance that Rawls assigns to it, when he compares justice to truth. A concept of justice at some remove from the concept of the right institutions to adopt is required for it to be a substantive claim that the first responsibility of such institutions is to serve justice. We indeed want the principles that regulate the structure of society to serve *justice*, as much as such principles in all due reason should and can. But if constructivism were true, if "justice" denoted nothing *but* the right rules for regulating society, then we would be conceptually barred from making that nuanced judgment. When we look at rules of regulation, we want to ask: do they serve justice, as much as it's reasonable and feasible for them to do so? That question cannot be posed, on the suggested revisionist conceptualization.

In short there's a reason why Rawls calls his principles principles of *justice*, rather than (nothing but) first principles of public policy. Rawls says that each "person possesses an inviolability founded on justice."[40] That inviolability is not *founded* on the first principles of public policy.[41]

But suppose now that, chastened by my demonstration that Rawls was indeed interested in justice per se, Rawlsians simply abandon that

39. "Justice as Reciprocity," p. 198 (emphasis added). I cannot see how this sound aspiration is consistent with the texts—see n. 37 above—that forswear analysis of the *concept* of justice. Cf. ibid., p. 204, where Rawls describes his proposals as contributing to "an analysis of the concept of justice."

40. *Theory*, pp. 3/3.

41. Note that if we adopt the difference principle not *because* justice requires it, but because it falls out of the right procedure for optimal choice of rules, it is questionable whether the worst off have an appropriately *strong* right to the preferment that the principle bestows upon them, in the sense of "strong right" that I introduced on p. 288 above.

aspiration and declare that they are concerned solely with rules of regulation as such, and not anything more ultimate. That would diminish but not extinguish my challenge. For it would remain necessary to respond to my wholly unterminological point that rules of regulation require principles of justice, as such, as part of their justification.

Rodney Peffer says, and many would agree, that "the entire raison d'être of moral, social, and political philosophy and theory, in general, and theories of social justice, in particular, is to guide our actual practice,"[42] and that it is therefore a pedantic fuss to insist, as I do, on the difference between justice properly so-called and fundamental rules of social living. On the stated premise, that insistence could not constitute a contribution to political philosophy.

I reject both premises of Peffer's argument, to wit, that the whole purpose of political philosophy is to guide practice, and that what I call justice does not bear on practice.

I address the first premise first. Not all philosophy that discusses the background to, and the right form of justification of, practice is oriented to recommendations regarding practice. Large tracts of meta-ethics constitute a massive exception to Peffer's generalization. And consider, too, theories of the ground of induction. Induction is the practice of drawing conclusions from empirical evidence. It is an extremely interesting, and difficult, philosophical question what grounds that practice. But contributors to that question are typically quite uninterested in reforming, or reconstructing, inductive practice.

Even if, moreover, *a* principal aim of political philosophy *is* recommendation with respect to practice, it does not follow that *all* questions within political philosophy are directed to that aim, that the stated aim is political philosophy's "*entire* raison d'être." One may or may not care about practice, but one may also care about justice, as such, one may be interested in what it is, even if one does not care about practice at all. Political philosophy is, in my view, a branch of philosophy, not a branch of normative social technology.[43] "What matters is not simply the conclusions we arrive at, but how we arrive at them."[44]

42. Rodney Peffer, "Rawlsian Theory," p. 17.
43. Cf. Chapter 6, end of section 19.
44. Joshua Cohen, "Is there a Human Right to Democracy?" p. 229.

It would, of course, be unusual to be interested in what justice is while not caring at all about practice. Being interested in what justice is standardly goes with caring about it, and, therefore, with caring about whether practice is appropriately responsive to it. But to care about both justice and practice is not to believe that justice is the only consideration worth caring about for practical purposes, any more than to care about human welfare is to believe that it is the only consideration with practical moment. It would be crazy to care about welfare (irrespective, for example, of its distribution) and nothing else, when it comes to practice, and, so I believe, it is similarly crazy, a piece of fetishism (see section 6), to care only about justice. I want to know what justice is whatever I or anyone else may think is the right form and amount of the contribution that justice should make to political and social practice. I personally happen also to be exercised by the latter question, but one need not be exercised by it in order to care about the first one.

Thus, not all political philosophy questions are practical questions. That is not the "*entire* raison d'être" of political philosophy. The first premise of the Peffer argument is false. And so is the second, because, as I have had occasion repeatedly to insist, fundamental principles *do* bear on practice, since they are needed to justify the practice-guiding ruler of regulation. And it makes a big difference, moreover, whether we think the optimal rules of regulation by which we abide are in conformity with or in some tension with fundamental justice in particular. It affects the attitude we have when we obey them, and that can have further effects, such as, for example, on how we transform them when we find that we can do so, or on how we react to situations where the rules of regulation seem not to give us the right directives.[45]

Now unlike the late Rawls, Peffer does not deny that it is the aim of political philosophy to establish certain truths. The late Rawls holds, by contrast, (a) that *the* aim of political philosophy is to reach a consensus on reasonable principles, not to discover truths, and that (b) whether there are truths about, e.g., justice is a question that his philosophy suspends. But these positions are in tension. For unless, in contradiction of (b), one expressly *denies* that there are such truths, how can the specification of the aim of political philosophy provided by (a) be other than arbitrary? Why, that is, should a political philosopher not seek truths if it is not excluded that there might be truths about, for example, justice?

---

45. Compare the point about adopting rules that can be broken, on p. 269ff. of Chapter 6.

5. Two Illustrations: Social Insurance, Property Taxation

People tend to reduce the care that they apply to things and people that are in their charge when they know that (some of) the slack induced by that lesser care will be picked up by others, such as government, or insurance companies. And crucially for my forthcoming purposes, they reduce that care to different extents. This fact, which I shall label the fact of *differential care*, has many ramifications, and it must be taken into account by intelligently designed rules of regulation. It follows that the said fact must influence the choice of constructively selected (supposed) principles of justice, but the upshot, I shall argue, is a discrepancy between justice and the principles constructivism selects.

Differential care occurs for two importantly contrasting reasons. Some reduce their care more than others do in the hope and expectation that they will thereby provide less care than others do, and thereby exploit and benefit from others' pains. We can call them "exploiters." But others, mere "free riders" who are not also exploiters, just happen to reduce their care more than others do: they do not aim at exploiting others, but they benefit *innocently* from the greater care provided by others. Their lesser care is innocent if, for example, it reflects nothing but less risk-aversiveness, since no particular degree of risk-aversiveness is morally prescribed. To eliminate a further possibility of moral taint that may exercise sticklers, we can also suppose that the inadvertent free riders falsely believe that others are as risk-unaversive as they themselves are.

Facts about differential care, and about the difficulty of detecting it, constitute relevant information in the enterprise of choosing rules to live by, and, therefore, for a constructivist, they constitute relevant information in the enterprise of determining fundamental principles of justice. While those facts are undoubtedly relevant to the selection of principles that are designed to cope with them, principles reflecting the relevant facts are not fundamental principles of justice, precisely because their selection reflects, in part, the stated facts. The principles that reflect differential care are not fundamental principles of justice but, sometimes, principles for minimizing injustice and, sometimes, principles that trade justice off against other desiderata.[46]

46. Some nonfundamental principles of justice apply fundamental principles, in light of the facts, without thereby inducing a deviation from justice. The principles that cater to differential care *do* induce such deviations. See the trichotomy laid out on p. 285 above: (2) and (3) are at issue here.

Now you cannot seek to minimize injustice, in the light of facts like that of differential care, unless you have a conception of what justice itself is, or, at any rate, a view of what would be more and less just, independently of such facts. Nor can you, under the pressure of the facts, trade justice off against other desiderata, unless, again, you have a conception, which constructivism *ex hypothesi* cannot supply, of what justice, independently of such facts, is.[47] The root cause, moreover, that induces a compromise with justice in the "exploiter" variant of the differential care phenomenon is a certain human moral infirmity: Constructivists are, therefore, in the questionable position that they must defer to facts of human moral infirmity in the determination of what *fundamental* (nonrectificatory)[48] justice is.

It might be thought that the exploiter case is ultra vires here: is it not disqualified by the governing Rawlsian assumption that the society for which we are legislating displays full compliance with the rules of justice? But the *danger* of exploiting is too pervasive for Rawlsians to set it aside for attention only when "non-ideal" or "partial compliance" theory is on the agenda, and that is not how Rawls in fact treats it. Consider his explanation of how and why a residual threat of coercion is still required in the well-ordered society, which I had independent occasion to quote in Appendix I of Chapter 3:

> It is reasonable to assume that even in a well-ordered society the coercive powers of government are to some degree necessary for the stability of social cooperation. For although men know that they share a common sense of justice and that each wants to adhere to the existing arrangements, they

47. And also what the right rate of exchange is between justice and other values: see pp. 271–272 of Chapter 6.

48. Principles of rectificatory justice tell us what to do when those principles that are such that there is no injustice if everyone abides by them are violated. It might seem appropriate to defer to the fact of human moral infirmity within that branch of rectificatory justice that treats of punishment. But, properly understood, even fundamental principles of rectificatory justice are fact-independent: principles such as that miscreants (if any) should be punished, and that victims (if any) should be compensated, do not presuppose that there exist miscreants or victims, and (the mere fact) that there exist miscreants is not a *ground* for punishing them, or certainly not a stronger ground for punishing them than it is for rewarding them. To be sure, it is not possible, strictly speaking, to punish other than miscreants, but the possibility of doing something isn't a reason for doing it. See, further, the discussion of what David Miller calls "presuppositional grounding" on pp. 335–336 below.

may nevertheless lack full confidence in one another. They may suspect that some are not doing their part, and so they may be tempted not to do theirs. For this reason alone, a coercive sovereign is presumably always necessary, even though in a well-ordered society sanctions are not severe and may never need to be imposed. Rather, the existence of effective penal machinery serves as men's security to one another.[49]

Rawls does not say here that exploiting is *itself* pervasive, but he suggests that a fear of exploiting is pervasive, and that rules must be framed in recognition of that fact about, or related to, people's not unreasonable apprehensions. And that indirect influence of the "exploitation" consideration suffices for my critical purposes.

For ease of exposition, I shall supply a single familiar example of differential care, but it has many other illustrations, and it must, perforce, be a consideration to which Rawlsian selectors of principles are thoroughly alive, and to which they respond.

Suppose that initially there is no insurance coverage for the damage done to dwellings by bad weather, and everyone works and spends on an equal scale to protect their dwellings from meteorological misadventure, at least partly because that is self-regarding good husbandry, but perhaps also more high-mindedly, because their effort helps to preserve the social stock of housing. We might then think it right that people whose dwellings are nevertheless damaged by the weather should be compensated equally for similar amounts of damage,[50] and we might therefore introduce a state scheme, $S1$, that does precisely that. Two contrasting things might now happen, the second being more likely than the first.

First, we might find that $S1$ induces no drop in anyone's disposition to keep his dwellings as weatherproof as he strove to keep them before (call that fact F). In that case, under those factual circumstances, we would no doubt retain $S1$, and we could say that justice, in this context, prevails in an uncompromised form: people are rewarded, and penalized, according to the degree of care that they show (which happens to be the same for everyone)—there would be widespread agreement, encompassing, for example, many libertarians and all "luck-egalitarians,"[51] that justice is

---

49. *A Theory of Justice*, pp. 240/211. Cf. pp. 268–270/237–238, pp. 315/277, and pp. 336/295–296.

50. To make that thought plausible, let us suppose that, in the given situation, justice with respect to everything else already prevails, so that there is, for example, no reason to apply a means test before deciding levels of compensation.

51. "Luck-egalitarians," such as Richard Arneson, G. A. Cohen, Ronald Dworkin,

fully served by the stated principle of reward (which happens to penalize no one under our stated first assumption *F*).

But, second, it might now be true (and almost certainly would be in real life) that *some* people would indeed hope to benefit from others' pains, or merely that *some* people would, quite innocently, be less careful than others, and that *S1* therefore would indeed benefit some at the expense of others[52]: call those facts *not-F.* We might then replace scheme *S1* by *S2,* under which everyone has to pay (an "excess" or "deductible" of) the first £100 of all weather damage, because we judge that the said figure is likely to reduce the difference in care to a minimum, and, consequently, to reduce to a minimum the amount to which some people benefit at other people's expense. We choose the £100 figure that defines *S2* in the light of facts about the weather and guesses about people's differential dispositions to be careful or otherwise in maintaining their dwellings, under different financial incentives.

Under the second hypothesis (*not-F*) about the facts, scheme *S1* would compensate more and less careful people equally, and the more careful would thereby be landed with higher costs of effort expended upon care. Under scheme *S2,* careful people continue to be penalized, as they were under *S1,* for the foul dealing or mere lesser care that others show, *but in different measure,* since the care differential, while indeed diminished, is not eliminated, by the £100 excess payment. Each of *S1* and *S2* visits an injustice on the careful, because they are forced to pick up (some of) the tab for the others, but *S2* is *(ex hypothesi)* less unjust than *S1.*

Let me state the lesson of this example. The chosen scheme, *S2,* reflects two considerations: justice, which would, if it could, compensate with sensitivity to the *individual* (and which is fully achieved under *S1* as long as the facts are *F*) *and* facts about differential human moral infirmity, and about innocent variations in carefulness, and about the indiscernibility of all those variations. It would be transparently wrong to say that the facts about moral weaknesses and so on make *S2* just (without qualification), as opposed to more worthy of selection, because it produces less injustice than *S1* does, on hypothesis *not-F.* We know when we institute *S2* that we are merely doing the best we can: we are aiming to produce as much justice as we think possible. In instituting *S2* we are seeking to fix the excess at a level that minimizes injustice, but we

---

and John Roemer, hold that justice endorses deviations from equality if and only if the unequally placed parties are relevantly responsible for that deviation.

52. That is, even *ex ante:* all insurance benefits some at the expense of others *ex post.*

cannot set about doing that unless we have some prior conception of what justice itself is (in the present case, so I am supposing, it is a certain equality in the distribution of burdens across similarly insured people). And no constructivist theory can tell us what justice is (in this domain), since the principles that a constructivism calls "justice" already take into account facts such as that of differential care. Constructivists cannot regard a distribution of insurance premiums and awards that is congruent with differential inputs of care as a privileged, because undistorted, realization of the value of justice.

I said that we select S2, with the same excess for everyone, because we cannot determine how exploitative, or innocently risk-unaverse, different people are. But suppose now that differential levels of care are indeed discernible, but only at great cost, and that a just scheme, S3, one that compensates with sensitivity to individual inputs of care, is therefore feasible. We might nevertheless justifiably reject S3 and retain S2, because the great cost of securing the justice that S3 provides might make it reasonable to sacrifice justice in favor of an unjust scheme under which, so we can assume, everyone would fare better.[53] In electing S2 we would not now be maximizing justice, but trading it off against considerations of efficiency. But that familiar operation cannot be perceived (as what it is) in the constructivist optic. Constructivism about justice lacks the conceptual resources to describe justifiable trade-offs between justice and other desiderata, because those desiderata (improperly) constrain what constructivism deems to *be* just.[54]

To conclude: the way we treat the fact of differential care shows that some justified principles merely maximize, without realizing, justice, and that some trade justice off against other desiderata, such as, here, the desideratum of efficiency. But constructivists must (mis)call each such set of principles *just,* without qualification, should it be eligible, all things considered. Nor can they say which aspects of a justifiable scheme reflect

---

53. My view of the relationship between justice and efficiency contrasts starkly with that of Ronald Dworkin, who rejects the idea that "fairness requires that people pay in proportion to the risk that they impose on the risk pool, no matter how expensive it would be to discover that risk. That seems an irrational definition of fairness, because a fair system, on that account, would be an economically wasteful one" (*Sovereign Virtue*, p. 451). My non-Dworkinian view is that its being economically wasteful can be a reason for not instituting a (perfectly) fair system.

54. Note that a constructivism about justice that frees itself from factual information—see subsection (iv) of section 3—continues to lack the stated resources.

the demands of justice as such and which not, because they cannot factor the influences on the scheme into those that do, and those that do not, represent justice.

I have discussed here, a particular (supposedly) just *scheme*, rather than a fundamental *principle* of justice as such. But there is a principle that justifies each scheme, and the principle that justifies S2 would be chosen in the original position and would therefore be misclassified as a fundamental principle of justice by Rawlsians—misclassified as such because it reflects the fact of differential care.

In my view, the principle of justice that properly operates in the insurance domain is that, against a background of equality of access to advantage, people should internalize the costs their lack of care imposes upon others. That putative principle of justice is, in my view, fact-insensitive. But even if it isn't, even if *its* basis is in facts about human beings, the difficulties of applying it in unmodified form that were reviewed above disqualify it as a rule of regulation. As I pointed out previously,[55] the contrast between principles of justice and rules of regulation does not require the claim that principles of justice are, as such, fact-insensitive.

Let me now provide a different kind of example, which lacks the element of strategic interaction between governors and governed.

"Council tax," a British local property tax, works like this. Properties are divided into seven bands, according to their estimated market value. The tax varies from municipality to municipality, but in any municipality there are seven levels of tax, corresponding to the seven market value bands.

Council tax bands illustrate the proper influence of the non-justice considerations of feasibility and Pareto optimality on rules of regulation. The bands are justified by a principle of justice that says that the broadest backs should bear the greatest burdens: so the richer you are, the more tax you should pay. But the bands ensure that same-band people whose properties are of different value pay the same tax, and so the very principle of justice that inspires the banding scheme *also* condemns it of an *in*justice, because, for example, across a £90,000–99,999 band, the £90,000 person pays the same tax as the £99,999 person. Yet, although that is a flaw in the scheme from the point of view of the very principle of justice that inspires it, that flaw, from the point of view of justice, does

55. See the remarks in the penultimate paragraph of section 1.

not condemn the scheme *as* a rule of regulation. If Mr. 90,000 were to complain about the injustice of his paying as much as Mr. 99,999, the right thing to say to him would be that the only way to eliminate such injustice would be by designing a more fine-grained scheme that would impose so much extra administrative cost that everyone, including Mr. 90,000, would lose.[56]

I say that it is the very *concept* of justice that tells us that justice is not fully realized by a rule that embodies a step function of the sort that the council tax employs. You don't have to accept the principle that the broadest backs should bear the greatest burdens to see that such a step-functional rule of regulation could not fully realize a principle of justice.

Someone has objected that, in my claims about property taxation, I am contentiously supposing that justice itself is a precisely specifiable relation (between, in this case, tax and wealth), whereas it is in fact only a rough relation. According to the objector, justice says that tax should correspond merely *roughly* to wealth: within an extreme form of the objection, it might be said to suffice for justice that tax be merely weakly monotonic with respect to wealth. The objector claims that justice itself can say no more than that about this sort of taxation: the rest is a matter of practical detail. Inspired by justice, we decide to adopt some such scheme, but we leave the domain of justice behind, and therefore institute no injustice, when we work out the practical details.

I have three responses to this objection. First, that while we can maybe just about tolerate the thought that it is not unjust, from the "broadest backs" point of view, that Mr. 90,000 pays the same as Mr. 99,999, it is much harder to accept that justice smiles on the circumstance that Mr. 90,000 pays significantly more than Mr. 89,999 does. More generally, the strongest objection to the property taxation scheme from the point of view of justice is not to the spread within the band, a spread that justice might be thought to permit, but to the step-functional character of workable bands.

Second, consider how the proposed supposedly "post-justice" purely practical discussion of exactly what divisions we should have would go.

---

56. The very concept of the *precise* value of a piece of property is, moreover, obscure, unlike the concept of what it will *actually* command on the market, which is not quite the same thing. And that complicates the practical problem of identifying it. (By itself, without the practicality point, the conceptual point cuts no ice with respect to contrasting fundamental principles and rules of regulation. But it does so indirectly, by enriching the practicality problem.)

Suppose someone says that there should be twenty-five bands. The reply will be: that would be impracticable. But suppose someone says: let's have two. The objection could not now be that *that* would be impracticable: two bands are more practicable than any larger number of bands. So the objection to the two-bands proposal would be . . . what? What conceivably other than: that two bands would be *too* unjust? So the idea that justice, being rough, is left behind when we discuss how *many* rungs we should have is false.

Third, suppose, perhaps impossibly, that a supercomputer could calculate, cheaply, all property values with precision, within the limits of the conceptual barrier that was explained in footnote 56. The function from house price to property tax would then approximate to a straight line. Who could deny that the distribution of tax burden would then be *more* just than the distribution we are actually able to achieve?

I conclude that, as I said, the example shows that rules of regulations can run counter to the very principle of justice by which they are inspired, because of the legitimate influence on the formation of rules of regulation of considerations other than justice.

6. *Justice and the Pareto Principle*

(i) I now discuss the theme of justice and Pareto, which played a role in the previous section, in more general terms. The discussion also continues the critique of the difference principle that was lodged in Chapter 4.

Among those who think, as I do, that the fact that it would constitute a Pareto improvement is a reason for favoring a change, some will think, at least on reflection, and as I think, that it is not a reason of *justice* to make that change, while others will think that it is indeed a reason of justice. The position struck in subsections (i) and (ii) of this section is that Pareto improvements deliver not justice but benefits that, in general, contradict justice. In subsection (iii) I shift into more relaxed gear and I allow, *arguendo,* that the fact that it would constitute a Pareto improvement may indeed be a reason of justice for making the change that the Pareto principle recommends. On either view, I expose a difficulty for constructivism in the construal of Pareto improvements that it mandates.

Now I argued in Chapter 3 that "The Pareto Argument for Inequality" fails, because the grounds upon which that argument recommends an unequalizing Pareto improvement are inconsistent with the grounds upon which it recommends the initial equality that the Pareto-improving inequality upsets. I mention that chapter here not because the remarks that follow build upon it, but precisely because they do not, yet might readily be misinterpreted as doing so. Here I suppose, for the sake of exploring the relationship of justice to the Pareto Principle, and whether or not this is ever true, that, in a certain given instance, an egalitarian distribution and a particular unequalizing Pareto improvement on it exhaust the feasible set. But here, and in contrast with the feasible set under discussion in "The Pareto Argument," the feasible set is constituted as stated for reasons that are entirely independent of human will. In particular, and unlike what was supposed in "Pareto," it is not because those who have more than others do under the Pareto-improvement are unwilling to redistribute their surplus to those others so as to restore equality at a higher level that equality at that higher level is unattainable. Equality at that higher level is here *strictly*[57] unattainable: its unattainability is dictated entirely exogenously with respect to human will. The relevant context can be modeled as follows.

We have a world of two persons, A and B, who have identical preferences and powers, and between whom full distributive equality prevails: each of A and B has an external endowment consisting of five units of manna. The assumption of identical preferences and talents here ensures (or if you think it doesn't, then please add the premises that you think are needed to ensure this) that, in the present case, every egalitarian view, regardless of the metric it favors, prescribes precise equality of manna bundles.

Three indivisible chunks of manna now fall from heaven, and facts about physics, location, transport, and so forth mean that although A can have two further chunks of manna and B one, there is no way of reversing that[58], or of giving them $1\frac{1}{2}$ each, or of transferring other resources so that, although one of them gets two chunks, they remain equally endowed, all things considered (but at a higher level than originally). Nor can we withhold just some of the manna: we distribute all of it or none of it. So the feasible set is as follows[59] :

57. This use of "strictly" is related to the distinction between "strict" and "lax" interpretations of the difference principle introduced in section 12 of Chapter 1.
58. I impose this assumption to preclude a coin-flipping solution (whether or not that would promote justice).
59. I here ignore feasible distributions (if there are any) that are Pareto-dominated by I.

	Distribution I	Distribution II
A has	5	7
B has	5	6

Many would concur with the relational egalitarian intuition that says there is an injustice if society chooses Distribution II, in which A has more manna than B through no fault or merit or choice of either. In this conception, socially sustained inequalities due at any rate to *this* kind of brute luck constitute an injustice.[60] ("*This* kind": I do not need to claim here that *all* socially sustained inequality-producing brute luck is unfair; it suffices for my purposes that *some* brute luck inequalities are unfair (because brute luck causes the inequality). Thus I could grant that there is no reason to prefer a world in which all are blind to one in which some are blind and some are not: I could, that is, affirm that the former world is *in no way better* (which is not to say that I do affirm that), while nevertheless affirming the position advanced in the present section).

Now my own belief is that while unequalizing Pareto improvements on equality may represent sound policy, such (possibly) sound policy does not promote justice. In order to see whether you agree with me, decide what your attitude to Jane is in the following example. Imagine a peaceful anarchy, a state of nature with no state, in which manna falls from heaven and gets shared equally because the sharers think that's the right way to deal with manna from heaven.[61] Now suppose that an extra piece of irremovable but destructible manna falls on Jane's plot. Jane says: "I don't want this extra manna, I'm going to make a big bonfire with it to which you're all invited, because it's not fair for me to have more than you guys do, for no good reason." If you think Jane is being *merely* foolish, then you can reject the claim that justice favors equality in this elementary case. But I for one would not think that Jane is being

60. Some would say that if nature itself imposed Distribution II, then it would not be an injustice, because nature cannot produce injustices. I need not deny that here since, in the present instance, II constitutes a social policy choice. It is not imposed by nature (alone): nature presents us with two options. (Some would also deny that an irreversible inequality [that reflects no relevant merit or fault or choice] that is produced by nature constitutes an *unfairness*. My own view is that it clearly constitutes an unfairness but that it is debatable whether or not it also constitutes an injustice.)

61. Even Robert Nozick allowed that equality might be the right distribution for manna from heaven, although he signally and consequentially failed to observe that the raw resources of the planet Earth *are* on a moral par with manna from heaven. See his *Anarchy*, p. 198.

foolish. I would think that she is simply a remarkably just person, and I think we should commend her for being one, and perhaps reward her with the extra manna. Or even if we should not precisely *reward* her with the extra manna (since that *might* be thought to contradict the very principle of equality upon which *she* acted), we might nevertheless let her have it. Justice can be mean and spiteful, but it's still justice even then: we shouldn't confuse different virtues. Portia didn't when she recommended, in *The Merchant of Venice*, that mercy season justice.

Rawls must claim that the indicated Pareto-superior distribution, II, is required by justice, since principles mandating it would be chosen in the original position. Choosing, as they do, purely self-interestedly, contractors behind the Rawlsian veil have no reason to oppose the occurrence of accidental inequalities that make everybody better off. And Scanlonian choosers would regard the stated inequality as passing the reasonableness test that they employ. It would be unreasonable for anyone to insist on what egalitarians would consider to be justice.[62]

I accept the validity of the constructivist derivation of the Pareto-endorsing conclusion, but I deny its conclusion. For I am far more convinced that legislating for an inequality that incorporates this sort of brute luck produces an injustice than that either the Rawlsian or the Scanlonian procedure for determining what is just is sound. In my view the Scanlonian and Rawlsian procedures do not yield justice, precisely because "accidental" inequalities are unjust, and those procedures declare some accidental inequalities to be mandated, without qualification,[63] by justice, such as the one in question here.[64]

Of course, some readers will not share the egalitarian intuition (see page 317) that is at the heart of the present disagreement, and may therefore not agree that constructivism is false because it violates that intuition. But some of those dissenting readers may nevertheless agree that constructivism can be rejected because it can give no shrift whatsoever to

62. They could insist on what egalitarians consider to be justice only if, quite inappropriately, they were already egalitarians, and, moreover, egalitarians of an unreasonably fanatical, because Pareto-disrespecting, kind. But they are supposed to be *choosing* principles, not *applying* them.

63. See subsection (iii) below for a more qualified position, but one that is not open to constructivism.

64. In the present connection I find the following remark by Murphy and Nagel curious: "Clearly, no one could object to [a Pareto improvement], except perhaps on grounds of fairness ('why not me?')" (*The Myth of Ownership*, p. 50). Doesn't the possibility of a fairness objection spoil the "clearly"?

that intuition, and that the matter of whether, or to what extent, the intuition is sound cannot be settled by a meta-theoretical preference for constructivism. Why should the very many of us who have the intuition school ourselves out of it in deference to the fact that certain sorts, or even *any* sort, of choosers would choose to implement Pareto?

As I understand the position, we face the following trilemma:

    a. Constructivist criteria favor the Pareto improvement, and inducing Pareto improvements is, moreover, independently of constructivism, policy-plausible.

    b. Justice requires equality.

    c. Justice should dictate policy.

I reject c, and I therefore say that *even if* we suppose that constructivist procedures are indeed the right procedures for telling us what to choose by way of rules of regulation (I need not comment here on whether they are indeed the right procedures for *that* distinct purpose), it does not follow, and it is false, that what they tell us to choose is justice. Justice is *not*, once again, the (sole) first virtue of social institutions (see section 4).

There are three policy responses that one might make when presented with the feasible set exhibited on page 317.

    d. Justice requires equality, that is, Distribution I, so that's what we should choose.

    e. Justice follows Pareto optimality, so we should choose Distribution II.

    f. Justice doesn't follow Pareto optimality, and Distribution II is not just, but it's preferable on grounds of human flourishing and might therefore reasonably be chosen.

Justice fetishists say (d). Constructivists say (e). I say (f). I say that it's crazy to regard an irreversible 6/7 inequality of the kind that we face here as, quite simply, and thoroughly,[65] just—few would pre-theoretically be inclined to say *that* about it. But it might[66] nevertheless be bad

---

65. Subsection (iii) explains the need for this qualification.

66. Merely "might," not only because (see sections 10 and 17 of Chapter 1) we might defy Pareto where it *rewards* injustice (it does not do so in our manna example), but also because we might sacrifice Pareto to equality up to a certain limit.

policy to level down. Good policy might require a deviation from justice in the present case.[67]

(ii) Now manna, alas or otherwise, doesn't (any longer) fall from heaven, but the choice of principle (between Pareto and equality) that its descent would induce does have realizations in the real world. Some putative examples are provided by Philippe van Parijs in his "Difference Principles":

> . . . the most cogent efficiency-based case for capitalist inequalities (it is sometimes argued) does not rest on the fact that the expectation of huge gains lures entrepreneurs into working hard and taking risks but on the fact that capitalist competition keeps removing wealth, and hence, economic power from those who have proved poor innovators or unwise in-

67. I say above that the Pareto principle might trump justice, which is equality, and that the Pareto principle is therefore a principle not of justice, but of wise policy. Can we say precisely the same things about the relationship of the difference principle to equality and justice? We cannot, for reasons related to the fact that, whereas, in its canonical lexical form, the difference principle indeed recommends change wherever the Pareto principle does so, the difference principle also recommends changes where the Pareto principle is silent.

Let me explain. The difference principle relates to equality and justice exactly as the Pareto principle does when the feasible set is as it is in our manna example, when, that is, the choice is between equality and a single distribution that is Pareto-superior to it. Here, like the Pareto principle, the difference principle recommends a move away from equality and (what relational egalitarians believe to be) justice, but one that might be wise policy. But unlike the Pareto principle, the difference principle also recommends Pareto-*neutral* moves that are arguably in the interests of justice, since they both reduce inequality and render the worst off better off. Consider, for example, this feasible set:

	III	IV
A	34	27
B	26	32

Suppose we are in III. Then the difference principle mandates a switch to IV. But that switch is against *A*'s interests. So it is not mandated by the Pareto principle. So the difference principle does not relate to equality and justice as the Pareto principle does. The difference principle recommends change wherever the Pareto principle recommends change *when* the identity of the worst off is constant across the relevant choices in the feasible set. Where that identity changes, the difference principle makes recommendations among Pareto-incomparable options about which the Pareto principle is silent, and which are arguably in the interest of justice.

vestors, while concentrating it in the hands of those who find and keep finding the cheapest ways of producing the goods that best satisfy consumer demand. This mechanism would be destroyed if profits were redistributed in egalitarian fashion or collected by a public agency. Thus, inequalities of income and wealth may be no less significant as enabling devices than as incentives. This possibility is even more obvious in the case of inequalities of powers and prerogatives attached to social positions.[68]

Van Parijs clarifies the investment example as follows:

The key condition for the mechanism to work is that the good investors/innovators (or selectors of good investors/innovators, or selectors of selectors etc.) should have power over that wealth, whether or not it is deposited on the account used for their household's consumption. The key condition for the mechanism (in its pure form) not to operate via incentives is that the contribution to efficiency does not rest on the stimulation generated by the anticipation of a reward but on the judicious allocation of a capacity. The key condition for this mechanism to be at the source of a genuine inequality is that having power over these resources counts positively in the measure of benefit-burden bundles.[69]

Similarly, in Van Parijs's second, "powers and prerogatives," example—see the last sentence of the excerpt from "Difference Principles" given above—as long as hierarchy of command is efficient (which it may be), and higher posts are more rewarding (in a nonpecuniary sense), then a further inequality that is not incentive-based appears to be justified by the difference principle. My present claim is that there is an injustice in the result, and that, like the Pareto principle, the difference principle therefore sometimes endorses injustice.

Finally, and to the same effect, there is the case in which the training required for certain posts counts positively "in the measure of benefit-burden bundles." That is a third example of an inequality that is not designed as an incentive and that is endorsed as just by the difference principle, even in its "strict" reading.

If there were a mechanism for imposing counterbalancing penalties on people who benefit from the productive inequalities that have just been noticed, then these inequalities would *not* be *strictly* necessary. If they remained necessary, then they would be necessary only in the "lax" sense

68. Philippe van Parijs, "Difference Principles," pp. 203–204.
69. Private communication, November 8, 2000.

that incentive-based inequalities are: because the relevant agents would refuse to carry out their socially useful functions if the compensating penalties were imposed on them, if, that is, the rewards inextricably attached to those functions did not *also* operate as incentives. But there may sometimes be no such counterbalancing mechanisms, within the bounds of efficiency, and yet, so I claim, acceding to the Pareto improvement, while wise, will introduce an injustice.

(iii) The position struck in subsection (i) is that respecting Pareto induces policy that deviates from justice but that might nevertheless be wise, so that, once again, the constructivist identification of fundamental principles of justice with the principles that should guide policy fails. But that objection of constructivism stands even if the claim that Pareto-inspired policy deviates from justice is too simpleminded, and a certain more nuanced view is required.

Let me explain. It might be claimed that at least certain failures to respect Pareto constitute *in*justices. Thus suppose that we begin with a situation of equality, and a distributor either (a) fails to realize an equality-preserving Pareto improvement or (b) depresses everyone's condition, while preserving equality. Such a distributor, many would say, would be acting unjustly. And some would say that it is also unjust (c) merely to refrain from inducing a Pareto improvement *even if it is unequalizing*. That is because "justice requires us to display an appropriate level of concern for each individual as well as not display an inappropriately greater concern for some individuals than others."[70] In a word: justice, so it might be suggested, compares not only what a person gets with what another gets, but also what a person gets with what she might otherwise have got.

I am not entirely sympathetic with an implicit premise of the present objection, the premise, namely, that if it is unjust not to produce situation *s*, then (that is because) *justice* prefers *s* to the status quo. The distributor may be behaving unjustly in some or all of cases (a) through (c), but I believe that one can behave unjustly other than because one induces or sustains an injustice,[71] and I am not sure that the relevant dis-

---

70. Andrew Williams, private communication, October 12, 1999.

71. In the course of his discussion of the leveling-down objection to egalitarianism, Larry Temkin suggests that it might be wrong to produce a good result. I am here suggesting that among the goods it might be wrong to produce is a certain form of justice. See Temkin, "Equality, Priority, and the Levelling Down Objection," p. 156, n. 4.

tributor would be doing the latter. Suppose that A has 5 and that B has 5 but that B could be caused to have 7, with no effect on A. Then it might be unjust of C to fail to raise B to 7, because C would thereby be "failing to display an appropriate level of concern for each individual." Yet, so I claim, one might still affirm that raising B to 7 introduces an injustice that is absent in the 5/5 distribution.

But suppose that I am wrong, and that Pareto inefficiency is not only inefficient but unjust, because justice indeed has the asserted non-interpersonal component. This would not obliterate my Pareto-centered criticism of constructivism. And that is because the present objection to that criticism does not say (what no one could, which is not to say that none have tried[72]) that distributive justice doesn't have a comparative aspect at all. And as long as it (at least also) does so, then the Pareto improvement on which I focused will be (at least) *in one way* a deviation from justice, and constructivism will be unable to acknowledge that weaker claim. Just as it cannot distinguish the different virtues that may combine to justify a principle (see page 286 above), so it cannot distinguish different *aspects* of justice, if justice has different aspects.

To argue further for the ineliminability of the interpersonal aspect in justice, consider that cousin of the Pareto Principle and the Difference Principle that travels under the label "Weighted Beneficence," according to which it is permissible to favor the better off when they can be benefited much more than the worse off can be. Weighted beneficence may be the best theory of policy, but I doubt that it's the best theory of justice in particular.[73] Suppose that Sam has 3 and Saul has 9. If we give Saul the widget, he goes up to 15. If we give it to Sam, he goes up to 3.1. Can anyone believe that it's *simply* more *just* to give the widget to Saul? I can't.

7. Justice and Constraints, Notably Publicity, on Choice of Optimal Rules of Regulation

Consider the old slogan which says that "justice must not only be done but be seen to be done." The slogan is usually applied to retributive justice. It says, for example, that the right person must be convicted, which is justice, but also that it must be *seen* that the right person has

72. Such as Harry Frankfurt and Joseph Raz.
73. As Liam Murphy says, "the [weighted-beneficence] view that benefits to worse-off people matter more is not based in some idea of fairness" (*Moral Demands in Nonideal Theory*, p. 154, note 8).

been convicted. Court procedures respect the slogan when they are designed partly in order to promote that second aim. Since that aim is for various reasons a good one, it might justify court procedures that achieve less justice than they otherwise might but that make it more likely that such justice as they *do* achieve will be open to view. (The police often know that a certain person is guilty of a crime, but they do not pursue her because they do not think it possible to prove that she is, to the high standard of proof demanded by the transparency norm.)

One might also make a case for transparency in distributive justice: it is desirable not only that the right sort of redistribution takes place but also that people at large *see,* are *assured,* that it *is* the right sort of redistribution. Many considerations support this extension of the slogan, one of them being that, when justice is visible, there is then a reduced sense of grievance on the part of those who get less than they hoped for from justice, and that reinforces the propensity to be just. Existing taxation may *in fact* serve justice, but if people doubt that, they may obstruct the purpose of that taxation by reducing their work input in the face of high taxation, to the detriment of the achievement of justice.

Notice that the old slogan implies, as my examples illustrate, that it is possible for there to *be* justice, and injustice, which are *not* seen to be done, which are, that is, *not* publicly manifest as such: the right man might have been convicted, even if nobody really knows that. And the stated implication of the old slogan is, as that example shows, pretty obviously true. But the slogan, *when taken literally,* also presupposes that one always *could* tell whether justice was done, since it would be impossible always to *be* assured, as the slogan directs, that it was done if one could not always be assured that it was done. The stated presupposition is, however, false, and the slogan is therefore unacceptable in certain contexts.[74] So, for example, the justice of absence of racism, about which much will be said in Chapter 8, will often be invisible, because it will often be impossible to tell whether or not a person, say a person doing some hiring, has acted on racist bias. With respect to such a context, one could not say "justice *must* not only be done but be seen to be done," since it *could not* always be seen to be done in such a context.

Now Rawlsians would of course agree that justice might be done yet

---

74. Such contexts no doubt fall outside the contemplation of those who utter the slogan, so the relevant contexts constitute no objection to it, under its normally intended scope: that is why I emphasized *"when taken literally"* above.

might (as a matter of fact) not be seen to be done, but at least for certain contexts, they could not agree that justice, and injustice, might be done where it is not possible to be assured that it has been done. For that possibility of assurance is a desideratum of rules of social regulation in at least some contexts, ones, for example, in which it is wise to attach certain forms of penalty to their breach. Publicity is therefore something on which constructivists (who identify optimal rules of regulation with principles of justice) must insist in such contexts, and that suffices to raise an objection against constructivism. For constructivism will therefore dub principles "just" that might involve a sacrifice and, indeed, a judicious sacrifice, in the interest of publicity, of what we should otherwise think is justice.

In short, since the rules of regulation that the constructivist procedure produces are to qualify as principles of *justice, and* a publicity requirement sometimes properly influences the shape of rules of social regulation, constructivism must say that it belongs to the *nature* of justice, in certain contexts, that it can not only *be* done but be *seen* to be done. But while publicity *is* indeed a desideratum of rules of social regulation in certain areas,[75] it is surely not a requirement of justice itself.[76] So here is a further gap that can open between the output of constructivism and justice.

Robert Nozick explains how justice may legitimately be sacrificed for the sake of publicity:

> Justice, it is said, must not only be done but be seen to be done. Yet, what should occur when what can be dependably seen and recognized is less complex than (fully) adequate justice requires? The interpersonal function of assuring others that justice is being done or that principles are being followed might necessitate following principles that are less subtle and nuanced [than what justice would require—GAC] but whose applications (and misapplications) can sometimes be checked by others.
>
> Thus, there can be a conflict between fine-tuning a principle to a situation and producing public confidence through the principle. The more fine-

---

75. For considerations that show that it is not always a desideratum, see the final paragraph of section 4 of Chapter 8.
76. I do not deny that it can be an injustice to fail to publicize something, and that might include failure to publicize that justice has been done. But that sound normative judgment does nothing to vindicate the contested conceptual claim. It does not make publicity a constraint on what can count as justice.

tuned the principle, the less easily can its applications be checked by others. On the other hand, beyond a point of coarsening, a principle may fail to inspire confidence, not because it cannot be checked but because its applications no longer count as desirable.[77]

Nozick here exercises a sound distinction between the principles that define a virtue—in the present case, that of justice—and the principles that are adopted in the service of that virtue, under epistemic and other constraints—principles that I have called *rules* of regulation. Nozick's point, expressed in my terms, is that rules of regulation that serve justice will often need to respect a publicity requirement that is foreign to the nature of justice itself. Since rules are to be obeyed, they must be shaped with sensitivity to sociological facts about obedience, facts that have no bearing on the content of justice.[78]

Nozick also alerts us to considerations other than publicity that affect the choice of rules of regulation (called "principles" in his vocabulary):

Because adoption of a principle itself is an action that affects the probability linkages among other actions, some care is appropriate in choosing which principles to adopt. One must consider not only the possible benefits of adherence but also the probability of violation and the future effects that violation would have. It might be better to adopt a less good principle (when followed) but one easier to maintain, especially since that principle may not always be available as a credible fallback if one fails to adhere to the more stringent one . . . No doubt, a theory of the optimal choice of principles could be formulated, taking such considerations into account. [Nozick's footnote here: The promulgation of a principle also affects how third parties will carry it out; a designer of principles will take account of how others might distort or abuse them.][79]

The projected theory of optimal choice of rules of regulation treats those rules as a function of the relevant fundamental principles, for ex-

77. *The Nature of Rationality,* pp. 11–12. Note the contrast between Nozick's view and the one espoused by Rawls in "The Independence of Moral Theory," p. 295.
78. For an excellent exposition of the constraints that principles of justice must meet, on the assumption, which I have rejected here, that "principles of justice . . . are to play [the] distinctive social role . . . [of] controlling or resolving conflicting claims . . . on scarce resources," see Allen Buchanan, "Justice as Reciprocity versus Subject-Centred Justice," pp. 241–242.
79. *The Nature of Rationality,* p. 20, with footnote on p. 185.

ample, of justice, *and* considerations that are manifestly extraneous to justice as such, such as publicity, the sociology of obedience, the social psychology of "promulgation," and so forth. The desired theory tells us how much justice we should strive to realize (as in the illustrations in section 5). Constructivism promotes the extraneous (to justice) considerations that properly figure in the justification of rules of regulation to the status of constraints on what justice *is*.

Nozick also remarks that

> If a principle is a device for having certain effects, it is a device for having those effects when it is followed; so what actually happens when it is followed, not just what it says, is relevant in assessing that principle as a teleological device.[80]

And my point is that a principle that purports to state what justice *is* is unlike a rule of regulation in *not* being "a device for having certain effects."

I have sought in this section merely to refute the publicity requirement, without a proper examination of its motivation or a survey of possible arguments for it. That closer examination of publicity is reserved for the final chapter of this book.

8. Justice and Stability

Consider now the requirement of *stability*, the requirement, that is, that principles, once instituted, have a propensity to *last*. It is entirely understandable that constructivist choosers should want the principles that they choose to be stable. Stability is a requisite of wise social choice: outside special contexts, it is utterly pointless to choose principles to which people will not (continue to) conform.

Now since well-formed constructors must seek stability, Rawlsians, who believe that justice is what well-formed constructors choose, must claim that stability is a requirement that justice satisfies. But that is a good reason for rejecting the constructivist view of justice. For to treat the evident desideratum of stability as a constraint on what justice might be thought to be, to judge that principles qualify as principles of justice only if, once instituted, their rule has a propensity to last, is absurd. It would mean that one could not say such entirely intelligible things as

80. Ibid., p. 38.

"This society is at the moment just, but it is likely to lose that feature very soon: justice is such a fragile achievement"; or "We don't want our society to be just only for the time being: we want its justice to last."[81] It would mean that Plato was conceptually confused when he argued on empirical grounds in Book VIII of *The Republic* that a just society was bound to lose its justice over time.

Why might people who want society to be just, or, to describe their aspiration in the terms that I have insisted are more appropriate, why might people who want society to be as just as it is reasonable to want it to be, seek stability in the rules they choose? The obvious answer is that they want justice, or such amount of justice as it is reasonable to hope for, to *last*. But that hope is inexpressible when stability is treated as a condition of *counting* a set of principles as principles of justice, since, under that treatment, it is true by definition that there is no danger that justice won't last. And that is absurd. The reasonableness of seeking principles that will (or can) endure might mistakenly be thought to support the constructivist doctrine that just principles must be stable. In fact, it refutes it. We of course don't want justice to be permanently at risk. But the very coherence of that *fear* shows that stability is not a feature of justice itself.[82]

Take a partly parallel case, which I shall have occasion to revisit in section 7 of Chapter 8, namely, the virtue of loyalty. Suppose an organization is seeking to formulate rules of loyalty, and its members reasonably judge that a certain set of rules should be rejected because they are too demanding, so demanding that they would readily be flouted, with the result that loyalty (as such: that is, *loyalty*, not merely loyalty as it is defined by the rules in question) would break down. The members reject over-demanding rules not at all because they don't formulate what loyalty is, but simply because they are too demanding, and therefore coun-

81. Rawls himself writes that "a just scheme of cooperation may not be in equilibrium, much less stable" (*Theory*, pp. 496/434–435). I am arguing that he has denied himself the conceptual resources needed to say so, and that he there employs. See, further, the final paragraph of this section.

82. Vandenbroucke writes: "Maybe our ideals of social justice and individual behaviour are bound to be *fragile*—forms of life one has continuously to argue for, which cannot be guaranteed support by an overlapping consensus, which are, even if realized in practice, continuously endangered by erosion." (*Social Justice*, p. 280). For a similar opinion, see David Copp, "Pluralism and Stability in Liberal Theory," pp. 203–206.

terproductive. They are the wrong loyalty-inspired rules of regulation, perhaps *just because* they express what loyalty *is* better than laxer rules of loyalty would.

And all of that applies, *mutatis mutandis,* to justice and rules of social regulation. Just as intelligently formulated rules of loyalty must take stability into account, and therefore cannot be expected to specify what loyalty *is,* so rules that are optimal from the point of view of justice must take stability into account, and therefore cannot be expected to specify what justice is. The best, it is often said, is the enemy of the good. But constructivists must infer that it therefore *isn't* the best. And that is absurd.

Now by "stability," thus far, I have meant plain, ordinary stability, that is, the propensity of a thing, for whatever reason, to last. Specifically Rawlsian stability entails ordinary stability, but it also includes the feedback property that adherence to the rules strengthens the propensity to adhere to them in future, and, for Rawlsian stability, that property must, moreover, have a particular basis:

> Finding a stable conception is not simply a matter of avoiding futility. Rather, what counts is the kind of stability, the nature of the forces that secure it . . . citizens' sense of justice, given their traits of character and interests as formed by living under a just basic structure, is strong enough to resist the normal tendencies to injustice. Citizens act willingly so as to give one another justice over time. Stability is secured by sufficient motivation of the appropriate kind acquired under just institutions.[83]

It is by no means evident that this undoubtedly desirable property would be of interest to choosers in the original position, but that possible criticism of Rawls falls outside my agenda. Nor do I want to discuss whether, desirable as it is, Rawlsian stability is a required feature of a just *society,* because of complexities in the understanding of the phrase "just society" that can be set aside for present purposes.[84] It suffices to say, here, that, whether or not selectors will favor Rawlsian stability, and

83. *Political Liberalism,* pp. 142–143. Cf. *A Theory of Justice,* pp. 138/119, pp. 177/154, pp. 398–399/350, pp. 454–456/318–319, pp. 496–502/434–440, pp. 567–568/496–497; "Distributive Justice: Some Addenda," p. 171; "The Independence of Moral Theory," p. 294.

84. For the relevant complexities, see the last few paragraphs of section 3 of Chapter 3.

whether or not the latter is required by justice, the selectors will favor ordinary stability, as such, and the objection, stated above, that they will therefore put a justifiable constraint on the rules they are to choose that is not a proper constraint on justice itself, stands independently of the answers to the questions that I am largely bracketing off here.

Only "largely," since I do wish to comment on one of Rawls's remarks about stability, because of its relationship to other themes in the present study:

> However attractive a conception of justice might be on other grounds, it is seriously defective if the principles of moral psychology are such that it fails to engender in human beings the requisite desire to act upon it.[85]

But what might make the stated conception attractive, other than its (*ex hypothesi* unrealizable) justice? *Of course* rules that formulate the stated conception are "seriously defective," because they are *ex hypothesi* hopeless as rules of regulation, but not at all because they are defective as an interpretation of justice. To reject a presumptive principle of justice *precisely* and *solely* because it is unworkable (as a rule of regulation) is to endorse it *as* a principle of justice. In which case, why does Rawls respond to the discrepancy between the stated "attractive" conception of justice and people's moral capacities by assigning a defect to that conception of justice (it is surely not a defect in it, considered *as* a conception of justice), rather than to people's moral capacities?[86] Is it an axiom that human beings are *capable* of justice? Is "original sin" a contradiction in terms?

It seems to me evident both that selectors of rules of regulation must have regard to stability and that just principles might be (my argument requires no more than "might be" here) fragile: accordingly, justice is not what those selectors select. And note that the present argument, while delivered by my view about facts and principles, does not require that view. What matters is the contrast between two desiderata, justice and stability, and whether both are fact-sensitive, or fact-insensitive, or one is one and the other is the other, is here quite immaterial.

85. *Theory*, pp. 455/398.
86. Speculations presented in section 9 of Chapter 4 may help to provide the required explanation.

9. The "Circumstances of Justice"

It has been objected to me by many people that the circumstances of justice, as Rawls (following Hume) defines them (that is, roughly speaking, limited altruism and limited scarcity)[87] constitute facts that bear on the question of what the fundamental principles of justice are. I believe that the suggested objection collapses once we have separated four questions that proponents of the objection tend not to distinguish: (1) Under what circumstances is (the achievement of) justice possible and/or necessary? (2) Under what circumstances do questions of justice arise? When are judgments of justice (and injustice) appropriate, or in place? (3) What is justice? (4) Does the answer to (3) depend on the answers to questions (1) and (2)?

I have views that I shall presently air about the answers to questions (1) and (2), and my views are at variance with those who press the stated objection. But my principal reply to the objection, which is elaborated in the final two paragraphs of this section, is that the answer to question (4) is no. Far from the answer to the question, what is justice? depending on the answers to questions (1) and (2), their answers depend on the answer to that prior question.

I believe that Hume's doctrine of the circumstances of justice is principally an answer to question (1), and that "justice," for him, denoted, in its primary application, a virtue of persons rather than, as it does for Rawls, a virtue of the basic structure of a society:[88] For Hume the virtue

87. See the discussion in pp. 126–128/109–110 of *A Theory of Justice*, which contains this summary: "Thus, one can say, in brief, that the circumstances of justice obtain whenever mutually disinterested persons put forward conflicting claims to the division of social advantages under conditions of moderate scarcity."

88. Beyond this categorial difference between them, there are at least two respects in which Rawls might be thought to depart from Hume's identification of the circumstances of justice. First, he does not exclude the transcendence of moderate scarcity, consistently with a continued role for justice: see "Kantian Constructivism in Moral Theory," *Collected Papers*, p. 326. Second, he defines the "subjective circumstances of justice" with less emphasis than Hume lays on conflicts of selfish interest and more on conflicts of "religious, philosophical and ethical doctrine" (idem., and cf. ibid., pp. 323, 329, and *A Theory of Justice*, pp. 129/112). The second departure makes the first departure possible, since the second departure allows for conflict under unlimited abundance. For simplicity of exposition, I shall treat the circumstances of justice as Humean, but my arguments will apply, *mutatis mutandis*, to the Rawlsian variant.

of persons that justice is, to wit, a disposition to observe rules of promising and property, cannot develop under extreme scarcity, and is unnecessary, has no scope for its exercise, under abundance. The same virtue of justice would, moreover, be unnecessary if people were fully altruistic, and it would be impossible if people were fully selfish. Compare craftsmanship as a virtue of persons. We might say, imitating Hume on justice, that it depends on limited scarcity and limited talent. Under extreme scarcity, so one might say, craftsmanship would be impossible, because there would be no time for it to develop, and one might also say that it would be unnecessary under a Cockaigne abundance in which all desirable artifacts grow on trees; that it would, again, be impossible if people lacked a certain modicum of raw talent, and that it would be unnecessary, and also impossible (in at least one sense of "craftsmanship") if the most complex productive achievements came as easily to people as they do to an omnipotent god: if it's as easy as falling off a log, it ain't craftsmanship. But all of that *follows* from what craftsmanship is and has no bearing on *what* it is, just as Hume's circumstances of justice *follow* from what (he thinks) justice is and have no bearing on what *it* is.

Whatever may be said about justice as a personal virtue, with respect to whether it is impossible and/or unnecessary for it to appear under any of the four extreme circumstances envisaged by Hume, consider for a moment justice as a property not of persons but of distributions. It's hard to see what might make *such* justice impossible: whatever the circumstances, such justice might at the very least, *happen* to be there, if only by accident. And the idea that a just distribution might be unnecessary arguably embodies a category mistake: unlike justice as a personal virtue, a just distribution serves no purpose other than, if this counts, the purpose of realizing justice.

Now, for Rawls, justice is not primarily a property of distributions[89] but of rules and, secondarily, of the persons who follow them. So let us ask the rather difficult (1) type question about Rawls: might there obtain what Rawls could consider to be justice in each of extreme scarcity and limitless abundance, and under each of extreme selfishness and extreme generosity?

I believe that the right way to answer question (1) *might* depend on

89. The nonprimacy of "distribution" as the canonical subject of the predicate "is just" follows from Rawls's view that the distribution produced by obedience to just rules counts as justice under the canon of pure procedural justice: see *Theory*, pp. 87–88/76–77.

whether we are to take the rules of justice, as Rawls sometimes represents them, as essentially coercive, when it is said to be of the nature of justice that its rules are *enforced*, and not merely observed; or, as at other times he represents them, and as I have argued they must be represented, as not essentially coercive.[90] I take the stated alternatives in turn.

First, then, assume a coercive conception of just rules, and consider the case of extreme scarcity, in which at least some must die soon, and in which everyone will die if resources are distributed equally. Now some kind of egalitarianism lies behind the Rawlsian architectonic, an egalitarianism that he thinks justified by the arbitrariness of the natural and social lotteries, and that is articulated in the general conception of justice. But there *is* a rule that respects the general conception under extreme scarcity, to wit, some sort of (deliberately contrived) lottery. It may be that most people would be unwilling to introduce that rule or sustain it or submit to it under scarcity, but that does not make the rule impossible. Consider what Rawls might, or would, or must, say of that rare and powerful someone who could have seized the only life preserver but who instead rolled dice to determine who would get it, and who had the power to enforce his will, which is to say to impose a just, because equal-chances, structure. Would Rawls say only that he was amazingly generous? Would he not also say, should he not also say: what a just man he was, to impose an egalitarian structure to his own detriment, under those conditions?

The case of abundance is different, as long as we continue to suppose that the rules of justice, to be such, must have coercive force. The egalitarian rule under true abundance is, I believe: take whatever you like. People's opportunities would then be radically identical, and no inequality that would disturb an egalitarian could ensue. But this would not be Rawlsian justice, as long as we stay with the (in my view misguided) coercive conception of the latter. For under the assumption made by Rawls that no one would be motivated to deprive another of anything without benefit to himself, there could be no role for coercion in the situation. Only in the presence of contrastingly "spiteful" motivation might coercion be necessary for justice under abundance.

Still staying with the coercive conception, what should Rawls say about whether just rules would be possible and/or necessary under each of the two logically possible ways in which limited altruism might fail to

90. See section 5 of Chapter 3.

obtain? I believe he should say this: that if altruism were unlimited, then justice would indeed be unnecessary (though not impossible), and that if selfishness were unlimited, then it would be necessary if it were possible but that it would almost certainly be impossible.

We may make much shorter shrift of the opposite assumption, under which the rules of justice need *not* be coercively enforced. Then even under scarcity a set of unusually just people might willingly conform to just rules, and everyone could do so painlessly under abundance.

So much by way of the answer to question (1). But a more important point is that the answer to (1) does not settle the answer to (2), which is the question whether judgments of justice *apply*, in specified circumstances. Thus, to take Humean (personal-virtue) justice first, we could judge whether people have or lack the relevant disposition even in circumstances where it is impossible and/or unnecessary for the disposition to develop or to be exercised. As for justice in distribution, it will always be possible to characterize a situation as either just or unjust: it's false that the question will sometimes fail to apply.[91] And, for Rawlsian justice, in either its coercive or its more generally rule-governed form, we can always ask whether or not just rules are observed. Thus even if, and contrary to what I have argued, there could not *be* Rawlsian justice under extreme scarcity, it would not follow that Rawlsianly just rules for such circumstances could not be described, and it therefore would not follow that we could not describe such circumstances as productive of injustice, by virtue of the fact that people in them are bound to proceed without regard to Rawlsianly just rules.

But the central polemical point is that these speculations regarding questions (1) and (2) have little bearing on what justice is. Return to Humean justice, which is a virtue of persons, and to the virtue of craftsmanship, which served as a partial parallel to it. The "circumstances of craftsmanship" that I laid out in the third paragraph of this section have no implications for what craftsmanship *is*. On the contrary, they follow from what it is. And, similarly, Humean justice, the observance of rules of promise-keeping and property and so (though not much) on, is what it is independently of whether circumstances make it necessary and/or possible, and independently of whether or not they make judgments of justice appropriate, and Hume gives no sign of thinking otherwise. In a situation in which promises are precarious and property is unsustainable,

91. See Cohen, *Self-Ownership*, p. 139, and cf. Chapter 3, pp. 125–127.

there is no justice, but whether or not we or anybody else is so situated has no bearing on what justice is, and Hume did not himself confuse the question of what justice is with the question under what circumstances it may be expected to appear. (Nor is there much reason to think that Rawls did so. The objection discussed in the present section [see its first sentence] is pressed on Rawls's *behalf,* but I find little textual justification for it in Rawls.) Indeed, *if* not only Humean but also (contrary to what I have argued) Rawlsian justice fails to appear, or even fails to apply, in the relevant extreme circumstances, then that would *follow from* what justice is, and could therefore have no bearing on the determination of what justice is.

Accordingly, the claim that the character of fundamental principles of justice is immune to fact is untouched by these complicated considerations about the circumstances of justice. That there are factual answers to the questions: when can justice obtain? and: when can we ask whether or not justice obtains? has no tendency to show that fundamental principles of justice are fact-sensitive. Facts that determine whether or not a principle applies do not, by virtue of doing so, help to determine the content of the principle in question. So, for example, the principle of rectificatory justice that says offenders are to be punished does not presuppose that there exist, or even *might* exist, offenders. Whether or not that principle is held fact-insensitively,[92] whoever believes it to be sound must believe it whatever view he holds about how many offenders there are, and the same is true, *mutatis mutandis,* of the relationship between beliefs about the content of principles of distributive justice and beliefs about the (perhaps) restricted conditions under which conformity to those principles might be observed, or under which they might be thought to apply.

David Miller has resisted my attempt to free principle from grounding in fact by urging that principles are "presuppositionally grounded" in facts, such as the facts that form the circumstances of justice.[93] As far as the "presuppositionally" part of that adjectival phrase goes, it is false that (the truth or endorsability or whatever of) principles *themselves* presuppose any such thing. What rather presupposes certain facts is the

---

92. It is held fact-sensitively if it depends, for example, upon views about the effectiveness of deterrence and fact-insensitively if it depends on no such factual views, but, for example, on a certain conception of desert.
93. See section II of Miller's "Political Philosophy for Earthlings."

applicability of principles: but it requires no demonstration or polemic to show that *that* rests on fact.

The "grounded" part of the quoted adjectival phrase is, moreover, wholly unjustified. So-called presuppositional grounding is not a form of grounding, where that means, as it has always meant in the present discussion, providing a reason for affirming. It is, in fact, obscure what Miller means by the quoted phrase, given that he expressly eschews the normal understanding of "presupposition,"[94] under which it is a feature of presupposition that a statement and its straightforward denial[95] have the same presuppositions, so that, for example, "The King of France is not bald" presupposes that there is a king of France as much as "The King of France is bald" does. But whatever Miller may mean by the phrase, his illustrations of so-called presuppositional grounding prove the weakness of the objection he seeks to press. One of his illustrative claims is that it is a "presuppositional ground" of the principle of liberty, which tells us to respect people's wills, that people are self-conscious formers of intentions. But even if it were true, contrary to my first point, that, as Miller claims, the principle of liberty (itself) presupposes that people are capable of self-conscious willing, their merely being so, absent further propositions, no more supports the principle of liberty than it does the principle of frustration, which tells us to frustrate people's wills as much as possible. That a certain action is possible is no more a reason for directing it than it is for forbidding it,[96] nor is it *part* of the reason for either, since nothing can be part of the reason *for* something if it is equally a reason for its opposite. If you have no more reason to affirm principle P than its opposite in the light of F, then F is not even a *partial* ground for P: P-grounding-wise, you are no better off than you were before the news that F arrived.

Miller writes that facts like those of human self-consciousness "bring . . . the liberty principle into play—if the facts were otherwise there would simply be no reason to propose such a principle."[97] But the same is true, *mutatis mutandis,* for the principle of frustration: there would be no reason to propose it if there were no deliberate intentions to frustrate.

94. See ibid., p. 34, n. 7.
95. "It is false that the King of France is bald" is the *un*straightforward denial of "The King of France is bald."
96. Compare what is said about grounds for principles about causing and preventing pain and pleasure in the final paragraph of section 8 of Chapter 6.
97. Miller, "Political Philosophy for Earthlings," p. 36.

10. Conclusion

Before passing on to Chapter 8, I remind the reader that I have made in general terms just one criticism of constructivism, to wit, that it mistakenly identifies fundamental principles of justice with the optimal rules for the regulation of social life. That mistake makes fundamental justice sensitive to facts and to non-justice values to which, in truth, it is immune. The mistake has various expressions, four of which were traced over the course of the last two chapters, in which I have sought to separate justice from (1) facts; (2) the Pareto principle; (3) considerations of publicity and related desiderata of rule formation, and (4) considerations of stability.

Constructivists can reply in one or another of two ways to each of those claims; they can, that is, in each case say *either* that, contrary to what I have argued, rules of regulation *need* not be sensitive to the relevant consideration *or* that, contrary to my view, the consideration truly *does* affect justice. Recourse to a facts-free constructivism illustrates the first strategy, in relation to the "facts" objection (see section 3(iv)): the proposal is that constructivism should be used to select regulating principles for *all* possible worlds. The first strategy is, I am sure, unavailable for the Pareto and stability objections, and the second is a starter in relation to Pareto but not, surely, in relation to stability. Neither strategy has much prospect in relation to publicity, which, as I proceed to demonstrate in Chapter 8, is comprehensively alien to justice.

Appendix: Is the Original Position Justification of the Two Principles Contractarian?

Rawls describes his justification of the two principles of justice as contractarian, but it is not, in my view, contractarian, given one plausible necessary condition for the application of that term. And whatever anybody wants to say about the term "contractarian" (which lacks a canonical definition within moral and political philosophy), one point of the present Appendix is to make what appear to me to be some neglected but important distinctions,[98] whether they be regarded as distinguishing

---

98. They are not the same distinctions as those that appear in the late Jean Hampton's "Contracts and Choices," which raises issues that are different from those that occupy the present Appendix.

kinds of contractarianism (in a broad sense of the term) or as distinguishing contractarianism (where the term is used with greater discipline) from partly similar forms of justification.

Here is the plausible necessary condition for the application of the term "contractarian" to justifications that Rawls's original position justification of his principles, in my view, fails to satisfy: a justification of an obligation, whether to obey the sovereign, or to comply with a principle, is contractarian only if it grounds that obligation for each individual either in an undertaking that the individual has made or in one that she would make under specified circumstances. The contractarian obligation is then binding for the reason that, or for a reason akin to the reason that,[99] promises are binding: she is bound because she (in particular) agreed or would agree to whatever is in question.

Three contractarians, on the stated understanding of the term, are John Locke, Thomas Hobbes, and David Gauthier. Locke's contractarian theory of civil obligation grounds it in an actual act of consent, whether express or tacit, to comply with the civil order. Hobbes is a more complicated case. On the one hand, there are elements in his thought that similarly point to an actual submission to the sovereign being the ground of the obligation to obey. But there are also other elements in Hobbes that are not to be found in Locke and that point to the idea that it is because you *would* agree to the authority of a sovereign in any situation in which there isn't one, that is, in any state of nature, that you are bound to obey the sovereign.[100] Gauthier's contractarianism justifies not obedience to a sovereign but compliance with selected moral principles, and, like one of the contractarianisms in Hobbes, it is hypothetical in form: Gauthier's rational self-seeking individual would agree to the relevant principles in a condition of unruly anarchy, and that is why she is bound to observe them.

In contractarianism, so understood, the individual's obligation to obey or comply rests on *her own* undertaking, be it actual or hypotheti-

---

99. I add that phrase because the undertaking in question need not qualify as a promise strictly so called: consenting, for example, need not, for my purposes, be treated as a species of promising. The precise category to which the relevant performative belongs does not matter here. What matters is that it is the individual's *own* performative that binds her.

100. On p. 167 of "Reason, Humanity, and the Moral Law," I distinguish four arguments for the obligation to obey the sovereign in Hobbes, three of which are contractarian in the sense identified here.

cal. True, that the undertaking induces the obligation may, as it does (at least) in Hobbes, depend on others making a similar undertaking,[101] but that does not deprive her own self-binding of its pivotal role in explaining the individual's obligation.

Rawls does not propose a contractarian (in any sense) theory of political obligation: we are obliged to obey the state not because we have or would have agreed to its authority, but because and insofar as the state enforces justice. There is no actual or hypothetical choice in favor of the state—its existence is assumed, and it is owed obligation if and because it is (sufficiently) just. Rawls might, however, still be a contractarian in the way that Gauthier is, that is, a contractarian of principles rather than of obedience to state law. But I do not think his use of the original position, on its best interpretation, is contractarian in character.

When I speak of the "best interpretation" of Rawls's use of the original position, I do not mean the interpretation of Rawls's words that he himself provides, for he interprets them ambiguously, and differently at different times, relative to the distinction under development here. I mean, rather, the interpretation that yields the best theory that can plausibly be said to be borne by Rawls's words. And with respect to the present issue, that best interpretation is, I believe, as follows: that the two principles would be agreed to by everyone in the original position establishes, because of the nature of that position, that they are principles of *justice,* and *that,* the fact that they are principles of justice, is what obliges each of us to observe them. So I am bound by them not because I (in particular) would have agreed to them, but because we would all have agreed to them. And *we* are obliged not (directly) because we would have agreed to the principles, but because the fact that we would all have agreed to them in this position of supposed impartiality makes them principles of justice.[102] You could *say* that we are bound by them because we would have agreed to them, but that does not mean that we comply with them because we thereby honor an undertaking to do so. That everyone would agree to the principles under the stated conditions, so Rawls, best interpreted, claims, establishes that they are principles of

101. See the *"That a man be willing"* formulation and the *"I Authorise"* formulation on pp. 190 and 227 of Hobbes's *Leviathan.*
102. See Rawls, "Distributive Justice: Some Addenda," *Collected Papers,* p. 175, for what I believe to be a conflation between the interpretation of the role of the original position that I recommend and a more properly contractarian interpretation. Cf. *Theory,* pp. 16/14–15.

justice, and it is *that,* and not, directly, that we would have agreed to them, which obliges us to follow them.

To repeat: my reason for abiding by the chosen principles is not that *I* would have agreed to them. It is true and required but not the essential point that *I* in particular would have agreed to them. The thing to say to me if I resist the principles is not that I would have agreed to them, but that everyone would have done so in the original position, and that they are therefore principles of justice. There is nothing that we are obliged to do precisely because not doing it would violate an agreement, whether actual or hypothetical.

Consider a partial parallel. For some domains in which the European Union legislates, a mere majority of states is required for an act to become law. But other laws require unanimity. Suppose now that a certain law is unanimously passed, in a domain where unanimity is required. Why is Britain obliged to enforce that law? Not because Britain voted for it—Britain would not be required to enforce a law, in the relevant domain, for which it had voted but some other state had not—but because all voted for it, and thereby rendered it legitimate.[103] For further comparison, consider a European law in a domain that requires only a majority vote. In that case, Britain's obligation to enforce it is the same whether it voted for it or not, and its obligation is not grounded on *its* having voted for it even in the special case where its vote was indispensable, to break what would otherwise have been a tie. In the unanimity case Britain's vote is necessary for the result to *count* as unanimous, but it is not the *ground* of its obligation to enforce the law. And I claim that the structure of the obligation to comply with the two principles in the Rawlsian case is analogous.[104]

It is worthy of note that on the construal of the original position that I favor, Rawls's use of it escapes an objection to which it has been subjected, one that we can call the anti-contractarian objection. The anti-contractarian objection says that any hypothetical contract that occurs in the original position is not binding, because a hypothetical contract is

103. Legitimate, rather than just: that is one reason why the parallel is merely partial. But in each case unanimity confers a property that explains my obligation, in contradistinction to its being explained by my own agreement.
104. To be sure, it is because of a promise, that is, its accession to the Treaty of Rome, that Britain is bound by the European Union rules, but that is analogous to the "larger contractarian framework" (see p. 343 below) in Rawls: it does not spoil the different analogy that is articulated above.

no kind of contract at all. If I *would* have agreed (but did not) on Monday to pay you £1,000 for the painting you were to paint on Tuesday, it does not follow that I have *made* a kind of agreement with you to pay you that money and that I am therefore now obliged to pay £1,000 for the painting. Accordingly a hypothetical contract is not worth the paper it isn't written on, and, the objection concludes, the original position is therefore an unsound device. Note that the anti-contractarian argument employs the construal of "contractarian" that I have offered here: it says that *my* hypothetical agreement does not oblige *me*.

The anti-contractarian argument rests upon two premises, a major premise, which says that hypothetical contracts do not bind, and a minor premise, which says that the original position is a hypothetical contractarian device.

Now I reject the major premise of the anti-contractarian argument in its stated (and required) general form: there is at least one kind of case, so I presently argue, in which a hypothetical contract *does* bind. But as you will see, this particular resistance to the major premise of the argument won't help Rawls. (What will help him is my rejection of the argument's minor premise, which says [as Rawls himself mistakenly does] that the original position is a contractarian device.) I nevertheless proceed to rehearse the case that spoils the argument's major premise, because of its intrinsic interest, and because it is of further interest that the hypothetical contractarian claims of Thomas Hobbes and David Gauthier illustrate the case in point.

In the case that I have in mind,[105] you *would* have agreed to the current dispensation (be it a rule, or a law, or a government) not merely in some special circumstances, for example, those of Rawls's original position, but in *any* circumstances in which the dispensation did not prevail, and that is why you are bound to honor it now. None of us, born into a coercive order and not the state of nature, had the opportunity to decide whether or not to agree to obey a coercive state, but if, as Hobbes claims, we would have agreed to that no matter what the stateless state of nature had been like, then, so I believe, we are obliged to obey a coercive state. It strikes me as plausible that, in general, if I would have agreed to X in *any* circumstances lacking X, then I am bound to accept X; and that contradicts the unrestricted rejection of hypothetical contracts that characterizes the anti-contractarian argument. If *wherever* the

105. I do not say that it is the only one.

existing dispensation was not in force, I would have agreed to it, then it seems to me a very powerful answer to any resistance to it that I may seek to mount that I would have agreed to it if it hadn't been there.[106] This does not mean that I have to do whatever the state in being tells me to do, but rather that I cannot object to it *just* on the ground that it's a coercive state to whose rule I have not consented. Hobbes argues *(inter alia)*[107] as follows: "Either we accept the sovereign or we are in a state of nature. But it is so bad to be in any state of nature that we would (or would have) accepted the sovereign were we (or had we been) in one. Therefore we are obliged to accept the sovereign." The argument says that we must accept state sovereignty if in its absence we would have agreed to create it. That major premise seems to me to be sound,[108] whatever we may think about the minor premise of the Hobbesian argument, which says that any state of nature would indeed be sufficiently bad to generate a preference for a sovereign.

But this counterexample to the wholesale rejection of hypothetical contracts doesn't help to defend Rawls against the anti-contractarian objection. For the Rawlsian agreement on principles of justice is emphatically not one that people would make under any and all conditions, whether or not they would make it under the specific condition of the veil of ignorance imposed by Rawls. And the *mere* fact taken just by itself, and supposing that it is one, that we would have agreed to those principles under such special circumstances does not, indeed, just in itself, oblige us to observe them. But if what I have called (see page 339) the best interpretation of Rawls's use of the original position is correct,

---

106. A similar point vindicates the so-called fair play principle against *one* objection, namely, that one might have had no choice about receiving the relevant benefits. If I would have sought the benefits, no matter what, then my protest against paying (at least the lowest amount that I would have paid) for them is silenced (see Rawls's defense of the principle of fairness in section 52 of *Theory*, and Nozick's criticism of it on pp. 90–95 of *Anarchy*, a criticism that, I believe, falls to the present point).

107. See n. 100 above.

108. Accordingly, and to the stated limited extent, I disagree with Ronald Dworkin's statement that "hypothetical contracts do not supply an independent argument for the fairness of enforcing their terms." Of course "a hypothetical contract . . . is no contract at all" but the material question is whether the fact that you would have contracted thus and so can itself have normative force, and I think it does, on the condition that you would have so contracted, no matter what. See Dworkin, "The Original Position," pp. 17–18.

the minor premise of the anti-contractarian argument fails, and his view therefore escapes its grip.

The demonstration of the irrelevance of the anti-contractarian criticism against Rawls does not, of course, clear his original position derivation of the two principles from all criticism. There is nothing self-evident in the claim that any principles chosen under the veil of ignorance qualify as principles of justice, and that has been subjected to independent criticism that I do not reject here (or elsewhere).[109]

While I have sought to show that the original position device does not make Rawls a contractarian, the larger framework within which he sets recourse to the original position is indeed contractarian. The original position device is conceived as settling the principles for a society of co-operators who wish to deal with each other justly and who *actually* agree that the original position is the way to determine what is just. But that does not contradict my view that they comply with the principles because they (think) they bear the stamp of justice, as opposed to in fulfillment of a hypothetical agreement.

Hobbes, Locke, and Gauthier are true contractarians, because it is *my* actual or hypothetical agreement that obliges me to obey Hobbes's sovereign, Locke's rules of civil society, and Gauthier's moral principles. But Scanlon's "reasonable rejection" test is not contractarian in the present sense: What obliges me to observe the principles that his device generates is not that *I* could not reasonably reject them but that no one could.

So, to conclude, on my understanding of the form of Rawls's and Scanlon's arguments, it runs as follows: everybody (under the veil of ignorance, or who is reasonable) would agree to these rules, therefore they are the right rules, therefore everybody is obliged to comply with them.

109. What I differently and expressly criticize in the opening parts of the present chapter is the claim that the principles chosen behind the veil are *fundamental* principles of justice.

8

THE PUBLICITY ARGUMENT

1. Andrew Williams on Publicity and the Egalitarian Ethos

Andrew Williams claims that my attempt to apply the difference principle to the domain of personal economic choice falls to the objection that principles of justice must satisfy a publicity requirement, which says that it should be possible to *tell* whether or not a principle of justice is being followed.[1] That requirement, Williams claims, defeats my contentions that a just society possesses an egalitarian economic ethos, and that it is therefore not just by virtue of the character of its state-legislated basic structure alone.[2] I hope to show that publicity, as Williams explicates that notion, is demonstrably not a requirement of justice, and that the egalitarian ethos that, so I say, justice demands meets every *defensible* publicity requirement on justice. To clarify: whether or not publicity is a *constraint* on, or, differently, a *desideratum* of, *rules* of *social regulation,* I shall argue that it is not a constraint on what *justice is* (see sections 3–6) and that the weaker suggestion that, even so, it might be a *desideratum* of justice, is unintelligible (see section 7).[3]

Williams is in broad terms a defender of Rawls, so it is worth noting that it is not at all clear that, by contrast with stability, publicity, in Williams's strong sense, would be favored by legislators in the original posi-

1. A fuller statement of the requirement is presented in section 2 below.
2. See Williams, "Incentives, Inequality, and Publicity." Except where otherwise indicated, all page references in the text of this chapter are to the cited article.
3. Williams also invokes stability, in the specifically Rawlsian sense (pp. 244–245), but that part of his case can readily be dismissed, since, as I showed in section 6 of Chapter 7, stability has nothing to do with justice. To be sure, I have also already maintained (in section 7 of Chapter 7) that publicity itself is alien to justice, but that is a more controversial contention, and I supply further argument for it here.

tion.[4] Publicity might be thought to be demanded by contractarianism, because contractors require clear terms of contract, to keep the line bright between compliance with and violation of the contract. But however that may be, it is my own view that a correct understanding of the role of the original position within the structure of his thought shows that Rawlsian constructivism is *not* a contractarian doctrine,[5] or, this being the essential point, not a contractarian doctrine in the sense that the argument just stated requires.

And whether or not constructivism and/or contractarianism imposes a publicity constraint on justice, Williams's case for publicity does not depend upon Rawlsian constructivism: although his is a defense of Rawls against my incentives-centered critique, his case does not presuppose that principles are to be chosen in a Rawlsian original position. We may therefore set Rawlsian constructivism aside here and address Williams, as it were, directly.

Note further that the concept of the basic structure plays no role in Williams's argument: see my reconstruction of that argument on page 348 below. The argument is intended to show that the difference principle doesn't govern individual economic choice and that an egalitarian ethos that informs such choice is therefore not a requirement of distributive justice, and neither that conclusion, nor the reasoning adduced to sustain it, employs the concept of the basic structure.

A word before I proceed to a detailed presentation and refutation of Williams's claims. An early draft of Williams's paper bore the title "In Tax We Trust," and, on page 246 of the published version, Williams *counterposes* redistribution through taxation to redistribution that is (entirely) due to an egalitarian ethos. But that is a false contrast. Rather, the two work together: the more egalitarian a society's ethos is, the more scope there will be in that society for Pareto-consistent redistributive taxation (see section 1 of the General Appendix). And in that context, "the kinds of informational issues that Williams identifies are not likely to be crucial."[6] I don't distrust tax. I say we should not trust

---

4. By contrast, original position legislators must aim at stability, even if they have no reason to aim at specifically Rawlsian stability: see section 8 of Chapter 7.
5. See the Appendix to Chapter 7 for a defense of that view.
   Williams's own view *is* akin to a kind of contractarianism, because of the strategic role of the *assurance* consideration in his argument (see sections 2 through 4 below).
6. Joseph Carens, "An Interpretation and Defense of the Socialist Principle of Distribution," p. 172.

in tax *alone:* if we do so, we can't trust tax to deliver what it otherwise could.

2. An Anatomy of Williams's Argument

Williams holds that for a rule to be a rule of *justice,* it must possess a publicity property: it must be discernible, in principle, what the rule requires and whether or not it has been satisfied, since "justice must be seen in order to be done" (page 246). The quoted claim is not equivalent to the idea carried by the old slogan that says "that justice must not only be done but be seen to be done," which I discussed in section 7 of Chapter 7. The seeing in Williams's remark is knowledge of what the just rule *is,* whereas the seeing in the old slogan is knowledge that the just rule is being *implemented.* What Williams denies, *inter alia,* is that there might be justice that *could not* be seen to be done.

Williams explicates what he means by "public" when he lays down that the rules of justice must be public in the threefold sense that

> individuals are able to attain common knowledge[7] of the rules' (i) general applicability, (ii) their particular requirements, and (iii) the extent to which individuals conform to those requirements.[8]

I understand the (somewhat curiously formulated) condition (i) to require that it be possible that everyone should know (that everyone knows that everyone knows that . . .) what the rules are: it excludes, for example, what Bernard Williams famously called "government house utilitarianism," according to which the government lays down rules conformity to which is utility-maximizing, but citizens obey those rules under the inspiration of nonconsequentialist deontic considerations. The government's principle is not *their* principle: it is the secret principle that explains why they are to follow their different principles. Williams's condition (i) excludes that sort of manipulation. It says that "individuals [must be] able to attain common knowledge" of what the governing rules of justice (simply) *are,* by contrast with (ii), which demands possi-

7. Individuals enjoy *common knowledge* of *p* when each knows that *p,* knows that the others know that *p,* knows that each of the others also knows the latter, and so on, ad infinitum, if that is possible, or as much as possible, if ad infinitum is impossible.
8. Ibid., p. 233.

ble common knowledge of what the implications of those rules are for particular cases.

There is an ambiguity in (iii), which Williams resolves in favor of an especially strong version of (iii). For if I understand him correctly, Williams means condition (iii) to be taken distributively rather than merely collectively: that is, with respect to (at least most) individuals, it must, Williams thinks, be possible to know, at any rate under favorable conditions of information, how much *each* of those individuals conforms to the requirements of justice.[9] If I understand Williams aright, his condition (iii) is not satisfied if we could have common knowledge that 98 percent of us conform to a rule, but we could not know which of us belongs to the 98 percent and which to the 2 percent. I shall argue later that condition (iii), thus interpreted, is an absurdly strong requirement on principles of justice (see sections 3–5).

Condition (i) will not be challenged here, but (ii) and (iii) will be subjected to criticism: I shall show that, understood in the strong form that Williams's argument requires, they are not conditions that justice must satisfy. I shall also show that the egalitarian ethos that I claim to be demanded by justice satisfies conditions (ii) and (iii) to a greater extent than Williams supposes.

Why does Williams insist on these conditions? Why does he think that matters that cannot be subjected to a form of public regulation that is possible only where (i) through (iii) hold are therefore beyond the writ of justice, however profound their effects may be on people's life chances? He thinks so because he believes that a certain ideal of social unity (pages 243ff.) that is integral to justice is unachievable in the absence of that form of publicity: justice, for Williams, is a cooperative enterprise the cooperators in which must know that others are cooperating—they are bound by justice to cooperate only when they know that others, too, are cooperating: it would be unfair to expect them to take up the burden of justice unless (they can know that) others are doing so.[10] And since the rules of an egalitarian ethos cannot be stated in a form that enables indi-

9. The stated understanding of Williams is strongly suggested by the material on pp. 233–234 of his "Incentives," and more or less demonstrated by his focus on individuals on pp. 238–239.

10. The fairness motif is not so manifest in Williams's presentation, but Adam Swift plausibly suggested to me that it is integral to the Williams position. Whatever Williams thought, the motif certainly strengthens his position, so I take it on board here. See, further, the third paragraph of section 3 below.

viduals to know, with any precision, how they apply to their own case, and whether others are complying with them, such rules cannot be rules of justice. Considered as candidates for rules of justice, they are exposed to an insoluble "assurance problem."

I propose the following reconstruction of Williams's argument:

     1. Justice is a set of demands.

     2. Demands of justice are to be discharged (only) collectively.

∴ 3. An individual is not obliged by a (putative) demand of justice unless others in general are disposed to observe that demand. (By 1 and 2.)

     4. You are not obliged to discharge a demand of justice unless you can know that you are obliged to do so.

∴ 5. No one *can be obliged* by a demand of justice unless it can be known, unless one could be *assured,* that others are observing it. (By 3 and 4.)

∴ 6. Nothing *is* a demand of justice unless one can be *assured* that others are observing it. (By 5.)

But

     7. One cannot be assured that others are observing a demand unless (ii) the implications of the demand are clear in particular cases, and (iii) one can tell whether or not given individuals are observing the demand.

∴ 8. Demands of justice satisfy (ii) and (iii) (by 6 and 7).

But

     9. The egalitarian ethos does not satisfy (ii) and (iii).

∴ 10. The egalitarian ethos is not a set of demands of justice.

3. Racism, Justice, and Assurance

I now proceed to evaluate various elements in the foregoing argument.

I begin with a counterexample to subconclusion 3. If anything is unjust, racism is. But I am obliged by justice to eschew racism even when I know that the majority of my fellows are racist. I am also obliged by justice not to exploit other people, even when I know that exploitation is rife. And that falsifies 3.

I consider the judgments lodged in the immediately preceding paragraph to be consistent with proper appreciation of the *fairness* consideration whose mention preceded my step-wise presentation of William's argument. A person's burden, under justice, may be greater than it otherwise would be when others do not take up theirs: so, for example, I may have to choose between exploiting, or practicing racist hiring, and otherwise going bankrupt. There is then undoubtedly an unfairness in my situation, but it remains true that I treat people of the wrong color, or exploited workers, unjustly if I, too, join the justice-violating crowd, and that is the sole point of contention here. An injustice can be done to them even if it is unfair to expect its agent to act otherwise. Perhaps in certain extreme cases of the relevant unfair shouldering of burden, I might even be *justified* in not doing what justice requires. That is a question on which I need not take a stand: I need only insist that justice nevertheless requires it.

Since 3 is false, at least one of 1 and 2 is false. And the examples, racism and exploitation, that I used to show that 3 is false also shows that at least 2 is false.

Premise 1 might also be challenged, but only if it is interpreted as I do not mean it to be interpreted here. For premise 1 is open to at least two different interpretations, which correspond to contrasting senses that the word "demand" may bear as it appears in the statement of the premise. If, as I do *not* intend, we take "demand" to mean "injunction," and, what seems reasonable, one cannot be enjoined to achieve the unachievable, then although justice can *demand* (in the stated sense) nothing that is unachievable, something unachievable might yet *be* justice[11]: and that would falsify premise 1. Justice *generates* demands, so understood, according to the circumstances that obtain, but, contrary to premise 1, it is not itself a set of (injunction-)demands. If, on the other hand, we understand a "demand" of justice as merely something that is *required* for justice to obtain, whether or not anyone is required to bring that something about, then premise 1 is unobjectionable. I shall henceforth interpret "demand" as "requirement" in the noninjunctive sense, and premise 1 will therefore not be in dispute.

A certain objection might be mounted against my swift use of racism to refute 2 and 3. It runs as follows: it distinguishes racism that there is an element of unjust *intention* in its structure. Not all judgments of justice are sensitive to intention, so 2 and 3 might remain true in

---

11. Compare the discussion of "'ought' implies 'can'" in section 13 of Chapter 6.

nonintentional cases, and, so it would further be claimed, assessing economic justice is one of those cases: it does not require the assessment of *intentions*.

But the contemplated objection would grossly beg the question here. We are arguing about whether an ethos can be a requirement of justice, and ethoses comprehend intentions. So the appeal to absence of intention in an attempt to restrict the scope of 2 and 3 and thus to save the conclusion with respect to a certain *form* of justice begs the question. As to the exploitation example: either exploitation, too, involves intention, and then the same reply to the objection—it begs the question—applies, or nonintentional exploitation is possible, in which case the contemplated objection doesn't get off the ground. And it would, of course, be even more transparently question-begging to demarcate the relevant form of justice as what we discharge *collectively*. I, for one, see no prospect of a non-question-begging demarcation, but I do allow that I haven't *shown* that no non-question-begging demarcation is possible.

I shall not challenge premise 4. I am confident that, if it is false, then it is false for purely formal reasons that favor neither side in the present dispute. In other words, if 4 is false, it could yet be repaired so as to yield what Williams requires at this stage of his argument.

I turn to subconclusion 5. Since subconclusion 3 has been refuted, 5 now lacks support. And racism shows, once again, that 5 (and for good measure 6) are, moreover, false. You are obliged as a matter of justice not to allow a person's race to influence your hiring decision, despite the fact that you indeed cannot always assure yourself that others (or even, sometimes, you yourself) are complying with that principle. I am confident that someone makes an unjust decision if he is moved by a racial consideration in hiring, whether or not others, or even he, can tell that that he has done so. And you are obliged not to exploit even when you know that almost all employers do. So it is false that assurance of compliance by others *must* be possible, in the case of principles of justice. Why should that assurance have to be possible, when compliance by others is itself unnecessary for a demand of justice to lie upon you?

Williams claims that citizens are bound by justice only when they know that others will cooperate with it too. Racism and exploitation show that justice does not *bind* only under assurance. But even if justice did not *bind* without assurance, it would not thereby lose its identity *as* justice. You need not queue in an orderly way if nobody else does: justice then releases you from that obligation. But orderly queuing surely remains the system recommended by justice.[12] Something can be required by justice, required, that is, for justice to prevail, even when no one is obliged to ensure the fulfillment of that requirement—insoluble coordination problems might, for example, ensure nonfulfillment of a requirement of justice. Accordingly, the inference from 5 to 6 fails.

But suppose that however weak the Williams argument for proposition 6 may be, you nevertheless find 6 inherently persuasive. Then, as I hope to show in section 4, premise 7 is, in any case, false: Williams's conditions are not required for assurance (and I go on to try to show, in section 5, that they are also not required for justice).

4. Does Assurance Require Williams-type Determinacy?

Recall (see page 347 above) that Williams's condition (iii) is intended very strongly: it is to be taken distributively, rather than collectively. And that makes it an unjustifiably strong requirement for assurance. Why should knowing that 98 percent conform, on the basis, for example, of "reasonable beliefs about human nature and socialization,"[13] or on the basis of causal inference, be insufficient for social assurance, for eliminating the danger of being a sucker, even when one cannot know who in particular conforms and who doesn't?

Let me illustrate the "causal inference" point. Fifteen tenants of bedsitting rooms in a large house share its large refrigerator, in which each keeps her own food in a separate, unlocked, box. For the most part, no one takes anyone else's food. But *only* for the most part: from time to time, a tenant finds that some of her stock is missing. Yet thus aggrieved tenants rarely retaliate by taking someone else's food, because they believe that if they do, then the convenient arrangement from which everyone benefits might begin to unravel. Everyone knows that most people conform to the "don't take from others" rule, and none would conform unless they believed that, but nobody knows who the nonconformers are. Someone might say: "If everybody littered, I would litter too, but most people don't, so I also don't, but I don't have to know who belongs to that 'most' to be motivated by the stated happy fact."

12. To appreciate my point, note that there are two reasons why I might not be bound by justice to do A: because justice does not declare in favor of A, and because, although justice favors A, A is unattainable, and I am therefore not bound to pursue it. My argument rests on the coherence of the latter reason.

13. Frank Vandenbroucke, *Social Justice*, p. 272.

The refrigerator model shows that condition (iii), in Williams's strong because distributive interpretation of it, is not required for assurance, but it leaves (ii) untouched, since the rule that forbids taking others' food (like the rule against littering) is absolutely determinate. The rules of an egalitarian ethos cannot, by contrast, be formulated in crisp terms. But it does not follow that one might not know that there is, or is not, a reasonably efficacious[14] societywide *good faith effort* to forswear market maximizing in favor of the restraint that an egalitarian ethos prescribes, and therefore, most importantly, in favor of the acceptance, without detriment to their input of effort, of very high progressive taxation by individuals who command high market incomes. Insofar as the point of publicity is to solve the assurance problem, and thereby to establish the desired social unity, knowledge of widespread good faith effort by individuals at large should surely suffice, even if one not only cannot, as in the refrigerator problem, sort out the great majority of good-faith-effort makers from a minority of backsliders, but one also cannot be sure precisely what the implications of the rules are for particular situations.

For an illustration of that further point, consider a camping trip where we all contribute roughly equally and enjoy the fruits of our cooperation roughly equally. We proceed communistically, under understandings of mutuality and forbearance that cannot be formulated crisply: we all try to put in comparable effort but no one can say how big a piece of effort has to be for one to have qualified as doing one's bit,[15] *or* what size a share has to be for one to be able to say, "I've taken no more than my fair share." Despite the ineliminable vagueness, that all or most devote effective good faith effort can be known, and this will surely suffice "to harmonize the pursuit of equality and social unity" (page 245) in the camping context (or, if it does not suffice, then Williams is setting an absurdly high standard of "harmonization"). Now it may be more difficult to know about good faith effort on a larger social scale, but that is not Williams's argument. His argument is that a knowability condition far stronger than what knowledge of good faith effort satisfies must be satisfied, if "the pursuit of equality and social unity" is to be harmonized, and the camping trip example refutes that. It shows *both* that the "particular requirements" of a rule of justice (see condition (ii)) can, *salva ju-*

---

14. I add "reasonably efficacious" to exclude the case of known good faith effort that is not known to have pertinent effects.
15. For a fuller presentation of this example, see my "Why Not Socialism?," pp. 58–60.

stitia, be vague, and also, pace Williams's distributive reading of condition (iii), that it can be unclear who exactly is conforming.

But *can* knowledge of good faith effort to conform to a principle that eludes crisp statement obtain on a large social scale? During World War II in Britain, a social ethos induced people to sacrifice personal interests for the sake of the war effort, and everyone was expected, as a matter of justice, to "do his bit," to shoulder his just share. It is absurd to suppose that someone could have stated precisely what amount of sacrifice that injunction required, and it is true, therefore, that, with respect to many people, one couldn't tell, and, with respect to some, they couldn't even themselves tell, whether they were sacrificing on the required scale. There are too many details in each person's life that affect what the required sacrifice should be: Max has a bad back, Sally has a difficult child, George has just inherited £20,000, and so on. "Yes, Jack only goes out once a week, not, like most us, twice, on guard duty, but then Jack has to take care of his mother." But "the extent to which individuals conform[ed] to"[16] the requirements of sacrifice could certainly be known, in rough terms, collectively, and also to some extent distributively: the sacrifice ethos *was* amenable to sufficient sub-Williamsian rough-and-ready public checkability for social assurance. Despite its vagueness, "do your bit" was understood and applied as a principle of justice. It would have been crazy to ask for it to be carefully defined, and it would be crazy to deny that it performed a task of social regulation, in the interest of justice.

I therefore reject premise 7.

Let me add that it is certainly not always regrettable that the amount of contribution that should be expected from a person defies nice measurement. Sometimes it would be a nightmare if we could measure precisely, because we might then be tempted to do so, in the interest of justice, and that would make life a nightmare. For an illustration of that point, consider again the camping trip introduced on page 352, in which a group of friends cooperate in the production and consumption of fish, berries, and so forth, under an understanding that each will contribute and benefit on egalitarian terms that resist precise statement. The trip would lack its distinctive and attractive character *both* if it were not characterized by equality *and* if that equality were formulable as a set of precise rules that all were required to observe.

---

16. The phrase belongs to Williams's condition (iii).

And even when justice *can* be stated precisely, it is often wise to forgo that statement of it. To see that, consider two contrasting ways of taking turns in the practice of buying rounds of drinks in a pub. It is expected, within many sets of friends who are comparable in wealth, that each will take his turn at buying a round for everybody. But nobody counts how much each friend spends, and, within the sets that I have in mind, nobody says, at the beginning of the evening, "OK, Jack, you have to buy the first round, since they called 'time' before you had a chance to buy a round last time." No balanced person wants justice to obtrude in life in that way: we agree with Portia that justice can bow to other considerations,[17] and, as I have said elsewhere, "we let justice remain rough, in deference to other values."[18] But it would be a mistake to conclude that we don't care about justice. The very same reasonably laid-back folk would be indignant if Jack never paid his share. In the foregoing example, justice *could*, we may assume, be precise, but we forgo precise justice. But that is not to agree that justice can always be made precise, as I now proceed to show.

5. Does Justice Require Precision?

The demise of premise 7 ruins Williams's case for 8. But we should also note that 8 is false: whether or not justice requires assurance, it doesn't require precision of application and verification.

I begin with a concession that Williams makes whose reach, I think, is greater than he realizes:

> . . . though Cohen may be correct that we can verify excessive self-seeking by those who benefit most from the present income distribution, it is quite possible that, in typical cases, we will lack a sufficiently precise public standard by which to justify, or criticize, each other's self-serving behaviour. (page 140).

Suppose that, as Williams claims, verifiability applies at most to *excessive*, that is, very considerable,[19] self-seeking. We are nevertheless, on the

17. See p. 304 of Chapter 7.
18. *Self-Ownership, Freedom, and Equality*, p. 31.
19. "Excessive" is an unfortunate choice of word here, since it implies, given the context of the quoted excerpt, that Williams is prepared to concede that it may be possible to tell (more or less precisely) when an individual's self-seeking is in excess of that

view he defends, not to condemn even *excessive* self-seeking as unjust, simply because we can't verify what's going on in less conspicuous cases. This seems to me to be groundless. Why should justice be silent where it *can* speak, even if it cannot always speak? Similarly, and more generally, it may be harder to tell in some societies than in others whether good faith efforts are being made to conform to the self-same principles: people and circumstances may be less scrutable in some societies than in others. But why should that mean that an ethos cannot be part of justice where good faith efforts *are* substantially assessable? To revert to the previous example, why should its rough-and-readiness disqualify "do your bit," as it was understood in World War II in Britain, as an injunction of justice?

One may, however, go further. For as Martin Wilkinson has pointed out to me, excessive self-seekers tend also to be flagrant: that is why, as Williams concedes, they can be detected. But it is absurd to think that flagrant self-seekers are unjust whereas unflagrant self-seekers who differ only in being unflagrant are not. So the applicability of justice in the flagrant case carries over to the unflagrant case, to the detriment of (ii) and (iii) as conditions on justice.[20]

The example of racism shows that (ii) and (iii) fail as proposed conditions of justice. Much racial injustice involves agents' motivations, but, pace condition (ii), it is difficult to formulate a criterion for color-blind motivation that the agent herself can be sure she is respecting; and, pace condition (iii), it can (partly consequently) be very difficult, in many cases, to observe whether racism has occurred. Racism cannot, therefore, be eliminated by legislation alone, because legislation cannot (thank heaven) penetrate to people's attitudes, and, if it could, it would still be true that it shouldn't, on grounds of freedom. But people, like

---

allowed by the Schefflerian personal prerogative that I accept. But that is exactly what Williams is denying: by "excessive" he must mean "self-seeking *greatly* in excess of what a personal prerogative would allow," and it is on the basis of that understanding of him that I criticize him in the rest of the present paragraph.

20. Let me quote from Will Alter's 2006 Oxford Undergraduate thesis "Does Justice Require an Egalitarian Ethos?": Suppose "somebody deliberately pretends her work is a good deal more onerous to her than it really is, in order to qualify for so-called compensating differentials in her pay. That she disguises this information well does not mean she is not acting unjustly. Imagine that the reality is accessible to her and she knows that she is feigning special burden. Does it stop her knowing she is acting unjustly to know also that other people are unaware, or that she is fooling them?"

(real-world) Rawlsian legislators who legislate against racism *so far as the constraints of law-making allow them to do so,* in the interests of justice, surely behave unjustly when they practice racist choice wherever the law cannot forbid them to do so (because the publicity that legal instruments require is impossible to achieve in the present case). We could not legally institute a principle that says: "cleanse your soul of racist bias," because we could not tell, sufficiently well, whether people (including we ourselves) were being true to it. But that doesn't mean that racism isn't unjust, or that "do not practice racism, even *in foro interno*" is not an injunction of justice. And I see no *relevant* difference, with respect to publicity, between racial justice and economic justice. I claim that there are matters of economic justice that the law cannot or should not regulate, for various reasons. And it fortifies my position that some forms of clearly unjust racism cannot be legally forbidden, and others that can be should not be.

Michael Otsuka adduces other examples that show that "the fact that it is very difficult to know what a rule requires" in specific terms does not show that the said rule is not a principle of justice:

> Nepotism and cronyism in hiring and promotion are . . . generally unjust. But it is often difficult to know whether one is being moved by friendship or familial relationship instead of merit. Moreover, there are some contexts (e.g., small businesses, political appointments) in which a certain amount of nepotism or cronyism is permissible. And it is difficult to tell when one is crossing the line in these contexts. Similar points can be made about fraternization with those whom one has the power to promote (or between teacher and student) and about the line between sexual harassment and acceptable behaviour in the workplace. In some cases, one has an agent-centered prerogative to favour family or friends to a certain extent in employment, or to fraternize. And it is hard to know, as Williams points out, how extensive this prerogative is.[21]

And Paula Casal draws a telling parallel between justice in the matter of remuneration and justice in the matter of sharing the burden of environmental protection.

> The requirement of publicity or the idea that we should know how much we are required to do, are not always decisive considerations. They are

---

21. Personal communication, June 1998. Cf. Frank Vanderbroucke, *Social Justice and Individual Ethics in an Open Society,* p. 277, which points to the importance in economic life of ethoses that defy crisp statement.

definitely not decisive in the case of our environmental duties. We know that there are going to be many free-riders who will continue to pollute and to destroy the ozone layer, etc. But that does not exempt us from our duties. Neither can the fact that we don't know how much we are supposed to do or how much other cooperators are going to do. Whatever it is that we think people should do for the environment, we can also apply to incentive payments.[22]

I agree with what I take to be three points that Casal makes here: An obligation of justice can bind (1) even if, contrary to Williams's premise 3 and subconclusion 6, it is predictable that there will be widespread failure to discharge it; (2) even if, contrary to his condition (iii), and therefore to his premise 7, one cannot tell how much failure there is to discharge that obligation; and (3) even if, contrary to his condition (ii), and therefore, once again, to his premise 7, one cannot tell with any precision what it asks one to do: it can be unclear what justice requires in a certain context, but it doesn't follow that justice can't be fulfilled, or violated, in that context. Williams argues that justice requires assurance of general compliance, which requires that (1) be false, which requires that (2) be false, which requires that (3) be false. He is multiply wrong.

He is also demonstrably out of step with Rawls himself. Publicity is one of what Rawls calls "the formal constraints of the concept of right."[23] But, as Rawls articulates that constraint, it cannot demand anything so stringent as Williams's conditions (ii) and (iii). It requires merely transparency in what the rules are, and the possibility of everyone knowing that everyone accepts them: I tried to explain the constraint in the third paragraph of section 2. The most Williams could claim is that Rawls's description of the publicity constraint is open to further specification, and that Williams's conditions (ii) and (iii) represent a sound further specification of the constraint. But the latter claim is defeated by the fact that what Rawls calls "principles for individuals" fall under the concept of right,[24] and at least some of Rawls's principles for individuals display the vagueness that Williams thinks publicity condemns. So, for example, the "duty of justice"

22. Personal communication, July 1998.
23. See *A Theory of Justice*, p. 433/115.
24. See the tree-structure of *Theory*, p. 109/94 and the accompanying explication of it in the surrounding text.

requires us to support and to comply with just institutions that exist and apply to us. It also constrains us to further just arrangements not yet established, at least when this can be done *without too much cost to ourselves.*[25]

Rawls does not say how much cost is too much, and Aristotle and I don't think he has to. But Williams, who purports to be Rawls's champion, must tell us why the duty of justice, with its reference to the vague "without too much cost to ourselves," is not, despite its vagueness, defeated by a publicity constraint, when a duty to forgo economic benefit "without too much cost to ourselves" is, according to Williams, defeated by the same vagueness.

Or consider the "natural duty to bring about a great good." Although we are under that duty if we can discharge it "relatively easily, we are released from [it] when *the cost to ourselves is considerable.*"[26] But what constitutes a "considerable" cost, and how can we know how considerable the cost is that someone would have to incur to discharge the duty? The Williams questions apply as much here as they do to the egalitarian ethos. And I say that they have no bite in either case. Speaking of the natural duties in general, Rawls allows that "their definition and systematic arrangement are untidy"[27] but he does not therefore set them aside. I propose the same conceptually and epistemically relaxed attitude to the claims of egalitarian duty in everyday life.

An examination of the characterization of publicity offered by Rawls in "Kantian Constructivism"[28] confirms that his own publicity requirement for justice is quite different from that of Williams. It has less to do with possible epistemic hurdles to the application of principles and more to do with shared knowledge and belief about acceptance and justification of principles. Note that if Rawlsian publicity were Williamsian publicity, then those "traditional conceptions of justice" that regard undetectable racism as unjust would be clear counterexamples to Rawls's claim that the five "constraints of the concept of right," of which one is publicity, "exclude none of the traditional conceptions of justice."[29]

Note, finally, that I do not conceive the egalitarian ethos as embracing "principles for individuals" in the Rawlsian sense of the phrase, under

25. Ibid., p. 115/99, emphases added.
26. Ibid., p. 117/100, emphases added.
27. Ibid., p. 339/298.
28. "Kantian Constructivism," p. 324.
29. *Theory,* p. 135/117.

which it denotes principles that are *additional* to those that apply to the basic structure. I have argued, instead, that there is no good reason why the *very* principles that govern the basic structure should not extend to individual choice within that structure, and that in particular the partial indeterminacy of application that those principles suffer under that extension is no such reason.

6. Egalitarian Ethoses at Home, in the Market, and in the State

I turn to premise 9, which says that the egalitarian ethos does not satisfy conditions (ii) and (iii). I shall not try to contradict it, to show, that is, that an egalitarian economic ethos satisfies conditions (ii) and (iii). I shall instead show that injunctions that Williams judges, and must judge, to be ones of justice *also* fail (demanding forms) of (ii) and (iii): he cannot, therefore, use (ii) and (iii) to impugn the egalitarian ethos (in particular).

Williams contrasts an egalitarian ethos that governs the distribution of household tasks with an egalitarian economic ethos that would restrain the use by powerful economic agents of their bargaining power. He thinks that the domestic ethos satisfies the publicity constraint but that the economic ethos doesn't. The egalitarian domestic ethos satisfies conditions (i) and (ii), he says, because its "requirements can be stated quite clearly," and it satisfies condition (iii) because "any serious failure to conform with these requirements is readily apparent to the victims of injustice, and likely to be exposed even more widely" (page 242). Williams thinks that nothing similar is true of the egalitarian economic ethos.

Now one might suppose that failure on the part of, say, husbands to do their proper share of household tasks is, as Williams says, "readily apparent" to their victims but not to others, simply because only the victims, only their wives, are *there,* in the kitchen. But that, I believe, is importantly false. There surely are violations of egalitarian domestic rules that household nonmembers would fail to observe even if they were in the kitchen, because they lack the special sensitivity that spouses acquire. In some cases only his wife can know whether the backache that he pleads as a reason for not washing the dishes is substantial or contrived. In other cases only he can know that. And in still other cases even he can be puzzled.

Accordingly, and to the detriment of his employment of condition (ii), the requirements of a just domestic ethos "cannot be stated quite [so] clearly" as Williams appears to suppose (how much backache justifies how much exemption from dish-washing?). As a result, and, to the detriment of his employment of condition (iii), public checkability of conformity to the domestic ethos is not so straightforward a matter as Williams supposes. But Williams would not wish to deny that an egalitarian domestic ethos serves justice. He therefore cannot insist on so strict a publicity requirement on justice (that is, one that incorporates conditions (ii) and (iii)) as he does. The difference between a just domestic ethos and what I regard as a just economic ethos is not so great, with respect to publicity, as Williams, to sustain his critique, must claim it to be (unless, what is surely false, he would be happy to abandon his belief that justice requires an egalitarian domestic ethos).

Williams claims (page 242) that "the force of Cohen's [domestic injustice] examples derives partly from the manifest injustice they involve." But unmanifest (that is, *unobservable*) injustice can be manifestly (that is, *patently*) unjust. It is manifestly (that is, patently) unjust to fake a bad back, *even to yourself,* as a way of avoiding kitchen duty, however unmanifest (that is, unobservable) it may be that you are doing so. Because "manifest" bears these contrasting meanings, the sentence in which the quoted remark appears fails of its object, which is to show that I am committed to what precedes its semicolon. The whole sentence says: "These requirements can be stated quite clearly; indeed the force of Cohen's [domestic injustice] examples derives partly from the manifest injustice they involve." If the second part of the sentence appears to support the first part, that is because of equivocation across the two meanings of "manifest," namely, "observable" and "patent."

There is a remarkable inconsistency between Williams's treatment of an egalitarian economic ethos and his treatment of an egalitarian domestic ethos. Whereas he regards his condition (iii) as satisfied in the case of the domestic ethos because, as we saw (see page 359), "any *serious* [my emphasis] failure to conform with [its] requirements is readily apparent to the victims of injustice" (and even if, we may infer, less serious failures are not "readily apparent"), he does not, as we also saw (see page 354), regard the observability of "excessive self-seeking" as sufficient to vindicate the satisfaction of condition (iii) in the case of the economic ethos. But "serious" and "excessive" come to roughly the same thing in the present context.

In a further attempt to demonstrate that an egalitarian domestic ethos fares better with respect to satisfying condition (ii) than an egalitarian economic ethos does, Williams writes:

> although a market ethos resists being institutionalized, it still may be feasible, perhaps through educational campaigns in schools and the media, to institute a domestic ethos that prohibits the types of gender injustice Cohen opposes. (page 242)

I believe that, once again, this statement exaggerates the extent to which a domestic ethos justice can satisfy (ii) and underplays the extent to which an ethos of economic justice can do so. I do not know how closely Williams means here to associate his master requirement of publicity with a requirement that a set of rules of justice be acquired through being *taught*. But whatever Williams means, let us note that neither requirement entails the other. Certain highly public rules might not need to be taught, but might merely need to be stated, to be understood and followed: in respect of such rules, talk of "educational campaigns" would be hyperbole. Other highly public rules might, moreover, become common property without even having to be stated. And, contrariwise, certain perfectly teachable, and widely taught, rules plainly lack full Williamsian publicity. An ethos may be eminently teachable, despite the fact that it cannot be embodied in crisply stated rules. Consider an ethos of antiracism, one that is surely necessary to sustain the primary good that Rawls calls the social basis of self-respect. Here, once again, despite the unavailability of transparently applicable rules, the point of antiracism can be explained, and taught, and the justice of society can thereby be improved.

Williams says merely that it "*may* be feasible" to institute an egalitarian domestic ethos, which implies that he allows that it also may not be feasible. Does he believe that what would otherwise be gender injustice would not count as such if an ethos opposed to it could not be taught (or otherwise instituted)? That would surely be a crazy conclusion, but I believe that Williams is committed to it.

In sum, I do not accept this further attempt by Williams to contrast an egalitarian market ethos with an egalitarian domestic ethos, with respect to their capacity to meet conditions (ii) and (iii).

Moving away from the domestic sphere, I should like to make a further, and at least in respect of condition (ii), even more damaging tu quoque point.[30] For consider the extraordinary (and surely unobtainable) knowledge that a government would need to have to enable it to satisfy the difference principle,[31] knowledge, that is, that would enable government to select an economic policy that is optimal with respect to enhancing the lifetime primary goods prospects of the least well off. How could government know, for example, that rises in provision for the worst off enabled by a shift from a universal to a means-tested distribution of some benefit compensates adequately for a decline (because of the stigma that attaches to means testing) in the strength of poorer people's "social bases of self-respect"?[32] Where is the index needed to answer such a question, and where are the prescient and even clairvoyant researchers who could supply relevant measures, in the fantasyland where such an index is at hand? So: if citizens can't be bound by the difference principle because its message to them is unclear, neither, by that criterion, is the government bound by it, which is a reductio ad absurdum of the Williams position. (Note that the fact that the *reasons* for unclarity differ across the cases doesn't affect the present argument.)

The present claim is that the difference principle fails condition (ii), so far as its application by government is concerned. It therefore also fails condition (iii), since *as (iii) is formulated*, its satisfaction presupposes the satisfaction of (ii). But Williams should not have formulated (iii) in that way: it could have been and should have been formulated logically independently of (ii), in some such wise as this:

> it must be possible for there to be common knowledge of (iiia) the extent to which individuals conform to the requirements *that are best judged* to satisfy the given rule.

It should have been formulated that way because it is, I concede, true and important that the (lax) difference principle, as applied to citizens, satisfies (iiia) much better than the demands of an egalitarian ethos do. For consider. Suppose the government imposes a set P of tax (etc.) poli-

30. The rest of this section is strongly influenced by suggestions provided by Seana Shiffrin.
31. Under the lax interpretation of it that Williams defends, in which it applies *directly* only to the behavior of government. I mean "difference principle" laxly up to the end of this section.
32. The widespread (at least in Britain) left-wing objection to means testing is not grounded in economic innumeracy but in the stated nonfinancial consideration.

cies under the guidance (such as it is) of the difference principle. It is then comparatively easy to tell whether or not citizens are conforming as required: it is a matter of whether they pay their taxes, observe contracts, and the like.

But in respect of the lax difference principle, if *citizens* pass the (iiia) test easily, the same might not be true of government. And it might be easier to tell whether citizens are faithful to the strict difference principle that characterizes the egalitarian ethos than whether government is faithful to the lax difference principle. How can observers know whether a government has sought to pursue the best economic policy it could discern, and thus whether, for example, its failures are attributable to unpredictable market forces rather than to bad faith? Seana Shiffrin writes:

> it seems a lot easier for the average citizen to have a sense of whether his/ her fellow citizens are grasping or not . . . than whether the best economic policies . . . are being responsibly pursued . . . There's no reason to think that citizens will be able to know that the government is pursuing the policies that benefit the worst off the most: such knowledge requires an enormous amount of information about the economy . . . and a lot of information about the internal workings of government . . . There's no reason to think citizens will know that justice is done—the opacity of economic systems and of government will work in some of the same ways that Williams thinks the opacity of other minds will prevent confidence that other citizens are acting in good faith . . . From daily life and participation in the workplace and marketplace, we tend to . . . [have] information [about] how materialist and self-oriented the culture is and our peers are. That information seems much more easily at hand (if not finely calibrated down to the individual) than some of the macroeconomic information necessary for evaluating government policy.[33]

My reply to Williams, in the round, has been that an egalitarian ethos would satisfy as much publicity, as strong a publicity requirement, as justice needs to satisfy. In other words, I have, by implication, responded disjunctively to his challenge: *either* a given specification of the publicity requirement is too strong, as a constraint on justice, *or* it is not too

---

33. Personal communication, July 2001. It is of considerable interest here that Rawls himself says that the (lax) difference principle is not constitutionally essential, *because* it is *inter alia* too "difficult to ascertain" whether the principle is satisfied. See *Political Liberalism*, p. 229, and *Justice as Fairness*, pp. 48–49.

strong but it can be met by an egalitarian ethos. In certain contexts one of the disjuncts is a more appropriate response than the other.

A number of examples introduced above, such as the camping trip ethos, the "do your bit" rule in wartime Britain, and the rules governing a just division of domestic labor, show that a rule does not lack the authority of justice simply because it does not always tell the agent precisely what she ought to do. But suppose there is no conceptual or cognitive bar to tracing the implications of justice for a particular agent in a particular circumstance. Suppose, for example, that people have the power to tell precisely how well off they are, in comparison with others, in the sense relevant to the issue of justice at hand. It could nevertheless be urged that people have a tendency to favor themselves in judgment, and that the rules we choose must therefore be sensitive to that: so perhaps an egalitarian ethos should be more stringent than what it would be if people were disposed to judge themselves more impartially. That may be so, but the point doesn't affect what justice *is*: justice is not hostage to human weakness and insufficiency. And if our tendency were the reverse, to judge ourselves too harshly, then that too might affect what rules we should adopt and promote, but not, again, the nature of justice, which is not hostage to human virtue either.

7. Publicity as a Desideratum of Justice

If there is widespread good faith effort and highly public rules, then, in all probability, we shall get closer to justice than if there is widespread good faith effort without very public rules. (I say only "in all probability" because a very high degree of justice might perchance be achieved under widespread good faith effort even when rules are vague.) But, so I have argued, it does not follow that justice itself must be capable of being expressed in highly public rules, even if it is, typically,[34] welcome when justice happens to be capable of being so expressed.

But Williams suggests that publicity might be seen not as a *constraint* on justice but as an (overrideable) *desideratum* of justice. In response to an earlier version of the present chapter, he said:

> I also have a doubt about whether I actually claimed, or needed to claim, that publicity is a constraint rather than merely one amongst a number of

34. Typically, but not always: see the last two paragraphs of section 4.

important desiderata. Here it's worth noting that my suggestion that Rawls believes that "our evaluation of competing conceptions of justice should proceed along a number of dimensions" (243) does not commit me to any claim about publicity as a constraint. Furthermore, my later remark "Suppose we accept that the relative merit of competing conceptions of justice depends, *in part,* on their capacity to play the same social role as a well-ordered society's conception of justice. . ." (244–5) supports the desideratum reading.[35]

In oral elaboration of this point, which he has allowed me to report, Williams said that the publicity desideratum might be more readily overridden or modified where the prospective burden on those who are to be protected by a candidate rule of justice was severe: thus, he said, it could be relaxed for racism but not for the economy, since racism imposes far more serious consequences on its victims than an acquisitive ethos does. Accordingly, the insistence on publicity in principles might be less appropriate in the racism case.

I find the *desideratum* proposal, thus elaborated,[36] unintelligible, and, also, *if* intelligible, then utterly implausible. Let me first say why I find the *desideratum* proposal unintelligible.

Publicity might, of course, as I have amply agreed, be a desideratum of rules of regulation: there is nothing unintelligible in that thought. To see why, as I nevertheless think, it cannot be a *desideratum* of justice itself, consider a distinct virtue, loyalty. An organization might demand loyalty from its members, and might think it advisable to establish criteria for deciding whether a member has been loyal. If wisely formulated, those criteria will, Nozick-like,[37] take into account not only the nature of loyalty but also other concerns, such as publicity, strain on individuals (we do not want them to leave), and so forth. But I do not see how concerns of the latter sort could be thought to contribute to an understanding of what loyalty *is:* they contribute, rather, to the justification of choosing *rules* of loyalty of a particular shape for some particular organization. Consider, too, the legal presumption of innocence, which is a

35. Private communication, October 12, 1999.
36. I do not, of course, deny that it is more desirable for justice to be fulfilled than for it not to be fulfilled, and that publicity may enhance the prospect of its fulfillment. I deny what Williams's fresh articulation of his claim differently affirms: that it counts (albeit overrideably) against a principle's *being* one of justice that it fails his publicity requirement.
37. See the Nozick passages quoted in the second half of section 7 of Chapter 7.

rule crafted to suit constraints of information, basic human rights, court procedure, and so forth. We could not form such a rule unless we already knew what innocence, itself, is, and it would be absurd to regard a good presumption-of-innocence rule as contributing to the specification what innocence is.[38] In order that we may form a suitable presumption-of-innocence rule and recognize it as such, we need, what we undoubtedly have, a conception of innocence that is wholly independent of practical constraints. To bring the point even closer to home, consider that courts pursue *justice,* but that their rules don't formulate what justice *is,* even though the whole point of those rules is to serve justice: they are formulated in the light of an understanding of justice, together with an awareness that rules of court procedure can at best imperfectly deliver justice, as well as an awareness that justice isn't everything (if only because another thing that is also something is the Pareto-threatening cost of various complex procedures that might bring decisions closer to justice).

And so, too, for general rules of social regulation (which are to be informed by justice) and justice itself. As long as there is such a thing as justice about which we can ask "What is it?," all talk of desiderata of it is a category mistake, a misprojection of discourse appropriate for what is right for regulative rules onto the specification of the principles that define a virtue, where such discourse is inappropriate. Merely because they *are* rules of regulation, rules of regulation (elected in the light of—often unruly—facts) do not constitute what justice *is,* and it is not the role of rules of regulation to specify what a virtue *is.* As I remarked in section 1 of Chapter 7, we do not ask what justice ought to be but what it *is,* and that shows the contrast in status between principles of justice proper and rules of regulation.

38. It is sometimes quite impossible to formulate sensible rules that codify the demands of a virtue. Consider the Antioch College dating code, which seeks to formulate rules of conduct for erotic engagements and instructs participants in such an engagement not to proceed from a given stage of it to a "hotter" one unless express consent from the would-be partner is forthcoming, typical stages being holding hands, caressing, kissing, unbuttoning, and so forth. There is no gainsaying the virtues (that is, mutual respect, freedom of choice, etc.) that the Antioch rules are intended to serve, but it is also evident that the Antioch rules endanger the activity they are introduced to govern. That is not because consensuality is not imperatively required, but because the often subtle marks of it defy characterization in publicly applicable rules.

But suppose I am misguided and Williams's desideratum proposal is indeed intelligible. Then, so I believe, it is nevertheless preposterous.

I experienced anti-Semitic attitudes as a Jewish child in Montréal, but the consequences of that for us were not very severe, since, unlike many other victims of racism, we Jews had assets (not least ones of culturally induced self-confidence) that made the ambient anti-Semitism relatively ineffectual with respect to our life chances. Are we therefore to say, in line with Williams's desideratum proposal (see pages 364–365) that Montreal's anti-Semitism was not unjust, since the inescapable vagueness of injunctions against *attitudes* could not in *this* case be overridden by the severity of racism's consequences? For reasons that have nothing to do with the possibility of public prohibition of attitudes, the racism in question was much less savage than antiblack racism in the American South in, say, 1930, but how could anything show that Montreal racism was not unjust? Was it only because American antiblack racism was so severe that one could consider it to be a proper target of less than optimally public rules, and *therefore* unjust (despite and in face of the stated unavoidable publicity deficit that would thereby be incurred)?

It is of course true that, at the level of rules of regulation, it is more important to enforce or otherwise direct the fulfillment of justice when the deleterious consequences of not doing so are greater. But that doesn't show that the more momentous the consequences, the more they qualify as a matter of justice. And it is also *pro tanto* more important to enforce justice where the injustice would be more severe, even if its consequences, considered apart from their injustice, are less considerable. So, for example, it may be more urgently required to control racism than to control economic greed, not because the consequences of the latter are smaller, but simply because racism is a worse injustice. But none of that tells us anything about the character of justice itself. Justice is an input into, not an output of, these trade-off decisions.

We must also sometimes trade one form of justice off against another, at the level of rules of regulation. So, for example, we may trade off the justice of distributive justice against the justice of not placing an unfair burden on someone, when that someone's contribution to justice would be unaccompanied by similar action by similarly placed others.[39] We may form rules of praise and blame of individuals with both sets of constraint in mind. We might thereby be described as deciding what rule is

39. See p. 349 above.

most just, or least unjust, all things considered, but *ex hypothesi* the rule that we come to form does not deliver pure justice: it represents a decision about how much of each sort of justice is to be sacrificed.

8. Publicity and Occupational Choice

In my view, a strong publicity requirement on principles of justice would distort justice with respect to issues of *occupational choice*.

Consider a society in which most people don't much like their jobs. Now consider two doctor-gardeners,[40] G and H. Society would benefit greatly if each of G and H switched from gardening to doctoring, and both G and H know that. But each of them prefers gardening to doctoring, and each consequently refuses to doctor unless he is paid a substantial premium.

Now there is a considerable difference between G and H, for while each prefers gardening to doctoring, G dislikes doctoring, whereas H loves it, even though, *ex hypothesi,* H loves gardening even more than he loves doctoring. Gardening is much more fulfilling, *in every sense,* for H than most people's jobs are fulfilling for them, whereas gardening is no more fulfilling for G than most people's jobs are for them. (*In every sense:* "fulfilling" here concatenates high scores on a number of relevant metrics, including degree of psychological satisfaction and extent of realization and exercise of creative powers. That which is fulfilling provides and/or sustains a high degree of well-being, in a comprehensive sense of that term.)

Neither, we may suppose, is seeking rent,[41] but only a salary that would make doctoring as worthwhile for him, all things considered, as gardening is. In my view, H's demand contradicts egalitarian justice, because egalitarian justice disallows an insistence on retaining enjoyments way beyond the norm. G's demand, by contrast, is plainly consistent with egalitarian justice.

Williams cannot recognize, as material for judgments of justice, distinctions of the sort that I just employed, since how much a given person

40. Doctor-gardeners, who can both doctor and garden but who prefer (the socially less useful) gardening, were introduced in section 2 of Chapter 5.

41. Notice that rent seeking cannot be an injustice, in Williams's view, since one cannot readily tell who is and who is not a rent seeker. In any case, not all rent seeking contradicts egalitarian justice, since a recipient of rent need not be better off than others: rent is a purely *intra*personal concept. See my *Self-Ownership,* pp. 217–219.

enjoys, or otherwise finds fulfillment in, or, contrariwise, is burdened by, a given job is not publicly (very) scrutable. Yet as I had occasion to remark earlier,[42] it seems absurd that labor burden should (therefore) be excluded from the ambit of justice when justice is conceived, as Rawls conceives it, as the principles that set out how we are to share the benefits and burdens of social cooperation. What burden of social cooperation is more significant and more pervasive than labor burden? How could it fail to be a matter of concern for justice that some people's jobs (usually, in the contemporary real world, those of the less well paid) are far less fulfilling than those of others, however difficult it may be to be precise about that difference, especially in individual cases, but also in an average sense?

This is not to concede that labor benefit and burden are wholly inscrutable. It is true that, as I have said and as Williams reports, labor burden "fails the test of public checkability laid down for primary goods."[43] But what I said there is that it fails the (very demanding) test that Rawls lays down for characterizing a good as "primary." It does not follow that labor burden fails less stringent but nevertheless significant publicity tests.

Here we can take a leaf from Joseph Carens's *Equality, Moral Incentives, and the Market.* For Carens, the extent to which a person fulfills his social obligation is measured by how large a fraction his *actual* income is of the maximum that he *could* earn.[44] Randomly chosen citizens cannot, of course, tell how much randomly chosen other citizens can earn, but, Carens points out, the latter's intimates can know that, and that might constitute a sanction that suffices for social regulation.

Now I do not endorse the stated view of social obligation, which Carens himself wisely abandoned, following sapient criticism of it from Donald Moon.[45] Carens's *Equality* scheme oppresses (some of) the talented, and indeed anyone who hates the jobs whose pay is in the region of their top earnings. The scheme fails precisely because it ignores the

42. See the second paragraph of section 5 of Chapter 2 and pp. 200–202 of Chapter 5.
43. Williams, p. 239, quoting "The Pareto Argument for Inequality," p. 170, n. 34, which is now n. 33 of Chapter 2.
44. In Carens's scheme actual earnings are redistributed equally. People seek earnings not to enrich themselves but to carry out what they recognize to be their social obligation. See, further, Chapter 5, pp. 189–191.
45. See Moon, review of Carens, pp. 146–150, and Carens, "Rights and Duties in an Egalitarian Society."

welfare effects that are salient in my own different view that people's job-and-income packages should, other things equal, be comparable in welfare terms. But a form of publicity similar to the Carensian also applies to the dimension that I consider central: one's intimates at least often know how repugnant or rewarding one's job is for one.

As I argued in section 4 of Chapter 5, the "slavery of the talented," where that implies settling an especially bad fate on them, is impossible within the broadly welfaristic perspective that I would affirm.[46] My egalitarian rule says that no one should seek such compensation as makes him all things considered (far)[47] better off than anyone else. Now many will find that egalitarianism too tough, the egalitarianism, that is, which says that no one should demand a salary much more than what is required for her to be roughly on a par with others, given the satisfactions, and frustrations, that attach, for her, to her job. Many will find the idea that you are answerable to others in this respect too invasive of an unconstrained personal prerogative in these matters. But that ground for rejecting my view has nothing to do with rejecting it on grounds of publicity failure, which is what we are discussing here. I have considered the charge that the egalitarian rule is oppressive, that it violates liberty (as opposed to publicity), in Chapter 5.

I say that egalitarian justice requires H to be a doctor, at a salary no higher than what he gets as a gardener, and despite his preference for gardening. Egalitarian justice therefore demands more than that H get a wage comparable to that of others, a demand that he can meet while indulging his preference for gardening, for it demands that he *be* a doctor. In other words, egalitarian justice corresponds to what Williams calls a "wide" ethos rather than a "narrow" one, to use the terms that he introduces in the course of his discussion of "Sophie," who would rather be an artist than a commercial designer. Egalitarian justice requires people to have some regard to equality not only when negotiating for rewards but also when making career choices, just as, on a camping trip, it does not restrict its demands to the domain of consumption: it is hostile not only to greed but also to shirking. Williams is right that equality requires

---

46. Indeed, and ironically, given the resourcist position that he espouses, Ronald Dworkin himself rejects slavery of the talented on what are essentially welfarist grounds. This is but one inconsistency in that multiply flawed treatment, on which see Miriam Cohen Christofidis, "Talent, Slavery, and Envy."

47. I insert "(far)" to cater for the personal prerogative to which I allow a certain scope in these matters: see section 5 of the Introduction and p. 61 of Chapter 1.

a "wide" ethos, and he is also right that such an ethos imposes formidable informational requirements.

But all that the wide ethos requires is that one does not violate equality in career choices. It will typically be difficult to know whether or not one is violating equality, but one cannot be expected to do more than not violate it where one has reason to think that one would. One cannot be expected not to violate it where it is unclear whether or not one would be violating it,[48] especially when it allows a certain due regard to one's personal preferences. "Due regard" is something that no one can specify, any more than anyone can specify how much regard is due to decor in restaurant selection, yet, despite that, we all know what an excessive preference for good decor is. The parallel that Casal draws between environmentalism and egalitarian justice (see pages 356–357 above) remains instructive here. It is hard to know in many cases what egalitarianism demands, and it is perfectly reasonable for self-interest to be a tiebreaker in such cases, but it hardly follows that one may do as one likes even in those cases where one can make a reasonable guess at what one should and should not do, from an egalitarian point of view.

The more general point was made in the context of the camping and Word War II examples of section 4. How much may I, with my legitimately particular needs, take from the common stock? I can't know exactly how much, but I can know *roughly* how much, despite all the incommensurabilities and indiscernibilities. There is such a thing as taking too much by *any* standard. The lamb of justice should not be sacrificed on the altar of vagueness and incommensurability.

Now, once again, expecting Sophie to be a designer, at no greater pay, might seem particularly oppressive, a denial of her freedom. But Williams's publicity objection to the wide ethos is not based on considerations of freedom: he excludes that appeal on p. 228. His objection is that the principles borne by the egalitarian ethos have inscrutable implications and are therefore inapplicable. I have replied to the publicity objection in this section. The problem that Sophie raises for freedom proper was dealt with in Chapter 5.

---

48. It is an important unrealism in the G and H example with which I began this section that they know all the relevant truths of their situation.

GENERAL APPENDIX:
REPLIES TO CRITICS

For the most part I respond here to critics of the material in Chapters 1 through 3. Section 1 *(Public and Private Action)* takes up the complaint that I overestimate the contribution that private individuals can make, and I therefore underestimate the contribution that the state must make, to the achievement of distributive justice. Section 2 explains that *The Site of Justice Is Not Where It Gets Caused.* It refutes the argument that assigns normative priority to the basic structure on the premise that it is *itself* a major influence on the ethos (or on the related ground that it is the optimal medium of *policy*). I argue that these claims confuse what justice is with what causes it to obtain, and philosophical questions with causal and practical questions. The objection that I confront in section 3 *(Prior Principles, Self-Respect, and Equality)* says that I overestimate the amount of inequality that Rawls's system tolerates, because I ignore the egalitarian effects both of the principles of justice that are lexically prior to the difference principle in Rawls's system and of the centrality of self-respect in that system. Section 4 *(Incentives and Prerogatives)* addresses David Estlund's contention that irresistible extensions of the Scheffler prerogative that I have honored[1] substantially diminish the difference between Rawls's position and my own. Section 5 replies to what Thomas Pogge says about *Mastergoals and Supergoals.* It takes up Pogge's criticism of what he considers to be the moral *monism* of my position, that is, my supposed general affirmation that what's moral sauce for the state goose is moral sauce for the private-citizen gander. Pogge argues that monism

1. See Chapter 1, p. 61.

373

is either of the "supergoal" or of the "mastergoal" variety, and that both varieties are deeply problematic. I argue that the difference between "mastergoals" and "supergoals" has nothing to do with monism as such, and that Pogge has failed to identify a relevant problem for my position. Section 6 *(Pogge's Failure to Address the Standard Case)* examines Pogge's quite minute, and misguided, critique of what I say about incentives. Section 7 *(The Currency of Distributive Justice and Incentive Inequality)* examines, and rejects, Susan Hurley's claim that there is a tension between my position on incentives and the central thesis of my essay "On the Currency of Egalitarian Justice." Finally, in section 8, I review criticisms of the incentive and Pareto arguments that anticipate my own, in various respects, and that were formulated by Thomas Grey and Jan Narveson.[2] I also examine a curiously ineffectual defense of Rawls's Pareto argument by Brian Barry.

1. Public and Private Action

Return to the passage on page 70 of Chapter 1:

> Suppose I am a doctor contemplating a hospital post that I know I could obtain at, say, £100,000 a year. I also believe that, if—and only if—I took something in the region of £50,000 for filling it, then any difference between my reward and what the less-well-paid get would be justified by what I strictly need to do the job, or by its special burdens. Then how can I say, with a straight face, that justice forbids inequalities that are detrimental to the badly off and be resolved to act justly in my own life, unless, should I indeed go for this particular job, I offer myself at £50,000 and thereby release £50,000 for socially beneficial use?

Passages like that one have given some people the false impression that, in my view, the principal relevant effect of the egalitarian ethos that I champion would be a multitude of doctorlike acts of forbearance and/or charity. So, for example, Norman Daniels reports that "Cohen says we must *replace* Rawls's focus on the basic structure and its accompanying division of responsibility with an ethos of justice that governs individual choices."[3] That is a misunderstanding, because I never suggest that gov-

2. I acknowledged that Grey and Narveson anticipated my argument on p. 263 of the original publication of "Incentives, Inequality, and Community."
3. "Democratic Equality," p. 265, emphasis added. For a similar misunderstanding, see Daniel Weinstock, Review of *If*, p. 407.

ernment should abandon *its* service to the difference principle in favor of replacement of that service by private-citizen action, and it is surely clear that what I call the strict difference principle has no tendency to favor private over public action when public action suffices for the desired maximinizing effect. Daniels's report would be correct only if "Not only but also" entailed "Not at all but only."

In fact, the most effective form of difference-principle-serving private-citizen action is not multifarious uncoordinated charity, that is, private action that *supplements* public action (such as the action that the doctor in the story on page 374 is in a position to perform), but private action that *enhances* the effect of public action. To explain the underlined distinction: private action *supplements* public when, for example, as in the doctor case, someone serves a principle within her own domain of choice, and possibly to good effect, even if her choice is not integrated with the choices of others. But private action *enhances* public when, to illustrate, a willingness on the part of the more fortunate to work hard at high tax rates enables government to set those rates under an expectation of high tax revenue and, therewith, the capacity to redistribute radically. Government tax policy is not then set against the grain of self-interest, and its range of options is thereby propitiously widened.[4] Awesome information/coordination problems indeed arise when the difference principle is honored exclusively through individual choices, but action under the inspiration of a tax-accepting ethos (which is to say, the action—or benign inaction—of accepting high taxation with comparative equanimity) faces no such problems.

Let me develop my illustration of the enhancing function of private action. Suppose that a country called Swedeland once had a strong welfare state that greatly benefited the worst off, but that the Swedeland state taxed the more successful at rates against which the upper and middle classes in time rebelled, through various forms of literal and "internal"

---

4. Rawls, by contrast, requires neither supplementation nor enhancement of government's service to the difference principle by the citizens of a just society: they need only comply, willingly, with just law. One might say, indeed, that Rawls calls for *compliance in daily life with law that serves principle, rather than compliance in daily life with principle itself:* "Ideally the rules should be set up so that men are led by their predominant interests to act in ways which further socially desirable ends. The conduct of individuals guided by their rational plans should be coordinated as far as possible to achieve results which although not intended or perhaps even foreseen by them are nevertheless the best ones from the standpoint of social justice" (*A Theory of Justice*, pp. 57/49).

emigration, to the detriment of, among others, the worst off, as tax take, and, therefore, the welfare state, sagged. (Some think that the story told here is true of Sweden, but I say "Swedeland" to cater for dissidence on that score. Whether or not the story is true of some actual state, it is not only coherent but credible, and its credibility suffices to demonstrate the extreme importance of the presence or the absence of the ethos for which I contend.)

The Swedeland case shows that my critic Kok-Chor Tan's character-ization of the "genuinely personal choices" that he seeks to protect against the encroachment of a Cohen-like ethos will not, contrary to Tan's intention, protect economic choices: "Genuinely personal choices . . . pertain only to those actions and decisions of individuals that have no direct implications for the kinds of institutions that can be established and supported in society."[5] But economic choices are not "genuinely per-sonal," by Tan's criterion, for any choices that belong to widespread pat-terns of choice *do* have strong implications for what sorts of institutions are possible. Economic choices therefore get no exemption from the judgment of justice under Tan's criterion.

The function of the doctor example (see page 374) is not to epitomize a comprehensive economic program but to demonstrate the incoherence of a certain package of declaration and of behavior. The doctor example serves to make a point of principle, not to describe a generalizable eco-nomic mechanism.

To see that point of principle, consider for a moment Rawls's first principle of justice, which mandates, *inter alia,* freedom of speech, or the second part of the second principle, which legislates, *inter alia,* against job discrimination. Could one suppose that the sense of justice of Rawl-sian citizens implies, with respect to their honoring of these principles, nothing more than cheerful compliance with laws that are designed to serve them? Suppose that the laws' designs could not eliminate certain forms of illiberal restrictions on speech, and some forms of job discrimi-nation, and that private action could bring some relevant relief. Would it not then be an obligation that is recognized and acted on by suitably placed individuals to try to diminish those injustices? If not, then their sense of justice could not be as described. If so, then why should matters be otherwise with respect to the difference principle, where a fuller real-ization of it than what the state can secure through law alone can be

5. "Justice and Personal Pursuits," p. 336.

achieved by individuals through their personal choices? Even if, and contrary to my view, there were no such personal obligations to promote justice, would not a person who engaged (beyond duty) in the relevant action qualify as especially *just,* and/or as bringing more justice to her society?

To be sure, it might be easier for government, on its own, to enforce the liberty and opportunity principles than it is for it to make the income of the least well off as high as possible, partly because talented people have information inaccessible to government about their salary and work preferences, whereas the problem of elusive information seems not as great in respect of the other principles. But that is a reason for people who are inspired, as Rawlsian citizens supposedly are by the difference principle, to promote its fuller application through their personal choices, and especially through acceptance of high taxation. If they are, as Rawls says, bent on being just, then why would they exploit their opportunity to impede fulfillment of the principle's aims, when they can help to ensure the achievement of what government alone cannot do (but would do if it could, given that it seeks to act on the difference principle)?

2. The Site of Justice Is Not Where It Gets Caused

It is sometimes suggested that the Rawlsian focus on the basic structure, and away from the social ethos, is justified by the preponderant influence of the structure over the ethos itself. Thomas Pogge:

> My book suggested, e.g., that a basic structure produces a certain rate of incidence of morally motivated conduct of various kinds . . . If [conditioning by the basic structure] is pretty strong, then the focus on the basic structure can be motivated (as it is for me) by the thought that this is the really independent variable: It is important what ethos and personal choices prevail, but lasting reforms at these sites can be achieved only through institutional reforms.[6]

And Rawls too gives it as a reason for focus on the basic structure that it strongly conditions people's attitudes and purposes.[7]

6. Personal communication, Nov. 30, 1999. "My book" is Pogge's *Reading Rawls.*
7. See *A Theory of Justice,* pp. 259ff./229ff., *Justice as Fairness,* pp. 55–57, and "Kantian Constructivism," pp. 325–326.

Pogge's argument employs two premises. The first says not only that the basic structure of society profoundly affects its social ethos, but, more strongly, that it is the "really independent variable" vis-à-vis that ethos. The second says that the primary site of justice is the site of causal power with respect to the character of society as a whole. Both premises are false.

While it is undoubtedly true that the structure profoundly affects the ethos, it is also true that the social ethos profoundly affects the character of the basic structure. It was not the character of Britain's basic structure in 1945 that caused it to be transformed in a socialistic direction after 1945, but a powerful democratic ethos that was formed in the experience of war. It was not the character of the American basic structure, but, perhaps, the consciousness-transforming consequences of the birth-control pill, and at any rate certainly changes in consciousness, the rise of a feminist ethos, that led to women-friendly changes in the American basic structure after 1970. There is too much influence of the ethos on the structure for the fact that the structure affects the ethos to possess any discriminating force. If the basic structure is said to be *the* site of justice because of its influence on the ethos, then, by the same argument, the ethos is *the* site of justice.[8] Neither the structural "variable" not the ethos "variable" is "independent" of the other.

Pogge's second premise, moreover, affirms the wrong criterion for determining the site of justice. For the site question is not "What causes a society to be just?" but "What makes a society qualify as just?" Thus even if the ethos of a society had no effect on its basic structure, even if the first premise of the argument were true, it would not follow that the character of its ethos does not count profoundly from the point of view of deciding whether a society is just. Indeed: to the extent that its causal power vis-à-vis the ethos is thought to show the importance of the basic structure for justice, if that, *inter alia,* is what makes it important for justice, then my claim that the ethos is a site of justice is vindicated, not compromised. What is causally fundamental for social justice is not identical with what is fundamental to making society *count* as just.[9]

8. Cf. Kok-Chor Tan, "Justice and Personal Pursuits," p. 356, who, citing Rawls, says that justice is concerned with institutions because the "effects of institutions are so profound and present from the start" (*Theory,* p. 7), as though the effects of the ethos could not *also* be profound and present from the start.

9. As Michael Otsuka has remarked (private communication), the present is causally dependent on the past, which is causally independent of the present. Does it follow that whether we enjoy social justice is not at all a matter of how things are now?

This is a suitable place at which to respond to Joshua Cohen's criticism of my reply to Ronald Dworkin's defense of Rawls's emphasis on the basic structure.[10] My reply identified what I consider to be an incoherent triad within the Dworkinized Rawlsian position:

(1) the difference principle is an egalitarian principle of distributive justice; (2) it imposes on government a duty to promote an egalitarian ethos; (3) it is not for the sake of enhancing distributive justice in society that the principle requires government to promote that ethos.

Joshua Cohen responded that

[i]t might be that changes in institutions and policies would change the distribution [favourably to the worst off] and produce that shift by changing the preferences, attitudes, and sensibilities that constitute the social ethos. Surely it could not be that principles of justice that require us to adopt the institutions and policies that make the greatest contribution to the least advantaged instruct us not to make the changes when the effects on the least advantaged come from changes in the social ethos that result from institutional changes.[11]

When confronted with the Dworkin proposal, we need to ask how a state that operates in the interest of justice conceives of itself, and, in my view, the Dworkin proposal attributes an incoherent self-conception to government. The Dworkin/Rawls government seeks to eliminate all inequality that is unnecessary to rendering the worst off better off: call such inequality, for short, "eliminable." Now how does the said government conceive an inequality that turns out to be ineliminable, because unmodifiable facts about society's ethos make it so? Such a government surely regards the ineliminability of that inequality as *unfortunate,* for when it embarks on its task, it hopes to end up having removed more rather than less inequality: it does not operate in a spirit of indifference as to whether any given inequality is eliminable. And my anti-Dworkin point, which is unaffected by anything that Joshua Cohen says, goes to what the government can conceive itself to be trying to do, when it tries to benefit the least well off as much as possible. It is trying, and sometimes failing, to produce as much justice as possible, yet, within the Rawlsian view, it is unable so to conceive what it is trying to do, since, if

10. See p. 127 of Chapter 3.
11. "Taking People as They Are," p. 377.

it *eliminates* all the relevantly eliminable inequality, the basic structure it produces is, *ex hypothesi,* maximally just: there could not, in the circumstances, be a juster one.[12]

Joshua Cohen allows that his defense of Dworkin fails "if the ethos— if attitudes, preferences, and sensibilities—are relatively unresponsive to institutions,"[13] and he goes on to argue that they are indeed appropriately responsive. But any defense of the Dworkin proposal against my criticism that turns on causal claims misses the mark, since no denial of any causal claim is implied by my criticism of that proposal. The question before us is not the sociological one of whether the state can influence the ethos, and, if so, by how much. The contested question is the noncausal philosophical one of what makes a society *count* as more or less just.

The philosophical question is not a causal question, and, for the same reason, it is also not a policy question, since a policy question is centrally one about causal levers. Accordingly, Martin Wilkinson exhibits misunderstanding when he asks "whether or not it is a good idea to extend the difference principle to cover social conventions and personal behaviour."[14] That phrasing misrepresents a conceptual question as a question about wise practice: the question I raise is whether on conceptual grounds, on the grounds, that is, of what constitutes a commitment to the difference principle, the difference principle necessarily so extends.

It is crucial here that the difference principle enjoys the status of being a principle of *justice*. It says that *justice* requires that no inequality ob-

---

12. Consider a field upon which a platform is to be erected. Its erectors drive struts into the ground so that, later, the platform will be placed on top of them. But now a great rain supervenes, and some struts get loosened. The erectors consequently now set about removing the loose struts, but they also set about removing the loosely rooted weeds, because they don't want lots of weeds growing through the timbers of the platform. So they remove loose struts, leaving the firm ones in place, and also loose weeds, leaving the firmly rooted ones in place, because, we can suppose, their removal isn't worth the effort. They act on exactly the same policy with respect to both weeds and struts, namely, remove the removable ones, but they are glad when a strut is irremovable but sad when a weed is irremovable. Is the Rawlsian government that seeks to eliminate what I called "eliminable" inequalities like a strut remover or like a weed remover? Intuitively, it is like a weed remover, but, by official doctrine, it is a strut remover, for there is officially absolutely nothing wrong with an ineliminable inequality. And I say: tell it to the judge.
13. Ibid., p. 380.
14. "Equality and the Moral Revolution," p. 278.

tain that harms the worst off. So I say, why should that not mean that justice condemns market self-seeking? I don't see how policy considerations can answer *that* question, as opposed to this distinct one: are there policy considerations that tell against outlawing, or otherwise discouraging, market self-seeking, whether or not such behavior is unjust?

It can be bad policy to seek to promote justice, whether because that would not in fact promote justice, or because seeking to promote it would prejudice other values.[15] That being so, I don't see how considerations about wise policy could *also* decide whether or not a piece of behavior, whatever we should do about it, is unjust.

Since I disparage the significance of policy here, one might say that my view lacks interest, since it has no *practical* upshot.

Both premises of this objection are false: that interestingness, in political philosophy, depends on practical upshot, and that my view has no practical upshot. We can disagree, substantively, about what justice *is* even when we agree completely about policy. But what justice *is* remains no less philosophically interesting than what knowledge, or rationality, is.

And the minor premise of the objection, which says that my view lacks practical upshot, is also false, partly because Joshua Cohen is undoubtedly right in his causal claim. We can indeed evaluate state action not only by what it does via the coercive structure directly, but also for the likely influence of that structure on the ethos. The Thatcherite free-market restructuring, for example, had disastrous ethos consequences. And one may add that our everyday actions greatly affect the ethos, because they change the norms to which we fall subject. Consider, for example, how environmental consciousness grew.[16]

3. Prior Principles, Self-Respect, and Equality

My critique of the incentives argument is a critique of an *argument* for inequality. I object to its failure to provide a promised comprehensive justification of inequality. My political disapproval of the inequality that the incentives argument purports to justify is, philosophically speaking, a secondary matter. My central criticism of Rawls is within political phi-

15. Those truths reflect the distinction between fundamental principles of justice and rules of regulation, which is introduced in section 19 of Chapter 6, and developed at length in the sections and chapters that follow that section.
16. See Chapter 3, p. 142.

losophy, not within public policy: it is not the *heart* of my contention that a society that is just by Rawls's lights exhibits *too much* inequality, although I indeed believe that, and that belief animates my work on these matters. But what I centrally reject is a certain justification for inequality, a certain representation of the conditions under which it is just. I reject that justification regardless of how *much* inequality it would actually justify, or might be thought by Rawls to justify.

To the extent that mine is a critique of a *justification*, it is no objection to that critique to say, as a number of my critics have said, that the *amount* of inequality that the Rawlsian justification of it would justify is for various reasons not great, that, for example, in estimating the size of the inequalities that survive Rawls's lax application of the difference principle, I wrongly ignore the *equalizing* effect of the two principles (equal liberty, fair opportunity) that are lexically prior to the difference principle. It is no answer whatever to "This justification of inequality doesn't work" to say "Oh, well, that shouldn't worry you too much, since the justification won't justify too much inequality anyway. *Other things* are helping to take care of that."[17] Rawlsian citizens think that the distribution of talent endowments is "morally arbitrary": that is part of the reason why they enter the original position. So we can ask: "If you think the distribution of talent is morally arbitrary, how can you think it consistent with justice for you to take advantage of your place in it?" They cannot reply by saying: "Oh, well, our taking advantage of that won't lead to very *much* inequality, given the full set of constraints that lie upon us."

The claim that the prior principles have an equalizing tendency does not touch the philosophically crucial distinction, which is not between large and small inequalities but between inequalities (however small) that are not unconditionally required to improve the condition of the

---

17. The proponent of this defense typically shows *satisfaction* that, as she thinks, not too much inequality will obtain. But why should she feel that satisfaction, given that if a lot of inequality turned out to be justified by the Rawlsian principles, just so much inequality would, in her view, be just? It is an indication that she treats the difference principle as what I call a "rule of regulation" rather than as characterizing justice itself that she is *eager* to show that it does not lead to "too much" inequality. (Compare section 9 [*Inequality: A Necessary Evil?*] of Chapter 2, and see also pp. 259–260 of Chapter 6 on how equality might be thought to control the validity of the difference principle.)

badly off and inequalities (however large) that are so required. Philosophy is interested in grounds, not ranges, of inequality.

Nevertheless, and as I have indicated, one of the things that motivates my critical stance toward Rawls is my conviction that his principles, as he interprets them, justify *substantial* inequality. The prior principles objection is therefore entirely in place as an objection to something that matters a lot to me, even if not, centrally, *as* a philosopher.

David Brink provides a statement of the prior principles claim:

> . . . there are general reasons for thinking Rawls's difference principle would not countenance significant incentive inequalities. The case for thinking that the difference principle would endorse significant inequalities is weakened considerably when we remember that (a) the conditions of self-respect are among the primary goods that the difference principle governs, and (b) the difference principle is lexically posterior not just to the equal basic liberties and equality of opportunity but also to the fair value of political liberties. *Ad* (a) As you note, unnecessary incentives erode the self-respect of the worst-off; given the primacy of the social conditions of self-respect (*A Theory of Justice*, p. 440), these incentives wouldn't maximize the position of the worst-off. *Ad* (b) Unless we can insulate the value of one's political liberties from the (comparative) level of one's social and economic resources, the fair value of political liberties will require substantial economic equality.[18]

The Brink objection says that I underestimate the equality-promoting tendencies of elements other than the difference principle in the Rawlsian system. In assessing the objection we must distinguish between what follows from the logic of his system and what Rawls thinks follows from it, in respect of how much inequality it permits. And in answering the first and more important question, we must consider the system with the *lax* difference principle in place, since it is a thesis of *my own* that what the system's logic actually requires is the *strict*, and more severely equalizing, difference principle. Hence any equality that the system produces that *I* can be accused of ignoring must be produced under, and in spite of, a lax interpretation of the difference principle. For my present

18. David Brink, private communication, July 1992 (*"Ads"* added). Cf. David Estlund, "Liberalism, Equality, and Fraternity," p. 110; Joshua Cohen, "Taking People as They Are," pp. 382–383; and Norman Daniels, "Democratic Equality," p. 252. For an interesting discussion of the prior principles claim, see Dong-Ryul Choo, "Cohen's Egalitarianism," pp. 18ff.

objectors say, precisely: don't worry about how much inequality the lax interpretation might allow—it can't allow much, given the pressure for equality *elsewhere* in the system.

Rawls himself frequently expresses, or betrays, a belief that contradicts Brink's, that the society his system prescribes will exhibit not, as Brink says, substantial economic *equality* but substantial economic *inequality*, at least in a wide range of circumstances: he says that deep inequalities in initial life prospects are inevitable[19]; he speculates that "differences in wealth and circumstances" across social groups will not be very painful for the less well off, because "we tend to compare our circumstances with others in the same or in a similar group as ourselves"[20]: there would be no pain from which their isolation would save the less

19. *A Theory of Justice,* p. 7. Perhaps that represents a liberal consensus: compare Murphy and Nagel, *The Myth of Ownership,* p. 80: "however egalitarian in spirit [one's] conception [of a just distribution] is, a just distribution will still involve substantial inequality of resources. This is simple realism."

20. *A Theory of Justice,* pp. 537/470. Let me quote the environing passage *in extenso,* since it testifies strongly to the presence of substantial inequality in the achieved Rawlsian society: "the plurality of associations in a well-ordered society, each with its secure internal life, tends to reduce the visibility, or at least the painful visibility, of variations in men's prospects. For we tend to compare our circumstances with others in the same or in a similar group as ourselves, or in positions that we regard as relevant to our aspirations. The various associations in society tend to divide it into so many noncomparing groups, the discrepancies between these divisions not attracting the kind of attention which unsettles the lives of those less well placed. And this ignoring of differences in wealth and circumstance is made easier by the fact that when citizens do meet one another, as they must in public affairs at least, the principles of equal justice are acknowledged. Moreover in everyday life the natural duties are honored so that the more advantaged do not make an ostentatious display of their higher estate calculated to demean the condition of those who have less. After all, if the disposing conditions for envy are removed, so probably are those for jealousy, grudgingness, and spite, the converses of envy. When the less fortunate segments of society lack the one, the more fortunate will lack the other. Taken together these features of a well-ordered regime diminish [but not to zero!—GAC] the number of occasions when the less favored are likely to experience their situation as impoverished and humiliating. Even if they have some liability to envy, it may never be strongly evoked." Cf. *Justice as Fairness,* p. 68: "we hope that the *observable* features of the distribution that result fall in a range where they do not *seem* unjust." (Emphases added). If I did not know that Rawls was free of cynicism, I would call the position that he expounds here cynical. It is an argument for, *inter alia,* secluded roads for liberal limousines.

well off if the inequalities were not big; and one way that Rawls suggests for delineating the "worst off group," namely, as those who earn less than half the *median* income,[21] suggests what many would consider to be substantial economic inequality. Rawls therefore *could* not agree that Brink's considerations (a) and (b) ensure substantial economic equality.

But Rawls is not always consistent, and although he *should,* for the reasons just stated, disagree with Brink, he in fact agrees with him on some counts. Let us now turn to the three supposedly equalizing factors adduced by Brink. We can ask two questions about each of them: whether Rawls shares Brink's view of their effect, and whether they would in fact have that effect.

Consider first the implications for equality of the fair value of political liberty. I do not think, and I do not think Rawls thought, that ensuring that people's opportunities to hold office and exercise political influence are substantially independent of their socioeconomic position requires substantially equal material holdings.[22] I believe that un-American experience shows that election regulation, of a sort that Rawls would endorse, can produce political democracy under a wide inequality of income and wealth. Note, moreover, that any equality to be credited to prior principles that would not also be provided by the difference principle itself obtains at the expense of making the bundle of material goods that the worst off get smaller than it would otherwise be: whatever the prior principles, for their own different purposes, mandate that happens to have a maximinizing tendency is, if required for maximinizing effect, anyway required by the difference principle. And I think it implausible that the fair value of political liberty requires a diminution in the income and wealth prospects of the worst off, relative to their prospects under a difference principle that is *not* lexically posterior to political liberty.

I turn to Brink's claim that protecting the social bases of self-respect rules out "unnecessary incentives." Here Brink's point is disqualified by the requirement, noted above, that the "prior principles" objection

21. *A Theory of Justice,* pp. 98/84.
22. See *A Theory of Justice,* pp. 197–200/224–228; *Political Liberalism,* pp. 327–329. On p. 328 of the latter Rawls writes: "one guideline for guaranteeing fair value seems to be to keep political parties independent of large concentrations of private economic and social power in a private-property democracy, and of government control and bureaucratic power in a liberal socialist regime." This implies that there can *be* large concentrations of wealth, and, therefore, significant inequality, in a Rawls-endorsable private-property democracy or liberal socialism.

must work under a lax interpretation of the difference precept principle. For laxity implies that economic agents are allowed to maximize their prospects *within* the policy chosen by the maximinizing state. So it is out of the question that the system should forbid "unnecessary incentives [which, because they are unnecessary] erode the self-respect of the worst off." If Brink is right that they do so, then the proponent of the system must either abandon laxness for strictness, and agree with me, or abandon the Rawlsian emphasis on the social bases of self-respect.

In the matter of fair equality of opportunity,[23] Rawls might agree with Brink, even though that agreement would contradict his general view, according to which fair opportunity *could* not generate substantial equality (since there isn't going to be substantial equality). For Rawls says:

> [W]ith many more persons receiving the benefits of training and education [in a society with fair equality of opportunity], the supply of qualified individuals . . . is much greater. When there are no restrictions on entry or imperfections in the capital market for loans (or subsidies) for education, the premium earned by the better endowed is far less. The relative difference in earnings between the more favored and the lowest income class tends to close; and this tendency is even stronger when the difference principle is followed.[24]

Rawls also makes a more remarkable claim about the equalizing effect of full equality of opportunity. He says that "in equilibrium the relative attractiveness of different jobs will be equal, all things considered."[25] This is inconsistent with the more moderate statement presented in the passage above, and as Richard Krouse and Michael McPherson point out, with the more general point, often made by Rawls, that people differ in their native abilities, a point that is crucial to his account of inequalities.[26] And one may add that, even with identical natural abilities, the equilibrium described by Rawls would eventuate only where utility functions were also identical.

How far would fair equality of opportunity induce more equality than

23. I prescind here from the doubts expressed in the last paragraph of section 4 of Chapter 4 about whether Rawls "really" puts fair equality of opportunity before the difference principle.

24. *A Theory of Justice*, pp. 307/207. For a similar statement, see *Justice as Fairness*, p. 67.

25. *A Theory of Justice*, pp. 305/269.

26. "Capitalism, 'Property-Owning Democracy,' and the Welfare State," p. 93.

the lax difference principle would induce? Recall that fair equality of opportunity is the circumstance that individuals with the same native talent and the same ambition have the same prospects of success. That has no immediate implications for the distances between the rungs of the ladder across which differently endowed and/or ambitious individuals have different prospects. It follows that, unlike what might seem plausible for equal political liberty and universal self-respect, there is no reason to suppose it in general likely that fair equality of opportunity, followed by the difference principle, produces more equality than would a difference principle unconstrained by fair equality of opportunity. Fair equality of opportunity should not have appeared on Brink's list.

4. Incentives and Prerogatives

My claim that Rawls endorses incentive demands that he ought not to endorse has been subjected to two contrasting lines of criticism. The first line affirms that Rawls is right to endorse the incentive demands that I think he is wrong to endorse, but the second line denies that he endorses, or, at any rate, is committed to endorsing, all of the incentive demands that I think he endorses.

The first criticism denies the pertinence of the difference principle to economic choice and attitude. That principle, it says, is to be applied to the basic structure of society only, because (these are three variants of the first line of criticism) the basic structure has especially profound effects on life chances, and/or because "an unrestricted difference principle" poses "excessive informational demands"; and/or because such a difference principle poses "intrusive informational demands."[27] Chapter 3 addressed the first variant of the first line of criticism, and each of Chapters 7 and 8 addressed the second and third variants of it.

In this section I address a variant of the second line of objection, which is

> that Cohen exaggerates the distance of his view from Rawls's, since Cohen acknowledges that at least some incentive demands are reasonable, and is committed to allowing that an even wider range is reasonable.[28]

27. The quotations are from a taxonomy of objections to my view that Joshua Cohen supplies on p. 365, n. 3 of "Taking People as They Are": the taxonomy given above changes his a bit.
28. Idem., with the number (2) added.

The first line of objection defends Rawls under the usual (and, in my view, correct) acceptation of his theory, according to which "anything goes" on the market once the right market rules are in place. The second line of objection, which was launched by David Estlund,[29] says no such thing, but proposes that a market governed by motivations that I cannot but countenance will be less different than I suppose from the sort of market that Rawls should and can, in all consistency, countenance. Estlund notes that I expressly allow inequalities that reflect a Schefflerian self-regarding personal prerogative,[30] but, so he urges, I cannot consistently acknowledge that prerogative without also acknowledging further prerogatives that induce further inequalities and, hence, more legitimate inequality than I had envisaged. In a society that I must consider just, "inequality-producing incentives will still be required by many conscientious citizens exercising" not only that prerogative but three other "prerogatives that Cohen must allow."[31] In sum, irresistible extensions of the Scheffler prerogative that I seek to honor substantially diminish the difference between Rawls's position and my own.

Before I respond to Estlund, let me say what I thought about prerogatives and incentives before I read his challenging article.

The heart of my objection to Rawls was to the argument which says that incentive payments are just solely and simply because they make the worse off better off and therefore whatever may be the motives that actuate the demand for incentives. My objection said that, in the "standard" case,[32] those motives reveal a lack of commitment to the difference principle on the part of the relevantly motivated agents, a lack of commitment that spoils the claim that the difference principle legitimates market incentives.

But I also endorsed two reasons for allowing income inequality with which I had no quarrel, reasons that have nothing to do with the incentive effect of income inequality. The first reason concerns the case of income inequality that counterbalances an inequality of labor burden.[33] Such inequality of income is justified not on incentive but on

29. See his "Liberalism, Equality, and Fraternity."
30. See p. 61 of Chapter 1.
31. "Liberalism," p. 101.
32. See p. 57 of Chapter 1.
33. See "the special burden" case described at p. 55 of Chapter 1. I believe that the example in Estlund that builds on a postulated difference between male and female job preferences ("Liberalism," p. 105) fails of its effect, because it is a complex

egalitarian grounds. And the second good reason for inequality is that it may supervene on exercise of a Schefflerian personal prerogative that entitles agents not to be fully constrained by egalitarian demands in their personal choices. I also claimed, essentially without argument, that, even when that prerogative was given its proper due, justice would dictate a society without very much inequality. (I didn't say what I meant by "very much.")

Note that it is no part of my critique of Rawls that I *endorse* the prerogative (that, so it happens) I endorse.[34] The important point for the Rawls critique, and the one I made, is that the prerogative justification of inequality is *different* from the Rawlsian. Michael Otsuka has recently argued[35] that the disposition of some egalitarians to concede any sort of prerogative to depart from equality is misguided. Otsuka has not convinced me, but as far as my argument against Rawls goes, I could come to agree with Otsuka and thereby deprive Estlund of the "concession" that he exploits.

Now before I read Estlund's article, I was disposed to *contrast* the incentives justification of inequality with its prerogative justification: I did not notice that, as Estlund shows, the prerogative and incentive considerations can be *combined*. My principal thought was that the Scheffler prerogative could not be an *argument* for the incentive justification, if only because the amount of inequality justified by the incentive consideration varies with circumstance: it might be more, or less, than what the Scheffler prerogative would license. It might be more, because the inequality that results from the use of prodigious market power might exceed what the Scheffler prerogative allows. And it might be less, because super-duper economists might discover ways of taxing people excessively, relative, that is, to the amount of what they earn that the Scheffler prerogative says they have a right to keep: if the Scheffler prerogative is sound, then it should influence taxation policy, but what it recommends could not, in the general case, be what the incentives argument recommends. So, as I said, "the compromise idea," the idea that justice is a compromise between legitimate self-interest and the interests of others,

instance of the special burden case: no prerogative is needed to justify the relevant inequality here.

34. What I said in Chapter 1, p. 61 was merely that "I do not wish to reject" the Scheffler prerogative.

35. In "Prerogatives to Depart from Equality."

"is, simply, different from the idea that inequalities are justified if they are necessary to benefit the badly off, given that agents are," to whatever extent they choose to be, "self-regarding maximizers on the market."[36]

Estlund makes three moves. First, he *combines* the prerogative and incentives motifs more clearly than I had seen could be done. It is, for Estlund, *in virtue* of her prerogative that a person's incentive requirement is legitimate, although the state accedes to the requirement only if doing so benefits the worst off. Second, Estlund claims that, if I endorse a self-interest prerogative, then I must also endorse other ones. Third, he infers that, once those further prerogatives are also recognized, the upshot is likely to be much more inequality than I seemed prepared to endorse.

I shall express a minor reservation about Estlund's second move and a major reservation about his third move.

The minor reservation concerns how many truly *further* prerogatives Estlund has identified. Estlund's first supposed additional prerogative relates to the *affection* that one may feel for other people, whom one may wish to serve with the money that one (therefore) requires as an incentive.[37] But motivation by such affection is already comprehended in Scheffler's prerogative, which allows one to devote disproportionate weight to one's own projects, among which are, indeed, projects inspired by affection for others. My error was not that I failed to *add* (to the Scheffler prerogative) a prerogative permitting the indulgence of affection for other people, but that I mischaracterized the Scheffler prerogative as a matter of (narrow) self-interest alone. We can, nevertheless, distinguish between a prerogative of narrow self-interest and one of affection, and Estlund is surely right that anyone who grants the first prerogative must also grant the second.

Estlund calls his second purportedly additional prerogative "inequality producing moral requirements,"[38] his illustration of which is a case where an incentive induces me to work harder so that I can pay for some damage that I have done to my neighbor's garden. Estlund's idea is that it was within my power to do that extra work for the worst off, but that the "moral requirement" prerogative justifies not going all out for them.

36. Chapter 1, p. 72.
37. Estlund, "Liberalism," p. 102.
38. Idem.

This might indeed be regarded as a further prerogative,[39] although one may wonder about how much inequality it would justify.

Finally, Estlund argues that if, as I grant, it is permissible for the claims of self-interest to override the claims of social justice within a person's calculus of priorities, then general social justice may also be overridden by other morally significant purposes within that calculus, even if those other purposes do not deserve greater weight from a neutral point of view. Incentive seeking might be justified by, for example, the desire to establish a foundation to promote the arts. But this, again, is comprehended in a Schefflerian prerogative.

The points pressed thus far are, as I said, minor, because they do not touch the *substance* of Estlund's second move, which is that I must allow more prerogatives than I expressly conceded. My point about Estlund's third move is more substantial.

Suppose I say that you should spend the afternoon working at the youth club, but that you can take an hour off to have your fingernails done, or to visit your beloved aunt, or to work off that moral debt that you incurred, or to pursue some independent moral purpose. I have then given you prerogatives that illustrate the four sorts of prerogative that Estlund distinguishes, but that doesn't mean that I have given you prerogatives that allow you to take four hours off. There may indeed be prerogatives of "self-interest, morality and affection" (p. 112), but it doesn't follow that there is more scope for legitimate inequality than a prerogative of narrow self-interest alone would justify. The fact that you can have more justifications than one for doing something doesn't mean that you are justified in doing that thing to a greater extent than you would be justified in doing it if you had only one justification for doing it. Estlund's third move is not one of logic.

There are three possible views here, and the third one is the most plausible. First, that you have *one* prerogative, which is to depart from equality to a specified extent, regardless of how you use it, be that self-interestedly, and/or affectionately, and/or morally. Second, that each prerogative justifies additional, and not just differently justified, inequality, and as much additional inequality as the amount of inequality that the

39. I express myself with the indicated circumspection because one might regard a prerogative as something that one can, with equal legitimacy, either exercise or not exercise, and the present putative prerogative, while *permitting* one not to have special regard to the worst off, is not something that one is straightforwardly permitted *not* to exercise.

prerogative in question would justify if (an admittedly weird assumption) it were the only prerogative. And the third and most plausible view is that the truth lies somewhere between the first two views.

I do not know how to establish the truth about these prerogatives. Perhaps I *did* underestimate the amount of inequality that the Scheffler prerogative, as I understood it, would *itself* allow, but I think it fair to say that Estlund has not *shown* that much more inequality is justified by prerogatives than what I thought the prerogative consideration, narrowly conceived, would allow.[40]

Notice, moreover, that in clothing the originally "naked"[41] incentives argument in the garb of personal and other prerogative, Estlund breaches the barrier between public and private on which Rawls insists. What you do *within* coercive rules structured by the lax difference principle is not, for Estlund, as it is for Rawls, beyond the judgment of distributive justice. According to Estlund, an incentive demand is open to criticism at the bar of justice if there is no prerogative-based reason for demanding it.

That is why Estlund rightly says that a concern for local personal justice as between, for example, spouses or partners serves "as a buffer (though not a barrier) to the intrusion of standards of social justice into

---

40. I was struck when I read this comment by Norman Daniels ("Democratic Equality," p. 267) on Estlund: "With agent-relative prerogatives this robust, we exclude explicit cases of greed but not many of the inequality-producing choices that individuals typically present. The space between Rawls's lax interpretation and Cohen's strict one suddenly shrinks." Daniels provides no evidence for the empirical part of his strong statement.

I should also like to comment here on an observation by Joshua Cohen about the standard case that puzzles me. Remarking that I acknowledge Scheffler/Estlund-type prerogatives, Cohen goes on to say:

> So Cohen accepts the justice of at least some incentive inequalities that emerge in Absolute Incentives cases, and surely must agree that it is difficult precisely to circumscribe the acceptable cases. For this reason, I put this case to the side. ("Taking People as They Are," p. 373)

Joshua Cohen's Absolute Incentives case is, give or take a wrinkle, my "standard case." I find it curious that we should suppose that Absolute Incentive cases, as such, can be set aside simply because some of them should indeed be set aside and the border of that set is hard to establish. A generalization of that procedure would extinguish a lot of discussion in moral and political philosophy.

41. See the penultimate paragraph of section 6 of Chapter 1.

the conduct of certain more local relationships and endeavors."[42] Because Estlund defends no *barrier,* because, indeed, he is happy to breach it, his critique of me sustains my objection to Rawls's teaching on the immunity of private economic choice to the judgment of justice. Rawls himself justified inequality when, and *simply* because, whatever the motivations of the high fliers might be, catering to those motivations could benefit the badly off. Estlund hasn't defended that.[43] I am, accordingly, confident that the challenging position that he develops is not, as Estlund sometimes suggests it is, entirely consistent with Rawls's own view, but a substantial revision of it, a kind of halfway house between Rawls's view and the one that I defended in Chapters 1 through 3.

Estlund is aware that he is not straightforwardly vindicating, but reconstructing, Rawls's position. He writes:

> Cohen's argument allows us to see that the theory *needs* to move to prerogatives if the difference principle is ever to justify significant inequality. Certainly, that was not clear from Rawls's original arguments.

Estlund is, rather, proposing a middle way:

> [The] distinction between the lax and strict readings of the difference principle presents a false dilemma. It is true neither that inequality is only justified when strictly necessary to benefit the least well off regardless of what motives people have, nor that inequality is justified if necessary to benefit the least well off given whatever motives people happen to have. Rather, between lax and strict there is what we might call
>
> *The Moderate Version of the Difference Principle:* Inequality is only justified when necessary to benefit the least well off given the actual motives that people have consistent with an ethos of justice as defined by the two principles.
>
> On the moderate version of the difference principle, if people seek incentives in order to pursue the prerogatives that Cohen grants are compatible

42. Estlund, "Liberalism," p. 106.
43. In a fascinating unpublished essay called "I Will If you Will: Leveraged Enhancements and Distributive Justice," Estlund supplies extremely interesting reasons for thinking that the amount of incentive inequality permitted in exercise of legitimate prerogatives might be considerably less than what he supposed it would be when he wrote the article under discussion here.

with the ethos of justice, then [substantial-GAC] inequality may be necessary in order to do as well for the worst off as possible.

... here's the importance I ascribe to Cohen's points: many have thought that Rawlsian arguments would justify inequalities that benefit the least well off even if this requires offering incentives to selfishly maximizing high flyers. Cohen's argument, for the first time, refutes this claim about what Rawlsian arguments would justify. Nevertheless, Cohen is wrong to suppose that just citizens could not be incentive seekers without being selfish maximizers, so the difference principle may yet justify significant inequality, but on a different basis than is commonly supposed. It may be that this new basis will not justify as much inequality as the mistaken interpretation would have done, but this is so far less clear.[44]

Estlund recognizes that there is no trace in Rawls of reliance on specific *prerogatives* to render inequality just: Rawls allows *whatever* incentives are "nakedly" called for, and thereby licenses them for reasons that are not endorsed by Estlund.[45] So whether or not Estlund vindicates more inequality than I thought justifiable—and we continue to disagree about that difficult matter of judgment—he yet does not vindicate my principal target, which was the naked incentives argument, and with it a certain understanding of liberalism. And as I have explained (see page 389 above), I need take no particular view about prerogatives for the sake of my critique of Rawls.

5. Pogge's Mastergoals and Supergoals

Sections VIII through XIII of Thomas Pogge's "On the Site of Distributive Justice" are devoted to the refutation of a view called "monism" that is affirmed by Liam Murphy[46] and attributed by Pogge to me, a view

44. Personal communication, April 21, 1998: I have indulged in a little helpful (uncheating) editing.
45. That being so, the last sentence in the long quotation from Estlund's 1998 communication is insufficiently concessive. How could allowing only a selected range of motives for wanting more justify as much inequality as allowing *any* motive for wanting more?
46. To prevent possible misunderstanding, I note that Murphy's monism is neutral with respect to the pluralism affirmed in section 3 of the Introduction to this book. Murphy's monism says, roughly, that the same set of goals (whether that set consists of just one or many goals) is to be pursued by all agents. The pluralism affirmed in my Introduction says that there is a radical plurality of goals (whether or not all sound goals are to be pursued by all agents).

from which it follows that what is moral sauce for the state goose is moral sauce for the private citizen gander. For monism says that any fundamental normative principle that applies anywhere also applies everywhere: thus, if to the basic structure, then also to personal conduct. Pogge divides monists into supergoal monists (one of which Pogge thinks I am) and mastergoal monists, and he argues that both forms of monism (and, therefore, monism) are untenable.

The proponent of a mastergoal says roughly this: "Let things be such, that a certain single goal is achieved, no matter how. Accordingly, if causal relations happen to be peculiar, and the goal will be better achieved if people seek to frustrate its achievement, let people seek to prevent the goal that is to be achieved from being achieved." In precise contrast, the proponent of the supergoal says roughly this: "Everyone should consciously seek the single worthwhile goal, regardless of how likely it is thereby to be achieved, and even if it would be better achieved if no one sought to achieve it."

I shall argue, first, that the distinction Pogge draws between two kinds of goals has nothing to do with monism as such; second, that it should embarrass monists neither more nor less than it does anybody else; and, third, that it should not in fact embarrass anyone.

The difference between "masterness" and "superness"[47] has nothing to do with the distinction between monism and pluralism, since the stated difference obtains even in the presence of a *plurality* (in every sense[48]) of goals. The root contrast is the perfectly general one between preferring a desirable outcome and preferring the intention to produce that desirable outcome: if I begin by thinking that people should promote a goal G because achieving G is worthwhile, then, *whether or not G is the only goal that I endorse* for everyone, including state and citizen, to follow, what should I say if it turns out to be counterproductive, with respect to the achievement of G, for people to seek to promote G? The poignancy of that question has nothing to do with monism, and it is therefore somewhat misleading for Pogge to present it in special association with monism. The dilemma that putatively arises is entirely general and, for that reason, entirely innocuous as far as the monism/dualism dispute is concerned. Note that a parallel question, and one that is equally peculiar, could be put to Rawls: Do you prefer a society whose government aims to satisfy the difference principle, but fails, to one whose gov-

---

47. As opposed to the names that mark that difference within the space of monism.
48. See n. 46 above.

ernment aims otherwise, but happens to make the worst off as well off as it could make them? If monists face a conundrum, then so does Rawls, and so does anyone who favors any sort of goal.

I suggested in Chapter 3 that, if we endorse the difference principle, then whether it *pursues* the difference principle decides whether or not a *society* is just and that the approximation of a society's distribution to what the difference principle directs us to pursue, namely, a maximinizing distribution, decides whether a society's *distribution* is just (whatever may be the means by which that approximation to the difference principle's demand is or is not achieved). Pogge asks me to choose between the "supergoal" of a just society and the "mastergoal" of a just distribution. He asks (p. 160, fn. 40) what, on my view, the relative weights of the (possibly) competing goals of a just society and a just distribution are.

There are contrasting perspectives within which this question can be posed. Consider first the perspective of the political philosopher who asks what we as a society should pursue. Within that perspective, we cannot choose between achieving justice and pursuing it, because, when we pursue justice, it is justice itself, and not its mere pursuit, which is our aim.[49] When I introduced Pogge's mastergoal/supergoal distinction, I distinguished the two goals by identifying different things of which one might say "let things be such . . ." But that is God's language. We lack the power to *let* anything be thus and so: we can only *make* things thus and so. For us, "master" vs. "super," and the more general distinction that it illustrates, are inoperable distinctions, within the perspective of agency.[50] God (or, for that matter, any other third party[51]) is in a position to decide whether He (or She) prefers justice or its pursuit, but those who seek justice cannot.

It's great when nature[52] does good things, and greater still, at least in one way, when the same things come from human intention and virtue.

---

49. As Dick Arneson has pointed out to me, I am not "committed to the position that if one truly embraces equality one will feel oneself morally required to act to express one's commitment to equality even when doing so is counterproductive" (private communication).

50. Similar considerations apply against Dong-Ryul Choo's contrast between an "equality-inspiring ethos" and an "equality-promoting" one in section V-3 (pp. 39–43) of his "Cohen's Egalitarianism."

51. Such as the state, vis-à-vis its citizenry: see the next-but-one paragraph.

52. Nature here covers anything that is unintended, and therefore *inter alia* the unintended consequences of our actions.

But it's a bit weird to ask which is *better*, for which one should be willing to sacrifice the other. We can't control nature, but only what we do. So we do not, when choosing how to act, choose between masterness and superness. The answer to Pogge's putative conundrum is: you should aim at what you think a well-inspired person would aim at, and you should hope that all goes well. Only in special cases should you (instead) aim at *being* a well-inspired person.

Consider now a contrasting perspective, not the one in which *we* act, but that in which the state, here conceived not as "us" but as a third party, has to choose between legislation that tends to render the citizens just and legislation that improves the justice of the distribution: perhaps promoting the justice of citizens through appropriate classes in civics would produce less distributive justice than spending the same money on raising social welfare payments for the worst off. So I *can* be asked which I would prefer the state to do. And the answer is: it depends on the circumstances. Neither goal dominates the other, in my (permissible) view. If things are dire enough, we should prefer justice to its pursuit. But in some circumstances its pursuit is preferable, even at some cost to justice.

I have argued that monists need not be more embarrassed by the supergoal/mastergoal distinction than any agent is by the more general distinction that it illustrates, and that in fact no one need be embarrassed at all by the distinction that Pogge draws. I now add that I am not myself, in any case, a monist, or a denier of monism, in the relevant sense. I have no definite view on the issue, not because I don't know my own opinions but because I am not sure what "monism" is: the defining formulation that I offered in the opening paragraph of this section can bear further clarification. By bracketing me with Liam Murphy in section IX of his paper, by treating Murphy and me as cotargets, Pogge exaggerates my commitment to Murphyan positions. Whether or not it entails my own position, I hold nothing so general as Murphy's moral monism. I don't say that the maximinizing goal must govern individual behavior (just) *because* it governs state behavior. I simply ask why it should not do so, and I reject various answers to that question because of their various insufficiencies, and not on Murphyanly general grounds. Nor do I say, in general terms, that "it makes no sense to require citizens to pursue [a] goal in one way . . . but not to require them to pursue it in other ways as well"[53]: if that is not contradicted by the competitive sports example of

53. Pogge, ibid., p. 159.

the final paragraph of section 2 of Chapter 3, then I don't know what it means, and I therefore do not know what monism is supposed to be. My ambitions are not general in this domain: I simply contrive to refute the *actual* reasons that Rawlsians give for why citizens need not pursue distributive justice in the particular way that they would if it informed the ethos that governed their choices.

I don't, then, "urge" Rawls "to endorse supergoal monism." The paragraphs that Pogge cites to this effect urge no such thing.[54] I simply distinguish a just society from a just distribution and I criticize Rawls's view of what suffices for a just society: I claim that it doesn't, by his own best lights.

6. Pogge's Failure to Address the Standard Case

a. Across sections IV through VII of his article "On the Site of Distributive Justice," Thomas Pogge presents five possible specifications of the "duty"[55] that I assign to talented persons, and he judges all of them to be wanting. Let me, then, state what I take that duty, if duty it be, to be, under the difference principle, and *modulo* a personal prerogative: it is the duty not to take more income than other people get, save where such wages are required to compensate for "special burdens."[56] Let me now review some elements in Pogge's discussion.

Pogge's first candidate specification (pp. 143–44) of the Cohen duty likens the self-enriching talented person who violates it to an ordinary kidnapper. But that sort of talented person illustrates my "bluff" or "bad" case[57], which I expressly ruled out of consideration. The talented person whom I condemn is, instead, analogous to an unordinary kidnapper who would actually prefer to keep the kid if he doesn't get the ransom money (p. 299). (At the beginning of section V, Pogge displays an awareness that his first specification is off the mark, but there is no ground for his initial report that I sometimes "suggest" that specification [p. 143].)

54. Ibid., p. 158. The cited paragraphs appear at *If*, pp. 131–132, "Where the Action Is," pp. 14–15, and on pp. 127–128 of Chapter 3 above.

55. I add scare quotes because I prefer to speak of how talented persons behave in a just society. The truth about that does not imply that this duty lies upon them in an unjust society: whether it does so is the topic of the inconclusive discussion in chapter 10 of *If*.

56. See p. 61ff. (on the prerogative) and p. 55 (on "special burden") of Chapter 1.

57. See Chapter 1, p. 57, and Chapter 2, p. 102, respectively.

b. In section V Pogge proceeds to introduce what I called the "standard" case,[58] which is quite expressly the case on which I invited focus: it is the talented person of my standard case, and only a fortiori his bluffing cousin, who violates the Cohen duty. But Pogge argues, incorrectly, that the standard case collapses into my bluff or bad case:

> Cohen himself, in any event, does not regard strategic conduct as central to his critique. In "The Pareto Argument for Inequality," he distinguishes three cases of economic inequality in a Rawlsian society, describing the strategic case as the "Bad case" and expressing the belief that the most likely is the "standard case" where "the work of talented people is not distinctively burdensome, but, on the contrary, characteristically more congenial than the work of others" ("The Pareto Argument," pp. 172–73). Now if high-productivity work really is more congenial, why would there be any pay differential at all in the standard case? The talented, after all, prefer the congenial work even without special rewards. So why would not a tax regime satisfying the difference principle reduce the reward multiple for such work to 1 or below? The answer Cohen indicates is that "talented people may, as in the bad case, successfully hold out" for a higher net pay rate, which Cohen then refers to as "a rate they secure by virtue of the bargaining power associated with their superior talent" ("The Pareto Argument," pp. 173–4). But with this answer, the standard case is collapsed into the bad case, showing once more that the only explanation (besides the "good case" of extra rewards for especially burdensome jobs) Cohen can imagine for the persistence of high reward multiples in a Rawlsian society is strategic behaviour by the talented.[59]

Pogge's economic reasoning works *at most* for the importantly unrealistic case in which the choice of the talented is binary: either to manage or to labor. If we introduce the minimal realism of three choices for managers, to wit, to work 8 hours as a manager, or 6 hours as a manager, or 8 hours as a laborer, then the manager's utility function might well lead him to prefer, and to choose, 6 hours as a manager instead of 8 hours as a manager, if tax rises, and to the detriment of the laborers. And the manager's exercise of that choice would not make him count as a "bad" or "bluffing" manager.

The difference between a "standard" manager and a bluffing one is indicated on page 57 of Chapter 1. The bluffing manager issues a *threat,* since even at the higher tax rate he would prefer working as he does now

58. See p. 57 *et circa* in Chapter 1.
59. "On the Site," pp. 144–145.

to reducing his work input. The standard manager issues a *warning*, since he genuinely prefers working less at 60 percent tax than he does at 40 percent tax (even though, what is manifestly consistent and of pivotal importance, he would remain better off than the laborer is when he works at 60 percent tax as much as he does at 40 percent). "Strategic behaviour" is conditioned by the anticipated response of others. Threats are thus conditioned, but warnings are not.[60]

Since the "standard" talented merely warn, "bargaining power" may have been an unfortunate choice of phrase on my part: in the standard case the talented credibly announce their genuine preferences, and government accedes to them out of regard for the worst off. They do bargain in that the announcement of their unwillingness to work for less than what the incentive provides is intended to, and does, secure what they want, although one may deny that the announcement constitutes a "bargaining" position. But the relevant substantial difference is between the preference orderings in the bluff and standard cases, which are clearly set out in the preceding paragraph, however we may want to use the word "bargaining."

Pogge's criticism of what I say about the standard case leads him to provide his second specification of my critique, which is that its target is economic rent.[61] But that is a serious mistake. That a person receives economic rent has no interpersonal implications: it says nothing about how his condition compares with that of others. The description of the standard case (which is the only pertinent case) includes information about interpersonal comparisons of welfare that does not bear on the assessment of economic rent. If Babe Ruth (Pogge, fn. 20) hated playing baseball but hated any non-baseball job much more, then, in my view, his high pay for playing baseball might have been warranted, even though it was loaded with rent.[62]

c. To sum up thus far. We can suppose for the sake of exposition that all talented maximizers fall into the standard case. Since that is the case

60. The distinction is due to Nozick. See his "Coercion," pp. 103ff.

61. See "On the Site," pp. 146–147. Pogge's criticism of my distinction between economic rent and producer surplus on p. 146 seems to me quite off the mark, but it is of no consequence to our dispute, since Pogge simply uses "economic rent" as a name for what I call producer surplus, and producer surplus, as I define it, is the relevant variable here (whether or not, as I think but Pogge doesn't, "economic rent" can mean something different from "producer surplus").

62. Toward the end of section V of "On the Site," Pogge slides into remarks about the metric that are oblivious to what I say about it in section 6 of Chapter 2.

that I (distinctively) condemn, the moral duty that I lay down, *modulo* a personal prerogative, is, as I said, not to take more wages than the worst off save where such wages are required to compensate for special burdens. And that doesn't amount to condemning either strategic behavior or economic rent.

d. The rest of Pogge's discussion of the identity of my incentives critique is vitiated by his conflation of the standard case with the bluff and rent cases.

I find it difficult to understand the situation of Pogge's Clara (see his section VI). *Ex* (Pogge's) *hypothesi,* managing and laboring are "objectively equally burdensome" in Clara's world, while Clara herself much prefers laboring to managing. But those facts don't tell us how well off Clara is in comparison with typical laborers, either when she labors or when she manages, at various rates of pay. The frankly interpersonal welfare comparison that I employ, and defend, is replaced here by an objective burden metric that does not match people's preferences. I do not exclude such contrasts, but they do not compensate for the fact that there is not enough information here for me to say whether "Clara's retreat to labouring" (p. 150) is permissible, by my lights.

Pogge says that "a third specification of [Cohen's] critique allows this retreat" to laboring (p. 150). But so far as I can tell, he doesn't actually describe the specification that is supposed to allow it.

e. Whatever that specification may be, Pogge thinks that I would not allow Clara's retreat. This leads him to his fourth specification: "The talented ought to contribute as they would in the society Rawls envisions even while receiving merely an equal share of the social product." And that is indeed near the mark, since I suppose that the jobs of the talented are not less fulfilling for them than the jobs of the untalented are for the talented.[63]

f. Pogge now raises a further supposed problem:

> Clara's latest complaint brings out an epistemic problem. When all talented citizens are known to be parametric maximizers, it is clear what a true commitment to the difference principle requires them all to do: They should work as they do now, yet redirect all special rewards.[64]

---

63. This is supposed to lead to an invidious contrast between Jeff, whose "respio" is 7 and Clara, whose "respio" is 5 (Pogge defines "respio" on p. 145 of "On the Site"). But I don't understand what commits me to "an entirely arbitrary cutoff" point (ibid., p. 150).

64. "On the Site," p. 151.

Pogge proceeds to contrast the clarity of that solution with what we can say in the case of partial compliance, and raises epistemic difficulties about that,[65] but that excursus is irrelevant here: our polemical space is that of full compliance theory.

g. Section VII presents Pogge's fifth specification:

> All persons should seek the most productive work each is capable of performing, no matter how hateful they may personally find such work; and all should accept no more than unit pay for their work (unless it is especially burdensome by interpersonally invariant standards) and should use the rest toward enhancing the lowest incomes.[66]

This conjures up a nightmare scenario in which the duty that I advocate is interpreted as making the productive work as much as they can to make the wages of the less well paid as high as possible. The scenario is quite unmindful of what I say about the resources and welfare metrics in sections 5 and 6 of Chapter 2. Note, as before, the tell-tale absence of interpersonal-comparative conditions in the specification of the fifth duty.

Pogge claims that I contradict myself: "Insofar as it entails such excessive demands on the very reluctantly superproductive, Cohen himself rejects then [*sic*] the moral duty that he urges upon Rawlsians."[67] I engage in no such gross inconsistency. For clarity, and fidelity to my position, the Pogge sentence would have to continue more or less as follows: "insofar as they stick, without good reason, to a pure resources metric." That being added, the supposed inconsistency in my view disappears.

Pogge's root error is to engage in what I called "inconsistent metrics" in section 6 of Chapter 2. I say that *if* the worst off are to be made as well off as possible *in resources,* then the superproductive must work until they drop, however ghastly their lives become. So I only "urge" the moral duty that I also reject *if* (as I do not think we should) we maximinize *in resources.* In my view, that's a crazy thing to do, and when the craziness is set aside, and we maximinize in a metric that has some regard to welfare, and, therefore, to the burdens of labor that people experience, then of course I urge no welfare-destructive duty. Nor is it quite correct to say that I *"urge"* it, even *modulo* a resources metric: I

---

65. "But in a society in which some citizens may, even partly, be complying with this moral duty, its content is unknowable, because such (partly) moralized dispositions affect the optimal reward multiple and tax rates" (ibid., p. 151).

66. Ibid., p. 152.

67. Ibid., p. 153.

simply say that the difference principle, with that metric, *entails* the oppressive duty.

7. The Currency of Distributive Justice and Incentive Inequality

In Chapter 8 of her *Justice, Luck, and Knowledge,* Susan Hurley purports to discern an inconsistency, or at least a tension, between the position that I articulate in my critique of Rawls's view of incentives and the central thesis of my essay "On the Currency of Egalitarian Justice."[68] I argue in the latter article that, within an egalitarian view of justice, and to a first approximation,[69] inequalities are just if and only if they reflect patterns of choice, and of failures to choose, on the part of the people among whom the inequality prevails. Hurley believes that there is tension between that position and my claim that inequality between more and less productive people is not rendered just by the consideration that unequalizing incentives make less productive people better off than they would be without the inequality that those incentives induce.

I shall describe the tension that Hurley claims to discern in a moment, but first let me demonstrate that the "Currency" view is consistent with the *conclusion* of my argument about incentives. The latter does not say that a just society displays no inequality of reward. It denies not that inequality of reward can be just, but that the incentive justification of it makes it just. And the incentive justification of it indeed does not make it just, from the perspective of "Currency," simply because the incentive justification of inequality does not require that the difference in reward between well and poorly rewarded people be wholly a matter of their choices, as opposed to wholly or partly a matter of luck. The central point is that the sufficient condition (a "forward-looking," or consequentialist one) for just inequality affirmed by the incentive justification is inconsistent with the necessary condition (a "backward-looking," or antecedentialist,[70] one) for just inequality laid down by "Currency." The claim of "Incentives" that benefit to the worst off does

68. Samuel Scheffler says that he is disposed to affirm such a claim on p. 37, fn. 77 of "What Is Egalitarianism," but he doesn't develop the point there.
69. "To a first approximation"—the ensuing statement neglects a nuancing of my view that I impose in response to certain arguments of Thomas Scanlon: see my "On the Currency," p. 937. That nuancing is ignored here because it is irrelevant to the matter discussed in this section, and so is the further revision of my original view that was offered in "Expensive Taste Rides Again."
70. I owe this term to George Sher: see his "Antecedentialism."

not justify inequality does not contradict but *follows* from the "Currency" view. (That is not to say that the stated claim is argued for on the *basis* of the "Currency" view in my critique of Rawls on incentives. Instead, what is argued is that the putative justification does not follow from Rawls's difference principle, unless we suppose we are in what that principle must condemn as an unjust society.)[71]

Now Hurley asks: if, as "Currency" says, choice produces an exemption from equality, then why doesn't the choice to work harder, which the talented make in response to incentives, produce such an exemption? Her rhetorical question does not say that the inequalities in question would then be justified *as* incentives, that is, under the difference principle, but as a particular case of inequalities that are justified by choice.

In elaborating my response I shall suppose, with no threat to generality, that the population divides into equally productive and equally unproductive people. Suppose that, initially, productive and unproductive people alike all supply the same amount of chosen effort but, perforce, different amounts of product, because of the difference in talent endowment that distinguishes productive from unproductive people. Then, according to "Currency," all should, ceteris paribus, enjoy the same rewards.

Suppose now that *some* productive people and *some* unproductive people choose to supply an identical measure of extra effort, while the rest in each category continue to supply the same effort as before. Then "Currency" prescribes inequality of reward, not, however, between the productive and the unproductive, but between the extra-effort suppliers and the extra-effort-withholders.[72] And that inequality of reward is not,

71. Having been provided by me with substantially the foregoing paragraph, Hurley claims that the distinction between forward-looking and backward-looking justifications is "artificial" (*Justice, Luck, and Knowledge,* p. 215). But I do not understand her argument for that: seeing things in what she describes as a (causally) dynamic perspective cannot obliterate the difference between rewards and punishments that are justified (antecedentialistically) by what has been done and rewards and punishments that are justified (consequentialistically) by what happens if they are offered or threatened.

72. This is a crude version of John Roemer's elegant articulation of equality of opportunity: see his *Equality of Opportunity* and, for a more compendious presentation, his "A Pragmatic Theory of Responsibility for the Egalitarian Planner." As Hurley pertinently reports (*Justice, Luck, and Knowledge,* p. 217), she mounts an assault on that articulation in chapter 7, but I was not persuaded that she succeeds, and, what matters more here, I do not think that what she says against Roemer af-

of course, prescribed because of its consequences as an incentive. The inequality in question is entirely different in shape from what an incentives justification of inequality would prescribe.

It is not, we are supposing, a matter of luck that some productive people *make* the effort-increasing choice that they do. But it is a matter of luck that, unlike the less productive, they produce as much as they do as a result of that choice. The relevant bad luck that helps to explain and thus, on the "Currency" view, to condemn the resulting inequality is that the unproductive lack the choice of producing what the productive can choose to produce by putting in greater effort, because, unluckily for the unproductive, they are, indeed, unproductive: their services are not at the relevant level of demand. That bad luck is ignored in the incentives justification of inequality.

Hurley writes:

> In virtue of their [i.e., the productive's] choice to produce, they are responsible at least in part for this extra product. Not all of it counts as a matter of luck for them. So some of it should not be up for redistribution, and should be returned to them.[73]

Under the appropriate assumptions, I agree with that statement, but the statement does not constitute an incentive justification of inequality. These people should, I can agree, get more in virtue of a choice that they made and others declined. That is a justification of unequal reward, but it is not an incentive justification of unequal reward. The extra reward is not justified *because* this extra reward causes the worst off to be better off, and it is justified even if no such consequence obtains.

So far as I can see, the foregoing explications fully reconcile my choice-centered conception of egalitarianism with my rejection of the incentive justification of inequality. And notice that my solution to the problem raised by Hurley does not employ what she calls the "regression requirement,"[74] which holds that "responsibility for something requires responsibility for its causes." I do not say that there is *no* responsibility for the results of increased effort (because part of the cause of those results is the endowment of talent, for which the productive are not responsible). Nor

---

fects my broad use here of the relevant idea, that is, my use of it in its very general (and not specifically Roemerian) form.

73. *Justice, Luck, and Knowledge,* p. 213.

74. Ibid., p. 218.

do I say that people lack choice with respect to how much effort they supply. They may or may not lack it: my conception of justice is neutral with respect to that difficult metaphysical question.[75] If there really is no such power to choose inputs of effort, then what *appears* to be choice justifies no inequality. If there really is that power, then some inequalities are indeed justified, but not because they represent the effect of incentives.[76]

8. Earlier Discussions of Rawls on Incentives

I was not the first to discern an inconsistency between egalitarian and inegalitarian motifs in Rawls, and Brian Barry in particular had shown an awareness that questions of the sort that I have pressed could be raised about the coherence of Rawls's position. Barry addressed critics of Rawls who

> say that if everyone accepted the [Rawlsian] argument for the *prima facie* justice of equality . . . incentives would not be needed because everyone would agree that it is just to work for the same income as everyone else. There would therefore be no room for a move from equality to inequality, and the final word on justice would be that it mandates an equal distribution of income.[77]

Barry said that Rawls had failed to defend himself against "this line of attack," but "that a satisfactory defense" could be given.[78] He claimed to offer that defense in Appendix C of his *Theories of Justice*.

I shall presently say why I believe that Barry's defense fails. But first I shall report the position of two critics of Rawls that Barry confronts.

The first critic is Thomas Grey, who comments in a review of *A Theory of Justice* on Rawls's stipulation that persons in the original position choose principles guided by their knowledge of human nature and human society. Grey emphasizes that competing social theories "will produce very different principles . . . Are the parties followers of Freud or Jung, Durkheim or Spencer, Marshall or Veblen, Watson or

75. Cf. my "Equality of What? On Welfare, Goods and Capabilities," p. 381.
76. Peter Vallentyne discusses the dispute between Hurley and me that is canvassed in the foregoing section in his "Hurley on Justice and Responsibility."
77. *Theories of Justice*, p. 234.
78. Ibid.

Piaget?"[79] And more pertinently to the central theme of Part One of this book, Grey remarks that "one who follows the anarchist notion that the acquisitive urge is not native to man, but is created by a social organization designed in the interests of a ruling class, will be disinclined to allow substantial inequalities in income as incentives for socially useful work."[80] One might add that "the anarchist notion" can allow for inequalities in the short run, because of bourgeois ideological inheritance,[81] but that, in a successful society inspired by the anarchist notion, people would gradually evolve to a condition where they would conduct their economic life unacquisitively.

Grey says that his main "objection to the difference principle is its failure to establish any limits of justice on the bargaining power of those with more than average productive abilities"[82]:

The principle apparently contemplates some extra payment to those with scarce or special skills. There is no other obvious ground than productivity for the inequalities in wealth or income which it allows. Apparently, Rawls believes that, even in the just society, paying differential incomes to those with extra skills will bring forth extra production from them. This necessarily implies that the exceptionally productive are morally justified in threatening to withhold their skills from the community to force payment of additional income.[83] A just society would not pay extra for something it had a right to in any case.[84]

We should revise Grey's idea that the appropriate contrast is a society in which there is "a social duty to work . . . to one's full capacity."[85] A just society, in the view to which, despite that incautious phrase, Grey is surely inclined, is not one in which people work as hard as they possibly

79. Thomas Grey, "The First Virtue," p. 305. For an excellent reply (in effect) to that particular question, see Rawls, *Justice as Fairness*, pp. 65–66.
80. Ibid.
81. See my *Self-Ownership, Freedom, and Equality*, p. 125.
82. Grey, "The First Virtue," p. 322.
83. It would be better to say, more simply: "are morally justified in withholding their skills from the community": no charge of threat is required.
84. Grey, "The First Virtue," p. 322.
85. Ibid., p. 323. Grey says that the socialist principle "From each according to his ability, to each according to his needs" implies such a duty. I am certain that it does not, at any rate in Karl Marx's interpretation of it: see *Self-Ownership, Freedom and Equality*, p. 126.

can, but one in which no one is better remunerated simply because her nonextraordinary effort produces extraordinary results. In such a society, remunerations reflect, perforce roughly, differences in how repugnant or attractive various forms of labor are, and nothing else. That condition is not perfectly attainable,[86] and the details of an approach to it need careful working out, but it clearly does not require people to work until they drop.

Grey discerns "a serious moral instability" in the arrangements proposed by Rawls. "As economic men," Rawlsian persons "have every right to . . . withhold their productive qualities unless they are fully remunerated":

> But when the individual takes off his producer hat and replaces it with his citizen hat, he is expected to vote for measures which directly violate the principles applied in economic life . . . The final distribution is not to be achieved through a second round of bargaining in the political arena, but by collective choice based on application of a supposed principle of justice which dictates that the worst-off are to receive as high an after-tax-and-transfer income as can be achieved for them. What that maximum will be can only be determined when the strong and productive again put on their hats as economic men, and self-interestedly calculate how much they will reduce the contribution of their productive skills to the community for each addition to the tax rate.[87]

The result, according to Grey, is an incoherent account of citizens' motivations:

> Within the economic system, they act as self-interested economic men, extracting what the traffic will bear. After office hours, they are expected disinterestedly to tax themselves a substantial portion of that income so that it may be transferred to others who are unable to gain it in the bargaining arena.[88]

A few years later Jan Narveson pressed similar objections.[89] He garnished them with details many of which I would not accept, and I do

---

86. For problems in articulating and achieving what is to be attained, see Joseph Carens, "Compensatory Justice and Social Institutions."

87. Grey, "The First Virtue," pp. 323–324.

88. Ibid., p. 324.

89. See "A Puzzle about Economic Justice in Rawls' Theory," and "Rawls on Equal Distribution of Wealth."

not, like him, regard Rawls's endorsement of unequalizing incentives as (inconsistent but) welcome. Nevertheless, and as the representative passages excerpted below indicate, Narveson anticipated much of the substance of what I myself argued in Chapter 1.

Narveson quotes Rawls's endorsement of incentives that are "necessary . . . to encourage performance,"[90] and he comments as follows:

> . . . incentives are psychological matters, which concern one's principles of action. If I hold out for, or accept, a greater payment for my services than someone else is getting for his, I am voluntarily consenting to an inequality. I cannot argue that this higher payment is "necessary," that I am *forced* to have more than you. Obviously, I *could*, if I wanted to, accept the same wage as everyone else . . . The question we are discussing is whether, in justice, I *ought* to do this. And to say that incentives are "necessary" for this purpose is to engage in confusion, or possibly even in self-deception.[91]

And Narveson concludes that

> if the difference principle is really the right principle for distributing economic goods, then any society manifesting any inequality other than what is naturally inescapable is to that extent unjust.[92]

This convinces Narveson that the difference principle must be rejected, since, as a friend of entitlement and desert, he finds egalitarian reasoning "outrageous."[93] But that does not reduce the similarity between his charge of incoherence against Rawls and my own.

Supporting that charge as I do, I am encouraged by how spare Barry's attempt to answer Grey and Narveson is. The insufficiency of Barry's reply, coming as it does from so penetrating an author, is indirect evidence of the strength of their (and, hence, my) case.

Barry addresses Grey's contention that Rawls's position displays

> a moral inconsistency in that the principled rationale for the market determination of incomes is incompatible with the principled rationale for redistribution . . . The charge is that, if it is accepted that productive advantages are [morally arbitrary],[94] there should be no need for material incentives.

90. *A Theory of Justice*, p. 151/dropped in 1999.
91. "A Puzzle," pp. 11–12.
92. *Ibid.*, p. 13.
93. Ibid., p. 22.
94. Barry writes "unjust," but content and context make "morally arbitrary" more

For the members of a just society should be motivated by thoughts of the injustice of inequality to work loyally in pursuit of the goal of maximum income equally distributed.[95]

But here (although quite pardonably, because he is following Grey) Barry misstates the problem in a way that makes it less poignant for the defender of Rawls. The demand that equal income (and, therefore, labor input) be maximized imposes unacceptably onerous labor costs. The case to answer is that talented people would not require handsome material incentives to work at ordinary levels of effort in their more than ordinarily productive ways, in a society in which they were themselves committed to the difference principle.[96]

Barry rejects various responses to that case, including the one that says the difference principle operates only after free choice of occupation has been secured. For he says, commenting on the latter, that

[t]he important question . . . is not so much whether or not Rawls does make the difference principle subject to free choice of occupation but whether or not he is entitled to do so, given his egalitarian premises.[97]

That having been said, we read on, expecting Barry to tell us whether, indeed, those premises permit an unfettered use of freedom of occupational choice that both upsets equality and restricts the way in which the difference principle can be satisfied. But no such discussion ensues. What we get, effectively in conclusion, is the mere statement that free choice of occupation comes first that Barry rejected as unsatisfying in the text quoted immediately above:

Now, I do not see that there is any way of showing that Rawls is being inconsistent in positing the priority of freedom of occupation. The priority of the first principle, equal liberty, over the second principle is built into the theory. And within the second principle, the clause stipulating that posi-

---

apt. According to Rawls, "the natural distribution is neither just nor unjust" (*A Theory of Justice*, pp. 102/87).

95. Barry, *Theories of Justice*, pp. 395–396.

96. For an effective elaboration of this case that constitutes a further substantial anticipation of Chapter 1, see section 6 of Joseph Carens, "Rights and Duties in an Egalitarian Society."

97. Barry, *Theories of Justice*, p. 99.

tions are to be open to all under conditions of "fair equality of opportunity" is stated by Rawls to have priority over the difference principle. I can therefore see no problem of internal coherence for Rawls's theory if we understand the application of the difference principle to be limited by the constraint of respecting freedom of occupational choice.[98]

But that is the reply Barry has already rejected. And whether or not it fails for the reason *he* gives,[99] it fails because nonmaximizing forbearance is *consistent* with freedom of occupational choice. Indeed, a good way to phrase the Grey/Narveson challenge would be as follows: even if free choice of occupation is a prior desideratum, why should the *ex hypothesi* Rawlsianly just people who enjoy that freedom use it without regard to the inequality it can produce? As Barry himself writes: "it is possible to say that some distribution of rights is just but also to say that only certain deployments of those rights are fair" (*Theories of Justice*, p. 314). That is what I myself say, more or less, in Chapter 5, where the issue of freedom of occupational choice is addressed in extenso.

The real question is how a maximizing posture could cohere with commitment to the difference principle or, more generally, with Rawls's "egalitarian premises" (see the text to footnote 97). In the face of that question, Barry merely reports that he can discern no inconsistency in the full set of Rawlsian principles. If, as may be unlikely, he means logical inconsistency, then what he says is true but beside the point. For the question at the head of this paragraph asks how a standardly self-seeking use of the opportunities conferred by the principle of freedom of choice of occupation can be justified in a fashion that coheres with the egalitarian justification of the difference principle. Barry appears to have forgotten, at this crucial final point in his discussion, that the problem, as he himself expressed it (see the text of footnote 95), was that there appears to be "a moral inconsistency" in Rawls "in that the principled rationale for market determination of incomes is incompatible with the principled rationale for redistribution." Barry thinks Rawls's own reply to the contemplated critic "begs the question," but it is impossible to discover a respect in which Barry's reply represents an improvement on Rawls's.[100]

98. Ibid., p. 400.
99. See the text to n. 97 above.
100. Barry, Theories of Justice, p. 393.

BIBLIOGRAPHY

Note 1: Dates that immediately succeed an author's name signify the original date of publication of the item, where that differs from the otherwise indicated date of publication.

Note 2: In most cases, when I quote or cite Rawls's *Theory of Justice,* I give reference to both editions in this style: *A Theory of Justice,* p. 25/18, where the first reference is to the 1971 edition and the second to the 1999. Where the parallel passages differ insubstantially, I do not note the differences. Where they differ more than insubstantially, I note that, and I sometimes remark upon the difference(s).

Action Aid leaflet. "How Do You Tell a Person Dying of Hunger That There's Nothing You Can Do?" *Action Aid,* 1990.

Alter, Will. "Does Justice Require an Egalitarian Ethos?" Oxford University undergraduate thesis, 2006.

Anderson, Elizabeth. "What Is the Point of Equality?" *Ethics* 109 (1999): 287–337.

Andrews, Kay and John Jacobs. *Punishing the Poor: Poverty Under Thatcher.* London: Macmillan, 1990.

Arneson, Richard. "Liberalism, Freedom, and Community." *Ethics* 100 (1990): 368–385.

———. "Property Rights in Persons." *Social Philosophy and Policy* 9 (1992): 201–230.

———. "Against Rawlsian Equality of Opportunity." *Philosophical Studies* 93 (1999): 77–112.

———. "Luck Egalitarianism and Prioritarianism." *Ethics* 110 (2000): 339–349.

Ashcraft, Richard. "Class Conflict and Constitutionalism in J. S. Mill's Thought." In Nancy Rosenblum, ed. *Liberalism and the Moral Life.* Cambridge, Mass.: Harvard University Press, 1989.

Baker, John. "An Egalitarian Case for Basic Income." In Philippe Van Parijs, ed. *Arguing for Basic Income*. London: Verso, 1992.

Barry, Brian. *The Liberal Theory of Justice*. Oxford: Oxford University Press, 1973.

———. *Theories of Justice*. London: Harvester Wheatsheaf, 1989.

Beauchamp, Tom L. "Distributive Justice and the Difference Principle." In Blocker and Smith.

Bedau, Hugo Adam. "Social Justice and Social Institutions." *Midwest Studies in Philosophy* 3 (1978): 159–175.

Bennett, Jonathan. "Analytic-Synthetic." *Proceedings of the Aristotelian Society* 59 (1958–59): 163–188.

Berlin, Isaiah. *Historical Inevitability*. Oxford: Oxford University Press, 1954.

Bilgrami, Akeel. "Secular Liberalism and the Moral Psychology of Identity." In R. Bhargava, A. K. Bagchi, and R. Sudarshan, eds. *Multiculturalism, Liberalism and Democracy*. New Delhi: Oxford University Press, 1999.

Blocker, H. G., and E. Smith, eds. *John Rawls' Theory of Justice*. Athens: Ohio University Press, 1980.

Britannica Book of the Year (A Record of the March of Events of 1944). Chicago: Encyclopaedia Britannica, 1945.

Buchanan, Allen. "A Critical Introduction to Rawls's Theory of Justice." In Blocker and Smith.

———. *Marx and Justice*. Totowa, N.J.: Rowman and Littlefield, 1982.

———. "Justice as Reciprocity vs. Subject-Centred Justice." *Philosophy and Public Affairs* 19 (1990): 227–252.

Burley, Justine, ed. *Dworkin and His Critics*. Oxford: Blackwell, 2004.

Carens, Joseph. *Equality, Moral Incentives, and the Market*. Chicago: University of Chicago Press, 1981.

———. "Compensatory Justice and Social Institutions." *Economics and Philosophy* 1 (1985): 39–67.

———. "Rights and Duties in an Egalitarian Society." *Political Theory* 14 (1986): 31–49.

———. "An Interpretation and Defense of the Socialist Principle of Distribution." *Social Philosophy and Policy* 20 (2003): 145–177.

Carroll, Lewis. *Symbolic Logic*. William Warren Bartley III, ed. Hassocks, U.K.: Harvester, 1977.

Casal, Paula. "Mall, Rawls, Cohen and the Egalitarian Ethos." Unpublished paper, 2006.

Choo, Dong-Ryul. "Cohen's Egalitarianism: Looking Through His Debate with Rawls." Equality Exchange website (http://mora.rente.nhh.no/projects/EqualityExchange), 2004.

Christofidis, Miriam Cohen. "Talent, Slavery, and Envy." In Burley.

Cohen, G. A. *Karl Marx's Theory of History: A Defence*. Oxford: Oxford University Press, 1978, and Princeton, N.J.: Princeton University Press, 2000 (expanded edition).

———. *History, Labour, and Freedom.* Oxford: Oxford University Press, 1988.

———. "On the Currency of Egalitarian Justice." *Ethics* 99 (1989): 906–944.

———. "Equality of What? On Welfare, Goods and Capabilities." *Recherches Economiques* 56 (1990): 357–383.

———. "Incentives, Inequality, and Community." In Grethe B. Peterson, ed. *The Tanner lectures on Human Values.* Vol. 13. Salt Lake City: University of Utah Press, 1992.

———. *Self-Ownership, Freedom and Equality.* Cambridge: Cambridge University Press, 1995.

———. "Reason, Humanity, and the Moral Law." In O. O'Neill, ed. *The Sources of Normativity.* Cambridge: Cambridge University Press, 1996.

———. "Where the Action Is: On the Site of Distributive Justice." *Philosophy and Public Affairs* 26 (1997): 3–30.

———. *If You're an Egalitarian, How Come You're So Rich?* Cambridge, Mass.: Harvard University Press, 2000.

———. "Why Not Socialism?" In E. Broadbent, ed. *Democratic Equality: What Went Wrong?* Toronto: University of Toronto Press, 2001.

———. "Expensive Taste Rides Again." In Burley.

———. "Luck and Equality: Reply to Hurley." *Philosophy and Phenomenological Research* 72 (2006): 439–446.

———. "Fairness and Legitimacy in Justice." Festschrift for Hillel Steiner, forthcoming.

Cohen, Joshua. "Democratic Equality." *Ethics* 99 (1989): 727–751.

———. "Taking People as They Are." *Philosophy and Public Affairs* 30 (2001): 363–386.

———. "Is There a Human Right to Democracy?" In Sypnowich.

Copp, David. "Pluralism and Stability in Liberal Theory." *Journal of Political Philosophy* 4 (1996): 191–206.

Dancy, Jonathan. *Moral Reasons.* Oxford: Blackwell, 1993.

Daniels, Norman, ed. *Reading Rawls.* Oxford: Blackwell, 1975.

———. "Democratic Equality: Rawls's Complex Egalitarianism." In Freeman.

Dupré, John. *Human Nature and the Limits of Science.* Oxford: Oxford University Press, 2001.

Dworkin, Ronald. "The Original Position" (1973). In Daniels.

———. *Sovereign Virtue.* Cambridge, Mass.: Harvard University Press, 2000.

———. "Equality of Resources." In Dworkin.

Enoch, David. "A Right to Violate One's Duty." *Law and Philosophy* 21 (2002): 355–384.

Estlund, David. "Liberalism, Equality, and Fraternity in Cohen's Critique of Rawls." *Journal of Political Philosophy* 6 (1998): 99–112.

———. "I Will If You Will: Leveraged Enhancements and Distributive Justice." Unpublished manuscript, 2003.

Eyal, Nir. "Distributing Respect." D.Phil. diss., Oxford University, 2003.

Feinberg, Joel. *Harmless Wrongdoing*. Oxford: Oxford University Press, 1988.

Flaherty, Joshua. "The Autonomy of the Political." Ph.D. diss., Massachussets Institute of Technology, 2003.

Freeman, Samuel, ed. *The Cambridge Companion to Rawls*. Cambridge: Cambridge University Press, 2003.

Gauthier, David. "David Hume, Contractarian." *Philosophical Review* 88 (1979): 3–38.

———. *Morals by Agreement*. Oxford: Oxford University Press, 1986.

Gibbard, Allan. *Wise Choices, Apt Feelings*. Cambridge, Mass.: Harvard University Press, 1990.

———. "Constructing Justice." *Philosophy and Public Affairs* 20 (1991): 264–279.

Grey, Thomas. "The First Virtue." *Stanford Law Review* 25 (1973): 286–327.

Griffin, James. *Value Judgment*. Oxford: Oxford University Press, 1996.

Hampton, Jean. "Contracts and Choices: Does Rawls Have a Social Contract Theory?" *Journal of Philosophy* 77 (1980): 315–388.

Hayek, Friedrich. *The Constitution of Liberty*. Chicago: University of Chicago Press, 1960.

Hobbes, Thomas. *Leviathan* (1651). C. B. MacPherson, ed. Harmondsworth, Middlesex, U.K.: Penguin, 1968.

Hurley, Susan. *Justice, Luck, and Knowledge*. Oxford: Oxford University Press, 2003.

Julius, A. J. "Basic Structure and the Value of Equality." *Philosophy and Public Affairs* 31 (2003): 321–355.

Kagan, Shelly. *The Limits of Morality*. Oxford: Oxford University Press, 1989.

———. *Normative Ethics*. Boulder, Colo.: Westview, 1998.

Kamm, F. M. "Owing, Justifying, and Rejecting." Review of *What We Owe to Each Other*, by T. M. Scanlon. *Mind* 111 (2002): 323–354.

Katz, Jerrold. *Realistic Rationalism*. Cambridge, Mass.: MIT Press, 2000.

Korsgaard, Christine. "The Reasons We Can Share." *Social Philosophy and Policy,* 10 (1993): 24–51.

Krouse, Richard, and Michael McPherson. "Capitalism, 'Property-Owning Democracy,' and the Welfare State." In Amy Gutmann, ed. *Democracy and the Welfare State*. Princeton, N.J.: Princeton University Press, 1988.

Kymlicka, Will. "Liberal Individualism and Liberal Neutrality." *Ethics* 99 (1989): 883–905.

———. *Contemporary Political Philosophy*. Oxford: Oxford University Press, 1990.

Laslett, P., and W. G. Runciman, eds. *Philosophy, Politics and Society*, Second Series. Oxford: Blackwell, 1962.

———, eds. *Philosophy, Politics, and Society*, Third Series. Oxford: Blackwell, 1967.

Laslett, P., W. G. Runciman, and Q. Skinner, eds. *Philosophy, Politics, and Society*, Fourth Series. Oxford: Blackwell, 1972.

Laslett, Peter, and James Fishkin, eds. *Philosophy, Politics and Society*, Fifth Series. New Haven, Conn.: Yale University Press, 1979.

Lessnoff, Michael. "Capitalism, Socialism and Justice." In Shaw and Arthur.

Lyons, David. "Nature and Soundness of the Contract and Coherence Arguments." In Daniels.

Macleod, Alastair M. "Economic Inequality: Justice and Incentives." In K. Kipnis and D. T. Meyers, eds. *Economic Justice*. Totowa, N.J.: Rowman and Allanheld, 1985.

Mandeville, Bernard. *The Fable of the Bees*. Many editions, 1714.

Marx, Karl. "On the Jewish Question" (1843). In Lloyd D. Easton and Kurt H. Gudat, eds. *Writings of the Young Marx on Philosophy and Society*. Garden City, N.Y.: Doubleday, 1967.

———. *Economic and Philosophical Manuscripts* (1844). In Tom Bottomore, ed. *Karl Marx: Early Writings*. London: C. A. Watts, 1963.

———. *Capital* (1867). Vol. 1. Harmondsworth, Middlesex, U.K.: Penguin, 1976.

McDowell, John. *Mind, Value, and Reality*. Cambridge, Mass.: Harvard University Press, 1998.

McMahan, Jefferson. "The Ethics of Killing in War." *Ethics* 114 (2004): 693–733.

Meade, James. *Theory of Economic Externalities: The Control of Environmental Pollution and Similar Social Costs*. Leiden: Sijthoff, 1973.

Mew, Peter. "G. A. Cohen on Freedom, Justice, and Capitalism." *Inquiry* 29 (1986): 305–313.

Mill, John Stuart. *Utilitarianism*. Many editions, 1861.

———. *Autobiography* (1873). New York: New American Library, 1965.

———. *Principles of Political Economy* (1848). In J. M. Robson, ed. *Collected Works of John Stuart Mill*. Vol. 2. Toronto: Toronto University Press, 1965.

Miller, David. "Political Philosophy for Earthlings: Against Cohen on Facts and Principles." In D. Leopold and M. Stears, eds. *Political Theory: Methods and Approaches*. Oxford: Oxford University Press, 2008.

Mishel, Lawrence, and David M. Frankel. *The State of Working America*. Armonk, N.Y.: M. E. Sharpe, 1991.

Moon, Donald. Review of *Equality, Moral Incentives, and the Market*, by Joseph Carens. *Ethics* 94 (1983): 146–150.

Murphy, Liam. "Institutions and the Demands of Justice." *Philosophy and Public Affairs* 27 (1998): 251–291.

———. *Moral Demands in Nonideal Theory.* Oxford: Oxford University Press, 2000.

Murphy, Liam, and Thomas Nagel. *The Myth of Ownership.* New York: Oxford University Press, 2002.

Nagel, Thomas. "Rawls on Justice" (1973). In Daniels.

———. "Libertarianism without Foundations" (1975). In Paul.

———. "Equality" (1978). In his *Mortal Questions.* Cambridge: Cambridge University Press, 1979.

———. *Equality and Partiality.* New York: Oxford University Press, 1991.

———. *The Last Word.* New York: Oxford University Press, 1997.

———. "Rawls and Liberalism." In Freeman.

Narveson, Jan. "A Puzzle about Economic Justice in Rawls' Theory." *Social Theory and Practice* 4 (1976): 1–28.

———. "Rawls on Equal Distribution of Wealth." *Philosophia* 7 (1978): 281–292.

Nozick, Robert. "Coercion" (1969). In Laslett, Runciman, and Skinner.

———. *Anarchy, State, and Utopia.* New York: Basic Books, 1974.

———. *The Nature of Rationality.* Princeton, N.J.: Princeton University Press, 1993.

Okin, Susan. *Justice, Gender and the Family.* New York: Basic Books, 1989.

———. "Political Liberalism, Justice, and Gender." *Ethics* 105 (1994): 23–43.

———. "Justice and Gender: An Unfinished Debate." *Fordham Law Review* 72 (2004): 1537–1567.

Otsuka, Michael. *Libertarianism Without Inequality.* Oxford: Oxford University Press, 2003.

———. "Liberty, Equality, Envy and Abstraction." In Burley.

———. "Prerogatives to Depart from Equality." In Anthony O'Hear, ed. *Political Philosophy.* Cambridge: Cambridge University Press, 2006.

Parfit, Derek. *Reasons and Persons.* Oxford: Oxford University Press, 1984.

———. *Equality or Priority?* Lindley Lecture. Lawrence: University of Kansas Press, 1995.

Paul, Jeffrey, ed. *Reading Nozick.* Totowa, N.J.: Rowman and Littlefield, 1981.

Peffer, Rodney. "Rawlsian Theory, Contemporary Marxism, and the Difference Principle." Unpublished manuscript, 1999.

Plato. *The Republic.* Many editions.

Pogge, Thomas. *Realizing Rawls.* Ithaca, N.Y.: Cornell University Press, 1989.

———. "On the Site of Distributive Justice: Reflections on Cohen and Murphy." *Philosophy and Public Affairs* 29 (2000): 137–169.

Rawls, John. "Justice as Fairness" (1958). In Laslett and Runciman, Second Series.

———. "Constitutional Liberty and the Concept of Justice" (1963). In Rawls, *Collected Papers*.

———. "Distributive Justice" (1967). In Rawls, *Collected Papers*.

———. "Distributive Justice: Some Addenda" (1968). In Rawls, *Collected Papers*.

———. *A Theory of Justice*. Cambridge, Mass.: Harvard University Press, 1971 and 1999.

———. "Justice as Reciprocity" (1971). In Rawls, *Collected Papers*.

———. "Reply to Alexander and Musgrave" (1974). In Rawls, *Collected Papers*.

———. "A Kantian Conception of Equality" (1975). In Rawls, *Collected Papers*.

———. "The Independence of Moral Theory" (1975). In Rawls, *Collected Papers*.

———. "The Basic Structure as Subject" (1977). In Rawls, *Political Liberalism*.

———. "Kantian Constructivism in Moral Theory" (1980). In Rawls, *Collected Papers*.

———. "Social Unity and Primary Goods" (1982). In Rawls, *Collected Papers*.

———. "The Priority of Right and Ideas of the Good" (1988). In Rawls, *Collected Papers*.

———. "Justice as Fairness: A Briefer Restatement." Harvard University typescript, 1989.

———. "Themes in Kant's Moral Philosophy" (1989). In Rawls, *Collected Papers*.

———. "Reply to Habermas" (1995). In Rawls, *Political Liberalism*.

———. "The Idea of Public Reason Revisited" (1997). In Rawls, *The Law of Peoples*.

———. *The Law of Peoples*. Cambridge, Mass: Harvard University Press, 1999.

———. *Collected Papers*. Samuel Freeman, ed. Cambridge, Mass.: Harvard University Press, 1999.

———. *Lectures on the History of Moral Philosophy*. Barbara Herman, ed. Cambridge, Mass.: Harvard University Press, 2000.

———. *Justice as Fairness: A Restatement*. Cambridge, Mass.: Harvard University Press, 2001.

———. *Political Liberalism*. Expanded edition. New York: Columbia University Press, 2005.

Raz, Joseph. *The Morality of Freedom*. Oxford: Oxford University Press, 1986.

Roemer, John "A Pragmatic Theory of Responsibility for the Egalitarian Planner." *Philosophy and Public Affairs* 11 (1993): 146–166.

———. *Equality of Opportunity.* Cambridge, Mass.: Harvard University Press, 1998.

Roemer, John, and Roger Howe. "Rawlsian Justice as the Core of a Game." *American Economic Review* 71 (1981): 880–895.

Sayre-McCord, Geoffrey. "Coherentist Epistemology in Moral Theory." In W. Sinott-Armstrong and M. Timmons, eds. *Moral Knowledge.* New York: Oxford University Press, 1996.

Scanlon, T. M. "Contractualism and Utilitarianism." In Amartya Sen and Bernard Williams, eds. *Utilitarianism and Beyond.* Cambridge: Cambridge University Press, 1982.

———. "The Significance of Choice." In Sterling McMurrin, ed. *The Tanner Lectures on Human Values.* Vol. 8. Salt Lake City: University of Utah Press, 1988.

———. *What We Owe to Each Other.* Cambridge: Cambridge University Press, 1998.

———. "Interview." *Imprints* 8 (2005): 102–111.

———. "Justice, Responsibility, and the Demands of Equality." In Sypnowich.

Scheffler, Samuel. *The Rejection of Consequentialism.* Oxford: Oxford University Press, 1982.

———. "What Is Egalitarianism?" *Philosophy and Pubic Affairs* 31 (2003): 5–39.

———. "Rawls and Utilitarianism." In Freeman.

Schwartz, Adina. "Moral Neutrality and Primary Goods." *Ethics* 83 (1973): 294–307.

Sen, Amartya. "Nature and Classes of Prescriptive Judgments." *Philosophical Quarterly* 17 (1967): 53.

———. *Collective Choice and Social Welfare.* San Francisco: Holden-Day, 1970.

———. "Liberty, Unanimity, and Rights." *Economica* 43 (1976): 217–245.

Shaw, William, and John Arthur, eds. *Justice and Economic Distribution.* Englewood Cliffs, N.J.: Prentice-Hall, 1978.

Sher, George. "Antecedentialism." *Ethics* 94 (1983): 6–17.

Shiffrin, Seana. "Moral Autonomy and Agent-Centered Conceptions." *Analysis* 51 (1991): 244–254.

Sidgwick, Henry. *Practical Ethics: A Collection of Addresses and Essays.* With an Introduction by Sissela Bok. Oxford: Oxford University Press, 1998.

Skillen, Anthony. *Ruling Illusions.* Hassocks, Sussex, U.K.: Harvester Press, 1977.

Swift, Adam. *How Not to Be a Hypocrite: School Choice for the Morally Perplexed Parent.* Falmer, Sussex, U.K.: Routledge, 2003.

Sypnowich, Christine, ed. *The Egalitarian Conscience: Essays in Honour of G. A. Cohen.* Oxford: Oxford University Press, 2006.

Tan, Kok-Chor. "Justice and Personal Pursuits." *Journal of Philosophy* 101 (2004): 331–362.

Taylor, Charles. "Neutrality and Political Science." In Laslett and Runciman, Third Series.

Temkin, Larry. "Equality, Priority, and the Levelling Down Objection" (1993–94). In Matthew Clayton and Andrew Williams, eds. *The Ideal of Equality.* Houndmills, Basingstoke, U.K.: Palgrave Macmillan, 2002.

Titelbaum, Michael. "What Would a Rawlsian Ethos of Justice Look Like?" Unpublished typescript, 2005.

Turner, Denys. "Religion: Illusions and Liberation." In Terrell Carver, ed. *The Cambridge Companion to Marx.* Cambridge: Cambridge University Press, 1991.

Vallentyne, Peter. "Hurley on Justice and Responsibility." *Philosophy and Phenomenological Research* 72 (2006): 433–438.

Vallentyne, Peter, Hillel Steiner, and Michael Otsuka. "Why Left-Libertarianism Is Not Incoherent, Indeterminate, or Irrelevant: A Reply to Fried." *Philosophy and Public Affairs* 33 (2005): 201–215.

Vandenbroucke, Frank. *Social Justice and Individual Ethics in an Open Society.* Berlin: Springer, 2001.

Van Parijs, Philippe. "Difference Principles." In Freeman.

Waldron, Jeremy. "A Right to Do Wrong." *Ethics* 92 (1981): 21–39.

Weinstock, Daniel. Review of *If You're an Egalitarian, How Come You're So Rich?* By G. A. Cohen. *Philosophy in Review/Compte rendus philosophiques* 20 (2004): 405–407.

White, Stuart. *The Civic Minimum.* Oxford: Oxford University Press, 2003.

Wiggins, David. *Ethics.* London: Penguin Books, 2006.

Wilkinson, T. M. *Freedom, Efficiency, and Equality.* Houndmills, Basingstoke, U.K.: Macmillan, 2000.

———. "Equality and the Moral Revolution." *Imprints* 5 (2001): 272–282.

Williams, Andrew. "Incentives, Inequality, and Publicity." *Philosophy and Public Affairs* 27 (1998): 225–247.

Williams, Bernard. *Shame and Necessity.* Berkeley: University of California Press, 1993.

CREDITS

I thank the following publishers for permission to draw on the indicated material:

Blackwell Publishing for material in Chapters 3 and 6 that appeared in, respectively, G. A. Cohen, "Where the action is: On the Site of Distributive Justice," *Philosophy and Public Affairs* 26 (1997): 3–30, and G. A. Cohen, "Facts and Principles," *Philosophy and Public Affairs* 31 (2003): 211–245.

Cambridge University Press for material in Chapter 2 that appeared in G. A. Cohen, "The Pareto Argument for Inequality," *Social Philosophy and Policy* 12 (1995): 160–185.

University of Utah Press for material in Chapter 1 that appeared in "Incentives, Inequality and Community." In Grethe Peterson, ed., *The Tanner Lectures on Human Values*. Salt Lake City: University of Utah Press, 1992, pp. 261–329.

NAME INDEX

I thank Michèle Cohen for her help.

(John Rawls does not appear in this index, because the whole book addresses his thought.)

Action Aid leaflet, 36
Alter, Will, 355
Anderson, Elizabeth, 8, 271
Andrews, Kay, 29
Aristotle, 358
Arneson, Richard, 81, 163, 206, 215, 217, 271, 310, 396
Ashcraft, Richard, 86

Barry, Brian, 87–90, 92–94, 99–100, 109–114, 164, 260, 285, 302, 374, 406, 409–411
Beauchamp, Tom L., 28
Bedau, Hugo Adam, 137
Bennett, Jonathan, 242
Bentham, Jeremy, 12
Berlin, Isaiah, 176
Bilgrami, Akeel, 290–291
Britannica Book of the Year, 37
Buchanan, Allen, 2, 86, 201, 326

Carens, Joseph, 53, 122, 189–192, 194, 205, 345, 369–370, 408, 410
Carroll, Lewis, 238–239
Casal, Paula, 198, 356–357, 371
Choo, Dong-Ryul, 383, 396

Christofidis, Miriam Cohen, 370
Cohen, Joshua, 12, 57, 76–77, 126, 145, 267–268, 296–298, 306, 379–381, 383, 387, 392
Copp, David, 328

Dancy, Jonathan, 248
Daniels, Norman, 374–375, 383, 392
Dupré, John, 232
Dworkin, Ronald, 8, 73, 98, 119, 127, 175, 188, 261, 310, 312, 342, 370, 379–380

Enoch, David, 199
Estlund, David, 1, 12, 68, 126, 373, 383, 388–394
Eyal, Nir, 294

Feinberg, Joel, 215
Flaherty, Joshua, 135, 142, 148
Frankel, David M., 143
Freeman, Samuel, 161, 197

Gauthier, David, 2, 110, 275, 295, 338–339, 341, 343
Gibbard, Allan, 110–111, 232, 292
Grey, Thomas, 374, 406–411
Griffin, James, 153

Hampton, Jean, 337
Hayek, Friedrich, 28
Hobbes, Thomas, 6, 11, 112, 338–339, 341–343
Howe, Roger, 201

423

SUBJECT INDEX

I thank Nicolas Vrousalis for his help.

abundance, 176–177, 331–334. *See also* justice, circumstances of
agent-centered prerogative. *See* personal prerogative
akrasia, 171–172
alienation, 66–68
altruism, 174–175, 331–334
analytic/synthetic distinction, 3–4. *See also* holism
anarchism, 1, 407
arbitrariness. *See* moral arbitrariness
Aristotelian Principle, 107
assurance, 21–22, 147–148, 245, 325, 345–357. *See also* publicity

bad case. *See* incentives, bad (or bluffing) case
bad faith, 63–64
basic liberties. *See* the liberty principle
basic structure (of society), 94, 162, 197–198, Ch. 3, 276, 331, 344–345, 359, 373–380, 387, 395
  and coercion, 144–148
  and the family, 117–118, 133–137, 140, 149
  dilemma, 137–138
  identity of, 132–140, 149–150
  informal, 133–138, 144–146, 149–150
  objection, 16–17, 117–118, 124–140, 183
  See also justice, site of
blame, 140–143, 173

blood donation, 188–190, 223–224
bluffing. *See* incentives, bad (or bluffing) case
Britain, 62, 65, 68
  World War II in, 219–222, 353, 355, 364
burden on the will, 203–205

camping trip, 352–353
"can't" or "won't", 170–177
capitalism, 12–13, 86, 163, 176–178. *See also* market
chain connection, 157
Chamberlain, Wilt, 17, 152, 169–170
clarity of mind requirement, 233, 245–247
close-knitness, 157
communism, 176, 179, 208, 225, 352
community, 32–33, 38, 41, 43–48, 53–54, 64–68, 82, 121, 178–179
comprehensive doctrines, 296–298
comprehensive justification, 41–44, 172, 381
constructivism, 2–3, 8, 20–21, 231–232, 239–240, 269, 345
  and fundamental principles of justice, 279–302
  and human nature, 177–180
  and justice, 20–21, Ch. 7
  and publicity, 345
  and truth, 302–307
  defined, 274–275
  Scanlonian, 294–296
  without facts, 298–300
  See also justice and constructivism, original position, political philosophy
consumer preference, 185

425